Camagüey

Holguin

Sierra del Cristal

O R I E N T E

Manzanilla

Niquero

SIERRA
MAESTRA

Guantanamo

Santiago De Cuba

CUBA

Island of Paradox

by R. Hart Phillips

CUBA *Island of Paradox*

McDowell, Obolensky : New York

To Phil

The author wishes to express her appreciation to Gene Carrier, Raul Casañas, and Doctora Sarita Rodriguez for their assistance.

Contents

December 1, 1956

After weeks of training in the mountains of Mexico under the tutelage of General Alberto Bays, who had fought in Africa and Spain, twenty-six men put to sea in a yacht, the "Gramma," at Tuxpan, Mexico. Recent storms had made the sea rough, and the young men, lawyers, technicians and engineers, were unaccustomed to the cork-like reaction of the small ship. There was nothing to eat except canned meat, fruit and vitamin pills, which the Argentine doctor, Ernesto "Che" Guevara, one of the five foreigners in the expedition, handed out in small daily rations. The food shortage was a deliberate sacrifice, for the men knew that in Cuba food would be easier to obtain than ammunition.

On the seventh day the yacht approached the coast of Oriente, where a rendezvous was to be made with Crescencio Perez, an old man whom the Batista government termed "the bandit of the Sierra Maestra," but who was to prove a tower of strength to the young rebels. Crescencio was prepared to meet the expedition with trucks and transport them into the vast jungle covered mountains which were *to be the base of operations against the Cuban government.*

The sky and the sea were dark as the "Gramma" neared land. The men put on their olive green uniforms, cleaned and loaded their weapons, and readied the equipment and provisions to be carried ashore. As the "Gramma" approached the beach, she was struck by a series of large waves, spun about, and the navigator hurled overboard and swept away. They could not find him in the darkness. They could hear him yelling, but it is extremely difficult to locate the position or direction of a voice at sea. The searchlight was useless; someone had forgotten to bring the kerosene which it used for fuel. Fidel Castro refused to go off and leave the man to drown. "While he has a voice," said Castro, "we will hunt for him."

A precious hour was lost. Finally the navigator was discovered and was hauled aboard, but in the process of circling they had lost their bearings. For a time they went the wrong direction. Then, unexpectedly, the yacht ran aground at Las Coloradas, in the midst of a swamp. Unable to free the boat, fearing that aircraft would spot them in the approaching dawn, the men decided to go ashore and try to make contact with Crescencio Perez further inland.

Unloading the yacht was difficult. The water was over the heads of some of the shorter men, rendering them useless. Even after they had left the sea behind them, the treacherous marshes embedded them in mud almost to their waists. During the nightmarish hour before dawn they struggled to find dry land, abandoning much of their equipment and supplies. By noon they had advanced inland into thick brush. The landing had actually taken place on December 1, 1956, but in the confusion and horror that followed, even Fidel Castro, in referring to it, always thinks of it as having happened on the following day.

A coast guard vessel cruising off the coast spotted the "Gramma" and, investigating, discovered some of the abandoned equipment. Within an hour airplanes were flying low over the district, bombing indiscriminately and blindly, in an effort to destroy the expedition. A thousand soldiers from Manzanillo and Niquero were rushed into the area.

Guided by friendly natives, the rebels moved into the foot-hills of the almost impenetrable mountains of the Sierra Maestra. There, hearing of the large army forces that were being concentrated against them, and to escape detection by airplanes, the expedition split into small groups. This would have been excellent strategy if the men had been more familiar with the terrain. Instead, many of them got lost. Some were captured and immediately executed by their captors. Others were killed in skirmishes. One youth told me how he and three companions struggled through the jungle for four days without food or water. He said a bridge on his teeth came loose and fell out because of the condition of his parched mouth. Then one morning he heard a voice calling, "Muchachos! Muchachos!" Peering through the brush, he saw an old man with a bag on his back, coming down a slope. It was Crescencio Perez, still trying to round up the expedition. He had been attempting for days to find the youths lost in the vastness of the Sierra Maestra. He gave them food and water from his bag, then led them to where Fidel Castro, Che Guevara, Raul Castro and others were waiting.

Thus, with only twelve men, Fidel Castro began the task of organizing a rebellion against Batista and his army of 30,000 men, many of whom had been trained by American technicians. Two years later President Fulgencio Batista fled from the island. His defeat was brought about by the te-nacity and determination of this small group of rebels. His defeat was brought about by the youth of Cuba, by boys and girls, some not more than thirteen years of age, who had sufficient faith in Fidel Castro to fight and to die for a free-dom which they barely understood and had never tasted. But the story of Fidel Castro is only a part, still undeter-mined, of the history of Cuba, an island that has had a strange way of revenging itself on all the men who have ruled over it.

I *Gerardo Machado*

1

In June, 1931, I persuaded my husband Phil (James Doyle Phillips, of Friendship, Arkansas) to accept the position of correspondent in Cuba for *The New York Times*. We had lived in Cuba for several years and I had developed a strong interest in the political life of this island with its pirate lore, its turbulent history under Spanish rule, and its strangely mixed culture. Havana was a fascinating city, still clinging to its traditional ways. I found pleasure in the narrow streets, the gracious old colonial houses with high ceilings and central patios, the high barred windows, the cafés with their dedicated coffee drinkers, the odors of far-eastern perfumes wafted out of small shops where laces, perfumes, and lovely delicate fans were displayed. In those days shopkeepers were proud of their wares and in no haste to sell them.

But the undercurrents of revolution were already stirring. In Havana University the students were plotting against President Gerardo Machado, who had retained his office without an election by the infamous prorogue of power in 1928. A month after Phil became correspondent, the August, 1931 revolt against the Machado administration occurred. It was a failure. Cubans have staged few successful rebellions. I mean a rebellion sufficiently formidable through force of arms to overthrow a government. The reason is lack of organization, a tendency to reveal plans prematurely, and traitors in the ranks.

All Cuban writers and many American journalists have depicted General Gerardo Machado as a monster in human disguise, a cruel tyrant who reveled in torture and bloodshed. That viewpoint is erroneous. Machado was the cleverest politician ever produced by the island, greedy, revengeful and unscrupulous, but he was the result of a system of government rather than the creator of a dictatorship. Under Spanish rule, Cubans had never been permitted to hold any but the most lowly public offices. When the Cuban Republic was established in 1902, those elected to high offices were men of arms who had fought guerilla warfare for many years, and it was inevitable that they should follow the rule by which they had lived—that to the victor belongs the spoils. The constitution centralized power in the executive branch, so that gradually, through patronage and graft, both the legislative and judicial branches of the government became servile instruments in the hands of the President. With this setup, it is truly remarkable that an open dictatorship did not emerge prior to the Machado regime.

Cuba had been governed by five presidents before Machado. Don Tomas Estrada Palma, 1902-1906, was known as the "Honest President." He was reelected to a second term, but the Liberal Party, of which General José Miguel Gómez was the candidate, claimed the election was a fraud, and a revolution broke out. The United States intervened, landing troops and taking over Havana. Intervention lasted until 1909 when elections were held under the supervision of American authorities. José Miguel Gómez, 1909-1913, was Cuba's most typical president. His administration was extravagant, and political plums were handed out to his followers in lavish fashion. General Mario García Menocal, 1913-1921, was a man of education and an astute businessman. Despite this, graft and unprecedented expenditures characterized his administration. Alfredo Zayas, 1921-1925, noted for his respect of the civil rights of the people but whose administration was marred by extravagance.

With the Cuban people accustomed to such government, it was not difficult for Gerardo Machado y Morales, 1925-1933, to build the most powerful political machine in the history of the nation, to increase the armed forces and use them to hold power, and to run the Republic into a hundred million dollar debt. Machado's greatest mistake was his attempt to suppress radical student elements by violence and assassinations. Despite the graft and excessive expenditures of his administration, Cubans would have overlooked these, had he not turned to bloodshed. Fearing elections even while in control of the ballot boxes, he retained office for a second and longer term through reform of the constitution in the Prorogue Measure of 1928, passed by a submissive Congress. Thus Machado gained a second term of six years instead of four, and the terms of representatives and senators were extended to six and nine years respectively. There was no resistance to the Prorogue Measure, neither by the public, nor by the opposition parties. When Machado made the announcement which made him a virtual dictator, former president Mario Menocal sat on the platform and clapped his hands benignly. Only Colonel Carlos Mendieta refused to attend the inauguration. Only the students of Havana University protested.

The August, 1931 rebellion was headed by Mario Menocal, who had seen the error of his ways, and Colonel Mendieta, who had been trying for more than three years to organize resistance against the government. Both men were captured at Rio Verde, Piñar del Rio Province, when the navy failed to join the revolt as had been planned. Following this, matters came to a slow climax. The ABC Revolutionary Organization, a secret terroristic society, was founded in December, 1931, and an extensive campaign initiated. No government official or sympathizer was safe from bombings and attacks. Armored cars were hurriedly imported as a mode of transportation. The government killed students in revenge and the situation became complicated.

It was during this period that my husband and I began to have difficulties with the government. The Secretary of Interior, Octavio Zubizarreta, called Phil down to the department and told him with wrath that the dispatch sent in the previous day was erroneous. There had been a riot in Principe Fortress Jail. More than a hundred *porristas*—Machado's strong-arm squad—had been turned loose in the political prisoners' cell block at midnight with knives and other weapons to attack the prisoners. The prisoners had tried to defend themselves with iron bedsteads and such articles as they could lay their hands on. Several prisoners were so gravely wounded that it was necessary to remove them to the hospital at Camp Columbia. Zubizarreta in anger threw the report of the prison authorities in front of Phil to prove his point. Phil pointed out that the prison report had a much larger number of wounded than we had used. We received no more complaints from Zubizarreta.

The Cuban government continued to make complaints to the *Times,* accusing Phil of having "sold out to the rebels." Finally, in January, 1933, Mr. Russell Porter was sent down to find out the truth about Cuba. He sat in the office for two days, with a skeptical look on his face, as we outlined the situation to him. He had never been in Cuba before, did not speak Spanish, and we felt it our duty to give him as much data as possible. We were rewarded with incredulity. "Surely you can find something to say in favor of the Machado government!" he declared. The next day he went to see Ambassador Guggenheim and spent considerable time at the Embassy. When he returned, he remarked, frowning, that we had not shown the picture of conditions in as dark colors as we should have.

Porter stayed for some time and wrote excellent articles on the Cuban situation. We turned over to him our files containing political, economic and financial information. The Cubans complained that Porter had been sent to "white-

wash" Guggenheim, whom they hated, believing that the
American Ambassador and Machado were friends. The
names *Guggenado* and *Machadoheim* were coined to express
Cuban contempt. Actually, the American Ambassador was
not at fault; his hands were tied by Washington and he
could do nothing. The Chase National Bank, with its influence in Washington, was determined that President Machado
should remain in office as long as he continued to make payments on the public works loans.

The entire island of Cuba celebrated when President Roosevelt was elected and took office. People felt that Cuba would
probably get a "New Deal" and their frantic appeals for
assistance would be heard in Washington. Nevertheless, the
history of this island since its liberation from Spain does not
record many examples of Cuban gratitude for contributions
made by the United States in lives, blood and dollars. On
the contrary, there is in many quarters reluctance to accept
that the United States was in any measure responsible for
securing Cuba's freedom. Many evils which have appeared
in public life and many things which have gone wrong have
been attributed to the Americans. I am afraid history in this
respect is about to repeat itself.

The brutal killing of two brothers named Valdés Daussá,
witnessed by Phil and me, was largely responsible for attracting the attention of Washington to the terrible things
which were going on in Cuba. These boys were killed under
the dreaded *Ley de Fuga,* which really isn't a law at all but
an old Cuban custom. A prisoner is taken to a selected spot
and told to run. If he runs, he is shot; if he doesn't run, he
is shot; and the record reads: "killed while trying to escape."

It happened on Good Friday, April 14, 1933. Our house,
on Twenty-ninth Street, between E and F Streets, faced
Principe Fortress Jail. Phil's bedroom opened onto a balcony. After lunch Phil went to his room, put on a bathrobe,
and was lying on the bed, reading. I was playing with my
puppy, Blackie. We heard a burst of rifle fire. We both ran

to the balcony. Slightly downhill to the left of our house was a hospital. Below that, Avenida de los Presidentes, a new thoroughfare, cut through the hill at that point, with high cliffs on both sides. The cliff ended abruptly at the edge of the hospital grounds, giving a clear view of the Avenida for quite some distance. The sunshine makes the streets and buildings seem much more white than they are. We saw a youth come running. He was alone in the street, his shadow the only other moving thing. He was weaving wildly from side to side, as if he did not know where he was going. Then I saw him halt, raise his arms and wave them. In the still hot afternoon his voice was perfectly audible as he cried, "No tire mas, no tire mas." (Don't shoot any more.) Several men posted on the cliff nearest our house raised their rifles. The first fusillade struck him in the back. He stumbled, falling. The second smashed through his head and shoulders. He fell in front of the huge statue erected to former president General José Miguel Gómez.

My first reaction was that it couldn't be true. Then another burst of firing came from farther down the cliff, but we could not see. I simply stood there. Phil reacted in a different manner. He tore off his bathrobe, got into his clothes, and was out the front door and into the car before I could realize that we had witnessed a murder. Phil backed the car into F Street and circled the hospital. Reaching the sprawled figure, Phil saw that he was only a boy. He was breathing his last in a huge pool of blood. His chest was the only part of him that still moved. His eyes were no longer focused on anything. The boy seemed not to realize his wounds, but only to be trying desperately to catch his breath. As Phil stood there, the mulattoes who had shot the boy leisurely strolled down the cliff with trailing rifles. They paused and looked down at the dying boy without the slightest emotion. A uniformed policeman ran up. He made no inquiries, apparently knew exactly what had happened. He ordered Phil away from the body. The two killers, dressed in uniforms of the crude cloth worn by the guards at Príncipe Fortress, sauntered off.

Phil has a good memory for faces. One day he pointed out to me a man standing among the army officers who were assembling in the National Hotel prior to the encounter with Batista's forces known as the "Battle of the National." This mulatto stood near the entrance. They later tried and convicted those whom they claim to be the killers of the Daussá brothers, but both Phil and I know that the men condemned to death did not do the actual killing.

When Phil returned to the house, he looked sick. People are queer. Phil had been in the front lines during the First World War. He had seen men die in trenches and on muddy fields. He said it wasn't the sight of the boy lying there that had made him ill, but the method of execution, the coldness and indifference, as they shot him down like a wild animal. We climbed into our car and headed toward downtown Havana, passing along the Avenida de los Presidentes where a crowd had begun to gather in spite of the police. I wanted to find out who the boy was. Farther down the street we came upon another excited crowd gathered about a patch of blood and were told that a second youth had been shot, that a government car had taken away his body. We found out later that the car had taken the boy to a hospital. Of course he was dead.

Phil wrote the story just as we saw it happen. That it was a dangerous story never occurred to us, and no newspaperman would have hesitated to write it. This was the first time an American correspondent had ever witnessed a killing by Machado henchmen under the *Ley de Fuga*. Washington was shocked by the report and the attention of President Roosevelt was drawn to the Cuban situation.

Before ten o'clock that night we received information from police headquarters that President Machado had expressed stern disapproval of our eyewitness story of the killing. We were warned that the *porristas* were out to "get Phillips."

The *porristas* were a gang of criminals organized by Professor Leopoldo Fernandez Roz, member of the Havana high school faculty, to do private, unlawful acts for the government. They were provided with arms, ammunition and identification cards and took orders directly from Machado. They killed, assaulted and tortured. Roz had been shot down the month previous by members of the ABC Revolutionary Organization as he stood on a street corner. The plan, as explained to Phil, was typical of the swift, silent vengeance of Machado. Two *porristas* were to enter a café where Phil was often seen. They were to start an argument between themselves, draw their pistols, and instead of shooting at each other, to kill Phil. It would be merely another case of an innocent bystander unintentionally shot.

Phil could think of no way to prevent it from happening. A correspondent cannot go into hiding or avoid public places. I insisted that he cable *The New York Times* and have them ask Washington to request the Cuban government for a guarantee of his life. Phil sent the cable. Within twenty minutes we had a cable from the *Times* saying they had telephoned the State Department. Half an hour later a second cable arrived stating that Washington had called the American Embassy in Havana on the telephone and ordered them to demand protection. Frankly, I was amazed by such quick action, especially from the State Department in Washington, which usually leaves American citizens abroad to get out of their difficulties as best they can. Much relieved, we went to bed.

The next morning when we arrived at the office, we discovered that apparently the entire city knew about the affair. There is really little need for newspapers in Cuba; news travels much faster by word of mouth. There was no Ambassador here, Guggenheim having already returned to the States, leaving First Secretary Reed as chargé d'affaires. Reed had delivered a note to the Cuban State Department that morning and within an hour the matter was being discussed by the public.

Sr. Martinez Ybor of the State Department rushed to our office in hurt amazement to learn what had caused us to think so badly of the Machado government. Secretary of State, Dr. Orestes Ferrara, Italian-born politician, also was shocked over our evident misunderstanding of government policies. We were offered a police bodyguard which we declined with thanks. A policeman would be excellent protection, we thought, if government agents were out to kill one.

Two days later Phil was in the Salon H Café when he noticed two strange mulattoes hanging around. After you have formed the habit of drinking coffee two or three times a day in a particular café, over a period of years, you learn the people who patronize it, even though you may not know who they are. A secret police agent who had always been friendly with Phil came over to where Phil was drinking coffee at the bar and said, "See those negroes?" Phil nodded. "They're *porristas* and I have a hunch they're here on your account. Don't pay any attention to them. If one of them makes a move, I'll kill him and say I didn't know who he was." But Phil decided to drink up his coffee and leave the café. Later the bartender reported that the two negroes stayed in the café the greater part of the afternoon.

That was Saturday. Sunday was uneventful. Cubans never work on Sundays and put aside all forms of activity except those of gaiety and pleasure. I have never seen a riot on Sunday and in the revolutions the rebels retire into the hills and spend the day resting and feasting.

Monday afternoon Phil stopped in at the café. Cubans drink coffee all day long and Americans generally acquire the habit after a few years here. Phil did take the precaution, however, to stand behind the cash register at the end of the bar. Suddenly, in a perfectly still atmosphere in which there had been no loud voices, two men standing at the bar began to shout at each other. They stepped back, drew pistols from inside their coats, and spun about, looking not at each other, but at Phil. The proprietor of the café, Marcus, grabbed the arm of one of the men, while a waiter began to grapple with the other. Using the coffee urn as a shield, Phil hurried into the kitchen and out the side door. It was all over before the patrons of the café had time to become alarmed. The men put away their weapons and went out into the street, walking side by side. A few minutes after Phil arrived at his office a government man walked in and announced that the *porristas* intended to murder Phil within the next twenty-four hours.

I insisted that Phil call the chargé d'affaires, Reed, and ask for asylum. Our house was certainly not a safe place. He called Reed, who said he didn't believe he could offer assistance. We were amazed—a chargé d'affaires of the American government refusing to give an American asylum. I have often wondered if Reed is a typical example of our diplomatic career men. He knew so very little about the Cuban situation. He refused to believe that *porristas* existed until he saw them being slaughtered in the streets by enraged mobs the day Machado fled the island. Phil telephoned the American Consul-General, Dumont, who instructed us to come to his house immediately. Later, Reed informed Phil that he had called the Cuban Secretary of State, Ferrara, and had made arrangements for Phil to spend the night at the home of Ferrara. Reed seemed quite pleased with himself. The Machado government had given orders that an American was to be killed and Reed had asked the Secretary of State of that government to invite the target to spend the night under his roof! Phil thanked Reed politely and hung up.

We went to the home of the Consul-General. Mrs. Dumont had often asked me to visit her. I told her I had expected to do so, but not under such circumstances. We had known them casually for several years, but later became real friends and spent many pleasant hours in their company.

We stayed with them two nights, but went about our affairs as usual during the day. We decided the best thing was for Phil to be armed. I tried to buy a revolver, but I might as well have looked for a white elephant. Finally I remembered an old gunsmith who sometimes sold guns that had never been claimed by their owners. I went to see him. The government had confiscated his entire stock. He said he doubted if he would ever see any of it again, that he considered his official receipt as just so much paper. After much search, he found a .32 that belonged to one of the clerks, rather antiquated, but at least a gun. I gave it to Phil. He hesitated, but I told him at least he would be spared the indignity of being shot down like some helpless animal.

Then matters took a new turn. Representative Shoemaker publicly stated in Washington that he had received confidential information from an agent who had attended a meeting of the Revolutionary Junta in New York that the ABC planned to murder Phil and blame it on the Machado government, in an effort to stir American public opinion against Machado. Someone in Washington wired Consul-General Dumont, who called our office several times that Saturday afternoon. Ironically, we had gone to a board meeting of the Band of Mercy Humane Society. When we returned to the office, Dumont came in and said he thought we had better spend the night and Sunday at his house. He frankly admitted that when both the government and the revolutionaries began talking about killing a person, protection became almost impossible to guarantee. Further, the political repercussions of an attempt on Phil's life would be grave. It was impossible for Phil and me to go immediately to the Dumont residence, as suggested, because there were dispatches to send. But we did arrive late that night and stayed over Sunday.

Monday we were visited by dozens of indignant revolutionaries. The story had become known all over Havana by midnight on Saturday, having arrived in Cuba over the service wires to the newspapers. The ABC representatives stated that they had never contemplated such an act. They offered us a bodyguard, which we declined with thanks and inward smiles. What could be more absurd than having bodyguards who were being sought by the police, bodyguards that the police had orders to bring in dead or alive?

We stayed several nights with the Dumonts, then decided that with so much publicity it was no longer to the advantage of the government to harm Phil.

On May 7, 1933, American Ambassador Sumner Welles arrived. He was heralded by the long suffering Cuban people as their savior. It must be remembered that the majority of Cubans still looked to the United States to free them from oppression. Within a relatively few years, this attitude was to change into a fury against any form of American influence or intervention in Cuban political affairs.

A small revolution broke out in Santa Clara and Camagüey Provinces on May 15th. Rebel bands gathered in the hill country and guerilla warfare began. The rebels would attack a small town with a military post, kill the soldiers stationed there, seize supplies and arms, then scurry back into the hills. By the time the government could send soldiers after them, the entire band would have vanished. Amusing stories are told of the amnesties offered by the soldiers. President Machado tried this several times. The rebels would be invited to come in and lay down their arms with impunity. They would come down from the hills, ceremoniously surrender their arms, useless old shotguns, rifles so rusty they could not be fired, revolvers from the Spanish-American War. The rebels would go to their homes to visit their wives and families, or sit about in the taverns, drinking and having fun. On an appointed day they would return to the mountains, where their good rifles and ammunition had been wrapped in moisture-proof materials and buried or hidden. In this way a rebel band could be ready to fight within twenty-four hours. These tactics were destructive to army morale, and forced the government to keep troops in all sectors of the provinces, since it was never known where or when the guerillas would strike.

From Santa Clara and Camagüey came stories of atrocities committed by Major Arsenio Ortiz, one of the most hated and feared men in Cuba. Machado had placed him in charge of operations there. Ortiz, as military supervisor of Oriente Province in 1931, killed so many, both by shooting and hanging, that the people demanded he be removed. A civil judge even had the temerity to order his arrest. Newspapers printed so many stories of atrocities committed by Ortiz that Machado was finally forced to bring him to Havana under guard. He stayed at Atarés Fortress, certainly not a prisoner, and later was assigned to the Havana police force where he continued his brutal methods. When trouble started in Santa Clara, he was sent there. Ortiz was a practiced, professional killer. He belongs to that cruel class of men who consider murder a matter of efficiency and expediency. His specialty was killing a helpless prisoner by placing a pistol at the back of his head and firing. I have been told he was a very religious man, widely read, and of fair education.

On May 26th, Ortiz was brought to Havana to answer charges of wantonly murdering and torturing *guajiros*, small farmers, to get information concerning rebel bands. His arrest was due to strong pressure from Ambassador Welles. Ortiz never faced a court-martial. Instead, he was sent to Germany on money furnished by the government.

On June 1st, President Machado called the American newspaper correspondents to the palace. The interview took place at night. He talked about reforms of the constitution but vehemently affirmed that he had no intention of resigning. We all knew that Welles had urged Machado to give the interview and be nice to the press for once in his life, probably outlining what the President was to say in a general way; but the General was a poor pupil. He could not resist the chance to say loudly and with emphasis that he had no intention of resigning. He was undoubtedly sincere. He had no such intention. He had planned to deal with

Ambassador Welles as with other ambassadors and if possible to use him as a pawn. We all knew the game. Government officials here bragged before Ambassador Welles arrived that they would *ponerle rabo* (tie a can to him). They said the first thing would be to give a series of lavish entertainments, with plenty of liquor, repeating the word "liquor" with great significance. Imagine their amazement when the Ambassador turned out to be a tea drinker, a man with the bearing of a true diplomat, and as suave as any Cuban.

The interview was written and the refusal to resign played up because other statements were merely worn-out platitudes concerning patriotism. The Ambassador must have been very much provoked, although one would never have known it except for the gleam in his eye.

Ambassador Welles maintained at all times an unruffled exterior. I remember a correspondent who during troubled times in Cuba called up the Ambassador with a piece of really startling news. The reaction to his story was, in a dry voice, "how interesting."

Privately, we all knew the President was "in disgrace." President Machado then tried to conciliate the opposition. He announced "reforms to the constitution." The opposition met the announcement with loud guffaws. Reforms—Machado had reformed the constitution once too often when he put himself in power without elections in 1928. In fact, a little more reform and he would have been in the presidency for life.

Ambassador Welles had already begun his famous Mediation Plan by which he hoped to bring about an agreement between the Machado government and its enemies. I often wonder if Welles really had any idea this could be done.

The mediation idea was received with reluctance and suspicion. No group cared to be the first to accept it. President Machado refused to say that he had accepted it. Finally, about the middle of June, Ambassador Welles called the foreign correspondents down to the Embassy and told them exactly what he hoped to accomplish. He also asked their help in gaining the consent and confidence of the different opposing factions, saying he knew the correspondents were in close touch with all of them. It was a clever gesture on his part.

The Ambassador almost convinced Phil that mediation could be carried out. I had my own opinion, but kept it to myself. I made some telephone calls and that afternoon the office was full of the terroristic crowd. Many of them came out of hiding. I thought the matter urgent because I knew they were planning an assassination the next Monday. I talked until I was hoarse. They liked the mediation plan not at all. Finally, I persuaded them to call a meeting for that night and to appoint two members to see the Ambassador. They asked me for suggestions and I offered the name of Luis Fuentes, who had been our best contact for many months, and another youth of good education and excellent family as the delegates to see the Ambassador. I didn't know whether or not the Ambassador would see them but I thought an assassination in high government circles would certainly ruin any possibility of carrying out the mediation plan.

Saturday, Phil and I went to see the Ambassador. The Ambassador sat behind his big desk in the Embassy with the window at his back and listened gravely as I explained that I thought an assassination might be avoided. The Ambassador appeared surprised but almost immediately agreed to see the youths, although he did ask me what type they were. I told him they were well educated, one spoke perfect English, both were quite charming boys, outside of their tendency to throw bombs. I have wondered what he had previously thought of the terroristic groups. Possibly he visualized them as being long-haired, bearded, typical anarchists.

The Ambassador talked with the boys that afternoon and later told Phil he was extremely glad to have had contact established and was much interested in getting the point of view of this group. They agreed to curtail terroristic activities, although in their meeting held after the interview, the boys told me they had a most difficult time persuading the others. On Wednesday of the following week the ABC Revolutionary Organization publicly accepted mediation and pledged themselves to refrain from terroristic activities.

But the government continued its arrests and murders. A policeman, Corbo, suspected of some connection with the ABC revolutionaries, was arrested while on duty and taken to Atarés Fortress. There he was tortured. They even slashed his throat twice with a knife. Believing him to be dying, the prison authorities sent him to Emergency Hospital. The police informed his wife that he had been fatally wounded in the performance of his duties. She hurried to the hospital and managed to reach his bedside. He told her the truth about what had happened. The police, who apparently believed he would not be able to speak with the throat wounds, and that he was dying anyway, had let her get past them. But when they saw him speaking, they literally grabbed her and pulled her away from the bed and ordered her out of the hospital, telling her she could not see him again. She went to the office of a lawyer and waited from eight A.M. until noon for him. She explained that she wanted to find a man named Phillips, although she had no idea where he lived. The lawyer knew Phil and brought her to our office. She told us what had happened. If ever I saw blank despair, it stared out of that woman's eyes. Phil gave the story all the publicity he could. Ambassador Welles called the attention of the authorities to the report and Corbo was sent to Camp Columbia military hospital. He is now a police major. He visited us later to express his gratitude and showed us the scars on his throat and arms.

Phil failed to save Sergeant José Angel Hernández, Battery B, Engineers Corps of the Cuban army, because Ambassador Welles accepted as fact the word of a minor Cuban official. Hernández was arrested on suspicion of having aided the ABC Revolutionary Organization in some manner never made clear. We were advised that he was undergoing torture for the third time and that he would not survive. Phil rushed to the Embassy as soon as the information reached us but the Ambassador, being informed by a minor official that Hernández had been removed to the Isle of Pines Penitentiary, decided not to follow the matter further. The body of the sergeant was later excavated from the gruesome graveyard of torture victims in the horse corral at Atarés Fortress.

While the American government had no legal right to interfere on behalf of Cubans, it has often been done and, in the peculiar situation which then existed, with Cuban officialdom trembling in their shoes as to the final action which would be taken by the United States, a word from the Ambassador was usually sufficient. The memory of United States intervention in 1907 still gave an American Ambassador considerable prestige.

I do not really know how many others went to the trouble Phil did to try to save lives. Of course, that is not the primary function of a correspondent but Phil was never able to isolate himself from the fact that human beings have obligations to each other which transcend their occupations. Phil was much admired by the Cubans for having written the eyewitness story of the killing of the Valdés Daussá brothers. It made the Cubans trust Phil and made them feel that he could help them.

The week before I left Cuba for a vacation in the United States, an unusual case was brought to Phil by members of the Feminist Party. A girl named Leonor Borja was being held in the City Hospital, under police guard. She was seventeen, a University Freshman, had been arrested twenty-one times and had served two sentences in the women's prison at Guanabacoa on charges of anti-administration activities. Anti-administration activities with the Machado government covered a multitude of offenses, even criticism of the administration. A law was finally passed making it ninety days in jail and a fifty-dollar fine to criticize the government in a public place. I don't remember the last charge on which the girl had been jailed, but it seemed every time the authorities saw her they arrested her. However, the sentence of ninety days given her had expired and for more than a month she had been in the hospital. The authorities refused to release her.

Phil took the case to Ambassador Welles, who promised to look into it. The morning I left for New Orleans the girl's mother came to the office to show me a picture of her. She was small, slender and very pretty. As the mother sat in the office talking with me the telephone rang and Ambassador Welles told Phil that the girl would be released immediately. The mother wept for joy. The girl later told us that she had never been sick. The authorities had simply not wanted to release her and had used this method in order to hold her indefinitely.

2

July 24, 1933: I arrived home today. After many years' residence in Havana no other place seems so much like home. When I saw shadowy, gloomy Morro Castle at the entrance of the bay, it seemed as though I had never been away. As the ship turned into the narrow channel at the mouth of the harbor, I spied our rather ancient and hard-used car coming along Malecón Drive. A white clad arm went up in salute—that was Phil.

A few minutes later we docked. Phil came on board. We were soon on land and walking through the huge dim warehouse of the United Fruit Company, where laborers were leisurely arranging incoming merchandise in orderly rows. We came out into the blinding, glaring, tropical sun. It was hot but I like the heat; I like the narrow streets, the glimpses of green patios through open doorways, the smell of burning coffee, the cry of the newsboys and peddlers who sell articles for the entire household in the streets.

I have been away five weeks. I went to Oklahoma City to visit my parents and I enjoyed it thoroughly but I was just a little out of step with the tempo of the States. I could not be enthusiastic over the return of beer. People seemed to talk so excitedly about things of little importance. I suppose I was somewhat at fault, for I could see that they were try-

ing, in their way, to entertain me. Several fairly well educated people asked me if Cuba were not a province or something of the United States. I told them perhaps they were
thinking of the Platt Amendment, and they said probably
that was it, and then asked if everyone in Havana did the
rumba . . .

Havana is much the same as when I left, a little more
sullen, a little more depressed—the capital of a country
which has had its hopes of freedom dashed to the ground a
dozen times in the past six months; a city which seethes with
rumor, intrigue, murder, and strange disappearances; a city
whose inhabitants amaze me with their long endurance of an
oppression which long ago would have aroused the Anglo-
Saxon race to open fighting. But perhaps I overrate Anglo-
Saxons.

Phil tells me there is no real news. Nothing has happened.
Ambassador Welles is trying to arbitrate between President
Machado and the ABC Revolutionary Organization, which
can never be done, no matter what Welles thinks. It is impossible to talk reason to a man incapable of reasoning.
Machado is convinced that nothing can shake his position.
He is brutal and treacherous, with Machiavellian cunning,
understanding his countrymen, their strength and their
weakness.

John, our 240 pound Jamaican cook, smiling broadly, told
me they had gotten along fine in my absence. Our shining
tile floors, high ceilings, shutter windows without draperies,
wicker funiture and old mahogany look good after rugs, cur-
tains and small rooms. People in the States simply stuff their
houses with furniture. Even the house at home with polished
floors and wide expanses of glass windows seemed stuffy
after eighteen foot ceilings. The one thing I miss is a lawn
and grass. Dad says my idea of a lawn is 360 acres with a
house in the middle. Our house here has a yard the size of a
pocket handkerchief. The neighbors' chickens find our flower
beds so enticing that seed is scratched out before it gets a

chance to sprout. There is only one rooster and three bantam
hens, but to look at the flower beds one would imagine a
good sized lion had been digging.

Lunch was ready. We had red snapper, of which I am very
fond, lettuce, boiled potatoes, sherbert and cake. I didn't
gain but three pounds on my vacation, which is a miracle
considering the amount of food I ate. One can never get food
in Havana like in the States. The average Cuban drinks
coffee and usually eats bread—butter among the richer
classes—for breakfast. Noon lunch, called *almuerzo,* consists
of rice in some form, eggs, black beans, potatoes, meat, fried
bananas and a dessert. Dinner is more or less a repetition of
lunch. The amount of rice consumed by the island of Cuba
is simply astounding. It arrives here from the Far East in
cargo lots.

When we first came to Havana green vegetables were a
rarity. Later the Chinese began to establish small truck
farms and now vegetables are plentiful except in June, July
and August when the sun is too hot for anything except cane
to grow.

July 26: President Machado restored full civil rights to
the people today—an empty gesture. Machado is so univer-
sally hated by the people that he can stay in power only by
force of arms. Military supervisors will continue to command
every district; civil authorities will do as they are told or
resign.

I wonder how far Machado is going with this mediation
idea? He has no intention of relinquishing his power and in
my opinion is playing for time. *How many times have we
heard this old mediation story?* There can be no mediation in
Cuba and I don't blame the students for refusing to have
anything to do with it. Phil is quite sold on the idea but I
am not.

Dr. Guillermo Belt came to see me today. Nice young
chap of about twenty-seven or twenty-eight. He is a protegé

of Colonel Carlos Mendieta and perfectly fitted for a political role in my opinion. His father died some time ago and left his three sons with sufficient money so there is no need to make much of an effort in that direction. Guillermo is soft spoken, almost shy, speaks English well and has some excellent ideas. His brother Alberto is a blond, takes nothing seriously and has an engaging laugh. Guillermo handles the finances of the revolutionary groups. Alberto belongs to the active terrorists and specializes in sabotage.

Dr. Belt has implicit faith in Ambassador Welles and believes the mediation is going to be a success. He is so enthusiastic over the situation that I didn't have the heart to discourage him.

Everyone is impatient for something to happen and for negotiations to be speeded up.

There wasn't much news this afternoon so Phil and I went swimming at the National Hotel pool. It is closer and more convenient than the beach. I can only swim after four when the sun loses its force, otherwise my skin simply comes off. When Phil gets tanned he resembles an Indian. He is dark anyway and might be taken for a foreigner, despite the fact he was born in Arkansas. I remember a tourist who came into the office once and heard Phil talking Spanish to someone. The woman turned to me and said sweetly, "My dear, does your husband speak English?"

Oclassen, the hotel auditor, told a story that seems to me to explain an important difference between the Cuban and the American. The American was named Bowman and he was a resident of Cuba for many years. It seems that once some Cuban challenged him to a duel. Duels appeal to the Cuban sense of drama. I am afraid many Cubans find more honor in a dramatic demonstration of courage than in being reasonable. This man sent his seconds to Bowman who had the privilege of choosing weapons. Bowman sat at his desk and looked at the seconds gravely for a minute and then said: "I am an American and am not accustomed to fighting duels. Here is the only way I will fight. We will enter a room naked, each armed with a knife. The door will be locked. The one who comes out alive wins the duel." There was no duel.

We came back to town at six and Phil wrote a short dispatch. Then we went home. I was so sleepy I could hardly sit up. Swimming always affects me that way. I was sleeping soundly when Blackie, my small dog, jumped off the bed, barking. It was two A.M. I looked in Phil's room and found him still reading and, after lecturing Blackie on learning the difference between a cat and a burglar, and then lecturing Phil on reading all night, I went back to sleep.

July 27: Machado exploded the negotiations this afternoon when he told the Cuban Congress that he had accepted Welles only in an individual capacity. He said, "You can be assured that the mediation is not being carried on by a government or I would not continue as President of the Republic. Our land must be maintained free, independent and unhampered by the Platt Amendment." Machado must be playing politics, either that or he is preparing to defy the American government. Members of Congress are becoming nervous because the Opposition is talking loudly about what Ambassador Welles is going to do and how the American government is going to oust Machado.

If mediation should really go forward it will mean that Congress must first approve the new constitution; then it will take six months to call a constituent assembly. But suppose Congress refuses to approve the draft constitution and Machado loses control of Congress because the legislators fear the United States is helping to take their jobs away from them? What then? Many of the Senate, for example, have terms running until 1935 under the modification of the constitution which Machado caused to be approved in 1928 and which the ABC Revolutionaries claims is illegal. It is the same old game of politics played all over the world;

the stakes a little more alluring; the graft a little easier to get perhaps; the ones at the top a little more confident that nothing can shake their position.

We have been deluged by telephone calls and visitors since Machado made that statement to Congress this afternoon. It spread over Havana like wildfire; it was not even necessary for the newspapers to publish it.

July 29: Washington has quite pointedly stated that Ambassador Welles is acting under instructions from the United States Government. This is in direct conflict with Machado's statement to the Congress yesterday, thus putting Machado in an embarrassing position. The Opposition breathed a sigh of relief and there were loud cheers for the U.S.A.

July 30: Perseverance had its reward. Blackie almost caught a burglar. Suddenly in the early hours of the morning she literally fell off my bed with such a clamor that I awakened. She dashed into the bathroom and I dashed after her. With one leap she jumped into the bathtub and tried to climb out the open casement window above. As I turned on the light I stumbled over Phil's trousers and saw his key ring, checkbook and his numerous credentials from the government neatly spread out on the washbasin. I then realized that Blackie had really found a burglar. I walked into Phil's room and shook him—no amount of noise can wake him—and demanded to know how much money was in his pockets, telling him it had been stolen. He opened one eye and said sleepily, "Seven cents, I think."

Imagine the disgust of that burglar! I am sure he will never again have a kind feeling for Americans, whom he had always heard were simply rolling in wealth.

John, our cook, wants to get a big dog to protect the household. I might get a big dog but I'll keep the little one. Dad always said it was a good idea to have a little dog around to wake up the big dog, because he had seen many a large dog snore while thieves carried off the piano.

August 3: Small things sometimes grow into big things, even in politics. When the bus drivers walked out on strike no one paid any attention to them, but now it looks as though there will be a general strike. How effective it will be is another question. There are some whispers that Machado would like to see violence between the strikers and the police so he can break off negotiations with Ambassador Welles, place the island under martial law and handle the situation through military control. He reportedly feels that the Cuban people are getting too much of a taste of freedom with Welles here as moral support.

No streetcars this morning, no taxicabs, no trucks. A few private cars are running at their own risk. Nails are strewn in the streets, also staples with one side bent upward so that it is practically certain they will penetrate any tire which touches them. I saw several cars with brooms tied in front of each wheel. It seems to work. But I also saw two with punctures. Gasoline is giving out. The garage where we usually buy was closed but when we honked the horn the doors rolled back and we drove in. We filled up the tank but they haven't much left. All deliveries have stopped.

Phil had Mendez, our printer, print a sign, *The New York Times, Periodico* and paste it on the windshield so the strikers won't throw rocks or shoot at us, as they have been doing at other cars.

We went to the market and loaded up with vegetables and then bought a filet roast and some canned goods. There are still vegetables but there won't be any more, the Chinaman told us, because the countrymen are afraid to bring them into town. The strikers are threatening all vehicles, especially delivery trucks. The head of the chauffeurs' union is quoted as saying that every vehicle on the streets will be wrecked and burned but perhaps with our sign we will not be molested.

August 4: Didn't arrive home until early this morning. The situation is becoming more tense all the time. No ice or milk deliveries this morning. We are furnishing our neighbors on each side with ice from our refrigerator.

Streets are deserted; everyone is afraid to go out. More strikes this morning. Railway employees plan to walk out tonight. At noon newspapers will shut down. Now we shall be forced to cover the town and island literally by ourselves. The telephone rings incessantly. People call us from all directions and in every part of the city telling us what they have heard and seen and asking for news. Everyone wants to know when the American marines will land. ABC Revolutionaries flood the office asking for news and bringing us rumors, some of them fantastic. It is a good thing we have lived in Cuba long enough to know what to believe and what not to believe.

Gonzalo de Quesada came in today laughing about how he crossed the bay since all the ferries have stopped running. Quesada occupies a rather singular position. He is the son of Cuba's first minister to Washington, one of the island's real patriots. He is strongly opposed to Machado but also dislikes the former president Menocal, as everyone knows, and that seems to have kept Machado from taking the risk of imprisoning him. I know Quesada works all the time with the ABC Revolutionaries and has a tremendous amount of information. He said he walked down to the waterfront where a navy launch was getting ready to bring some Machado politicians across to Havana. Being acquainted with everyone, he stopped to talk with them. When the boatman said, "Ready," he stepped in with the rest of the *Machadistas* and came across. He wondered if he could return the same way, so, with an air of importance, he asked the boatman what time the launch returned in the afternoon. Possibly he can pretend he is one of the favored few until the launch crew finds out differently.

There is something unusual about this strike. It seems to be spontaneous and there are no leaders. The ABC Revolutionaries deny they are organizing it, although they are doing everything to stimulate the movement. We were told that Martinez Villena, the young Communist leader, is behind it. I doubt that because the striking unions are not communistic. It seems like a snowball. I certainly would like to see the Cubans make a success of it.

Midnight, and I'm still in the office. I'm terribly tired. I had to tell Joe, our office boy, to stay and answer the phone while we wrote dispatches. It rings all the time. My telephone conversations contained such comments as these: "No, the American marines have not arrived. That was a merchant vessel, not a warship you saw in the harbor . . . No, I don't think they will come . . . No, Mr. Welles has said nothing. 1 have no idea what his plans are . . . No, I don't know when the strike will end and if I were you I would buy some groceries and sit tight and wait."

August 5: The telephone rang at six this morning. Someone wanted to know when the United States was going to intervene. Imagine, at that hour! I simply staggered out of bed. We went to bed at three this morning. People never think of those things. John came at eight, having walked the twenty blocks from his house. I arrived in the office to find Joe doing nothing but answering the phone. With no newspapers, the town seems to think that foreign correspondents are here to furnish them with news.

I noticed Chief of Police Ainciart and his gang trying to force the stores to open. As we came along Galiano Street, someone stopped us and told us Ainciart had just been there, waving his revolver in the air and threatening to shoot the watchmen at the stores if they didn't open the doors. They opened them but as soon as Ainciart went farther down the street they closed the doors again. The merchants are in a predicament. The strikers come by and threaten them, the police arrive and threaten them, they spend their time opening and closing doors. But there are no clerks and customers and it is all a useless procedure.

Ainciart also went to the Cosmopolita Restaurant, across Central Park from our office, where many Oppositionists gather. He was accompanied by two henchmen, with drawn revolvers. The police chief stopped outside the door where a group stood talking. He cursed and raved like a madman, telling them to come on and fight if they were so brave. The men had sense enough not to say a word and stood perfectly still. As one of the young men told me afterwards, "If I had so much as sneezed I would have sneezed myself into the next world."

There were small riots in the city today, with several killed and wounded. The police are walking the streets, stepping warily like belligerent tomcats, and waiting for someone to make a wrong move so they can shoot. With the strike in progress, the meetings of Welles and the mediation committee are ridiculous. People are getting more and more impatient, while Machado sits grimly in the palace and demands that his armed forces break the strike.

August 6: This general strike is a marvelous thing. An entire nation folds its arms and quits work. I don't know exactly what they can accomplish and apparently the strikers themselves are more or less vague on that point. They intend either to starve themselves to death or force the United States to take pity on them and intervene. Anyway, they are determined to see this through, no matter what happens. There is no leadership to this strike; it is entirely spontaneous—a nation without a leader, acting in perfect accord.

Waiters, cooks, bellboys, room service and other employees of all hotels walked out this morning. One can't get a cup of coffee for love or money. Phil sent Joe out scouting. He managed to get a couple of sad-looking sandwiches and three bottles of mineral water, without ice. The bottles of water, imported from Spain, must have been in stock for years, and we paid forty-five cents for each bottle. Hotels are refusing to serve anyone other than their own guests. In most hotels you find the manager cooking, the office force acting as waiters and everyone helping to clean up the rooms. I saw a few distracted looking American tourists on the street. Poor things! They can't get anything decent to eat, nor are there any cars, or any places to go. When they leave they will have to walk to the docks and heaven knows how they will get their luggage down. Carry it, I suppose. There are no dock workers and vessels land only passengers who think they must come to Cuba. Some of the steamship agents complain their boats have been hauling Havana bound freight around the ocean for days with no place to land it.

Machado once more ordered his soldiers to "restore public order." But the soldiers are perfectly helpless in the face of the present situation. Ambassador Welles admitted today that the Mediation Plan has struck a snag over shortening the terms of the present government officials. The Ambassador had a conference with Machado this afternoon. The Secretary of one of the cabinet officials came breathlessly into the office after climbing the five flights of stairs. He was afraid to use the elevator. He repeated in detail what each had said. It is good copy but of course we can't use it. Welles has bluntly ordered Machado to resign. Now watch the fun start. It is a wonder Machado didn't have apoplexy on the spot.

Outlaw radio stations keep on broadcasting in spite of all efforts of the Machado government to stop them. The ABC's are telling the people to hold out and force Machado to resign.

August 7: About three this afternoon a crowd began to collect around the Capitolio where Congress was in session. Some very foolish people got the idea that Machado might resign. Why the immense crowd collected in front of the Capitolio is just one of those Cuban mysteries.

Phil and I had gone downstairs to the café. Marcus, the proprietor, personally made coffee for us behind closed doors, although of course there was no milk. We stopped in the doorway of the Manzana to look at the crowd. The Prado in front of the Capitolio, which is very wide, was packed with people. There must have been somewhere near 5000.

As we stood there a sudden shout went up. We were too far away to see what happened but later we learned a mulatto had rushed out of the Capitolio and, pausing at the top of the steps, screamed: "Machado has resigned."

One moment, thousands of people were sweeping across Central Park, yelling like maniacs. Some of them climbed the statue of Marti. It happened so quickly we remained motionless in the doorway, as did the doormen of the building. Phil looked down toward the Plaza Hotel and noticed two American women tourists walking toward Central Park, right into that mad crowd. How they could have been so foolish is incomprehensible. Phil dashed out, grabbed them both unceremoniously by the arms and, despite their protests, hustled them onto the sidewalk and into the building. The doormen slammed the big, heavy mahogany doors just as the first wave of the mob hit the sidewalk and started down Zulueta Street toward the palace.

We stood there in the dim light of the foyer. The protests of the two American women died down when they saw the look almost of horror on the faces of everyone in the foyer. We didn't have long to wait. There was the crack of a rifle. Then a machine gun opened up. Revolvers barked. The crowd shrieked like the cry of a single animal, and fought to reach shelter from the hail of death. We hurried upstairs. The two American women didn't have to be invited. They followed. When the women were all safe on the second floor, Phil went back down in the elevator. I was frantic. Although the gunfire had ceased, I knew it was only a lull. But of course Phil wanted to find out how many had been killed and wounded. Then the firing broke out again.

The phone began to ring constantly. People were being shot down in the streets in other parts of the town. The gunfire was spreading to all sections of Havana. Others reported hearing a radio broadcast that Machado had resigned. Much to my relief Phil, some twenty minutes later, returned. I noticed a piece of skin missing from the back of his hand. He shamefacedly admitted it had been caused by a bullet. He

had just reached the Plaza Hotel when Chief of Police Ainciart passed in a car and raked the sidewalk with machine
gun fire. Phil had dashed for shelter behind a stone column
but his exposed hand was struck by a bullet.

The hospital is surrounded by a huge crowd trying to find
out if their relatives are dead or dying. Hospital authorities
will permit no one to enter, so the crowd waits around outside, some crying, all struggling to see the faces of the
wounded as they are brought in. A call has been sent out for
doctors and nurses. Every first aid station and private clinic is
full.

It seems that at the same time the mulatto rushed out of
the Capitolio shouting, "Machado has resigned," a radio station broadcast the same report. Since it first identified itself
as the "ABC Station," the public believed that Machado had
actually resigned. In every part of Havana the people had
rushed into the streets shouting, cheering and celebrating.
Automobiles filled with plain-clothes men armed with rifles
and machine guns simultaneously appeared and started
shooting.

It sounds to me like a Machado trap in order to bring his
enemies out into the open. Oppositionists have repeatedly
warned their members to stay indoors; they were apparently
aware of some such plan. In fact, the ABC Station broad-
casted this warning every day to the public. Unfortunately,
the people were too eager to believe in Machado's resignation.

August 10: Our office continues to act as something of a
news center. It is fortunate in one way because we get news
from every section of the city. To drive a car is getting more
and more dangerous. We have had several blowouts—big
staples which went through the tires like paper. Yesterday,
in the outskirts of the city, strikers cut four tires off the car.
They threatened Phil with rocks and other missiles despite
the *New York Times* sign on the car.

We have no bread of any kind. I have eaten crackers so

long I feel like a parrot. Potatoes have gone up from four to fourteen cents per pound; chickens retailing at three for a dollar jumped to eighty cents each; there are no fresh vegetables and little rice and beans. Some of the *bodegas* (corner grocery stores) are still open but they have practically nothing left on their shelves. I can't imagine what the really poverty stricken are doing. A laborer cheerfully remarked to Phil that he had eaten only one meal during the past two days, but he was going to hold out until Machado resigned. That expresses the Cuban national feeling.

The interior towns are just like Havana. Everything is paralyzed, industries shut down, stores closed, streets deserted. On the National Highway, private cars are being fired on. Anyone with a loaf of bread is of the social elite nowadays. Cubans know nothing of the art of making bread at home; the majority of them have no ovens so that when the bakeries close there is simply no bread.

Dr. Orestes Ferrara, Cuban Ambassador to Washington, came back to Havana yesterday. We were informed that he told Machado to sit tight and call the bluff of the United States, because they would not intervene. He gave us a long statement saying he thought the general strike would fail.

The atmosphere is tense, no longer cheerful. People's faces are grim and drawn. The government is getting more and more nervous and worried. The Conservative and Popular Parties today accepted Ambassador Welles' Mediation Plan and wrote a letter asking Machado to sacrifice himself; in other words, to resign. Their bugaboo of course is American intervention. They tell themselves it won't come but they are frightened to death because either way their jobs are certainly ended. On the other hand, we hear stories that Machado is trying to force intervention, knowing that he will then be protected and permitted to leave the island with the fortune he has accumulated.

August 11: We came to town this morning about ten, as usual. The office was already full of people, excitement running high. Everyone felt something was sure to happen. We had been told two days ago of a planned revolt of the army. We were skeptical. This morning we were told the exact plans. At three this afternoon we were informed that the plans had miscarried and the officers heading the revolt were in jail. Three officers had already been executed. According to the story, these officers had gone as a committee to Major Castillo, chief of Camp Columbia, who had refused to join the plot. Instead of making him a prisoner on the spot, they meekly went away and he had them arrested.

Frankly, we were skeptical. We had lived among revolutions and rumors of revolutions too long. Phil went to the Embassy and talked with military attaché Gimperling, who professed to know nothing. However, as Phil sat there, Gimperling received a telephone call and was apparently much perturbed. Taking a pencil he wrote down the names of those whom Phil had been informed were arrested. He admitted that he had just been advised of their detention.

It was nearly four o'clock by then. War preparations were being made in Havana. Troops were moving in. The palace guard was tripled. Machine guns were mounted on the grounds and in Zayas Park facing the palace. Someone in the Horter Building phoned us that at El Castillo de la Fuerza, military headquarters, soldiers were being stationed on the roof, great activity was going on, with truckloads of soldiers coming and going. President Machado left the palace hurriedly and started for Camp Columbia. This hardly looked like a revolt at the camp. We were extremely puzzled by this peculiar situation.

Phil and Haas of the United Press decided to follow the President out to Camp Columbia. I tried to get them not to do it and later had a woman's privilege of telling them, "I told you so." They arrived at the camp and found cavalry, infantry, and artillery drawn up as if ready for action. Even mountain artillery packs were in place, as well as portable wireless apparatus. Then they discovered that all approaches back into the city were blocked. Finally they returned by coming miles around, through Jesus del Monte suburb. It was five-thirty by the time they returned.

We were receiving continual reports of revolt. Luis Fuentes called and told me that Machado had been ordered to resign and that Colonel Julio Sanguily had telephoned his home from Camp Columbia saying that Machado would resign immediately. General Alberto Herrera, Secretary of War and Navy, was with the President. Colonel Erasmo Delgado, Chief of Cabañas Fortress, we learned, had moved over into El Castillo de la Fuerza, taking it over with his own men.

In spite of all this, Machado returned quietly from the camp and entered the palace. We were still puzzled and time was getting short for a dispatch. We had so much information, but so much of it contradictory, that we hardly knew what to believe. Colonel Frederick Palmer, famous war correspondent, down here covering the story, dropped into the office about five-thirty P.M. He admitted he also was puzzled. At that point we remembered an officer we knew, Captain Torres Menier of the Aviation Corps, and we had the good fortune to locate him in the camp. He gave us the whole story, how the officers headed by Colonel Sanguily, Chief of the Aviation Corps and Colonel Erasmo Delgado, Chief of Cabañas Fortress, had decided to revolt and force Machado to resign. It was well planned and executed. Colonel Delgado came over from Cabañas with his men and occupied Castillo de la Fuerza, military headquarters, putting up sand-bag barricades, machine gun nests and other fortifications. Troops were moved into Havana from Camp Columbia. Cabañas Fortress guns were trained on the palace; palace guards were changed and reinforced.

General Herrera, Secretary of War and Navy, former Chief of Staff, was called on the telephone and requested to come immediately to El Castillo Headquarters. When he arrived he was placed under arrest and released about an hour later after he had promised to tell Machado he must resign. Machado refused to believe that the army had turned against him. He raved and threatened and told General

Herrera he would go to Camp Columbia and bring the army to its senses.

President Machado reached Camp Columbia. Captain Torres, who said he was one of the officers detailed to demand Machado's resignation, told how Machado had marched into the camp headquarters to find the officers there adamant in their demand and the troops drawn up for action. Machado was told that his resignation was the only thing which would solve the situation and prevent widespread bloodshed; that the entire armed forces both in Havana and the interior were behind the movement. He was given twenty-four hours to resign. Captain Torres said that Machado displayed little emotion during the interview, although of course it was a death blow to his pride and ambition. "This will be settled in such a manner that no aspersion will fall on the good name of the Cuban Army," Machado replied.

At ten tonight, Secretary of State Ferrara refused to admit that the military coup was a success. He told Phil over the telephone that, "The whole army is not in revolt."

Then came another report, news that the Aviation Corps officers are demanding that President Machado resign "in favor of General Mario G. Menocal." If I can judge a situation, the whole army is in accord. Camp Columbia controls not only Havana but the entire island and the government. Machado will have to resign in spite of his and Ferrara's efforts to find a way to avoid it. Ferrara is trying desperately to rally some of the officers to the aid of the President but he will meet with no success. They are more afraid of the United States than of Machado. Cuba's greatest burden is her army and the officers realize that if the Americans intervene the greater part of the army will be disbanded. The budget last year appropriated ten million dollars for the army alone. Imagine that for a small island which has no foreign enemies! Nearly a fourth of the national income!

3

August 14: Days and nights have so run together since the downfall of Machado that I shall merely put down what I can remember of the whole affair.

Machado resigned or rather asked for "leave of absence" and then fled for his life. The entire procedure was supposed to have been carried out in "legal form" according to the constitution. That is the influence of Ambassador Welles.

Congress met on the night of the eleventh. Only three congressmen had the nerve to go to the Capitolio in spite of the fact that it was in the hands of three hundred soldiers; but I suppose they were as frightened of the soldiers as of anyone. With not a light showing from the exterior, the three—one of them said to be Dr. Rafael Guás Inclán, Speaker of the House of Representatives, the names of the others we have not yet learned—went to the Senate chamber; and by the light of a few candles—they dared not turn on the lights— they granted Machado's leave of absence, signing the document for all the other congressmen and pretending it was legal. General Herrera, Secretary of War and Navy automatically became President but he was in just about as much disfavor as Machado, so they hurriedly put through a law repealing existing legislation. This was to clear the road for

Dr. Carlos Manuel de Céspedes, whom General Herrera, theoretically at least, appointed Secretary of State.

Visualize that session of Congress! The big dark Senate chamber lit only by a few candles. Three frightened congressmen hurriedly put into proper shape the measures which were to change the government of the Island. The ominous quiet of the huge building in which three hundred soldiers were stationed on the lower floor. I wonder where Herrera signed the documents appointing Céspedes Secretary of State? We haven't found that out yet but I imagine either at the palace or the farm of the President where Machado went that night. I suppose the documents were carried there by Colonel Sanguily or Colonel Erasmo Delgado. They visited the Embassy early the morning of the twelfth. We wonder whether they went for advice or congratulations. It would seem that Ambassador Welles gave at least tacit consent to the revolt of the officers.

When Phil and I reached town about nine Saturday morning, people were beginning to venture out into the streets. Groups gathered here and there conversing in low tones. There were no streetcars, buses or taxis as yet. The public could hardly believe that Machado had resigned. There were no newspapers, so the news went from mouth to mouth. Trucks filled with soldiers passed through the streets. Some of the soldiers made speeches and were cheered by the public. Slowly, the people realized that Machado was no longer head of the government. More people came into the streets; things began to assume a holiday air; the crowds were laughing, talking and cheering in spontaneous bursts of enthusiasm. Soon Central Park, the Prado Promenade and all adjoining streets and sidewalks were crowded.

Phil had gone to the airport to meet a German correspondent who was arriving that morning. I asked the elevator boy to take me up to the roof of the Manzana so I could see what was happening. I stood leaning on the parapet looking down six stories to the streets and Central Park thinking—"What a happy crowd." All at once people started running toward the upper end of the Prado, collecting at Virtudes and Neptuno Streets. A few seconds later there were scattered revolver shots, a fusillade, then two rifle reports. I couldn't see what happened but a few minutes later a group emerged into the street carrying a soldier on their shoulders and shouting and cheering. The killing of *porristas* had begun. They had just killed Captain Jiminez, Chief of *La Porra,* and his negro aide in the drugstore on the corner of Prado and Virtudes.

While this was going on an incident took place in Central Park which brought the tears to my eyes—the sheer pathos of it. A small group of boys of probably ten to twelve years, poorly dressed, some of them barefooted, came solemnly across Zulueta Street carrying a Cuban flag. They marched quietly up to Marti's statue in Central Park and waited while one of their number climbed the tall statue, no small feat in itself, and put the flag in Marti's outstretched hand. Then the small boy climbed down and they all walked quietly away.

We checked some twenty *porristas* killed that day. But that was only the beginning. One youth boasted that he had helped kill seventeen. Luis Fuentes came into the office on Sunday afternoon exceedingly drunk. When I scolded him he said, "Mrs. Phillips, I had to get drunk. I haven't killed any *porristas*. I couldn't kill a man in cold blood that way. But I've seen things I can't forget. I'll say one thing for them, they died fighting."

The terrible things which happened. Civilization was stripped away in one stroke. Relatives of boys who had been tortured and killed started on vengeance hunts and they knew the men they were seeking. The *porristas* never tried to keep it a secret as to whom they had killed. I remember in the killing of the seventeen-year-old student, Rubiera, that one of the secret operatives who had taken part in the murder, returned to the police station and washed blood from the lapel of his coat while he described the killing to others at the station. The ABC terroristic organization knew his identity in twenty minutes. So now it was their turn to hunt the *porristas*.

The young terrorists seemed to have killed cleanly and with some justification, if not with due process of law. But not so the crowd who gathered at the scent of blood, the same public who had shouted, "Viva Machado" only a few months ago in the streets. They demanded blood and more blood.

One *porrista* named Leblanc was killed in front of the Capitolio, that big white glittering building on the upper Prado. He left the Hotel Pasaje, apparently in an effort to escape. As he crossed the street someone recognized him. The horde was upon him. He drew his revolver, backed up against a light post and prepared to die fighting. A huge stone smashed against the side of his head; a bullet struck him in the breast. He sagged, clinging to the post for support. The crowd, howling like devils, closed in. Across the street, on the balcony of the hotel, his wife and two children saw him beaten to death. Several soldiers standing on the sidewalk looked on. Finally one pushed his way through the mob and sent a bullet crashing through the brain of the victim. The body was completely unrecognizable when the mob finished its work.

Another *porrista* was trapped by several youths on the third floor of a building. They shot it out and the *porrista* was wounded. The crowd, attracted by the shooting, surged up the stairway, grabbed the wounded man and hurled him from the third floor to the pavement below. They rushed down, picked him up and repeated the performance. Still he did not die. One of the boys, who had wounded him, ran downstairs to the pavement in an attempt to kill the victim outright. He thrust his revolver against the head of the *porrista,* who had somehow struggled to his knees, his hands outstretched imploringly. A huge negro knocked the revolver away, and, putting his foot in the face of the wounded man, kicked him violently to the pavement. He finally died. The boy who had shot the *porrista* told me this with tears in his eyes. He said he would never forget the incident so long as he lived. There is a curious ending to this story, for the boy died two weeks later. The diagnosis of the physician was that his heart simply gave out under the tremendous strain and excitement of that day. Those two incidents were told to me by people who saw them. Others equally fantastic and unbelievable occurred all over town and in the interior. What the total killings of the day were we shall never know. I am sure a lot of innocent people were ruthlessly slaughtered, people who probably had done nothing except talk too loud.

On that morning of the twelfth, I had remained on the roof a long while, watching the streets below. Some minutes after the small boys had placed the flag of Cuba in Marti's hand, a crowd began pouring down Zulueta from the direction of the Presidential Palace, many of them carrying queer articles. Boys ran along the street with ferns, uprooted *cannas* and other shrubs offering them to anyone who would buy— loot from the lower floors of the palace.

Such a joyful looting! One huge negro proudly pushed out of the palace grounds a water cooler on which reposed two bottles of mineral water; an old woman carried a couple of pillows, another a stalk of bananas—canned goods, chairs, typewriters, the side of a bed—someone else had the other side. They were perfectly useless articles to those who carried them, but the nation had gone mad. Every plant in the palace patio was uprooted, every shrub and flower. I suppose they would have carried away the palm trees if they could have.

The palace looting which yielded little of value spurred the crowd on to greater deeds. The home of every member of the cabinet was looted and wrecked. Fine collections of rare books were divided among those who could not read. Beautiful china, valuable objects of art were borne away. I saw an old negro woman sitting on the curb on Twenty-third Street. Beside her was a beautiful radio, a bird-cage and a china vase. How she had managed to carry them all and what she would ever do with them was a mystery, but there she was.

Louis Hamburg, photographer, tells the story of the looting of the Averhoff residence. Averhoff was Secretary of Treasury under Machado for only a few months. He took the position in opposition to the wishes of his entire family, who wanted him to stay out of politics. Hamburg, intent on taking pictures of the looting and looters of the Averhoff home, located on Malecón Drive, started to enter the lower floor. He glanced up to see a baby grand piano tottering on the upper balcony. He didn't have time to run. The piano crashed, its beautiful mahogany and delicate wires a tangled mass. The looters later burned all the furniture which they had thrown into the street.

Some families of the Cabinet members had fled, taking in many cases not even a change of clothing. Personal effects, letters, jewelry, everything was grabbed by the looters. Beautiful things were destroyed. Irreplaceable things. The books of Senator Wilfredo Fernández, a lifelong collection of rare volumes, many of which he had bound with his own hands, a collection started in childhood, was completely destroyed.

Nor was it only the homes of officials of the Machado regime which were looted. The houses of the mistresses of various high officials were sacked and burned. A pet store, owned by Villapol, Palace Paymaster, was raided. Many of the animals were killed—canaries, puppies, kittens, rare tropical birds—crushed, strangled, many of them torn to pieces.

Nothing of this sort should ever have been permitted. The commander of the troops should have thrown a thousand men into the city, protected life and property, and quelled mob spirit at the start. Instead, the soldiers themselves helped kill *porristas,* their comrades of the day before, servants of the same government which the soldiers had upheld by bloodshed and arms for the past four years.

Phil and I went home about the time the mob was sacking the *Heraldo de Cuba,* owned by Secretary of State Orestes Ferrara. We stopped to see it. The streets in front and alongside the building were knee deep in papers. The crowd was carrying away everything. Some with hammers were smashing the big presses. We saw one negro trying to roll a huge newsprint roll down the street, while another sweated over a motor he had yanked off one of the smaller presses. One enterprising Spaniard hired a couple of negroes to rush in and bring out an addressograph plate-making machine which he had sold the *Heraldo* a few weeks previously. Raul Casañas who used to work for us came by and told me that the Spaniard had managed to get it safely away, giving the negroes two dollars.

Our car, with the *New York Times* sign on it, was cheered everywhere. The people seem to think the *Times* helped get Machado out. They make a sort of hero out of Phil over the Valdés Daussá story. We arrived home in the small hours of the morning. At nine, Phil had to hurry down to the residence of Dr. Carlos Manuel de Céspedes—Ambassador Welles' candidate—to cover his oath of office.

While Phil was there, Quesada came in. I am always glad to see him. He is a mine of information on Cuban history. I asked Quesada what type of man Céspedes was. Quesada said he was a gentleman, honorable and intellectual; but he was indecisive and did not understand the Cuban people. Quesada told me something that throws an interesting light on Céspedes' character. He carries in his pocket a picture of his illustrious father. Whenever he gets in a tight spot and doesn't know what to do, he looks at it for inspiration. Rather pathetic in a way, a son trying to live up to his father's greatness, not trusting his own ability. Too gentle a man to rule Cuba.

Orestes Ferrara and his wife had a narrow escape when they left by plane Saturday afternoon. The seaplane was in the harbor warming up her engines when he and his wife were taken aboard. A mob rushed to the waterfront. They stormed through the offices of Pan American Airways out onto the docks and began firing at the plane. The pilot, without waiting for mail or other passengers, took off and headed for Miami. Several American passengers waiting to go aboard had their luggage seized by the mob. That was the last they saw of it.

The killing of *porristas* and sympathizers of Machado went on Saturday and Sunday and today but with less enthusiasm. They are and have been frantically hunting cabinet officials.

Machado left the island by airplane Saturday afternoon, August 12th, with a mob close behind him. Why the revolutionists didn't think of going to his home, *Nenita*, in the morning is a mystery. Machado, Averhoff, Secretary of Treasury, and Captain Crespo, Chief of Atarés Fortress drove out to the airport at *General Machado* and demanded an airplane. The company refused to permit them to charter a plane until they had obtained permission from the military authorities. They had to wait more than an hour. Another version of the delay is that the military authorities and Mr. Welles were extremely anxious to get Machado out of Cuba, but that he refused to go until the Ambassador would guarantee that he would not be extradited from the United States and would be protected there.

At any rate, as the plane roared down the field, several automobiles overflowing with ABC revolutionaries arrived, but had to be content with firing at the rapidly disappearing plane. So, all the principals of the government got away and only the "little fellows" got killed, just as usual.

Now begins that amusing and embarrassing period in which Americans here about-face. I mean the managers of branches of American companies. Americans in Cuba are divided into two classes, employees of big American companies, and the few who settled in Cuba and established their own businesses. Managers of the American companies usually gather at the American Club. As a whole they have supported Machado. They refused to believe that he had committed murders, terming it newspaper propaganda. They complained the Cuban revolutions have been "fought on the front pages of the American newspapers." Lots of them used to call Phil up and want to know why we sent in such stories. They were afraid business would be damaged. They haven't had any business for the past three years, so I can't see their reasoning. The manager of one of the largest companies has called Phil many times, angry over some dispatch. Saturday night this manager called Consul-General Dumont and said he had received threats that his home would be burned. He demanded protection. Dumont, knowing Phil has contacts among the army officers, asked him to get in touch with Camp Columbia. Phil telephoned Captain Torres Menier and a detail of soldiers was sent immediately to protect the home of the American.

Even harder to understand is the attitude of the American Chamber of Commerce. Machado consistently favored European exporters, to the detriment of American trade, and practically nullified the tariff preferential, giving special privileges to European nations. His customs department deals out favors with a lavish hand where it will do the most harm to American exporters. Yet the only time the American Chamber of Commerce protested, very feebly, was over the Emergency Tax Law. When Machado decided to register all foreigners and fingerprint them, the Chamber of Commerce remained silent, while both the British Minister and the Spanish Ambassador protested vigorously.

August 15: The trackdown of *porristas* and minor officials continues, but more as a dark undercurrent in an atmosphere of happiness and bright new hopes, and quite in contrast with the grim desperation of Havana a few days ago. The Cuban people are like children who have suddenly entered fairyland. They have a new government making new promises, and now, to hear the Cubans tell it, all they have to do is sit back and wait for the miraculous recovery of business and watch the dollars roll in from the United States. They confidently expect a loan of fifteen million dollars, although the island cannot pay what it now owes. Foreign obligations total almost $160,000,000. They cannot understand that, in view of the many defaulted Latin American bonds now held by U.S. investors, the Yankee dollar may become scarce.

There is an unprecedented amount of drinking going on. Cubans are getting drunk day after day—something never seen before on this island. It has always been the American tourist whose drinking has provided the natives with considerable amusement. Now it is the Cubans, particularly the youths. The terrorists spend their days and nights—they never seem to sleep—drinking. Salon H, the café downstairs, is crowded with a hard drinking crowd, all claiming they won the revolution. The ABC had no more than two thousand members during the years of the Machado regime. Now, three million people have suddenly become ABC members. Their green flag seems about to replace the Cuban flag. One cynically minded individual remarked that the *bodegueros* were celebrating, not the downfall of Machado, but relief from the ABC, which had obtained donations from the Spanish merchants under the slogan, "Contribute or be Dynamited."

The structure of the ABC was copied from a secret society formed in France prior to the French Revolution and was composed of "cells." Seven A men, the executive or directing body, each have under their control ten B men, who in turn each control ten C men. This plan of organization prevents traitors from betraying any members outside of their own immediate group. The A cell furnished arms and ammunition, collected funds, and approved and formulated plans to combat the Machado administration. Many of the lower cell members acted as spies; every branch of government, including the police and secret service divisions, was honeycombed with ABC members. The actual terrorists or "action squads" were composed of not more than one hundred fifty youths, the majority of them university students who were willing to sacrifice their lives. These groups were free to form their own plans, but had to submit them to the A cell for approval, after which the necessary arms and explosives were furnished.

Their assassination of government officials, including Captain Calvo, Chief of the Secret Police, and Dr. Clemente Vazquez Bello, President of the Senate, was made possible by a system called *chequeo*. Some forty youths, working in shifts, would watch every movement made by the intended victim. His daily and habitual acts were checked and rechecked until the most favorable place for his assassination had been chosen. In the case of Captain Calvo, the killing took place at seven-thirty A.M. at the foot of the cliff on which the National Hotel is located. He was accustomed to pass there each morning at that hour. Dr. Bello was returning home from his usual morning swim at the beach when two automobiles filled with youths holding sawed-off shotguns met him.

The ABC at present controls the government. Dr. Joaquin Martinez Saenz, new Secretary of Treasury, was in A cell. He is a young lawyer and should be excellent in this position. Dr. Carlos Saladrigas, Secretary of Justice, is also an A cell member. He is of good family and has considerable cultural background, speaks good English and is, in so far as the word can be applied to Cuba, a conservative. Dr. Guillermo Belt, also an ABC member, is Secretary of Public Instruction.

The students talk of reopening the university. Frankly, I think returning to Havana University will be impossible for many of them. One can't plant bombs, commit murders, become hunted outlaws and then return to the atmosphere of the classroom. Luis Fuentes is an example. He was expelled from the university by presidential decree for a period of eight years, when he and other students in 1928 protested against the Prorogue Measure. He left home because he did not want to involve his family and bring down on them the wrath and vengeance of Machado. For years he did not have enough to eat. He slept on park benches and in flop houses. Once, when he was sharing a tiny room with two companions, he escaped arrest only because he had gone with a girl friend to her home to spend the night. "Pure luck," he admitted to me, somewhat embarrassed. His girl friend, a university student, later left her home because her family objected to her joining the ABC. There are many such cases, young girls of good families living as the mistresses of young men. It seems queer to see such a sudden change in a Latin country with century-old ideas concerning women. A way of life has vanished. Young girls who had been living a cloistered, sheltered life now speak with pride of the bombs they have planted.

I remember a story Phil told me. On the sidewalk near our office, he encountered several students he knew standing in a circle. In this group was a girl, quite young, with a package under her arm, and as Phil approached he heard them making a lunch date. The boys greeted Phil and began chatting with them. The girl looked at her wristwatch, held it to her ear to listen to it, and then said, laughing, "I've got to hurry or I'll be late." After the girl had walked away, one of the boys drew Phil aside and told him that the package was a bomb she was going to plant, and they were meeting in a nearby café to have lunch and wait for it to explode.

What is going to happen to the younger generation? Will they be able to readjust themselves to a normal way of life, to the pattern of daily life, to the society of their parents and relatives? Can they discard their present bloody ideals and their reckless disregard for authority? Frankly, I don't know. Undoubtedly they will have the same difficulties returning to civilized ways of living that every nation has following a war. But terrorism, in my opinion, more quickly and permanently undermines the morals of a country than does open warfare. War between nations, terrible as it is, leaves both the victor and the vanquished with a certain unity, a common bond. But terrorism is a form of mutilation that breeds distrust and hatred, severing a people into irreparable factions.

Soldiers are everywhere. Saturday night, following the

orgy of killing *porristas,* a squadron of cavalry moved into Central Park. The park is now practically a stable, with bales of hay and sacks of oats piled high in front of the Manzana de Gomez. Machine guns are mounted on tripods. Troop patrols and night watches prowl the city with a businesslike manner. The khaki uniform is looked on with favor, but I cannot forget that it is the same army which killed under orders of Machado.

Colonel Perdomo, former Chief of Police, sat in a café today eating his lunch and conversing with friends. With tears running down his face, he expressed his sorrow for "pobre Cuba." He said the revolt of the army was the most terrible thing that had ever happened on the island. From now on the army would be the most important factor in Cuban life. From now on the army could never be trusted.

He is right. In the history of Cuba no president has ever before been ousted, nor any change of government brought about by a revolt of the army. The army never dared before because of the Platt Amendment. All previous revolutions in Cuba started in the outlying provinces and none of them had ever been successful. Now for the first time the people realize how easy it is for the army to force a change of government.

The United States during the occupation of the island following the Spanish-American War organized and trained the Rural Guards as a means of preserving order in the Republic. President José Miguel Gómez, the second president, began the real work of forming an army for an island which has no more use for an army than a child has for a stick of dynamite. Cuba has no foreign enemies. She is completely under the protection of the United States and always will be because of her proximity to our southern shores. The third president, General Mario G. Menocal, increased the size of the army. President Zayas paid little attention to it except to see that sons of wealthy families who did not care to become professionals were given soft berths in the military. President Machado during his first four years worked hard at bringing the army to the highest point of efficiency possible. American officers and aviation officials came down to train the Cuban armed forces; tremendous amounts of equipment were purchased and thousands enlisted. The United States simply sat by and watched the dictatorship grow. The United States thereby sanctioned it, knowing that any army in Cuba is a weapon in the hands of the government which will permit abuse and oppression of the people.

I remember when Machado put himself into the presidency a second time by modification of the constitution. Protests poured into the American State Department and Machado made a hurried trip to Washington. The Pan-American Conference was soon to be held in Havana and Machado was afraid other Latin American countries might boycott it. He returned from Washington beaming and ordered a hasty washing of the city. Havana was given a superficial beauty treatment. The Prado was hurriedly reconstructed. The Malecón was repaved so hastily that it was soon cracking and crumbling in hundreds of spots. President Coolidge attended the Havana conference, his visit tacitly giving a stamp of approval to the Machado government. At that conference Dr. Orestes Ferrara, later Secretary of State and Ambassador to Washington, declared, "American intervention is a splendid thing!"

August 16:   Last night I was coming out of the Pasaje Hotel, opposite the National Capitolio, where I had been paying a call on a sick woman. I encountered a negro soldier with a rifle thrust out in front of him and a bloodhound expression on his face. Behind him was a mob of drunken men. Fortunately there was a sidewalk café, and although the passage between the tables was narrow, I managed to use these tables to separate myself from the negro soldier and the mob. I hurried to our car, where Phil was waiting. Someone yelled, *"Porrista!"* The hue and cry started as a man darted out from the sidewalk café and ran down the street. The negro soldier,

waving his rifle like a club, followed by the howling mob, ran
after him. We left the scene hurriedly. I had no desire to
watch.

This morning I met Luis Fuentes. He laughingly explained
the whole affair. He and several companions were spending
the evening drinking in a bar. Luis, with a sudden burst of
patriotism, told everyone to stand up and cheer. One man
refused. Luis jerked him to his feet. The man struck Luis and
a fight started. One of the people watching the fight pointed
at the man and yelled, *"Porrista!"* All eyes suddenly focused
on this one man, who, frightened as he saw the crowd surge
toward him, ran out of the bar. Those in the bar ran after
him. A huge negro soldier with a rifle came from somewhere and still others joined the mob, which surged forward,
knocking down all the tables in the sidewalk cafés and frightening the coffee drinkers. Luis said that he and his companions took after the mob in an attempt to halt the chase. They
felt the "unpatriotic" man had learned his lesson. As the pursued crossed the Prado, an automobile filled with ABC men
blocked his way, grabbed him and were going to lynch him
when Luis and his crowd plowed their way through the mob
with guns in hand and formed a ring about the victim. They
explained the situation to the ABC men and then made a
speech to the mob. Having restored a semblance of peace,
they escorted the victim home. Luis said they don't dare go
to any of the cafés along the street because the owners are
furious over their broken tables and mirrors. Luis considered
it a great joke. But to me it is a highly dangerous situation. A
pointed finger or a single cry of accusation can set loose incredible and terrible violence. There isn't the slightest respect for authority. The police are treading softly, not knowing exactly where they stand, but aware that if they interfere
the mob might attack them. In front of the Marti Theatre the
other night a crowd had gathered and was blocking the sidewalk. A policeman ordered them back. Some of the crowd
obeyed, but one youth would not budge. He informed the
policeman that he would have him discharged, that his

brother was a member of the ABC. Then others in the crowd joined the youth. The policeman shrugged his shoulders and walked away. He knew how little authority he really had.

Just before dawn the other morning I was awakened by a terrific pounding at the front door. I leaned out of the window in my upstairs room. The night watchman who patrols our street, with pride in his voice, told me that he had just rescued a porch chair that belonged to us from a burglar. "Here it is," he said. "A negro was carrying it down the street."

"Did you arrest him?" I asked.

The watchman stood there in the dim morning light, looking up. "No," he said. "I just took the chair away from him."

That is about as much law as can be had in Cuba at present. It is perhaps more than you can honestly feel entitled to, when police are more afraid of being arrested than the citizens.

August 17:   We have astonishing information. The students and Communists are plotting with the soldiers to revolt against the army officers. The students heartily dislike Ambassador Welles and will do anything they can to embarrass him. They are convinced that Welles is as bad as Machado was, and that their patriotic duty is to cast off the yoke of the United States.

Someone is going to have to straighten Cuba out and if they let Welles alone he will do it and the island will start back on the road to prosperity. Cuba will probably get a loan. Welles has promised that, and a new reciprocity treaty favoring sugar. This will help Cuba of course, but without Cuba having to lift a hand to help herself, a policy that the United States may someday rue. My own opinion is that a general reduction of customs tariff by the Cuban government would do wonders for business. Cubans claim the high tariff was put into effect in retaliation for the Hawley-Smoot tariff. I always call their attention to the fact that Machado put the Cuban tariff into effect in October, 1927, and the Hawley-

Smoot tariff was not introduced in the American Congress until 1929. The Cuban tariff upped duties from an average of 16% to 46%, which, combined with 5% consular fees means that a 51% duty is paid on all imports.

Tonight we went to see Consul General Dumont. Phil told him what we had learned and Dumont said he had been informed that a number of sergeants were plotting at the Castillo de la Fuerza, military headquarters. He had received the information in an odd manner. A Cuban by the name of Medina was, during the Machado administration, a supervisor of labor activities on the docks, and had been useful to the Consul General in smuggling cases. After days of hiding, following the overthrow of Machado, Medina had managed to board a United Fruit steamer bound for New Orleans. Before departure he sent a friend to ask the Consul General to come aboard the ship, as he had information. He told Dumont that the enlisted men of the army were planning a revolt. Since none of the officers live in Camp Columbia, the sergeants and noncommissioned officers are in charge of the soldiers, a situation which would make a revolt by the enlisted men easy to carry out.

August 18: What a relief to be able to sit in the cafés and not expect shooting to break out at any moment. The merchants claim that business is picking up. Of course the poor are desperate and unemployment is widespread. The jobless of Havana have congregated in several small villages in and around the outskirts, where houses are built of palm leaves called *yagua*. One settlement was known as *Llega y Pon* (Come and Squat). The village has a mayor who receives no salary and a police force with no weapons except their fists. Three to four thousand people live in the tiny huts. At night there are no lights. There is a muddy creek where the women do their washing. The Public Works Department delivers them a tank of water each day for drinking, first come, first served. Why they don't all die of disease is beyond understanding. I suppose germs simply give up the ghost in such an atmosphere. The people beg, hunt around the markets for refuse, and sell penny articles in the streets.

The ABC made a gruesome discovery today. They went out to Fort Atarés and began digging in the horse corral. A soldier who had been stationed at the fort tipped them off. They found several skeletons. One of them was Sergeant José Angel Hernández, whom Phil had tried to save. Another was Félix Alpizar, student leader, who disappeared one night after being wounded in a gun battle with police. Also, the skeleton of a negro known as Margarito Iglesias, who disappeared in December, 1931. Iglesias had ruled the dock workers with an iron hand and had forced them to contribute funds which he and several others lived on and spent for their own pleasure.

People are complaining that *Machadistas* are beginning to appear on the scene again, particularly in the palace. Phil says that he sees quite a few. Rafael Ybor, former head of the Press Bureau of the State Department, is back at his job. Ybor is an excellent interpreter and an affable chap. He telephoned Phil, frightened and in need of help. It seems the ABC's informed him that they would kill him if he didn't resign. By some mysterious maneuver he had managed to get approval of the State Department. I suspect that he went to President Céspedes, whom he has known for years, then slipped quietly back into his job, hoping no one would notice. Phil contacted members of the ABC and asked them to reconsider, assuring them that Ybor was harmless.

We arrived home at noon to find John, our huge Negro cook, terrified. He told me he had suffered from a pain around his heart for three days and that it was getting worse. I advised him to take some soda. Knowing the quantity he eats, I was sure he was suffering from straight, uncomplicated indigestion. Tonight John still had the pain. I demanded to know if he had taken soda. He confessed with considerable reluctance that he thought soda might poison him. I fixed a teaspoonful in a glass of water and stood beside him until he drank it. I am sure he expected to die. Later, when he was serving dessert, he said, "Mrs. Phillips, I can feel that soda working around my heart." Phil and I laughed, and finally John began to grin. A couple of hours later he admitted that the pain had disappeared.

One of the terrorists dropped in today, a chocolate colored lad with an incredibly deep bass voice. He is the son of a famous black general of the War of Independence. During the 1931 revolution against Machado he led a band of 130 men. They never did surrender. When the revolt failed, they hid their weapons and separated. He is a protegé of former president Menocal. He came in to thank us for what he considered we had done for Cuba. He bowed with wonderful dignity and told me that if there was anything he could do for me just to let him know. I thanked him, mentally noting that if ever I wanted to start a revolution I would enlist his help.

Casey, the big, hefty, constantly perspiring correspondent for the *Chicago Daily News,* is here, together with Tom Petty of the *Herald Tribune* and Karl Decker of the International News Service. The other night, Casey, having imbibed less wisely than well, made a bet that he could start a riot. He went out into the street and yelled like a Comanche on the warpath. A large group of negroes appeared like magic and gathered around him. Not understanding, they nevertheless gazed at him with open-mouthed admiration. When he shouted, "Come on, boys," and started down the street, they fell in behind and began yelling also. The farther they went the more recruits fell into line. Finally, Casey, having yelled himself hoarse and feeling a need for liquid refreshment, stopped at a bar. But the negroes were so worked up that they didn't even notice his desertion and kept on down the street, a howling mob. "Casey's riot" lasted almost an hour.

August 19: Chief of Police Ainciart was finally cornered. He had escaped earlier by dressing up like a woman and had

rented a room in the suburbs, probably hoping to escape detection until he could book passage on a ship. Ainciart committed suicide when he saw he was trapped. Lieutenant
Gutierrez of the Aviation Corps was among those who surrounded the house. I personally doubt that Ainciart committed suicide; it was probably committed for him. But at
any rate, he is dead. He was stupid, cruel and brutal, and
with no feeling or compassion for his fellow men.

President Céspedes spoke via radio to the United States.
He will give Cuba a good administration if they don't overthrow him, as they are planning to do. We have considerable
information now about the new revolutionary plot. It may
never come off, but I fancy it will. The army knows it can
change the government at will.

August 20: Phil told Ambassador Welles about the plot to
overthrow the government and was laughed at for his pains.
The Ambassador simply cannot imagine trouble is brewing
when everything is so quiet. Phil came back to the office
much provoked. He remarked that if the Ambassador
wouldn't listen he would have to take the consequences.

General Mario G. Menocal, former president of Cuba, returned to Cuba today. He didn't announce his coming. Someone remarked that he came in quietly because he knew there
would be no huge welcoming crowd to greet him. He is a
wily politician but has about run his course in political life.
I asked Phil to describe Menocal to me today because I have
never met him. Phil says he is more the cold eyed businessman than the affable politician. I gather from the description
Phil gave me of Menocal receiving the press that he is more
intent on impressing his followers with his unapproachable-
ness than on winning them with charm. He is a slender, wiry
old man who carries his years well. He has gray hair and
wears a Van Dyke. He is one of the five Major Generals of
the Cuban Wars of Independence and it is said he was never
hesitant about leading his men into battle. He is well edu-

cated and a gentleman of the old school. Cubans say he was the hand-picked American candidate in 1912. When a revolution broke out after his reelection in 1917 the American government curtly informed the rebels that the insurrection would "not be countenanced" and that the United States would hold the leaders of the revolt responsible. That finished off the revolution. Of course, the United States was chiefly interested in the amount of sugar Cuba could produce, and was not going to have sugar production hampered by a revolution.

Menocal never really says anything and talks in vague generalities. The way Phil described his last interview went like this: The correspondent arrives at the luxurious home of the General in the Vedado residential section. He is greeted by the butler, turned over to a second man, delivered to the secretary, and finally ushered into the room where the General is receiving. The General is sitting on a raised platform, something like "the king on the dais" arrangement, flanked on each side by several advisers. In front of the platform, extending for some distance across the room, are two rows of rocking chairs facing each other from a distance of probably three feet.

The correspondent walks the length of the room and, after greeting the General, is forced to sit in a rocking chair. He must ask questions in a loud voice since the General is some distance away. The General starts to reply. Advisers on each side hold up admonishing hands. This usually starts a discussion among all the other advisers. There is a consultation concerning whether the question should be answered. The correspondent sits there with a "well, make up your mind, boys" expression on his face. Finally the General replies in the vaguest possible manner, stringing together all the meandering that the combined minds of the advisers have been able to devise. Their one aim of existence seems to be to prevent the General from committing himself to anything. The correspondent leaves, convinced that it cannot make much difference what opinion the General has.

August 21:   Late yesterday afternoon they dug up Ainciart's body in the cemetery out in Marianao where the army had interred it and took it to the University. A group of medical students were the ghouls. They strung the body up to a telephone pole after mutilating it, but the rope broke. Someone poured gasoline over the body and set it afire. All this occurred in the midst of a howling mob of the lower classes. Luis Fuentes said that most of the students were ashamed of the performance. They should be.

August 22:   Colonels Carlos Mendieta and Roberto Mendez Peñate returned to Cuba today. Thousands crowded the waterfront to see them. They head the Nationalista Party, which was outlawed during the Machado regime. Mendieta is the only political leader who refused to have anything to do with Machado. I am told by the students that Mendieta is absolutely honest and cannot be bought. Mendieta will probably be president when elections are held.

August 24:   President Céspedes dissolved Congress and declared the 1901 Constitution in effect to replace the Machado constitution. Students, now frankly opposing the government, are demanding an entirely revolutionary government composed of five members with executive and legislative powers.

I saw some of old Colonel Blas Hernández' men on the Prado today, wearing side-arms, and swaggering along in their big hats. Blas is quite a picturesque old revolutionist. He refused to surrender in the 1931 rebellion and was a fugitive from justice until the fall of Machado. He lived most of the time on the plantation of Antonio Mendoza and then took to the hills last January or February to fight against Machado. Now he is something of a hero.

We were shown interesting documents, original checks signed by Machado, thousands and thousands of dollars worth. The boys who have the documents, ABC members, were surprised to learn the identities of some of the people receiving checks from Machado's personal account. There was an interesting set of checks and vouchers signed by an American, a member of the police department of a northern American city. Another set of checks showed that the Chief of Police of a Florida town had received money regularly from the Department of the Interior of Cuba.

September 2: What a storm we had yesterday! It had been raining and squally for a couple of days. When we got up yesterday morning the wind was gusty, with bursts of rain. We had breakfast and came to town. Everyone was boarding up windows and taping plate glass windows, nailing doors, and getting ready for a real blow. Usually the trees in the parks and on the Prado are roped down but the authorities forgot it this time.

The storm struck Havana after lunch. The wind around the Manzana sounded like the winds that whistle on the prairies. Hurricane winds, of course, do not blow steadily, rather in spurts, so that the windows sound as if they are coming out. The pressure is tremendous for a second and then lessens leaving a sort of vacuum, then coming again with renewed force. The hurricane had struck Isabela de Sagua on the north coast during the morning and then veered north so that Havana didn't get the full force of it. Lights in the Manzana went off. We had to write dispatches by candlelight and walk up and down five flights of stairs.

Harold Denny, a *Times* staff man, started to the boat, the German steamer, *Reliance,* on which he was taking some kind of a tour. Just as he got to the dock the *Reliance* snapped her moorings, smashed into the pier and the *Margaret Lykes,* a British steamer. Denny came back to the office wet and thoroughly disgusted. He finally went home with us to stay all night. We waded around the house as water had come in at every point and crevice. There were no lights and candles are ineffective in high ceilinged rooms. However, Phil scrambled some eggs, and with salad and jam and leftovers we managed dinner.

September 4: Fuentes told me that a boy by the name of Soler had been tried, found guilty and executed by the *Directorio Estudiantil* of the University. I could hardly believe it but it is true. Soler confessed he had given information to Machado's *porristas* which caused several students to be killed by the authorities. The ABC had documentary evidence to prove his guilt which they found in the files of the Department of Interior. Everyone at the student court trial cried when Soler was pronounced guilty. The firing squad, Soler's own classmates took him to a farm near here. He himself gave the order to fire. Then they brought his body back to the morgue and stood over it with rifles to prevent the usual mob from dragging it through the streets. They had promised him that his body would not be mutilated. Neither the police nor the army paid the slightest attention to the affair, professing ignorance, although they must have known what was going on.

4

September 5: We heard rumors in the afternoon that the soldiers were much excited over a report their pay was to be reduced. Phil had a headache so he lay down. I received a telephone call telling me that Camp Columbia Army Headquarters was the scene of unusual activity, with cars rushing in and out. Also, something was going on in the Dragones Cuartel. Our night man called and said he had a story from a sergeant that the enlisted men were revolting but he was checking further. I awakened Phil. We were convinced that the soldiers had taken over the government. But we had to get absolute confirmation. Phil called Quesada and demanded to know the details, telling him we already knew what was happening. Quesada gave Phil the requested information. We got the story off while the rest of the correspondents were trying to check their information. The last I heard of Associated Press last night they were striving frantically to put the pieces together and complete the story.

This morning I found out that there were a number of conspiracies. Menocal and a number of the older officers were planning a military coup. The younger officers, together with the students, were planning a coup. The sergeants were planning one. The communists were planning a soldier-worker government. The way it looks, the American newspaper correspondents were the only ones on the island who weren't conspiring. The conspiracy of the younger officers and students was scheduled for September 10th or 12th. When the sergeants heard of the other conspiracies they decided to stage their coup without waiting. They chose as their leader Sergeant Fulgencio Batista, headquarters stenographer and a persuasive talker. They needed someone who could hold the soldiers in line. The leaders of the conspiracy at Camp Columbia declared the government theirs by changing the Presidential Palace guard and ordering all guards at Camp Columbia to accept only passes signed by Batista or the "Revolutionary Junta." All officers were ordered to leave the post. Realizing that the Cuban people would not support a military government headed by sergeants, they sent out cars and called members of the university faculty on the telephone, members of the *Directorio Estudiantil*. The students rushed to the camp, thinking it was their own conspiracy. When they arrived, they decided that, so long as they were in it, they would support the military revolt and everyone shouted: "Viva la Republica."

Sergeant Batista had the brilliant idea of calling all military posts on the telephone and advising them that the sergeants were in command of the government. The sergeants on duty at these posts, and it was of course sergeants on duty since the officers had gone home for the night, declared their allegiance to the sergeant government and sent word to the officers not to return to their posts because their jobs were occupied.

After staying up practically all night with the revolutionists, Phil and I returned to Havana.

Businessmen were greatly disturbed over the change of government. The public knew of the revolt because the first thing the sergeants did was to start broadcasting over the radio. The radio next door buzzed and cackled all night with the patriotic speeches shouted into it. The new government is trying to convince the people by sheer oratory that the millennium is at hand.

President Céspedes had been out in the interior inspecting the cyclone damage for the past two days and did not return until about noon. He then made what many people here say was the mistake of his career. He should have declared the army in rebellion and asked the United States government to land marines. Perhaps the United States would have done so. Instead, Céspedes merely refused to resign, stating there was no one competent to receive his resignation, and walked stiffly out of the palace. He went to his home in the Vedado residential section.

The Revolutionary Junta at Camp Columbia during its night session appointed five commissioners to form the new government:

Dr. Ramón Grau San Martin, Professor of Havana University, leader of the students, and physician with a fashionable clientele.

Dr. Guillermo Portela, Professor of Havana University.

Sr. Porfirio Franca y Alvarez de la Campa, formerly with the Banco Nacional, which went bankrupt.

Sr. Sergio Carbo, radical journalist, owner of *La Semana*. Carbo spent two years in Russia, but my personal opinion is that instead of being a Communist he is more of a Carboista.

Dr. José M. Irisarri, lawyer with socialistic tendencies and said to be highly intelligent.

Phil went over to the palace this afternoon to see the five Commissioners. Phil has known most of them previously, so we have contacts already established. He says the palace is like a political rally, crowded with students wearing huge guns and talking loud and long about what they are going to do if the United States dares to interfere.

U.S. Destroyer *McFarland* came in today. The U.S. Cruiser *Richmond* and several other destroyers will arrive soon. Ambassador Welles is sitting down at the Embassy in grim silence. I'll bet he feels sick. Sergeant Batista, Chief of Staff, went to call on Ambassador Welles this morning to see when recognition will be granted by the United States.

The Communists are displeased. They claim they organized the strike which ousted Machado and they got nothing out of it. The soldiers, knowing nothing about Communism and not particularly liking the name, decided the students were the best group to obtain the support of the people. The students wanted power by any means possible. The soldier who is stationed outside our house to guard a truck depot on Principe Hill told me quite seriously that now they would eliminate all the officers who had been the tools of Machado and free the nation from American influence, after which everything would be fine. The soldiers take their politics seriously, which may be dangerous when based on such childish mentality.

The Commissioners, Sergeant Batista, and the students have spent the entire day on the Palace balcony addressing the crowd which has surrounded the Palace since early morning. Sergeant Batista has proved to be a powerful and inflaming speaker. But he had better be careful the public does not get the idea that the island is now completely in their hands.

Sergio Carbo gave Phil a statement for the *Times*. "At daybreak on September 5th the Republic came of age, and with cries of joy escaped from the American Embassy. . . ." There was more in the same vein. The palace group is talking loudly about running Cuba without American interference. How stupid! Cuba will always be under the influence of the United States. Her strategic position in relation to the Panama Canal and the Gulf of Mexico forces such a relationship upon Cuba. Furthermore, a billion and a half dollars of American capital are invested here. Even more important, Cuba must in order to exist, sell 97% of her production abroad and the United States is the only market she has. So now we shall sit back and watch Cuba snub the United States!

This may be a revolutionary government supported by the entire nation, as the frenzied orators shout over the radio, but you never saw so many machine guns and rifles and revolvers in your life. As I write this, a sergeant, broadcasting over the radio, boasts of what the Cuban army will do to the American marines if they dare to land.

Communists with red flags marched into Central Park this afternoon to hold a meeting. They shouted and howled about things in general and particularly the warships around Cuba, demanding they be withdrawn instantly. A fine time was had by all.

September 8: Some one committed a blunder when they allowed the Secretary of the Navy, Swanson, to sail for Cuba. If there ever was a time when such a visit was inopportune! At the last minute it was realized and Swanson did not come ashore.

The Five Commissioner government is not working out well. A republic means a President to the Cubans and a President is what they are going to have. The students announced that all factions will meet and select a president, but we were informed that the selection is already made; and, if their choice cannot be imposed on the rest, the students will boycott the government.

Russell Porter, staff writer of the *Times*, is here again. He is to handle the "American angle." He arrived in Havana an ardent champion of the students. He is convinced that Cuba will have a splendid government made up of the "youth of the land." The *Directorio* is trying to impress Porter. Eddie Chibas is inviting him here and there and he is being served propaganda in huge slices on small plates. Porter would recognize propaganda if an American tried to feed it to him. What puzzles me is that he does not seem to recognize the Cuban brand. I have known the students in the *Directorio Estudiantil* for a long time. I have had arguments with them over "Yankee imperialism." They cannot understand that imperialism is economic rather than political. They are convinced that the United States is like a crouching tiger waiting to seize Cuba at any time the chance comes. They are sure that if the United States could not get sugar from Cuba, a sugar famine would occur. No government composed of young men with such ridiculous ideas as those will or should long endure.

Eddie Chibas, who is acting as master of ceremonies on the Cuban propaganda front, was arrested during the Machado regime for throwing a bomb at a streetcar. The police claimed to have found a car in the Chibas garage with a similar bomb in it. They even arrested the servants, one of whom was a Spanish maid. They brought her into headquarters for questioning. The officer in charge of the investigation asked, "Who do you think put that bomb in that car?" The maid looked at the police with a perfectly serene face, eyes innocent and unshielded. Like all women of her class, you could never be certain if her mind was functioning, since thought seemed to have no physical relationship with her face. Finally she said, with conviction, "I think the police put it there." The examination was hastily terminated.

September 9: The ousted army officers have gathered at the National Hotel. They began to appear early this morning. By noon the place was full and they seemed to be holding a meeting. The hotel management could hardly tell them to get out of the hotel. Night came and still they stayed on and began to request accommodations.

The army threw a cordon of soldiers around the hotel. At midnight another detachment surrounded the hotel and advanced into the grounds with the idea of arresting all the officers. When the sergeant in charge reached the entrance he looked in and saw Ambassador Welles and First Secretary Reed sitting on a divan squarely in front of the main door, talking quietly. The soldiers did not enter. The Ambassador, of course, did that on purpose to prevent bloodshed. The officers were determined to resist arrest and most of them had arms and ammunition, which they had brought into the hotel in packages. I imagine the hotel staff thought the officers were bringing their lunches and were amazed to see everyone suddenly walking about with ammunition belts and revolvers strapped about their waists.

The Mexican Government yesterday recognized Cuba. According to the Estrada Doctrine Mexico does not recognize governments, countries are recognized. They realize of course from their own experience what a task it would be to formally recognize administrations which change so rapidly, so they sent a little note wishing everyone a pleasant and happy future. The students fairly burst with pride over the Mexican note of cordiality and went around telling every American they saw. I asked one of them just how much merchandise Mexico purchased from Cuba yearly and how many loans they expected to get from Mexico. I think I won that conversational battle.

Luis Fuentes has deserted the ABC Revolutionary Organization and is now a supporter of the present government. He is wearing a .45 revolver and is head of a police station. He described his duties with a good deal of hilarity. He is the supervisor of the sergeant or lieutenant in charge of the police station; in other words, the supreme authority. Last night all the prisoners the police brought in on various charges of disturbing the peace and traffic violations he turned loose. There is nothing mean about Luis. Foolish, probably, but not mean. He saved the life of a *porrista*.

Tonight we met Luis and his bodyguard downstairs in the café. Just why Luis has a bodyguard is not clear unless he desires protection from the police whom he is ruling in a grandiose manner. The bodyguard is a baby-faced youth with a *café con leche* complexion, smooth black hair and a good tenor voice. As we sat talking with Luis, two negro musicians, carrying guitars, entered the café in the hope of picking up a few nickels. Luis called them over, then ordered the bodyguard to sing, which he obligingly did. The musicians perhaps realized they would receive no money for their efforts but they could hardly refuse in view of the revolver which Luis was showing me with pride. The incongruity of the situation, and how symbolic it seemed of all Cuba, amused me greatly.

Porter wrote a story about the sugar mills seized by the workers. Nearly all the sugar mills belong to American cap-

ital. The workers don't really care about the sugar mills, they
wouldn't know what to do with them. What appeals to them
is the food in the company commissaries. In several places
the workers have looted the stores. Quite frankly, I doubt if
they have had enough to eat for a year or so and one can't
blame them for looting. Workers formerly could make two
dollars a day. Now they are lucky to make forty or fifty cents.
With the sugar crop restricted by the government, the grinding season is only about two to three months long. How they
live the balance of the year is a mystery. Some American
companies have treated their men badly, especially with the
system of paying wages in scrip instead of money, and then
charging high prices in the commissaries. However, in checking the terrible tales of oppression, we often find the mills
in question under Cuban management. Certainly the laborers
deserve more money than they are now getting, but the majority of the mills are running at a loss as it is.

The root of the difficulty goes back to the *Dance of the
Millions,* 1919-1921, when American bankers came here and
loaned money without limit. An old Englishman of my ac-
quaintance used to make reports for American bankers and
knows more accurately the conditions of land, mills and all
phases of the sugar business than anyone I have met in Cuba.
He told me about one mill on which a New York banker
wanted a report prior to lending something like two million
dollars on it. He made the report and found that the mill,
which was an excellent one but worth only about five million,
already had a six-million-dollar loan by two other groups of
American bankers, divided into first and second mortgages.

The result of all this money poured out into new machinery
and equipment, and additional lands has been that each mill
is burdened with a tremendous bond issue on which, with
present prices of sugar and crop restriction, they cannot even
pay the interest. Many companies have gone into bank-
ruptcy. The American banks have taken over many mills, as
have the Canadian banks here.

September 10: Dr. Ramon Grau San Martin is Cuba's new president. His selection was made by the *Directorio Estudiantil.* Representatives of all other factions were called to the palace and told that Grau had been selected. The delegates of the other factions were astounded and angry and finally, after some argument, washed their hands of the entire matter. I doubt if any of the political groups will support Grau. Dr. Grau San Martin is a tall, thin, anemic looking chap. There is much doubt about his executive ability. He will be dominated by the students of the *Directorio,* who of course have no idea of practical government.

Quesada came in and announced that the new government was already a complete failure. Knowing he is a supporter of Grau and the students, I asked him what had happened. He said there was no ice water in the palace and, if an administration couldn't see that ice water was on hand for visitors and the press, then he felt sure they would not have sufficient executive ability to manage a government.

No foreign diplomatic representatives attended the inauguration. They are all waiting to see what the United States does about recognition. Phil came back from the inauguration looking as though he had been in a wreck, his tie under one ear, his collar wilted. His white shoes looked as if a parade had passed over them. He said that half the *Autenticos* (Grau supporters) had stepped on his feet and that he had never seen such a mad mob, especially the women. He said Grau must have a lot of women patients.

The Anti-Imperialist League met in Central Park today. Everyone enjoyed shouting, "Down with Yankee Imperialism" and "Down with Welles." Then the Communists arrived carrying red flags and denounced both the Americans and the Grau administration and proclaimed their ambition to place a red flag on top of the new Capitolio.

Phil and I went out to the National Hotel late this afternoon. The army has had the hotel surrounded for several days. I cannot see how the officers could be so foolish as to all get together and permit themselves to be surrounded. I have a hunch they think American intervention will come and that the army will not attack the hotel because it is American property, and because Ambassador Welles is living at the hotel. The hotel staff walked out today on strike so the officers will have no service.

Phil and I passed the guard around the hotel by showing foreign correspondent press cards. It is a queer situation. One day the soldiers refuse to let anyone pass through. The next day all the friends and families of the officers go in to visit them. The officers maintain an armed guard at the main entrance, no rifles, but with pistols swinging at their hips. We went into the lobby crowded with women, children, friends, officers and, I suppose, government spies.

Phil is acquainted with many of the officers. The one I know best is Captain Torres Menier, a Cuban aviator who received his training in the United States. I told him I thought it was stupid to gather in a hotel like that. He agreed with me and said that in his personal opinion they should have been fighting several days ago. However, it seems they all consider themselves under the orders of Colonel Sanguily and it is his idea.

We are told that Ambassador Welles has promised American intervention if they attack the hotel but of course we do not believe that. The United States lost the chance to intervene when the fourth of September coup was staged. Our *Cuban policy* will reach a new low before this is over. Backdoor diplomacy never worked and never will.

The ABC's today issued a statement that they will not support the present government. The rest of the factions will probably do the same.

September 12: The new cabinet was sworn in today.

Dr. Joachin del Rio Balmaseda is Secretary of Justice and Secretary of State *ad interim.*

Dr. Antonio Guiteras y Holmes is Secretary of Interior and Secretary of Public Works *ad interim.* Guiteras was a salesman of pharmaceutical products in Holguin, Oriente Province. He was known as a Communist during the Machado regime.

Colonel Julio Aguado y Andreu is Secretary of War and Navy. He was Chief of Cabañas Fortress during the Machado regime.

Dr. Carlos E. Finlay y Shine is Secretary of Health. He is the son of the famous Dr. Carlos Finlay who discovered that yellow fever is transmitted by the *aedes aegypti* mosquito.

The officers at the National Hotel are cooking, washing dishes, making beds and sweeping floors. Captain Torres told Phil and me laughingly that they had assigned the aviators to running the elevators, since they were accustomed to going up and down.

The merchants, industrialists and other businessmen, the majority of whom are foreigners, are going around with long gloomy faces and predicting the worst. Cubans really have little they can call their own on the island with the exception of the government. Wall Street owns the sugar mills or controls them through loans. English and American capital owns the railways. The Electric Bond & Share has a monopoly of electric power in the island; the International Telephone & Telegraph has a telephone monopoly. The bulk of city property and much farm land is owned by Spaniards; the majority of commercial firms are owned by Spaniards or Jews. Cubans have one ambition—to be professional men, preferably doctors or lawyers, and to become connected with the government. There are so many lawyers now that many of them cannot make a living. Legal procedure is complicated and expensive here due to the tradition of Spanish law. For example, a bill of sale or deed to some ordinary piece of property costs from $25 upward for notarization in comparison with fifty cents or a dollar in the United States.

September 14: The new constitution has seven clauses. Some wag remarked that the government didn't have time to put in any more clauses as they were all too busy talking. Visiting the palace is like visiting a lunatic asylum with all the inmates turned loose to do as they please. I approach the palace, leave my automobile anywhere I can find parking space, lock the car in gear, lock the doors, look to see if there is anything that can be twisted off by the crowd. Amid the screams of dozens of urchins who demand to *cuida la máquina,* I roar back that I don't need anyone to watch my car, give one backward glance, and hurry toward the Palace entrance. Having pushed through the mob at the iron gates, I show my five or six press cards to soldiers lounging about, leaning on their rifles, hastily put back in my purse a police card signed by the former chief of police, Ainciart. It is important to remember to discard such things. After some delay, I am admitted.

In the press room I find soldiers sitting on all the desks, smoking. Knowing I can't possibly get near the elevator, I take to the stairs and on the second floor find myself embroiled in another crowd. Finally I arrive at the cabinet room where President Grau receives everyone. It is a long narrow room with a long narrow table. The President sits at the head of the table, surrounded by the *Directorio Estudiantil.* Another American correspondent grins at me and asks, "Come to see the President?"

A couple of hours later I had progressed several paces toward the head of the table, where Grau is now totally obscured from my view by excited youthful nation savers. Eventually I get within shouting distance and, trusting that a woman's voice will make itself distinct in the midst of all the male roaring, I ask a question. The President replies, looking right at me, but not in answer to the question I asked. No one around the President pays the slightest attention to him, nor has the courtesy to stop talking long enough for him to make himself heard. I ask my question again. The President replies. Not having been able to hear a word of his reply, I nod brightly, try to make my face show comprehension, smile, nod again, and withdraw. Near the door I catch hold of the sleeve of the first member of the *Directorio*

Estudiantil I see and repeat the question I asked the President. After all, the students *are* the government. This young man's answer, to a single, specific question, lasted seventeen minutes, at which time I simply abandoned him. This is my life as a correspondent!

The first counterrevolution has started. Naturally with the revolution in power any one who starts an uprising must be a counterrevolutionist. Captain Aran, an ousted army officer, together with a number of followers, took over the army garrison at Consolación del Sur, Pinar del Rio Province. He probably has about one hundred men, including soldiers who are said to have joined from the military post at Consolación del Sur. Some two hundred troops have been sent out to combat this "counterrevolution."

Will we never finish with revolutions? Everyone who comes into the office has some complaint about the new government. Everyone thinks the United States should "do something." Businessmen are praying for intervention. So are the Spanish landowners. We stopped to get gasoline at the garage where we customarily trade and the proprietor came out to talk with me. He shook his head pessimistically and remarked that Cuba would never have a decent government. The only people in the island who do not want intervention are the politicians, those who have hopes of government jobs, and the students, now getting into office as fast as they can.

Alex, the youngster in the United Press office, told me of an incident which happened at the palace. He said the other night he saw a girl, probably seventeen or eighteen, very pretty—and Alex is very susceptible to feminine charm—walking along the corridor carrying a large portfolio. He approached her, told her he was of the *prensa* and asked if she worked in the palace. She replied that she was heading a committee to *depurar* the State Department; that is, the committee was deciding whether this or that ambassador, consul, or secretary should remain in service or be dismissed. She showed him a list of diplomats now holding foreign posts. Opposite each name was written such remarks as: "*Machadista*," "Out," "Remain." Alex could hardly keep his face straight as he thought how funny it was for this group of children to be ousting career ambassadors and consuls by one stroke of the pen.

Alex was raised in the United States. Although his family is Cuban, he affirms emphatically that he is an American. Environment is a curious thing. Alex declares that he cannot understand the workings of the Cuban mind and apparently he does not, judging from his reaction to events. The other night a Cuban man about town, who spends his time running around with American women tourists, was robbed and stabbed. Alex, who sometimes talks in headlines, said: "Havana's first gigolo stabbed in the belly."

September 15: Captain Aran surrendered early this morning. His men deserted one by one during the night. When the Captain awoke this morning he had thirty-seven men left and decided they could not fight two hundred. He expected support from the various factions, but didn't get it. Anyone who starts a revolution in Cuba has to fight it out himself. Those who promise to help usually have a bad cold and stay home.

Phil went to the station to take a photograph of Captain Aran and his men, who were brought in as prisoners this afternoon. Phil has a new camera and is rapidly becoming one of those "addicts."

Feeling against Americans is running high. A big crowd of negroes surrounded Phil and dared him to take a picture, making bitter and lengthy remarks about Americans. Being a southerner you can imagine Phil's anger.

Reports continue to come in about sugar mills being seized by the workers. One crowd of millworkers locked the manager and his family inside his home and took turns all day and all night running a stick along the picket fence. You can imagine that sound going on for hours and hours! One man from the interior said that swarms of communistic agitators had descended on the mills and were inciting the workmen.

The authorities are trying to starve the officers in the National Hotel. No food supplies are allowed to enter. It was reported that the water supply had been cut off this afternoon. According to our information the hotel has a couple of deep wells, so that cutting off the city pipelines will not leave them without water.

September 17: Phil came in, laughing. He said a checkroom for revolvers has been installed at the palace. It seems that the students, who are overrunning the palace, are so heavily armed their weapons get in everyone's way. The major-domo of the palace established a check counter on the ground floor. Phil said he had never seen such a miscellaneous collection of guns. He also saw one of the cabinet officials refused admittance by a soldier on guard at the presidential offices. The official started to pass through the door but was stopped by the soldier who demanded identification or a written pass. The member of the government drew himself up and said, "I am a cabinet member." The soldier didn't believe him. Fifteen minutes were lost trying to find some one in the palace to identify him.

September 22: A group of women attacked the wives of officers, who were leaving the hotel after visiting their husbands. Their clothes were torn off.

The officers at the National Hotel are practically without communication with the outside. The telephone wires have been cut. The officers come out in the garden and stand along the edge of the high cliff and wave at their families. It looks like an encampment around the hotel with soldiers sleeping in pup tents and lounging around. The officers must be insane. We know the army is going to attack the hotel but the officers do not believe it. Ambassador Welles moved out several days ago. He said the service was too poor with all the employees gone. Apparently he is going to sit here and let Batista and his army attack American property.

It seems strange that the officers would bottle themselves up in a hotel to be attacked and captured. Of course, they are depending upon American intervention, and they are going to be badly fooled. President Roosevelt is determined not to intervene regardless of what happens.

However, the American navy officers here have planned the taking over of the island down to the smallest detail, just in case it should be ordered. Consul General Dumont has planned the removal of all Americans from Havana. The plan is quite elaborate. The town has been divided into districts; in each district an American key man has been appointed and either he or his substitute is near a telephone constantly, so that at any time the Consulate decides to evacuate the Americans the key man of each district is advised. He will contact every American on his list. Trucks guarded by American marines will pick up the Americans.

I asked the Consul-General if we were on the list. He grinned and said newspaper people were supposed to take care of themselves.

No matter how much Cubans talk they will not attack Americans. I see no danger, if fighting breaks out, except from stray bullets. The soldiers talk about what they are going to do, how they will run the Americans out of town, whip the American marines, but it is pure talk and nothing else. When Phil and I stop to talk with a group of them, it isn't long before they are slapping Phil on the back, posing for their pictures and insisting if there is anything they can do they will be delighted to do it.

September 23: Everyone is sure there will be a revolution. The United States will, we hear, step in if a state of chaos reigns in the island. It looks to me as though such a state is practically here. Reports come in daily from the interior that conditions of uncertainty and unrest exist there which cannot be rivaled in Cuban history. Small groups are fighting in the interior. Laborers are on strike at every sugar mill in the island. Negroes are rising and demanding equality and signs reading "Pick your white woman" are reported in many localities. There is much talk of an armed group being formed here to go out and kill negroes. The negro revolt during the administration of President Gómez, when thousands of negroes were slaughtered, particularly in Oriente, Camagüey and Santa Clara Provinces, is recalled—negro women and children lying on the roadsides, killed by the soldiers. While the racial problem has only flared that one time in Cuban history, it is highly possible trouble may come again owing to the doctrine being preached by the radical agitators.

There are several negro cults in Cuba, the Nañigo being the largest. In the interior the ceremonies and rites of the Nañigo Cult are still held. A young Cuban member of the Red Cross, sent to Sagua la Grande after the cyclone to assist in the relief work, spent the night in a small village near the north coast, in that district. As I remember, his story was as follows:

"Sometime after midnight I awoke. The very air in the room seemed to vibrate to the steady beat of drums. I tried to go back to sleep but it was impossible. I dressed and went out into the street. The only person I could find was a rural guard who seemed in no way disturbed by the sound. He said it was a Nañigo ceremony somewhere out in the hills, probably five or six miles. Seeing that I was curious, the rural guard invited me to ride out with him to the scene and offered me a horse from the military post.

"We rode in the direction from which the guard said the sound came, although to me, with the unceasing rhythm in my ears, we seemed enveloped in the sound. Finally, we saw the light of the fire. We approached. The light of the flames glistened on the sweating torsos of the blacks as they writhed and twisted in harmony with the sound of the bongos beat with the heel of the palm by the drummers. The dance went on and on. The guard and I returned to the village but it was near daybreak before the drums ceased."

I asked Raul, our office boy, about the Nañigos. He was raised in Santa Clara Province and knows a few words of

the dialect of this cult. The god of the Nañigos is the *ceiba*
tree. The high priest is a mythical figure known as Changó.
The Catholic religion is mixed with and lost within the pagan
beliefs of Africa. Formerly no one could become a member
of the inner circle of the Nañigo unless he had killed at least
one person. Now they indulge in black magic in which a
white rooster figures. There is considerable difference in the
beliefs and practices of the cults of Cuba and those of Haiti.
Raul says he has gone to the Nañigo ceremonies and that he
has known of white people who joined the cult. He said that
the effect of the drums is mesmeric and that after one has
heard the drums for five or six hours one is ready to believe
anything or to do anything. That is undoubtedly the secret
of the influence which the priests of the cult exercise over
the members.

Students are now telling the negro he is being oppressed
by the whites. The *Directorio Estudiantil,* during Machado's
regime, put out a manifesto in which one of the points was
that no illiterate should vote. They call them *analfabetos.*
Now the students are rallying the *analfabetos* trying to fuse
them into a political party. This is the old trick of the Cuban
politician.

We have so many strikes that it is useless to talk about
them. The dock workers are striking, newspaper employees
walked out this afternoon, most of the tobacco workers are
on strike. Everybody puts on demonstrations. The streets are
full all the time with demonstrators, shouting first one thing
and then another. The only thing they all agree on is "Down
with the Americans."

Labor leaders and Communists are working overtime.
John, our cook, told me a man came to the house and asked
him to join the servants' union. John, being a Jamaican, is
keen on looking out for his personal rights so he said he was
going to the meeting. This morning he came in and with a
disgusted look told me that he was not going to join, despite
the fact that it had been agreed at the meeting to force every
servant in town to join. John said he didn't like the crowd. It

was low class riffraff from the streets with whom he was not going to associate. Phil and I laughed.

No one is paying rent; the landlords are helpless. A moratorium is going to be declared on rent.

September 26: The ashes of Julio Antonio Mella, Communist leader believed to have been slain in Mexico at the orders of Machado, arrived here today. A huge crowd shouted and screamed against the present government, proposing to establish a labor government. They paraded the ashes around town but have not decided what to do with them.

We are rapidly becoming a militaristic nation. We now have the *Pro Ley y Justicia* (For Law and Justice), the student militia, and today President Grau created the Revolutionary Guard. Anyone may join and he will receive food, uniform and lodging but no salary. The main attraction of the Revolutionary Guard is that of carrying a rifle and a couple of pistols.

Garage owners are in a furor. They say these uniformed boys drive up, demand gasoline and drive away without paying. If the garage man doesn't serve them gasoline, they use their rifles as persuaders. Cars are disappearing in every direction. Whenever the various revolutionary groups need a car, they take the first one handy.

September 27: Forty thousand Spaniards and Cubans belonging to the Spanish Regional Societies paraded today. There were no disorders. It was amazing to note the difference in these people from the usual demonstrators with torn shirts, ragged trousers, one shoe or maybe none, no hats, dirty and belligerent. This crowd was well dressed. They marched past Central Park to the Presidential Palace along Zulueta Street and the Prado Promenade in perfect order. The Societies are protesting a recent decree issued by President Grau forcing all doctors to become members of the Medical Federation or lose their license to practice. The Regional Societies and the Federation have been in controversy for the past year because the Federation attempted to force the Societies to remove from their membership lists all persons earning over one hundred dollars monthly. The Societies refused, stating that their maintenance depended on the upper middle class. Many doctors resent the fact that medical attention and hospitalization is given to the members for two dollars monthly. Hence the struggle. The present government sided with the Federation and approved the decree ordering all doctors to join the Federation or quit practicing.

The Regional Societies, headed and controlled by Spaniards, are rich and powerful, several of them having as many as fifty thousand members. They own hospitals and sanitariums. Nearly all the salaried and wage earning people belong to these Societies. It is a wonderful thing for them to be able to get medical attention and even operations for the two dollars monthly quota. The Societies are determined not to accede to the demand and are threatening to close all commercial establishments as a protest against the present decree.

September 29: Communists tried to place Mella's ashes in a hastily constructed monument of bricks and cement in Fraternity Park. The authorities permitted them to erect the monument without molestation. Phil and I passed there and took a picture of the monument and the crowd milling around. It looked like trouble was brewing. Secretary of Interior Guiteras had given them permission for the demonstration, then Colonel Batista apparently decided to stop it. Batista, in my opinion, is too ambitious to have radical leanings.

As we came into the Manzana de Gómez, Phil met a soldier whom he knew. He told Phil it was time a few Communists were killed to put them in their places; they were getting too bold running up and down the streets with their red flags.

Headquarters of the Anti-Imperialist League is on Reina

Street. The plan was to march from these headquarters up Reina Street to Fraternity Park where the ashes were to be deposited. Shooting started almost simultaneously with the parade, but as usual no one knows who started it. The soldiers tonight claimed that snipers posted on adjoining buildings started firing into their ranks.

Curiously enough, it wasn't the Communists who were killed. Phil and Alex went to the Emergency Hospital. They saw a boy of ten or twelve with the whole side of his head blown away. A Jamaican negro passing along the street had his foot shot away. He asked Phil to notify his wife, so she would know what had become of him. Joseph Gibson, Universal newsreel man, was shot in the legs. He and several other cameramen were on the balcony of the Hotel Nueva Isla taking pictures. Undoubtedly, the soldiers saw the cameras and in their excitement thought they were machine guns, because from all reports they fired directly at the cameramen.

I hope Gibson isn't badly wounded. He is quite a character. One of the photographers told me that after several days during which he had sent no pictures out of Cuba, he received a cable from Universal Picture Service reading: "What did you make today?" Gibson wired back: "One Cuban señorita."

The soldiers smashed the makeshift monument and trucks hauled it away within a few minutes. The ashes of Mella have been lost in the melée or the Communists hid them. The soldiers looked for them all afternoon but so far without success. Six people were killed and twenty-seven wounded. The soldiers detroyed the Anti-Imperialist League of Cuba headquarters and burned the furniture. The furniture, files and records of the National Confederation of Labor, located nearby, were thrown into the street and set afire.

September 30: The students say in one breath they do not care if they never get recognition; that they do not need it; that this is the first one hundred per cent Cuban government

Cuba ever had; and then in the next breath ask when the
United States will recognize the Grau administration.

Property owners are frightened to death; ragged mobs are
running through the streets, shouting, "Down with Americans." The merchants are so nervous that every time they
hear a yell in the streets they rush out and pull down the big
iron shutters which are used instead of doors on most small
establishments. The shutters make a terrific noise when they
are rolled up or down and, when one hears a shot and sees
people running, the next sound is the slam bang of the iron
shutters going down in every direction. It has the appearance of a fire drill carried out several times a day.

One thing which ultimately will defeat the Grau government is the question of revenue. No one is paying taxes;
people are afraid the next administration will try to collect
them again. None of the merchants are importing. Wholesale houses are shutting down on credit and demanding cash.
We are told that the government cannot get credit on arms
and ammunition but must pay cash.

The Cuban army yesterday attacked the National Hotel,
American-owned property. Residents in the vicinity were not
warned to leave and the first they knew of the attack was the
burst of firing at daybreak.

Troops were moving in from Camp Columbia the morning
of October 2nd, when we went home from the office and it
was necessary to go out by Carlos III Street in order to reach
Vedado. We live up the hill from the hotel so that the first
shots woke us up. Our telephone rang incessantly. People
who lived in the immediate neighborhood of the hotel kept
calling us up to tell us that the hotel was being attacked. The
residents of the big apartment building at Twenty-third and
O Streets were particularly indignant because they had to
vacate all apartments facing the hotel. Soldiers were using
the building as a barricade to fire at the hotel.

We dressed and started to town. We crossed Twenty-third
Street and took Calzada as far as the Hotel Presidente where

people in all kinds of costumes, bathrobes and slippers, over-
coats with nothing underneath, were watching the bombardment from the dining room on the eighth floor. Newsreel
men had their cameras on the roof and were trying to get
pictures with telescopic lenses. We stayed there and had
breakfast. While we were watching, the Cuban gunboat,
Patria, came wallowing out of the mouth of the bay in the
heavy sea and steamed around to a point just off the Malecón. The first shot they fired landed two blocks away in the
middle of the park and the second somewhere at the foot
of the hill kicking up dirt. The shots failed to damage the
hotel but they nearly wrecked the Patria. She rolled from one
side to the other and the sailors on board, after the gunboat
finally righted herself, decided to let the land artillery do the
work and made back for the harbor.

The fight was getting hot. The army brought into action
several 75 mm. French type guns, 37 mm., one pounders and
other small artillery. Later in the morning Phil got into
the university. He went up on the roof to see the guns and
was walking about when a soldier reached out and jerked
him unceremoniously behind the sandbags which they were
using as breastwork. Phil protested that the officers in the
hotel certainly couldn't shoot that far with a rifle but the
soldiers said snipers on various roofs around the university
were taking shots at anyone who showed himself.

Tonight a man described to me how the soldiers were
using the 75's. If they ever had any instruction they couldn't
remember it in their excitement, so they would get down and
sight through the bore and bring the gun around until they
could see the hotel through the barrel, then they would load
and fire. No wonder one shot hit the tower on top, the next
missed the entire hotel and fell into the sea, and the next
struck a room on the ground floor. Of course, the National
Hotel is a good-sized target and they made many hits. Bal-
conies were blown off, whole rooms wrecked, gaping holes
left in the walls where shells went through.

The officers are the best shots in the army. A number of

them were trained by the United States Army. They did telling work with their rifles. They killed over a hundred soldiers and wounded some two hundred. The army sent the dead and wounded to Camp Columbia and to the Emergency Hospital by truck loads.

Robert Lotspiech, American assistant manager for Swift & Co., was killed on the roof of the Lopez Serrano apartment building. He is supposed to have leaned over the parapet and a stray bullet struck him. It could hardly have come from the hotel. People living in the building say the soldiers posted around the building fired at the windows and at the roof—for what reason no one knows. At eleven A.M. an American called me from the Serrano building and said he and his family had been lying on the floor of their apartment for three or four hours. He asked me to get in touch with Ambassador Welles and arrange to remove the poeple from the building or have the soldiers stop firing at the windows. He said: "I have to hang up. This phone is in a dangerous spot. Another bullet just came through the window into the ceiling."

Americans in the building were pleading frantically with the Ambassador by telephone to do something, but Welles sat there and never did a thing. Phil, after having talked with the Ambassador, called Consul General Dumont and asked him why the American authorities did not evacuate the building. Welles hesitated all morning despite the insistence of Dumont that the Americans be evacuated. Finally he called Washington on the telephone. Consul General Dumont arranged a truce for an hour and the Americans, thirty-seven, I believe, were evacuated. Phil and Porter went to the Lopez Serrano building during the truce. Many other Americans, who lived in apartment buildings in Vedado, were in danger most of the day. Soldiers passing along the streets fired into their windows and many of them spent the day lying on the floor.

Then the firing started again. During the truce seventeen wounded officers were removed from the hotel, but none of the three hundred had been killed. There were three women in the hotel, the wife of Colonel Sanguily and two more, whose names I do not know. The officers had little ammunition. What they did have entered the hotel early the night of the first when a truck ran the gauntlet, and, despite soldiers firing at it from every direction, managed to get down Twenty-third Street and turn into the driveway by the Ford building.

The Manzana de Gómez building where we have our offices shook from the firing of the guns. Adding to the bombardment was the crack of rifles from first one side and then another. Civilians in sympathy with the officers fired on soldiers in the streets and soldiers fired without paying attention to whether their targets were really snipers or not. Many people were wounded, some killed. Cars loaded with students raced through the streets.

The officers surrendered at four-fifteen in the afternoon. As soon as we heard the white flag had gone up on the hotel, Phil left the office to go there, although the firing did not cease with the appearance of the white flag. Phil says the scene was indescribable. He got as far as the hill on Twenty-third Street and was looking down at the crowd rushing toward the hotel after the surrender. There were thousands. All at once shooting again started. Soldiers on the hill fired directly into the crowd. As Phil backed the car out to get away from the screaming, fleeing mob, he could hear the bullets singing. Twenty were killed and many wounded in that shooting. The whole thing had started with the killing of sixteen officers who were waiting to be removed to Cabañas Fortress as prisoners. Just who killed the officers is not clear. It was either the soldiers who were guarding them or members of the *Pro Ley y Justicia,* student militia, who had aided the army in attacking the hotel.

Even Bill Lander of the United Press, who was standing within a few feet of the slain officers, is unable to decide who did the shooting. He came into the office late last night and said he wouldn't forget that scene if he lived to be a hundred.

He and several other correspondents had gotten into the
hotel following the surrender, in advance of the mob. The
majority of the officers had been removed in trucks. There
was a group of officers standing in front of the hotel chatting
amicably with the soldiers guarding them. All at once a shot
was fired which clipped a leaf from a palm tree in front of
the hotel. The officers were mowed down with tommy
guns, the majority of them having their heads blown away.
Whether it was *Pro Ley y Justicia* or soldiers not even those
present can say. Bill Lander says he saw a soldier throw his
hands into the air and shout: "Por Dios, stop firing." Bill was
standing at the entrance of the hotel when the shooting
started and he sought protection behind one of the stone
columns.

With this burst of firing the soldiers on the outer edge of
the crowd thought they had been attacked and started firing
into the crowd. The quick witted fell flat on the pavement;
others ran panic stricken and were shot. Bill said when the
firing stopped he saw a student crouched beside a bush. He
wondered why the boy didn't get up and walked over and
touched him. The boy fell backwards. He had been shot between the eyes.

Who fired the shot through the palm tree? Nobody knows.

The following analysis of the fourth of September revolt,
was made by a former officer, who must remain nameless
even today, since he has been subject to considerable persecution and has spent many months in prison. "Machado himself feared the army officers, not the older and higher category, who were his close adherents and linked with him in
his flagrant and profitable misgovernment, but the group of
younger officers who were completely divorced from politics
and were career men. One hundred forty-six of this group
had been trained in American military schools and were imbued with the high ideals of the American armed forces.
Realizing that these officers were a potential danger to a dictatorship, Machado, following his illegal gesture of perpe-
trating himself in office without elections, tried by extension

of various favors to gain the active support of these younger officers. In this he failed. His next step was to have the higher and most trusted of his officers weaken the disciplinary hold of the subaltern officers on the troops. This subtle campaign went on for a period of nearly four years during which time the authority of the younger officers was gradually undermined. For example, in disciplinary cases where a soldier was accused by his lieutenant of insubordination or some other minor offense, the soldier, brought before the major of his division or to the Chief of Staff, was immediately absolved and the lieutenant reprimanded. On every occasion the authority of the subaltern officer was disregarded and belittled by his superiors. Therefore, the troops came to look on their immediate officers as mere figureheads without any real power.

"When Machado fell and the highest officers of the army fled, the troops, composed of the uneducated classes of the island, were completely disorganized. They had no desire to submit to the authority of the officers then in command. They had been taught to disregard them and to look to the higher category of officials as their commanding officers. Thus the next logical step was for the enlisted men to assume control.

"President Céspedes appointed Colonel Julio Sanguily, Chief of Staff, immediately upon his inauguration. Colonel Sanguily was formerly an aide to General Mario G. Menocal during his term as president. He was not only a close personal friend of General Menocal but completely dominated by him. The officers of the army noted with consternation that the appointments made by Colonel Sanguily of military supervisors of the various provinces were all former comrades of former president Menocal. The appointments were as follows: Colonel Emiliano Amiel, Santa Clara Province; Major Vilató, Camagüey Province; Colonel Arquimedes Mendez, Oriente Province; Lieutenant Colonel Erasmo Delgado, Havana Province; Major Ovidio Ortega, Pinar del Rio Province. The head of Matanzas Province was also an adherent of Menocal. It was immediately clear, knowing as we did the ambition of Menocal to become President again, that the foundation had been laid for a coup d'état. This aroused considerable discontent among the officers as it was evident that the army was again to be used as an instrument of power.

"The most youthful of the officers began a conspiracy in conjunction with the students and radical professional men toward the ousting of the Céspedes government. The news of these plots leaked to the troops, with demoralizing effect. The fourth of September rebellion started as a simple mutiny; that is, a movement within the ranks destined to force compliance with certain conditions or demands made by the troops with regard to their own status, and was never intended to become an insurrection with removal of officers and a change of administration. It simply got out of hand. An officer commands merely through long established obedience of troops to military discipline. If this discipline is relaxed an officer is only one man against a hundred.

"In my personal opinion the actual head of the conspiracy at Camp Columbia was not Batista but Sergeant Pablo Rodriguez. He, together with several other sergeants in active service, planned the mutiny, which became a revolt, and changed the history of the island. Sergeant Batista was a stenographer attached to military headquarters. In Cuba, stenographers of military courts, such as Batista, are merely civilians who pass the required examination and enter the service as office workers. Rodriguez in casting about for a man of, let us say, 'facility of words,' a man who could hold the troops in line by power of oratory, thought of his friend Sergeant Batista. Add to this natural gift of oratory which Batista possesses a pleasing personality, and, while he lacks education and culture, an agility of mind far greater than the average enlisted man of the armed forces—Batista was thus made the nominal head of the movement.

"The mutiny expanded into an insurrection. The leaders suddenly found the entire matter out of proportion to their expectations. They removed the officers, an easy matter as they were scattered here and there throughout the city. Then they found themselves forced to establish a government which would condone their action. In something like panic they called in the student element.

"On the morning of September 5th Batista can be likened to a man who finds himself holding a hot potato which burns his fingers, but which he is unable to lay down. Batista was not only willing but more than anxious to turn over the command of the army to any officer who could be found to take it. The basis of this desire lay in his belief that the revolt of the enlisted men and the ousting of their officers would undoubtedly bring swift American intervention. Not only did Batista and the army plotters believe this but the students and the five Commissioners were of the same opinion, notwithstanding their loud cries of defiance toward the United States.

"Let me stop here and explain that in view of the Platt Amendment, under which Cuba accepted the right of the United States to intervene in her affairs when and as the American government saw fit, and the fact that intervention had already taken place in the island under this Amendment, the entire island of Cuba looked on American intervention as logical and to be expected. This created in Cuba a sense of inferiority. Affairs of the island were administered always with one eye on Washington, so to speak, to see if such administrations met with approval. Therefore, when the enlisted men removed their officers and installed a new government, owing to a movement which actually got beyond their control, they were frightened over the result and convinced that it was merely a matter of days before American marines controlled the island.

"It was in such a state of mind that the Commissioners heading the government on September 5th, called to the palace Colonels Quesada and Perdomo and offered them the offices of Chief of Staff and Chief of Camp Columbia respectively. Batista and his fellow conspirators, as I said before, were not only willing but anxious to turn the command over to those officers who, it was expected, would call back to the army all the officers whose reputation and past record was clean. Thus the government hoped by restoring to command at least the majority of the officers to prevent American intervention. Here is where the American government through Ambassador Welles made its greatest mistake. Either Mr. Welles deliberately deceived the officers, which we hesitate to believe, or President Roosevelt conveyed to Welles an erroneous impression concerning the policy of the American government which was—no intervention at any cost.

"We do not know where exactly to place the blame but the facts of the case are these: Colonel Gimperling, Military Attaché of the American Embassy, who had many friends and acquaintances among the Cuban officers, and who, we believed, spoke directly for the Ambassador, advised the officers under no circumstances to return to their commands, stating that the American government would never tolerate a revolt of the enlisted men, such as had taken place, nor a change of government by them, and that American intervention was undoubtedly the next step.

"We must likewise consider the human element of this problem. The Céspedes government was the handiwork of Ambassador Welles, who, with the most excellent intentions, hoped to reconstruct Cuba both economically and politically. When his own creation was overthrown he was undoubtedly much perturbed and resentful against the student-soldier government and determined to prevent their recognition at any cost. He therefore used every weapon in his possession against the administration. He thus prevented the officers from returning to their commands, which would have strengthened the position of the student government and might have tipped the scales in their favor both with the Cuban public and the American government.

"Colonels Quesada and Perdomo immediately reported to Colonel Sanguily, whom we still considered as our Chief of

Staff, concerning the offer of the government and, while I cannot state as a fact that the American Ambassador directly advised Sanguily that American intervention was imminent, subsequent events verify that this understanding was conveyed to Sanguily. The officers, who were widely separated in their homes and demoralized by the sudden revolt of the troops, did not learn of the offer of the government until many days later when Sergeant Batista had become Colonel Batista, Chief of Staff. Naturally, it was then impossible to return to our commands and countenance a sergeant as Chief of Staff.

"Had the American Ambassador laid his cards on the table and stated frankly that the situation was an internal one and the American government would under no circumstances intervene, then the history of the island would have been written in a different manner. The younger officers would all have returned to their commands under Colonel Quesada as Chief of Staff and would have gradually regained control of the troops. I make this statement after talking with many of my brother officers and I believe I am correct in saying this was the sentiment which prevailed.

"However, Colonels Quesada and Perdomo were advised by Colonel Sanguily to reject the offer of the student government and to await American intervention; since if any of the officers returned it would mean, in the eyes of the American government, that the action of the troops had been condoned.

"Colonel Sanguily, who was recovering from an operation at the National Hotel, issued a request for all officers to gather there. We went blindly on the consideration that Colonel Sanguily was still our Chief of Staff. We were told to remain until the situation was cleared up and we could return to our posts. One group in the hotel was, however, not idle. They contacted members of the ABC and laid plans for a revolution. They were promised aid from the outside should the soldiers attack the hotel, which, however, was not expected as it was the general belief that American intervention was merely a question of a few days. From a military standpoint we all knew how stupid it was to congregate at one point as we had done but we were obeying Colonel Sanguily as commanding officer.

"Days went by but no solution was reached. We ran short of food; the staff of the hotel walked out on strike; we were surrounded by soldiers and not permitted communication with the outside world. We had no news of the attack, although we had come to expect it momentarily. The night before the attack a truckload of food ran the gauntlet on Twenty-third Street and reached the hotel. The soldiers undoubtedly believed it was ammunition but, as a matter of fact, it was only food.

"I was doing guard duty on the side of the hotel facing the Ford plant from a second-story window the morning of the attack. My turn was from four until six A.M. My relief had arrived and just as I started to leave we saw an armored truck speed around the corner of the Ford plant and come toward the hotel. Our first thought was that it was an attempt of the soldiers to dynamite the water tank which was on that side so as to starve us out. We lost sight of the truck as it came close to the building and a second later a burst of firing came from the guards on the ground floor on that side.

"The soldiers who descended from the truck were instantly killed with a machine gun in the hands of the guard at the kitchen entrance. The truck roared back the way it had come. The attack had started.

"In the hotel we had a total of thirty-seven Springfield rifles with sixty to eighty rounds of ammunition each. These rifles were issued to the best shots among the officers. One officer, who took second honors in an international sharp shooting contest several years ago, had his own rifle there with the special ammunition used in contests. Every time his rifle fired a soldier fell and the other thirty-six officers acquitted themselves with an average approximating this. This was the reason that the officers in the hotel with only thirty-seven rifles were able to kill more than one hundred soldiers and wound many others.

"The attacking soldiers made one costly blunder after another. They reversed the usual military procedure, attacking first with rifles, then with machine guns and later with artillery. One machine gun, with a range of some 2800 yards, was placed at the Beacon Light Monument on the Malecón within easy rifle range and many lost their lives at this point. Knowing nothing of the calculations of indirect firing, the soldiers were forced to place the artillery close enough so they could aim the guns as a rifle, rather than make the proper calculations which would have enabled them to fire from a completely safe distance.

"Only two of the officers were killed during the fight, although several were wounded. The deaths among the officers occurred largely after surrender when a total of sixteen were killed by the soldiers.

"A truce was arranged around three o'clock to remove the Americans in the district and to allow the removal of some of the wounded in the hotel. During this truce Colonel Sanguily ran a referendum as to whether to continue fighting. This is, of course, a military error. The officers, who had resolved to die fighting in the hotel, realized that without outside help, which did not appear, they were fighting a senseless battle and it was simply a matter of time until surrender was inevitable. When the hotel was surrendered there was not a single remaining shell for the rifles."

II
The Rise of Fulgencio Batista

5

October 6: Russell Porter today wrote a story saying the Grau government has gained strength by their victory at the National Hotel. I can't see where. They have the entire island against them now, except those who continue to go to demonstrations. Today I asked a boy who attends all demonstrations in favor of Grau why he supports the present government. The boy replied, "I don't think much of the government, but I get twenty cents every time I go."

Mr. Morris of Lykes Brothers saw a negro in the street with a red flag. He stopped his car, called the negro over, and asked him if he were a Communist. The negro proudly said, "Si, señor." Morris inquired as to just what a Communist might be. The negro thought a second, then said, "Un hombre muy guapo con una bandera roja." (A very handsome man with a red flag.)

The majority of Cuban Communists have inherited sufficient money to live comfortably and like to talk. Being radical is the fashion at present. But if anyone suggested they give away their property and live with the classes they are inciting against the upper classes, they would run squeaking for cover.

Quesada's son, a precocious youngster of twelve, recently informed his father that he had become a Communist. The other day when this youthful Red refused to eat what the cook served for lunch, his father said: "Now you're a Communist and should be glad to eat the black beans and rice which the cook has prepared; the majority of the people haven't even that." The son replied, "I'm a Communist but I'm not a pioneer!"

October 7: President Grau broadcast an indictment against American financiers tonight. The students are taking the point of view that the American people are going to rush to their rescue and demand that the United States government recognize this administration. They are criticizing American bankers and capitalists here in the hope of gaining the sympathy of President Roosevelt. They assume this attitude owing to certain statements of President Roosevelt concerning the "money changers." They do not realize that Roosevelt is playing politics.

It is like the fond mother who takes her child to visit a neighbor and spanks it when it doesn't behave. If the neighbor, thinking that the fond mother *really* desires her child to behave better, also spanks the child, the atmosphere of friendliness changes and the mother goes indignantly home. The reaction to Grau's speech isn't going to be what he expects.

October 8: One would imagine a battle was being fought nightly at Principe Fortress Jail. I never heard such shooting. If they were killing prisoners, as rumors state, they would undoubtedly have run out of prisoners by this time. Phil says he thinks it is automobiles filled with civilians passing along the opposite side of the hill from us and taking shots at the guards on the walls. Then the guards return the fire and every guard who is awake, and some that aren't, rush out of their quarters and fire their rifles.

The other morning an incident occurred just before we got home for lunch which illustrates of how little value is life today in Cuba. A negro boy of about fourteen attempted to steal a bicycle belonging to a youngster living on F Street. The owner of the bicycle came out of the house and saw the negro boy riding off. He yelled and howled until the neighbors came running. The negro, frightened by the racket, dropped the bicycle and started running. The boy whose bicycle he had attempted to steal gave chase. Negroes living in the public works yard in front of our house joined in the chase, yelling like Comanches. The negro boy was some distance ahead of his pursuers. A guard doing duty on the wall of Principe Fortress saw the boy running with the crowd behind him but was too far away to know what the trouble was. However, he raised his rifle and fired, killing the negro boy, much as one would shoot down a passing bird.

October 18:   Everything which happens in Cuba is blamed on Ambassador Welles. Gasoline is running short. The students affirm that the Ambassador ordered the Standard Oil Company, Shell-Mex and Sinclair Oil not to import any during the past three months. The truth is, garage owners got tired of furnishing free gasoline to the students, the *Pro Ley y Justicia* and the Revolutionary Guard so claimed they didn't have any and couldn't get it from the oil companies.

Phil called up Ambassador Welles who said he guessed that about the only thing he hadn't been accused of was kidnapping and murder. He expected by tomorrow to see that accusation in some newspaper.

I notice that Porter is writing an economic article. He went to see Colonel Despaigne, Secretary of Treasury, the oldest cabinet official and probably the one who knows most about his department. Colonel Despaigne, who is about seventy-five, was one of the "Honest Cabinet" appointed by President Zayas, upon pressure from the United States, when General Crowder tried to straighten out Cuba's financial affairs in 1922 after she had defaulted on her foreign debts. William P. Harding, a member of the Federal Reserve Board, was sent to Cuba to make a report on the financial situation. He stayed two months and then resigned, stating it would take a large staff of experts several years to make an accounting.

Colonel Despaigne was too honest. He refused to authorize

the Santa Clara Convent purchase by the government at a tremendous price, of which the greater part was to be divided by the politicians. He was forced to resign. Colonel Despaigne has little patience with the students. He has been besieged by young revolutionists demanding jobs. One young man stated that he had planted thirty bombs and believed he deserved a job. Despaigne peered at him over his glasses and said: "Then, young man, you had better put a bomb under me and blow me out of this job, because there is no place in the Treasury for you." Colonel Despaigne says they will not have money enough to finish the year without a deficit.

Each government department has a Depurating Committee which checks the list of employees and dismisses all *Machadistas,* ABC members and anyone not a student adherent. Then another Depurating Committee springs up and starts to depurate the first depurating committee. They have had fist fights and gun battles in the various departments.

Raul Casañas said he had just come from the Treasury Department, where he worked for two months before Machado fell. He hopes to again get a job by proving he is not a *Machadista.* He said that Despaigne, in exasperation over the fist fights in the Department, had called in the soldiers. Now a soldier with a rifle is sitting in the middle of each bureau of the Department.

October 21: Bombs and more bombs during the past few days. Today they blew a Santiago express off the track. The express is one of the trains of the United Railways, English owned.

If you haven't been in jail in Cuba you are a nobody. This administration has started out to arrest everyone who does not agree with them. ABCs are fleeing. Dr. Joaquin Martinez Saenz, head of the organization, has gone to Miami. Saenz's automobile was shot at a day or so before he left.

October 28: We are going to have a general strike. The issues have become vague but enthusiasm over striking is increasing. Standard Oil, Sinclair and Shell-Mex beat their workers to the strike and closed their doors. Shell-Mex acted intelligently. Company officials turned over the keys of the plant to the British Legation, and, when government troops arrived to force the companies to open their doors, Shell-Mex officials told them to see the British Government.

Bus drivers walked out in protest against a five cent round-trip fare. Electric light company employees presented a list of demands that would make any employer faint.

October 26:   Some one tried to kill Colonel Carlos Mendieta. The bomb tore out a window and smashed a chair in which Mendieta is accustomed to sit to receive visitors. However, entirely by accident, Mendieta was upstairs when the bomb exploded.

The homes of all political leaders of any note in Cuba can easily be found. If you know the district in which the man you are seeking lives, you don't need the street or the number. Just drive around until you see a big crowd, with the appearance of a wedding or a funeral. Go right in. You'll have to elbow your way through the people on the porch, then into the *sala,* also crowded, then into the salon. There, surrounded by his most prominent followers, is your politician.

The government has the jitters. The Graf Zeppelin passed over Havana and nearly frightened the palace into hysterics. I suppose they thought it was an attack. The antiaircraft gun on the roof was quickly unlimbered for action by the soldiers.

History repeats itself. *La Voz* was closed today and the edition confiscated. Police chased newsboys in the streets with some copies already off the press. The kids ran like Olympic sprinters, dodging, and selling the copies as high as thirty cents each. They are worth only a penny. One man found reading a copy on the street corner was arrested.

Martinez, came into the office this afternoon and sank into a chair with a sigh. I asked what the trouble was and he said he was "simply worn out with conspiring." Martinez is the most reluctant ABC member one could imagine. Having been raised in Philadelphia and having a none too good opinion of the aims and aspirations of the students, he became an ABC only through the influence of his best friend and temporary employer, who was formerly the family lawyer. Martinez spent his half million inheritance with gusto and now is practically on the breadline.

He said that the heads of the revolutionary group met in the office of a certain lawyer, whom he described as "dressed up like a boy scout and letting his practice go to the winds while he conspires to save the nation." The meeting had been called concerning the transportation of a couple of machine guns from Marianao to Havana over the Almendares River bridge. After much discussion and with each member mentioning an important engagement which prevented him from taking on this patriotic errand, they called in Martinez and brightly informed him they had decided to trust him with an important assignment, then went blissfully away leaving him to do the job. Martinez could think of no strategy. Putting the machine guns under the seat of his car, he arrived at the bridge. When the soldiers requested him to get out to be searched, he displayed eagerness, helped them to go through his pockets, acted drunk. The soldiers, no doubt bored with the continuous searching and not caring to do the extra work of lifting the seats, gave him a shove back into the car and told him to go home. With the machine guns across the river and safely delivered, Martinez went out and got drunk.

Being, as he says, terribly sensitive when he is drinking, he hit a marine and dislocated his jaw. The marine had looked at Martinez in a way which he considered an insult. Four marines marched Martinez to a cell at La Punta Naval Headquarters. Luckily, he was allowed to telephone his friend, the lawyer, who has influence in many places.

By three o'clock in the morning Martinez was out of jail. The delay was over a technical matter. There was considerable doubt that Martinez had used only his fist to dislocate the marine's jaw.

November 4: The students decided they will support Grau and will have nothing whatsoever to do with conciliating other factions. As one of the students expressed it: "Government by a minority has a freer hand and is able to give a better administration than a government which tries to please everyone."

Quesada tells me that the Presidential Palace is something like a trick house out in Hollywood. There are secret stairways and sliding panels. In the Salon of Mirrors on the second floor, one of the mirrors at the end next to the Cabinet Room slides back to reveal a stairway leading to the third floor. There are several other secret entrances and exits. That might account for one of the legends concerning former President Machado to the effect that he could stay up all night, appear at six in the morning before the astonished eyes of the palace employees, and enter his office to work undisturbed. He probably sneaked up one of those secret stairways and slumbered peacefully, while the guard outside the office door informed all comers that the President was working.

The palace was originally constructed during the administration of José Miguel Gómez as the Governor's Palace of the Province of Havana and was purchased by the government during the presidency of Menocal. The old building is now used as the Municipal City Hall.

November 6: Phil and I arrived in Cienfuegos, Santa Clara Province yesterday afternoon. Phil simply adores going to the interior. With strikes going on in almost every sugar mill and bandits running up and down the country, everyone warned us against coming; but, of course, we didn't pay any attention. I never saw anything very frightening in the interior. Phil and I have been down as far as Santa Clara a few times. Phil was much interested in seeing for himself how conditions were and what the people were thinking and how they felt about the student government.

A long distance call from Cienfuegos was the main reason we came. In a lawsuit going on between an American company and someone in Cuba, being tried in an American court, the testimony of two old Spaniards had to be taken at the consulate in Cienfuegos. The lawyer, whom we had known for a long time, couldn't find anyone who could take dictation in English, much less write up a court record, so he asked me to come down.

I am sitting in the anteroom of the consulate, waiting for the consul, and trying to keep awake. It is warm, much warmer than Havana and so peaceful. One would never imagine these people getting excited over politics, but they do, spasmodically. The consulate is located opposite the park, a big expanse of concrete, statues and a few trees. The consulate has been in this building for many years. Originally it was a beautiful old residence. The big salón, divided by a railing behind which the stenographer works, takes up the front part of the building. Back of this is a huge patio along which are the consul's office and several other rooms. There are no windows in the house, only doors with iron grills. Out in the hot sunny park are a few unemployed sitting on the benches. I suppose they are unemployed—half the island is at present. After noisy Havana, the quiet here is restful. Only a few cars are circulating; a pedestrian now and then passes; once in a while a man with a poor bony horse loaded with charcoal goes by; or peddlers wander along with stringy looking chickens.

Cienfuegos, located on the south coast of Cuba, was once a thriving port. It has a beautiful bay and large quantities of sugar were shipped from here, but nobody wants sugar any more. The town has a dismal rundown look. The Prado promenade has huge holes, the cement walk is cracking, benches are falling apart; even the trees have a ragged "don't care" air. We walked on the Prado last night but it was so gloomy we soon returned to the hotel. The Pan American Airways plane lands here on its way back and forth from Mexico. Formerly there was a night layover for the passengers and the hotelkeeper said he had a few guests, but now the schedule has been changed.

The Hotel San Carlos, where we are staying, is an old Spanish inn with an excellent reputation. The huge white and gold dining room has a forlorn appearance, with only two or three people dining where a hundred would not be crowded. The food is fair, especially the seafood. We have a room on the second floor, with a foyer, an excellent bathroom, solid mahogany furniture, potted plants and even cut flowers.

We came from Havana very leisurely yesterday. The country between Havana and Matanzas is beautiful, rolling, and with tall stately palm trees in profusion. I like Royal palms; I like the way they grow in straight rows as if planted by measurement, marching over a hill in single file. Some one told me that the uneducated natives of Cuba will not cut down a palm because they say the palms are the souls of dead soldiers always marching.

The Central Highway is good. It should be from the amount of money it cost. However, it is cracking here and there and the ditches alongside have been permitted to fill with weeds. In some places between Matanzas and Santa Clara weeds have grown six and eight feet tall. We have been in Matanzas many times. It is a queer, sprawled little town with narrow streets, wandering rivers and many bridges, built around a magnificent harbor. The big full-length painting of Machado has disappeared from the salon of the Hotel Paris. The Paris has a patio with a huge fountain, where they keep live crawfish and cook them for you while you wait. Flowering vines cover the walls and run up to the open windows of the second story.

Leaving Matanzas the road follows the sea past the best residential district and then turns inland. The country after a few miles becomes flat, more like a plain, particularly after one has passed into Santa Clara Province. There is no place one can obtain decent food after Matanzas. We ate a picnic-style lunch under a tree, while oxen gazed at us through the fence. Now and then we passed a *guajiro* on horseback wearing the huge hat and middy blouse with many tucks and buttons which serves both as a shirt and coat. Negroes tramped along the highway without shoes, with clothes hanging by threads. We expected to leave the highway at Santo Domingo but we were told that we could never get a car over the road and must go on to Esperanza.

At Esperanza we were informed that if it rained we might as well leave the car and walk. Over a rough rocky road we reached Ranchuelo, then the road began to show that it had recently been muddy. Outside Ranchuelo we stopped to ask about a turn and were told we would have to make a detour; we went on. Suddenly a small boy rushed out into the road and yelled so loudly we stopped. He proudly told us he was the guide to show us along the detour. We accepted his guidance and drove through his mother's backyard, out into a cow pen, around the corner of the barn, into a cane field and then across a pasture. The little boy, who had been talking volubly all the while about the cars he had piloted through this stretch of road, said to blow the horn. Phil obeyed. This, the youthful guide said, was to rout out his aides who were to open the wire gate which led back into the road. Two other small lads came running madly from another house and opened the gate. Phil, amused at our guide and the detour, gave him forty cents.

We drove out of the gate onto the worst road I have ever had the pleasure of traveling, and I drove the Ozark Mountains before there was a real highway. It was twelve miles and it took two hours to go that distance. We realized that if it rained we would undoubtedly remain fast until the dry season. All along this road, which is probably a hundred years old, were people traveling on horseback. During this two hour stretch we wandered through the *batey* of a sugar mill. The mill was deserted. The only person we saw was an old man who was trying to fix a particularly bad spot in the road near a makeshift culvert. He said he had made the culvert all alone and unaided and was at that moment trying to cut down the sides of the deep rut with a worn shovel. He also had nine children to support. Phil gave him a *peseta* after he broke down and confessed about the hungry nine children. I told

Phil he should be put in jail for trying to raise nine children. After a good deal of backing and sighting we managed to get safely across the culvert.

Running parallel to the road we were traveling was a half-finished highway with mixers, ditchers, even scrapers lying rusting. We asked when the highway had been started and why work had stopped. He said it was begun back in 1929, he thought, but that something happened to the appropriation and the crews walked off, abandoning their tools and equipment. Cienfuegos, he said, got tired of waiting for the highway and built a road of its own past Cruces. But this new road is useless so far as communication with the rest of the island is concerned. There are three roads now, which suffer the slight misfortune of never meeting each other, separated by twelve miles of farmland.

November 10:   Tuesday morning I started on the testimony, determined to get through so we could leave Cienfuegos. But it took longer than I expected: two wily old Spaniards who were afraid to say no and afraid to say yes. Finally their testimony was recorded, despite their reluctance to see what they had said appear on paper. We made a wild dash to the hotel, paid the bill, collected our belongings, and, despite the predictions of the hotel staff that we would never reach Havana that night, we left town just as the sun was setting. Phil was certain something was going to happen in Havana, although we had telephoned on Monday night and everything was quiet.

We went through the stretch of bad road again, and it was dark before we rolled onto the Central Highway. We had the highway almost to ourselves, only a down-island bus passing once or twice. Phil could not drive as fast as he wanted to because our headlights were not working properly and a queer mist, like swirls of smoke, hung over everything. This side of Matanzas, where the road makes the turn, at the edge of Ceiba Mocha, two soldiers in raincoats stepped into the middle of the road. We almost hit them. They asked us where we were going and apparently intended to search the car. Phil told them who we were and pointed at the huge *New York Times* sign pasted on the windshield. They asked if we had any American cigarettes. Neither of us smoke American cigarettes, but Phil handed them a package of a Cuban brand. Although the disappointment showed in their faces, they allowed us to proceed.

At Cotorro, fifteen miles outside Havana, we were again stopped by soldiers. We handed out more cigarettes. We came through Luyamo and into Vedado. The streets were deserted. It was two A.M. when we arrived at our home on Principe Hill. At two-thirty we heard the drone of an airplane, then another, and there was the sound of a heavy explosion near Camp Columbia. Within a few minutes antiaircraft guns were unlimbered in Camp Columbia. The sounds of lighter weapons being fired came from the roof of the Presidential Palace and from the university, while searchlights from the Capitolio and Cabañas Fortress played across the sky. Visibility was so poor that undoubtedly the pilots could hardly see the lights of the city at all. It is a wonder that some of the bombs aimed at Camp Columbia didn't hit the Prado. Several bombs fell in the camp, one of them clipped the corner off Batista's house. The antiaircraft guns banged away for an hour and of course didn't hit a thing.

We thought the planes were from the United States. We had been told they were coming from Florida for the night raid but later it turned out that three former officers of the Aviation Corps went out to Camp Columbia airfield and seized the bombers. One of the bombers fell several miles from Havana; another between here and Key West and the pilot, Lieutenant Aristides de Aguero, was rescued by the American coast guard. I suppose the third one came down. It was a failure so far as a raid was concerned, although it frightened the army.

Phil, remembering that it was election night in New York City, put in a long distance call to *The New York Times*. He got the first part of the story in. A few minutes later he called again with additional information. At least, we had the semblance of a story because we knew that it was a revolution involving some of the ABC. It was the beginning of a desperate attempt to oust Colonel Batista and the student government.

The revolution was badly managed as usual. The rebels failed to blow up the Twenty-third Street bridge over the Almendares River, and the bridge on Fifth Avenue, which would have cut Camp Columbia off from the city. In street fighting, soldiers have no advantage and artillery cannot be used, but the rebels let themselves be trapped in places where artillery could be used against them. A revolution must be offensive, not defensive.

During the early hours of the morning the revolutionists took all the police stations in town. By nine A.M. they actually had Havana and if they had followed up their advantage by hard street fighting they could have won. The complete absence of soldiers in Havana during the morning puzzled us a great deal. We saw the rebels in possession of the town, sitting around congratulating themselves on their victory. What Camp Columbia was doing during those hours will remain a mystery. Either they couldn't decide who should come to town and do the fighting or they were waiting to see which side they should take—the government or the rebels. According to our information the American government offered to take Colonel Batista aboard one of the battleships in the bay, if worst came to worst.

The airfield at Camp Columbia had been in the hands of the rebels since before the air raid started and it took the army two or three hours to force eighty rebellious soldiers and former officers to retreat from the field. The soldiers finally advanced on Havana. They captured the Tenth Police Station which commands the Almendares Bridge on Twenty-third Street, then progressively ran the rebels out of first one place, then another. Fighting went on all day. Many were killed. The soldiers captured Police Headquarters, two blocks from the Manzana de Gómez where we have our offices, with

armored trucks and machine guns. We could hardly carry on
a conversation in our office during the roar of the firing.

A group of rebels retired to Ambrosio Military Post, which
had been seized early that morning. A more stupid move
could not have been made. Immediately, they were surrounded and artillery began pounding the post to pieces.
However, darkness came and the soldiers had to stop.

The soldiers surrounding Ambrosio Post must have gone
to sleep on the job because sometime that night the rebels
moved out with trucks of ammunition, and retired to Atarés
Fortress, which was also in the hands of rebels. Here they
made another mistake.

The battle of Atarés Fortress began the next morning. It
wasn't a battle. It was merely a slaughter when the army
gunners finally got the range and began dropping shells into
the middle of the fort. The Atarés Fortress is located on a
high hill overlooking the bay. It was built by Conde de Ricia
in 1763-67 during the Spanish colonial days, and long served
as a prison. On August 16, 1851, fifty-two Americans and
Cubans under the command of Colonel William S. Critten-
den, who had come to Cuba to fight under General Narciso
López against the Spaniards, were executed in the fort. Later,
López died in the same fort in the garrote—a sacrifice to
Cuban liberty.

We will never know exactly how many were killed in
Atarés Fortress. Between one hundred fifty and two hundred and some two hundred wounded. The inside of the fort
is in shambles, huge blocks of stone blown off the walls, and
the buildings destroyed. The rebels in the fort did some good
work with the few long range guns which they had, but machine guns were useless. The distance was too great and the
soldiers made no attempt to storm the hill, simply battering
the fort with artillery. Several shells went over the fort, landing in the town. One woman, standing on a balcony, was hit
by a shell.

The rebels silenced the gunboat "Patria," and forced her to
retreat, incidentally hitting the S.S. "Morro Castle" of the

Ward Line. However, there were no casualties. Pan American Airways was forced to abandon its dock just below the fort.

For six hours the guns roared. The Manzana de Gómez Building seemed to shake with the vibration of the bombardment. No one attempted to do any business. Stores closed and the majority of the inhabitants stayed indoors. It was dangerous in the streets with soldiers patrolling.

At four in the afternoon the fort surrendered. The son of Pizzi de Porra, a boy of fifteen, committed suicide in the fort, blowing out his brains with a revolver, when he saw the white flag go up. There were three women in the fort. One girl went there with her father, who was killed. Sofia Blasco, a member of the ABC group, was taken prisoner. The soldiers killed two men who were trying to run up the white flag. A third got the flag up and fell from the parapet badly wounded. The soldiers didn't pay any attention to the white flag for almost half an hour. With a pair of field glasses from the fifth floor of the Manzana de Gómez we could see the flag but the firing went on for some time. When the gates were opened, after the shooting had finally ceased, the first group of prisoners who came out of the fort with their hands in the air were mowed down with machine guns.

After the surrender, soldiers marched twenty prisoners down the hill toward Swift & Company's plant. There is a wall nearby from some former building. They lined the prisoners against the wall and shot them. An official of a foreign legation here took pictures of the killing of these prisoners. The pictures were sent later to President Roosevelt.

One of the prisoners told the following: "The soldiers lined us up. We knew what to expect. I was near the end of the line. As the machine gun began firing I must have fainted. When I recovered consciousness I was lying on the ground with a body on top of me and covered with blood. The soldiers had departed; only a group of ragged negroes were staring at the bodies. As carefully as I could, I freed myself from the body on top of me and started to crawl away. One of the negroes opened his mouth to shout, which undoubtedly would have attracted the attention of the soldiers, some distance away, but another negro standing next to him quickly covered his mouth with his hand. I crawled around the end of the stone wall, and rising, walked away."

Hamburg, one of the photographers, says the scene at the morgue was horrible. They piled the bodies on the floor. There wasn't room enough. Emergency Hospital was a stench of blood with surgeons working frantically. No anesthetic was given. None was available.

Colonel Blas Hernández was killed after the surrender. An officer of the army bragged that he had shot the Colonel like a dog. Later that army officer—ironically his name was Hernández, was made Lieutenant Colonel and placed in charge of the military post of Artemisa, Piñar del Rio Province. He was killed when he resisted arrest by soldiers sent out from Camp Columbia by Colonel Batista who reportedly had learned that Hernández planned a revolt. Hernández was one of the chief plotters of the fourth of September revolt which placed the enlisted men in control of the army.

A former lieutenant of the army, who was standing alongside Colonel Blas Hernández at the surrender, tells the following story: "After the surrender we were marched outside the fort and were standing under guard near the gate. Colonel Blas Hernández was standing beside me. A captain walked up and asked, 'Is Blas Hernández here?' The old Colonel replied, 'I am Blas Hernández.' Without a word the Captain pulled out his revolver and shot the Colonel. We were so horror-stricken that none of us moved, not even the soldiers guarding us. The Captain demanded, 'Is Lieutenant—— here?' That was my name. Although I had never seen the Captain before and knew of no grudge he could have against me, I said, 'I think I saw the Lieutenant go with the first group of prisoners.' A man standing near me came to my aid. He said, 'Yes, I know him. I saw him taken away with the first group.' That saved my life."

Until late that night trucks bearing dead and wounded kept

rumbling into town. Every hospital and first aid station was
overflowing. People searched frantically for relatives believed
or known to be in the fort.

James O'Connell, an American who was watching the
bombardment from Talla Piedra docks, was badly wounded.
The soldiers fired into a group of civilians standing there
gazing at the fort. No reason was given.

The following story I overheard a man tell in a café several
months after the Atarés episode. It may be true or it may not
be true—the story I mean: "Someone wiped the blood off
of my face with a handkerchief and I opened my eyes. A
woman's voice said, 'Are you badly hurt?' I felt no pain, except that my head ached. I sat up. I was lying on the floor in
the morgue. God, what a feeling when I realized where I was.
Bodies covered all the floor space, some piled on top of each
other. The woman who had spoken took hold of my shoulder
and helped me to rise. 'I was looking for my brother and I
noticed you seemed to be breathing,' she said. Other people
were frantically seeking relatives in the place and the confusion was so great that no one had noticed me. She asked me
if I had any money. I looked in my pockets. They were
empty. Every paper I had was gone. The woman took me by
the arm and pushed me toward the door. No one paid any
attention. Outside the cooler air began to make me feel better.
The woman and I walked to a row of taxis and I got into one.
She pressed a *peseta* into my hand and walked away. I have
never seen the woman since but every day I look at the people on the street and wonder if I would recognize her."

After the surrender of the fort, rifle fire continued all night.
Soldiers in automobiles rode through the streets, firing in
every direction. Many people were killed and wounded.
Snipers on roofs killed soldiers now and then.

The revolution ended in failure as usual. It hardly seems
possible that the leaders were military men and had knowledge of warfare. Big fat Jim Warner, who has been around
Latin America for years, says that after the surrender, when
the smoke had cleared away, he started up the hill. He saw

a bundle come rolling down the hill. As it neared the bottom it struck a bump and bounced completely over a high board fence. When it struck the ground on the other side of the fence, a negro tore himself out of the blanket and lit out running. Warner said his heels were smoking, as he went out of sight. That was one revolutionist in Atarés whom the soldiers didn't capture. Warner laughed so hard he had to sit down.

The night of the ninth, the student government turned the floodlights on the Capitolio, lighted the revolving searchlights in celebration of the victory. The public muttered bitterly over the callousness of the students in flaunting their celebration in the faces of the many families in mourning.

The palace cat lost his tail or the greater part of it. He ran across the patio on the ground floor just as a bullet came singing through the patio. He was the only palace casualty.

The following description of the revolt which ended with the Battle of Atarés is by a Spanish youth, native of the Province of Asturias, who joined the Cuban rebels to fight against the student government: "None of us knew until eight o'clock in the evening that the revolution was to be staged the following day. The news spread quickly among us by word of mouth, and cars filled with ABC'ers sped through the city giving the secret signals agreed upon with their automobile horns. We learned we were to concentrate at various points at two in the morning. When I got to the place, I found more than two hundred men and we had only three rifles, although most of us had pistols. At two-thirty the airplanes passed over. We wanted to start fighting then but the leader of the group said to wait.

"At six o'clock a group went to Police Headquarters, which made no resistance, and brought back what rifles, revolvers and ammunition were there. We called Dragones Military Post and learned that the soldiers there had joined us. Most of us then went out hunting rifles and seeing how many police stations were in our hands. There was no fighting because all the police joined us.

"Three men and myself went out looking for arms. We had

one revolver and a long knife between us. We walked down San Ignacio Street and when we reached Muralla Street we saw two marines on the corner hiding behind some columns and looking upward. Apparently, some one had shot at them. My friend, who was later killed in Atarés, and I walked up behind the marines. My friend put the revolver between the shoulders of one marine, while I put the point of the knife against the other and we told them to surrender. I was frightened but the marines were more frightened. We took their two rifles, two pistols and ammunition and then picked up a taxi and went to Dragones Military Post, which was in our hands.

"We needed more rifles so we took another taxi and went to San Ambrosio Military Post, which had also joined us. We learned that all the police stations and military posts in Havana had joined up and that the town was ours. We stayed around San Ambrosio. We didn't see any soldiers.

"At three in the afternoon the gunboat, Patria, came close to the shore and began firing at San Ambrosio. We fired back and Atarés Fortress, also in our hands, fired at the Patria with an antiaircraft gun and forced her to retreat.

"About four-thirty my companion and I left San Ambrosio, found a taxi and rode to Fort Atarés. Everything was in great confusion there.

"At two in the morning, Colonel Blas Hernández arrived with the revolutionists who had been in San Ambrosio. There wasn't anything to do. Some of us went to sleep. We were told that we were not to leave Atarés until the revolution was over.

"At six A.M. the bombardment began. We had about six hundred people in Atarés, far too many, as it is a small fort and everything was terribly crowded. We had two antiaircraft guns, twenty or twenty-five machine guns, and 15,000 rounds of ammunition.

"Up to eleven o'clock in the morning no one had been killed. None of the shells fell into the fort and only hit the walls and knocked off stones. The gunboats, "Cuba" and

"Patria," fired at the fort from the bay and we fired back with the antiaircraft guns. Then a small piece of artillery was set up on Burro Hill and began firing. I was in the kitchen when a shell passed through, taking off the head of the cook. He fell partly into the huge pot of rice and black beans which he was cooking. There wasn't any more food so we lifted the cook up and carried him out so no one would notice. We had to feed the people in the fort something.

"The bombardment became heavier and every minute more victims fell. All the civilians were fighting, some on the walls, others on the roof.

"Major Leonard, who had been placed in command, walked along by the wall where we were firing and said: 'Well done, boys, keep it up, we are winning.' He walked through the door facing toward Burro Hill and drawing a revolver, placed it against his temple and fired. The death of Leonard so shocked everybody that no one knew what to do. Captain Dominguez took command but many wanted to surrender and others did not so that the confusion was terrible. At last it was seen that we must surrender or be killed and the white flag must be put up.

"The first white flag was shot down. Then a boy carried one up on the wall but he was instantly killed with the flag still in his hand.

"Colonel Blas Hernández wanted to keep on fighting. He had not wanted to come to the fort. He had wanted to fight in the open and even after the white flag had been put up Blas wanted to keep on fighting.

"The soldiers and marines came up the hill. At this moment, the fifteen-year-old son of the newspaperman, Pizzi de Porra, shouted, 'While I live I will not surrender; deliver me when I am dead,' and fired a bullet into his own head.

"The soldiers rushed into the fort and began grabbing everything they could carry off. Those who protested against the loss of their personal effects, such as watches, were beaten with rifles. I saw several lying on the ground with blood running out of their mouths. All I had was three dollars and I made no protest when a soldier wrenched that out of my pocket, tearing the pocket out also.

"I didn't go out of the fort until a lot of those in the fort had been taken away. I kept hearing firing but I didn't see the first batch of prisoners killed.

"The soldiers made the group of prisoners I was with sit on the ground. They threatened, cursed and reviled us. Some of the younger boys in our group began to cry.

"Captain Hernández then walked up and asked: 'Who is Blas Hernández?' Blas, who was in the group, said proudly, "I am Blas Hernández. I am a Cuban." Hernández fired and Blas fell to the ground. Hernández placed his gun against the head of the Colonel and fired again. Then he turned around and killed a boy, who, being frightened, was crying: 'Don't kill me. I have a mother in Havana and I want to see her.'

"As we waited for the truck I heard some of the soldiers complaining they had gotten nothing in the way of booty during the surrender. Others were showing the jewelry and money, which they had taken from the prisoners. Others were trying on the leggings and boots which they had taken from the dead. A negro soldier came by wearing the hat and belt of Blas Hernández. He shouted to Captain Hernández who had killed the Colonel: 'Look, Captain, I'm Blas Hernández.'

"In prison we slept on the floor for several days until the Red Cross came with beds and blankets and delivered half rations for all the prisoners. The soldiers took away our shoes, leggings, shirts and even pants. The first twenty-five days of prison were so awful I do not want to remember."

6

November 11: Fighting is still going on down the island in various places, but only small bands are involved. *This* revolution is over.

There is still shooting here in the streets. So few soldiers have been killed by snipers that I am convinced the army is taking this means to terrorize the population. Basilio Lira, a Frenchman, was killed yesterday as he walked into his roof-top apartment. A group of soldiers fired at him; they said they thought he was a sniper.

This afternoon I heard a commotion out by the elevator and asked the floor boy what had happened. He said soldiers with rifles and machine guns had gone up on the roof of the Manzana. In a few minutes the building shook as the soldiers fired again and again. They were firing at the roof of the Hotel Inglaterra, just across Central Park from the Manzana, where a group was firing in this direction. The battle went on for at least ten minutes. Finally, some soldier on this side, with a little better eyesight than the others, said he believed it was soldiers on the roof of the Inglaterra Hotel. A soldier was sent to investigate and found that the battle had been staged, not with snipers, but with another group of soldiers who were on the roof of the Inglaterra.

On the day of the battle of Atarés the Associated Press

bought up all the express space on the plane leaving Rancho Boyeros. All the photographers here from the States are accustomed to send their pictures by air express. I always send mine air mail. So about two P.M. that day I got ready what pictures I had of the Atarés battle and Phil took them out to the airfield and put them in the air mail. Associated Press thought they had a complete scoop. Imagine their surprise when today they received word from the head office that Wide World also had pictures. The A.P. men here were furious. I, in all innocence, got my pictures through on the plane which Associated had practically paid for, because, according to their contract, Pan American Airways is forced to carry the air mail.

November 12: The Judge Advocate of the General Court Martial, where the thirty-four soldiers of the Air Corps who joined the rebels against the government are being tried, is asking the death penalty. But that is a bluff. The government does not dare to shoot them. Sergeant Basilio Gonzalez of the Aviation Corps, who turned the planes over to the rebels, has the oddest alibi. He says he was told the movement was being staged to put Colonel Batista in as President of the Republic. The rest of the soldiers at the field say they only obeyed orders.

The students affirm that not only will the leaders of the revolution be shot but that all the *Machadistas* now in jail will be executed shortly. They will never do it. There are too many potential revolutionists in Cuba. It is no real crime to start a revolution. If you win, you're a hero. If you lose, you stay in jail a while and then are released, because the ones in power don't know how long they are going to stay in power. They may be in jail sometime too. The *Machadistas* are merely government officials out of power and if they are killed off, their friends may turn the tables on the group now heading the government. Everyone realizes the situation.

November 16: Nothing to write about except shooting and bombings. One gets a little out of patience with these people.

What progress are they making? Of course, the idea is to raise so much hell that President Grau and the students will be forced out.

We saw Eddie Chibás on the Malecón. I made him so angry that had I been a man he would have sent his seconds. Eddie, knowing I am losing patience with the student government, pointed out to me how loyal the soldiers were and how fervently they had supported the student government. I said, "Eddie, I can remember when you told me during Machado's administration that the army was a bunch of murderers. It is the same army today. Except now they are on your side. Tomorrow they may decide to remove the student government and put in another crowd."

Military court martial condemned Sergeant Basilio Gonzalez and Private Homobono Rodriguez, leaders of the soldiers who joined the rebellion, to face a firing squad.

Quesada came in today. He became librarian at the Capitolio the latter part of October. He is already disgusted. The library belonging to Congress is a magnificent collection for this small island, worth probably half a million dollars. Quesada says it is scattered around, uncatalogued, books being eaten up by *comejenes* and other insects, badly in need of organization. Quesada had great hopes when he went there of separating the more current books from the rare volumes, making a large part of it available to the public since there are no public libraries of any importance in the island. However, he is swamped with personnel, none of whom know anything about books or office work, the majority being revolutionists more interested in bombs and salaries than anything else. He will eventually have to resign; no one cares at present whether the library is looked after or not.

Dr. Joaquin del Rio Balmaseda resigned the portfolio of Secretary of Justice the other day. I asked Quesada why. He said the Assistant Secretary wanted to manage the department one way and Balmaseda another and that the Assistant Secretary had more friends among the students, therefore more influence. It is the same in all departments.

Ambassador Welles is going to Warm Springs to confer with Roosevelt on the Cuban situation according to reports.

Ambassador Welles has made no statements in Cuba for so long that an article in the *Diario de la Marino* reads: "Mr. Welles, upon being questioned, replied that he had nothing to say (Composing Room: save this setup for the next time the reporters go to see Mr. Welles)."

Cubans have an ironic sense of humor. One might call it the "humor of the gallows." Their jokes are all based on the discomfiture of some one else and they laugh at, not with, each other. They excel in political cartoons. As a whole their political cartoons are more pointed, and more applicable than those of any nation that I have noticed. However, they often descend to vulgarity and attacks on personal character. It is a good thing there are no efficient libel laws in Cuba or half the cartoonists would spend their lives in jail.

November 19: Don Enrique José Varona, noted Cuban writer and philosopher died today. His philosophical works have been translated into many languages.

Some seven hundred policemen in Havana have been discharged as suspected of aiding the recent revolution or having delivered over the police stations without resistance. I know one policeman who went out and fought all day on the side of the rebels. He returned to his station the following morning, telling the sergeant on duty he had been sick and, since he had not slept the night before and his eyes were bloodshot, the sergeant believed him and told him to get back on duty. He was downstairs drinking in the café and he told Phil about it as though it was a good joke. He was not among those discharged as suspects.

The soldiers must have cleaned out at least one beach to have collected the 1500 bags of sand they put on the roof of the palace today. I suppose they are expecting another attack.

November 20: Oppositionists crowded the office this afternoon demanding to know if Ambassador Welles had been recalled. Welles will leave as soon as he can. He intended to leave last September but couldn't on account of the overthrow of the Céspedes government. He is now in the States conferring with President Roosevelt and the State Department.

The students are wild with joy over what they think is their victory—they have forced President Roosevelt to recall Welles. Everyone knows that the Cuban government has asked his recall several times, with many complaints lodged against him, because he has not recommended recognition of the Grau government.

It certainly was no secret that Ambassador Welles had wanted to leave Cuba for a long time. It is the same old story. Every time the Cubans don't like their government they want Uncle Sam to step in and change it and then, of course, they won't like *any* government aided by the United States.

They are planning a demonstration, sponsored by Alma Mater, the unofficial but actual organ of the government. Alma Mater headlines declare, "Welles will not be permitted to land." All talk of course.

We still have destroyers and at least one cruiser in Cuban waters. Just what good comes of this I, for one, cannot see. It may doubtless be a sort of restraining influence on the lower classes and it furnishes the students with something to talk about. The only groups in the island who do not want American intervention are the students and politicians. The Spaniards, who make up the greater part of the commercial class and own a large proportion of the property, would gladly see the United States take over the island permanently.

We seem to make nothing but blunders in our policy toward Cuba. The United States has never shone brightly in the diplomatic field. The case of Cuba is a fair example. We did not want Spain or any other foreign country entrenched so close to our southern shores. Even England, when she ruled the colonies, cast a longing eye at Cuba. English troops did take Havana in 1762, but had to give it back to Spain. The United States wavered between purchasing it, grabbing it, or backing a revolution designed to oust the Spaniards. While we were trying to find some pretext or clever way by which we could wrest the island from Spanish rule, enterprising Cubans dreamed of the advantages of independence. Finally we were drawn into the Spanish-American War, a war promoted largely by Hearst and Pulitzer newspapers and the Revolutionary Junta in New York.

November 21: Admiral Freeman, Commander of the United States Naval Forces in Cuban waters, maintains a somewhat elaborate secret service system in Havana. Officers come ashore in civilian clothes. Major del Valle, head of the marines here, is in charge of this intelligence service. Del Valle, a Puerto Rican I think, is an efficient officer. Speaking fluent Spanish, he mixes socially with the student element of the government. One of the students, who dined on board the *Richmond* described this intelligence service to me. On the roof of the American Embassy the United States Navy has established a radio station to transmit messages from the city to the ships in the harbor. It is regrettable the American government did not have some system like this here during the Céspedes administration.

The work of secret operatives in Cuba should be easy. There is no such thing as a secret. We heard from Cuban sources all the plans made by the United States Navy in case of landing the marines. One foreign legation here receives advice of transactions which take place in the American Embassy almost before the ink is dry on the paper. An operative in Havana bragged that he knew practically all the conversations held by Ambassador Welles inside his office when the door was shut and no one in the anteroom. Perhaps he was lying, perhaps not.

November 24: We got a cable at two o'clock in the morning confirming the recall of Ambassador Welles. The students are celebrating, believing recognition will be granted immediately. We do not think so, although it is apparent that

Secretary of State Cordell Hull wants to recognize any kind of a government in Cuba, just so he can get off to the Pan-American Congress and receive the blessings of the Latin and South American countries, none of which *really* care what our policy is with Cuba.

November 25: The *Pro Ley y Justicia* and *Ejercito del Caribe* today kidnapped and killed five former army officers. The officers were being transferred from Havana to Santa Clara to stand trial. It must have been previously arranged with the guards of the prisoners because they offered no resistance.

November 27: Dr. Fernandez Medina, the Uruguayan Minister to Cuba, announces he will bring about conciliation between the Grau government and its enemies. It will take a better man than Medina to do it. Knowing the character of Cubans, I do not believe conciliation is possible.

Batista is doing everything he can to please Consul General Dumont who thinks that Batista is the only one in the government with brains. Batista sees the handwriting on the wall so far as the student government is concerned and is seeking a friend in the American government. Batista is highly ambitious.

The Opposition wants President Grau to resign on February 24th, known as the *Grito de Baire* and celebrated as a national holiday. It is doomed to failure. The ABC masses refuse to have anything to do with it, stating that the problem of Cuba is the problem of the army. They affirm that whenever the money begins to give out, Batista will force a change of government. He has the arms and ammunition and the soldiers. From now on Cuba is in the same category with all Latin American countries—the army rules.

Phil and I had dinner with Consul General and Mrs. Dumont. One of the guests summed up the situation. He said the conciliation plan is doomed to failure because no representative cooperative cabinet can be formed, as there are no candidates. No one wants to be a mere cabinet official, everyone wants to be President.

December 3: The Pan-American Conference opens today in Montevideo. The Cuban delegates hope to stir up feeling against the United States. The plan has an excellent chance. The Cuban delegates are Dr. Angel Alberto Giraudy, Secretary of Labor, Dr. Herminio Portell Vilá and Alfredo Nogueira. Carlos Prio Socarras and Juan Antonio Rubio Padilla, members of the *Directorio Estudiantil,* are there to egg them on. Not one of them has ever been to a conference or knows anything of international procedure.

Ernest Gruening, adviser of the American delegation to the Conference, which includes Secretary of State Cordell Hull, issued a statement in which he said that Hull favored recognition of the present Cuban government. The government here was quite elated over this. Gruening is one of the group which might be considered as "mouthpieces" in the United States for all the Anti-Yankee minorities in various Latin American countries. Hull, of course, knows nothing of the Cuban situation and is so bent on diffusing goodwill all around that he is not worrying about what is happening in Cuba.

December 4: A tremendous wave of nationalism has hit Cuba. It is now "Cuba for the Cubans." A Cuban is anyone born on Cuban soil no matter what nationality his parents were, provided of course he declares upon reaching the age of twenty-one that he is a Cuban citizen. During the Spanish Colonial period no Cuban-born individual could hold a public office. The Cubans still retain the inferiority complex engendered at that time.

The demand is now being made that every employer in the island must hire 80% native labor. As a matter of fact, I am surprised they do not demand 100%. The government recently signed a decree providing that 50% Cuban-born individuals must be hired, but still that does not satisfy the nationalistic spirit. Some 2000 of these eighty percenters today marched to the Presidential Palace.

Every employer in the island is horror stricken. They contend that only foreigners will do manual labor. There are some 500,000 Spaniards in the island, the majority either employers or employees. Added to these are Haitians, Jamaicans, Canary Islanders, Americans, English, French, Germans and Poles. Many of them, particularly the Spaniards, have held the same jobs for twenty or thirty years and to be thrown out of work with only a month's notice is hard indeed. Practically all cooks, bartenders, streetcar employees, railroaders and janitors are foreigners. Of course, technical personnel is exempted, provided there is no Cuban to fill the position.

December 5:   The Cubans didn't get away with it at the Pan-American Conference. The representatives of a group of American Republics advised the Cuban delegates that no attacks on the United States were permissible at the Conference. In the opening salutation which Cuba has the right to make, having been host of the last Conference in 1928, the Cuban delegates planned to attack the United States for not having recognized the Grau administration. However, they were forced to submit a copy of the address prior to delivering it and the Procedure Committee administered a sharp rebuke, so they had to write it again.

The employees of the *Cia. Cubana de Electricidad* are going to strike unless forty-two demands are immediately granted. The officials asked Phil to mention their company as an "affiliate" and not a subsidiary of the Electric Bond & Share, but I like the word subsidiary. This company has a monopoly on electric power in the island. One of the main complaints of the Cubans against it is that the company furnished the campaign money for former President Machado. The company's history goes back to when Machado was just coming into the picture politically. Machado and his associates owned several small electric plants down the island. Then Catlin of the Electric Bond & Share came to Cuba. He and Machado went into partnership. They purchased all the electric plants in the island. Actually, Cubans say, Machado bought the plants for moderate sums and then he and Catlin sold them to the Electric Bond & Share, and split the profit. The company claims an original investment in Cuba of some two hundred million dollars. They must have spent that amount, considering the prices paid for the plants, the new installations and power lines. However, the rates charged for electricity are outrageous, fifteen cents per kilowatt in Havana to the ordinary consumer, as high as twenty and twenty-two cents in the interior. Labor is cheap and there seems little excuse for these prices. On the other hand, one must consider the following factors:

1. They have been forced to pay high graft not only to Machado but to officials all down the line in order to operate without interference.

2. The City of Havana, as well as all towns of the interior, are months and in some cases years in arrears on their payments for service. Havana is now said to owe something like six million dollars.

3. Government officials pay their bills only when they are so inclined.

4. The Electric Bond & Share charges the *Cia. Cubana* high prices for materials, consulting fees and salaries for company officials. Thus when the officials here say they are nearly bankrupt one can hardly keep from believing them. But the poor public foots the bill.

This may be the beginning of a general strike. Thousands of tobacco workers are already out. Colonel Batista says even if the employees of the electric light plants strike the lights will not be cut off. He has thrown a heavy guard around the plant here as well as plants at other points of the island.

December 6: *Cia. Cubana* today was ordered by presidential decree to reduce its rate 45%. What consternation will now reign in the New York offices of the Company!

The students claim they are preparing a decree greatly reducing telephone rates of the Cuban Telephone Company, subsidiary of the International Telephone & Telegraph. However, I judge they will wait to see what happens in the question of the electric company. The students have the United States in a ludicrous position. The American government does not dare to intervene now to save the Electric Bond & Share or any other American investment here—not with the Pan-American Conference in progress. If they did, Cuba could shout from the housetops that it was imperialism, another indication of dollar diplomacy. With bankers and moneyed interests bringing every possible pressure to bear on Washington to save investments in Cuba, this small island defies President Roosevelt, reminding him of his policy of Good Neighbor, while they confiscate American investments. The rest of Latin America is sitting back, grinning over the discomfiture of Uncle Sam.

The Grau cabinet is like a merry-go-round—no one stays long in one department and new ones are continually getting on and off. I try to keep a list of the cabinet but it is practically impossible. Every once in a while we run across an entirely new member and everyone looks blank and says, "Never heard of him."

The other night soldiers stopped us on the Malecón. All cars were being searched. After showing our credentials, Phil grumblingly remarked that he wondered what they were looking for this time. I told him they were probably hunting for future cabinet officials.

December 11: Batista changed his mind. He had practically agreed to force Grau to resign and put in another man, preferably Colonel Carlos Mendieta. However, the students had a meeting with Batista either last night or the night before. Batista suddenly decided to support Grau again. Grau today issued a statement that he had no intention of resigning and would make no further efforts to effect an agreement between his government and opposing factions.

December 12: Today is my birthday. John cannot understand why it is a family tradition with us to put sixteen
candles on a birthday cake. He always thought one candle
stood for one year.

Carleton Beals came walking into the office today. I like
Beals personally, but the relations of the United States with
Latin America would be much improved if the entire group
of writers such as Beals, Professor Buell, Zimmerman and
Gruening would turn their attention to domestic rather than
international affairs. They cause Uncle Sam more trouble in
Latin America than do the Latin Americans. They come
down to these small countries, get in touch with the university professors and students and put all sorts of ideas into
their heads about the imperialism of the United States.

When Hubert Herring, another America writer bent on
improving relations by showing the Latin Americans just
where the American government has attempted to encroach
on their rights, told me not long ago about the Cultural
Relations Association, I told him bluntly I thought it was
nothing more than a racket.

I have asked several of these Latin American experts why,
if they wanted to criticize the American government, they
didn't make their criticisms in the United States, where some
good might come of it, instead of coming down here in these
little hot-headed countries, which have no love for any
American, and ruining what little prestige we still may have.

Yesterday the government issued a decree providing for
the coining of three million silver dollars and at the same
time three million dollars worth of silver certificates.

Cuba has no currency system. The American government
always feared that if the Cuban printing presses ever started
stamping out money, the flood of paper would be disastrous.
Thus in the Platt Amendment Cuba is prohibited from as-
suming any obligation she cannot pay. Broadly interpreted
it has meant that the American government would not only
prevent Cuba from borrowing money from any foreign

nation other than the United States, but would see that no
currency system was started here. However, some twelve
million dollars worth of silver coinage was issued, twenty
million of gold, and about five million in fractional silver.
Machado issued six million dollars in silver in 1932. Now
this government plans to issue three million more. The
foreign banks here make money on silver issues. The rate of
exchange for American bills increases, merchants and business men must have American money to use abroad, the
bank collects the percentage and then turns around and delivers the silver to the Cuban Treasury, which hands over
American bills. Thus the banks do not care how much silver
they issue. The government, on the other hand, forces payment of a large portion of the taxes in American bills, refusing to take silver, except in a certain percentage. Thus the
public is squeezed both ways.

December 17:   The National Federation of Labor attempted
to stage a demonstration this afternoon against the 50%
law which is forcing them out of jobs in every industry.
Result, six killed, ten wounded and the *El Pais* newspaper,
which yesterday attacked the Grau government, burned. The
attackers fired into the El Pais building, killing linotypist
Dassau.

In the midst of this confusion, while the building was
burning, soldiers arrived on the scene attempting to disperse
the crowd. Hamburg, the photographer, went calmly about
taking pictures. A soldier threatened to shoot him if he continued, but Hamburg speaks no Spanish so he simply replied, "Si, señor," and took another picture. The soldier
threw up his rifle to fire but another photographer, Delgado
of Fox Films, intervened and talked the soldier out of it.

Hamburg, speaking no Spanish, gets away with a lot of
things. His favorite way of boarding a vessel coming into
the harbor, when orders have been issued that no photographers are to be permitted on board, is to go down to the
pilot launch just before it is ready to leave the dock. He

walks calmly on board and then yells for the pilot to hurry up. The officers of the port, apparently stunned at such behavior or believing he must have authority from the President or Colonel Batista, usually make no protest whatever.

He went to take pictures of a religious procession recently just outside Havana. He got his camera ready but, finding that the wax figure of a saint was obscuring the view of the balance of the procession, he waved at a priest and shouted: "Hey, move Santa Claus over a bit." They moved the saint.

December 18: Jefferson Caffrey arrived today as the special representative of President Roosevelt. He could not come as Ambassador since the present government has not been recognized by the United States. The Oppositionists, who hope to oust the present government, went to the docks to meet him.

December 19: Riots all over town—the commercial employees, practically all Spaniards, struck against the 50% law. A group wearing badges "Cuba for the Cubans" ran through the streets like packs of wolves on a hunt, shouting, "Down with foreigners." Soldiers fired into a crowd of rioters at Zanja and Lealtad Streets, killing one, wounding four.

I must put down a good illustration of Cuban military discipline. During the rioting a sergeant wished to move a group of soldiers from one street corner to another, where it looked as though trouble might break out. Instead of the usual brisk commands, this sergeant said, "Hombres, por favor," indicating the other side of the street. He bowed when he said it.

The guard on the Manzana de Gómez roof was being changed during the recent search for snipers. As I walked out of the building, ten or twelve soldiers were lined up in front. The sergeant carelessly waved his hand and said, "Come on." One soldier standing at the end of the wavering line was so deeply interested in trying to flirt with a girl that he failed to hear the remark. The others marched or rather sauntered off leaving him standing there. The sergeant, noticing he did not move, stepped back and called again, "Come on." The soldier withdrew his attention reluctantly from the girl and shouted back, "Why didn't you talk a little louder, I can't hear whispers."

December 20:   If the government paid as much attention to organizing the departments as they do to organizing parades, this country might begin to improve. Another demonstration today of some 32,000 protesting against the Platt Amendment. The first killing by authorities after arrest has occurred. Mario Cadenas, nineteen-year-old student, was executed on the Camp Columbia rifle range several days after he had been arrested, on some minor charge. The government is now trying to explain it and hush it up.

December 21:   The Cuban government has taken over the sugar mills, Chaparra and Delicias, owned by the Cuban American Sugar Company, the original investment in these mills being some ten million dollars. The seizure order was issued by Secretary of Interior, Antonio Guiteras, well-known Communist. He plans to operate the mills this year. I wonder where he will get the money?

Quesada resigned his job as librarian of the Congressional Library. He committed a social error. He advised his numerous employees that within a period of six months he would give them an examination to find out if they were qualified for their particular jobs. Many did not appreciate this. They fled to the *Directorio Estudiantil* with loud complaints.

December 26:   We wrote a tourist article for the Resort page of the *Times*. We wrote as vaguely as possible. What we expect is a revolution, not tourists. Alex of United Press said advertisements of the winter season should read: "Tourists admitted to revolutions free of charge, but are requested to bring their own shotguns."

December 27:   Cuba is not going to pay the interest on the Public Works Bonds. Nor will any part of the sixty million

Sergeant Fulgencio Batista at
Camp Columbia Military Headquarters,
September, 1933.

Gerardo Machado and his granddaughter.

General Fulgencio Batista, 1934.

Colonel Blas Hernandez.

Fall of Machado regime August 12, 1933. Corporal Heredia, killed by public in Santiago de Cuba.

Body of Colonel Blas Hernandez.

Military Coup of March 10, 1952.
Batista marching into Palace.

Military Coup of March 10, 1952. Deposed President, Carlos Prío Socarras,
wife and children, board plane at Rancho Boyeros airfield.

The trial of
Major Jesus Sosa Blanco.

Fidel Castro and Camilo Cienfuegos.

Wide World Ph

Raul Castro and
Ernesto "Che" Guevara.

Wide World Photos

dollars be paid. Secretary of Treasury Señor Despaigne said today: "We are not going to pay those loans because they were illegal loans contracted by Machado's illegal Congress."

Legal or illegal, it will be paid sometime. Governments may rise and fall, but the obligations of a government must be paid if credit is to be maintained. Are the loans illegal? In 1928 Machado borrowed from the Chase National Bank, which in turn sold these obligations to the American public, eighty million dollars; that is, the public and contractors hold all except twenty million dollars, known as the bankers' credit, which is in the hands of the Chase National Bank, Continental Illinois Bank & Trust Company of Chicago, and The National City Bank of New York. On June 30, 1933, Cuba owed a total of $164,934,700. This consisted of $54,464,-000 Speyer and Morgan loans, $7,816,000 internal funded debt, $80,000,000 public works obligations, and $22,654,700 outstanding sugar stabilization bonds issued under the Chadbourne Restriction Plan of 1930.

Machado should never have been permitted to borrow such a large amount as eighty million dollars on such short terms (maturing in 1945), particularly in view of the situation of the sugar industry. But American bankers were at that time shoveling out money to foreign countries, not caring whether they could or would ever pay. The banks were passing the bonds along to the small American investor, collecting their commissions, and not bothering to find out if the financial condition of the borrowing country was such that it would be repaid. The American State Department tacitly, if not officially, approved the loan. Therefore, the Cubans blame the American government and the Chase National Bank.

On the other hand, as I point out to Cubans, Machado was elected by the people in 1924, he made himself President again in 1928 without any or very slight protest from the people. He borrowed the money and the money was spent on the Central Highway and the Capitolio, at least part of it. Neither the American government nor the bankers were responsible for what the Cuban government saw fit to graft. So, it boils down to this—Cuba received the money, it was spent, it must be repaid.

Added to the $164,000,000 which Cuba now owes is a floating indebtedness amounting to around fifty million dollars. The nation has been bankrupt for several years, but Machado managed to pay the foreign obligations through complicated and somewhat fantastic arrangements with the Chase National Bank. He knew that he must. The American State Department during the Hoover administration was willing to support Machado only so long as he paid on the foreign debts.

December 30: Cuba's 1934 sugar crop will amount to 2,315,459 long tons. The radical students are conforming to the International Brussels Sugar Agreement. The acceptance by Cuba of the Chadbourne Restriction Plan, a forerunner of the International Agreement, was the worst blunder Machado made.

Chadbourne, a corporation lawyer and mouthpiece of the American bankers, came to Cuba ostensibly to "save the sugar industry." Having glowingly painted the picture of how all countries would join Cuba in restricting sugar production to conform to the decreased demand, and affirming that he had a gentleman's agreement with the producers of the United States, he was able to get the Cuban producers to accept the plan. It is considered by many as the greatest mistake economically in the history of the island. Cuba must depend on her sugar and tobacco. With prices so low, the producers were clutching at straws; they might as well have drowned for that is eventually what happened.

At the beginning of the First World War, Cuba's average yearly crop was around two million tons. Then Europe clamored for sugar, as did the United States, and Cuba entered an era of unprecedented expansion of the sugar industry. Money poured into the island from the United States. American financiers came to Cuba, pockets bulging with gold. They purchased mills and land, tore out old machinery, installed new equipment, and production soared. Thousands of acres of virgin land were cleared and planted in cane. At the end of the War, Europe still needed sugar. Prices climbed to fantastic levels. In 1920, the sudden reduction of the world price of sugar brought disaster to Cuba. Banks suspended payments; hundreds of commercial firms failed; sugar mills owing large sums were taken over by banks. However, sugar production continued to increase as the mills strove desperately to pay debts and make expenses. 5,120,421 tons was reached in the 1928-29 crop. During this period beet sugar grown by various countries gradually replaced imported sugar. The American beet producers increased production by leaps and bounds. The markets of Cuba gradually declined. Cuba restricted her crop first in 1926 and again in 1927. Why the government did not see from that experience that the price did not increase is incomprehensible.

Any government which attempts to control supply and demand is simple-minded. It has never worked. Look at Brazil with her coffee, England with her rubber. What Cuba should have done was to tighten her belt, reduce operating costs and produce sugar at a profit, or at least break even, at so low a price that the rest of the sugar countries would not have increased production. Cuba has plenty of labor, one of the best sugar soils in the world, and she should have announced to the world sugar producers that if they wanted to enter the competition, come on in. Only the strongest would have survived, but it couldn't be much worse than it is now.

Another factor which worked against Cuba was the wave of nationalism which swept the world. Every nation decided it would be self-supporting, while at the same time selling its surplus. The idea is ridiculous. How much more sensible to say to one's neighbor, "We will buy this, if you will buy that!" No wonder the average individual, like myself, has lost respect for the statesmen of the world. They may have great learning, but simple common sense is beyond them. Now the United States is embarked on a policy of upping her tariff walls to protect her industries, which never needed protection. The tariff wall therefore simply bleeds the American public by raising prices on all the protected products.

The American bankers, believing in 1930 that they were practically omnipotent, set the course to be followed by the Cuban sugar industry for the next five years. The result— Cuba has practically lost her only remaining sugar market, the United States. The "gentleman's agreement" turned out to be nonexistent and the name of Chadbourne is hated in Cuba.

The present sugar mills of Cuba, all either directly or indirectly controlled by the banks, are practically bankrupt. Their stocks are worth next to nothing on the market; their bond issues are so heavy they can hardly pay the interest; their mills, full of the best equipment, are operating only two or three months a year. Thousands of acres of cane remain uncut every year and the cane planters are almost starving. There is no real hope for the Cuban sugar industry unless a war breaks out somewhere in the world. Then the countries involved will be too busy fighting to raise sugar.

January 1: I looked back over my diary today. Murders, revolutions, hurricanes and disasters. The end of the Machado regime has certainly not brought peace to Cuba. Bloodshed brings more bloodshed, violence more violence, and the folly of government multiplies. One of Cuba's greatest burdens during the Machado regime was supporting an army of ten thousand, which required a yearly budget of ten million dollars. Now Colonel Batista brags that he has eighteen thousand soldiers, three thousand police and three thousand marines. I don't believe he has that many, but he soon will have. One of the aims of the revolution was to decrease the size of the army and lessen the burden on the taxpayers. Now, with a 100% Cuban government, it is necessary to double the size of the army to keep such a government in power. And now, according to President Grau, there will be an election of members to the Constituent Assembly—in short, a new Constitution. If there is anything Cuba does not need at present, it is a new Constitution. They can't follow the seven clauses in the one they have!

If there is an error that can be made, the Cuban politicians will find some way of making it. There are one hundred twenty-eight representatives and thirty-four senators, twice too many for the size of this island. Cuba is divided into six provinces, each with full governmental machinery, utterly useless, except to act as soft berths for politicians. There are far too many municipalities and Machado continually created new ones to provide jobs. The national lottery was the weapon by which the President controlled Congress. If a congressman became refractory, the President simply took away his *colecturas,* his right to purchase a certain number of lottery tickets which in turn were sold to the wholesalers at a handsome profit. The lottery law was not a part of the Constitution, but it was passed soon after the Republic was established. It seems to me there is an irony involved when the control of government depends on a gambling device. But ring in the new year! Perhaps I am mistaken, perhaps the old mistakes will not be repeated, perhaps Cuba will be blessed with an era of peace and happiness, which she so much needs.

January 5:   The high school students marched to the National Theatre, where *King Kong* is being shown. A horrible, huge cardboard cutout of the giant gorilla was standing in front of the entrance. The students tied a big card around its neck, reading, "King Kong Batista," and carried it to the Capitolio, where they made speeches against him. Strange to say, the police and soldiers used good judgment and paid no attention.

In one of the local theaters which features political burlesque, a sketch was recently offered concerning the Grau administration. Soldiers threatened to shoot the actor taking the part of Grau, not liking his impersonation. The other night when it was time for the actor impersonating Grau to appear, a small mechanical dog which barked, "Graw! Graw!" was brought on the stage. The audience shrieked with laughter. Soldiers in the balcony expressed their displeasure by throwing a few chairs at the audience on the lower floor and the show terminated in a free-for-all fight. It is a miracle the soldiers didn't start shooting.

January 6: The high school children are having one secret anti-Grau meeting after another in the high school building opposite Central Park. The meetings are so secret that it is impossible to hear the speeches for more than a block. Mrs. H., who lives in the Pasaje Hotel, her room facing on Zulueta Street so that she looks directly into the high school auditorium, is so disgusted with the continual oratory that she declares the entire bunch should be sent to a reformatory. From thirteen years upward they all carry revolvers. The other night a group of them decided to put a bomb in the home of a government official. When they arrived at his address they found a soldier with a rifle guarding the front gate. They beat a hasty retreat. When they got to Central Park they discovered it was nearly time for the bomb to go off. Their one idea was to get rid of it. Any place would do. Looking around they noticed the beautiful building of the Spanish Regional Society *Centro Asturiana* and placed the bomb in one of the numerous doorways and hurried off. It went off on schedule.

Colonel Carlos Mendieta has written President Grau asking him to resign. Mendieta is the logical man for the presidency. He has considerable following as head of the Nationalista Party. He is known throughout the Republic as an honest man. The greatest criticism of him is that he is of the old political school. He is somewhat indecisive. He is now trying to decide whether he would rather be provisional president or become a candidate for the presidency. He had better decide in favor of the provisional presidency, in my opinion. He may be too old to serve by the time this country gets around to holding presidential elections. He is friendly with the United States, which is one thing in his favor.

January 8: Now the school teachers have gone on a strike all over the island. They want more wages. There has been no particular attention paid to education in Cuba since the American occupation. There aren't half enough school buildings. In the majority of instances the government does not own the buildings where schools are now functioning despite the fact that sufficient money has been appropriated at various times. Every once in a while the property owners renting to the government demand their rent and threaten to turn the schools out into the street.

While the government issues optimistic figures concerning the small percentage of illiteracy in Cuba, some authorities on the subject affirm it is from 53% to 60%. Rather depressing figures.

At present the entire school system has become contaminated with politics. The high school pupils of Cuba are not like any normal children. I feel very sorry for them. They have no gymnasiums, no athletic organizations, no parties, no class dances, no real school life. The same is true of the university. It is politics first, last and always; studies are merely incidental. They are divided into Rights and Lefts, the Lefts being a little more Communistic and radical than the Rights, although the difference is very little. They stage demonstrations, hold fiery political meetings, plant bombs, call strikes, make demands on the government; in short, meddle in the nation's affairs. The majority are thin, anemic looking youths, with pale solemn faces, giving one the impression they are carrying the weight of their nation's history on their shoulders.

January 9: Negroes in Santa Clara, influenced by the student propaganda to rise and take the privileges so long denied them, tried to oust the whites from the park in Trinidad, where a concert was going on. The whites replied with revolver shots and a general gun battle ensued, with four people gravely wounded. Every day tales of battles between political factions in small towns reach Havana. The President appoints a youthful student as mayor of some town; the political leaders of the town decide they will not allow the appointee to take office; more than one mayor has been literally shot out of office.

January 14: The government took over operation of the *Cia. Cubana de Electricidad* on the grounds that if the company could not reach an agreement with the employees the government would. The government did not give a receipt to the company when they took over the properties, so we hear.

Phil and I came to town about ten and found all the elevators stalled. Streetcars were scattered here and there wherever they had happened to be when the power was cut off. We sat in the café downstairs and drank coffee because I refused to walk up five flights of stairs.

Finally, about noon, the lights in Central Park began to burn feebly and then power came on gradually. Trucks, filled with employees of the company, circulated through the downtown section and the employees cheered and shouted. One more dragon had been slain.

I hope they are in the same cheerful frame of mind when they begin receiving their pay like government employees; that is, only now and then and usually several months in arrears. The only government workers who get their salaries on due date are the soldiers and marines. They must be paid; if not, they might decide to change the administration.

7

January 15: It is long after midnight, but none of the American correspondents dares to go to sleep for fear they will change presidents again without warning. President Grau resigned. As usual, all action took place after midnight. The minds of the Cuban politicians apparently do not begin to function until after dark.

Last night at ten o'clock the Revolutionary Junta went into session at Camp Columbia. The Junta consists of those who signed the proclamation issued on September 4th when the enlisted men staged their military coup. However, in a crisis everyone of any importance in the present government goes to lend his presence and advice.

The Junta held their meeting in the ballroom of the Officers' Club, a beautiful building where the pride of Machado's army used to strut about. I remember going to a dance there during the Machado regime. Now the former sergeants and corporals are stepping gingerly over its glistening polished floor. It must have been quite a dramatic scene, speech after speech, plea after plea to save the 100% Cuban government. Outside, three hundred soldiers, sailors and police milled around, waiting to see who would be the next President.

The first action of the Junta was to bar all newspaper reporters. Gutierrez, a tall, slim, excitable chap, who used to be our night man, and who almost lives at Camp Columbia covering military matters, told me he was unceremoniously escorted out of the Officers' Club.

The sudden meeting of the Junta to select a new President was because Colonel Batista saw that revenue was getting scarcer and scarcer. The United States government has been bearing down on Batista to put into power an administration which the people will support. It is an odd situation. The American government directly engineered the fall of Machado and the establishment of a new government, the Céspedes administration. Batista and his cohorts ousted the Céspedes administration, declared themselves free from American influence, seized American property, and, before long, Assistant Secretary of State Welles finds himself backing Batista.

Yet Colonel Batista has seen the error of his ways and realized that no government can exist in Cuba without American recognition. So, he told President Grau to resign.

Yesterday afternoon Colonel Batista, President Grau, Colonel Mendieta and Dr. Gabriel Landa met at the farm of Enriqué Pedro outside Havana. Batista told Grau he must resign and that Mendieta was to become President. Grau was not pleased, particularly over the choice of his successor, who represents the conservative elements of the nation.

Dr. Antonio Guiteras y Holmes, the most powerful of the cabinet members, has drawn around him all the leftists. In fact, he may supplant Grau as the radical leader in Cuba. Guiteras is half Irish, and a mixture of Latin and Irish is dangerous in a tropical country. He has reddish brown hair, freckles, and does not look like a Cuban. He is tall, excessively thin and somewhat stooped. He talks little and makes decisions swiftly.

The strained relations between Guiteras and Batista are almost bringing about civil war. Guiteras and the students, in a desperate effort to save the present administration, backed Carlos Hevia, Secretary of Agriculture, for President,

while Batista and the army backed Colonel Mendieta, who
is the choice of the United States. Hevia can hope for no
support. Mendieta undoubtedly could gain the support of
the public.

At two this morning Grau resigned. Guiteras and Batista
were at dagger points. Guiteras threatened there would be a
fight if the army refused to accept the decision of the Junta.
The tension spread to the outside, among the soldiers and
sailors, who were never on very good terms. The National
Police are supporting Guiteras, we hear, and a lot of them
were present in brand new uniforms.

Today Havana is in a furor of excitement. The Junta ad-
journed at five A.M. without reaching a decision. Then a
lot of things occurred which are completely unexplainable
and which could only happen in a country like Cuba.

Colonel Batista, after backing Mendieta as candidate all
night, suddenly called a few members of the Junta to Camp
Columbia and appointed Carlos Hevia President. During the
night a group of students went to Colonel Mendieta and
asked him if he would support Hevia for President. The
Colonel, still tottering on the fence of decision, and probably
having none of his group at hand to help him reach a decision, said that he would support Hevia. The students rushed
back to Camp Columbia and gave Mendieta's statement to
the press.

About noon it became known that Hevia would take over
the presidency at four that afternoon. The confusion was
pitiful. Members of the Junta, dazed with sleep, tumbled out
of bed, and frantically phoned other members demanding to
know who appointed Hevia. Everyone denied they had anything to do with it. Reaching the conclusion that Batista had
appointed him, the Junta declared they would accept no responsibility.

Even Guiteras, who had supported Hevia so staunchly, declared he would not remain in the cabinet so long as Batista
was Chief of the Army. The Guiteras plan was daring. Believing he could dominate Hevia, it was apparently his idea

that Hevia should remove Batista and appoint Captain Pablo Rodriguez as Chief of Staff.

The *Nationalista* Party declared that if Mendieta had said he would support Hevia, he was talking personally and not for the Party.

The university students held a meeting at the university and decided they would oppose Hevia's administration "with all the means at our command."

Soldiers, heavily armed, have been pouring into town all day. The Palace guard has been doubled, the machine guns and antiaircraft weapons stripped for action. Navy Headquarters at La Punta bristles with small cannon. There may be a war, the navy and police on one side, the army on the other.

Apparently Batista decided to appoint Hevia as President and see how much support Hevia actually had, intending of course to bow to the storm of protest from the military and put Hevia out and Mendieta in after the reaction. Thus Batista was giving Hevia the political kiss of death, since Hevia's supporters will no longer trust him as being anti-Batista. Clearly, Batista has become Cuba's "maker of Presidents." Hevia cannot last a week. I feel sorry for him. Imagine his bewilderment to find that his enemies are his friends and his friends are now suspicious of him.

Phil went to the palace early in the afternoon. Sometime later I heard rifle fire in that direction. Phil telephoned, saying the soldiers had just killed and wounded many people in Zayas Park. It had happened as Grau was leaving the palace. As his automobile came out from the ground floor patio, the crowd cheered and surged toward it. An officer gave the order for the soldiers to fire into them. Four killed and fourteen wounded is the official figure, and the military defends itself by calling it an attempt to assassinate Grau. The Presidency was assumed by Hevia at around four o'clock. There was little formality.

Hevia is imbued with many of the impractical theories of the students. Educated in the United States, a graduate of the Annapolis Naval Academy, he commanded the Gibara expedition in the 1931 revolt against Machado. He is thirty-seven, short, slender, with black hair and eyes so black they glitter. Yet he has a rather retiring personality.

Alex, the young man who works for United Press, was helping Haas cover the palace this afternoon. He described the scene in the President's office. "They kicked everybody out except me. I was sitting at one corner of the President's desk, pretending to use the telephone. When an aide asked me to leave, I said, 'Sure, wait'll I get this cable off to New York.' I called the Commercial Cable girl and said, 'Leave the line open. I'm going to talk and talk, but don't pay any attention. I'll explain later.' So I talked in English about anything that came into my mind, while she giggled. I hoped they would forget about me and they did.

"Grau was sitting in front of the desk. Beside him was the Secretary of Justice, Almagro. They had a small table between them on which Almagro was writing the resignation of Grau. Ruben de Leon, a member of *Directorio Estudiantil,* and Almagro started arguing. Leon grabbed the resignation and ripped it across, shouting: 'Grau is not quitting.' All the students jumped up, waving their arms in the air and shouting.

"Almagro rose from his chair and said sarcastically: 'Well, what about Batista? Batista doesn't want Grau!' Leon called Almagro a traitor and several other names. I saw Leon hit Almagro and they had to be separated.

"Grau rose from his chair, followed by the crowd of students and cabinet members, and went into the adjoining office. I looked around and saw that only Colonel Aurelio Alvarez and myself were left in the room. I don't know how he got left, but there he was. We talked aimlessly, Aurelio raving against the Americans, against Batista, against everybody. I didn't pay much attention as I was trying to hear what was going on in the next room.

"Not having anything else to do, and sitting in the President's chair, I rummaged through his desk. It was completely empty except that in the upper left hand drawer were three small pasteboard boxes with what looked like Chinese characters on the outside. I opened one and found some funny little tubes. I smelled one and got a whiff that nearly knocked me off the chair. I put it back. Then I noticed the little bronze key in the center drawer. The head of the key had a hinge. I hadn't collected a single souvenir in the whole revolution. I thought what a nice one the key from the center drawer of the President's desk would make. I put it in my pocket.

"I had smoked about a package of cigarettes, when in came a navy aide from the other room. He glared at me and asked what I was doing. I said I was waiting for a statement Grau had promised me.

"Alvarez jumped up and said he wanted to see Grau. The aide said, 'The President is too busy to see anyone now.' Alvarez said he had as much right to go in the other room as anyone but the aide walked away and slammed the door. In a minute or so he came out again. Alvarez had gotten in a state of rage by that time. He walked over to the aide, grabbed him by the arm and whirled him around: 'You go in there and tell Dr. Grau that Aurelio Alvarez is waiting to see him. You tell him that all the support he has in Camagüey Province is on account of me.' The aide jerked loose and said: 'Shut your mouth, the President isn't going to see anybody.' Alvarez squared off like a big rooster. I sat back and thought —boy, here's where I see a fight right in the presidential office, but no such luck. The door burst open and the students poured out, still arguing. When they saw there was going to be a fight, some of them grabbed Alvarez, and some grabbed the aide.

"Grau paid no attention. He said he was washing his hands of the whole thing and going home. He walked out. That left Hevia as president. I grabbed the phone and called Haas downstairs and told him Grau was leaving.

"In a few minutes shooting started down in the park. I went to the balcony to see. People were lying on the ground.

I saw one fellow, covered with blood, running toward the market place.

"About that time somebody said, 'How the hell did you get here.' It was Captain Franco Granero. He was pretty provoked. He said: '*Ratón,* is what you are, never do I go any place in this palace but what I stumble over you. I suppose the next time I raise up the lid of my soup plate I'll find you there.'

"I said I was covering the palace and I had to stay. He said, 'Get out!' So I left."

Down the island the army has taken over all municipal and provincial governments.

January 16: Carlos Hevia took formal oath of office this morning as president. Every president seems to take a different oath. It was a quiet affair, no crowd, no students. Dr. Federico Edelman administered the oath. Colonel Aurelio Hevia, father of Carlos, shook hands with his son and said: "Good morning, Mr. President, congratulations." No foreign diplomats were present. Hevia told correspondents, speaking perfect English, that he was a friend of the American people.

Something happened to the twenty-one gun presidential salute. After eight shots the cannon on Cabañas Fortress, across the bay from Havana, ceased to fire. One story is that the powder got wet; another, that the soldiers misplaced the ammunition; a third, that the soldiers in the fort decided, after they had fired a few shots, that they didn't like Hevia. Take your choice.

I was told today by a man close to Hevia that the students belonging to the Revolutionary Junta were the ones who appointed Hevia and that Colonel Batista was as surprised as anyone when he found Cuba had a new President. It is difficult to know what to believe. Colonel Batista did not attend the inauguration, which lends color to this last report. Undoubtedly, Hevia has no support and is merely a sort of stopgap until another President can be selected.

January 17: Colonel Carlos Mendieta will become Cuba's new president tomorrow. Paying no attention to poor Hevia sitting alone in the palace, the political factions have finally agreed upon Mendieta. Batista and the American government are in accord. Phil went out to see Mendieta but he was deep in conferences, everybody giving him advice.

Mendieta's house looks like a camp meeting. All the politicians are getting on the band wagon because they know the new administration will have a lot of jobs to give out. There is no civil service in Cuba. It is merely a matter of influence as to the job you get.

Government employees are out on strike. The employees of the *Cia. Cubana de Electricidad* are threatening to strike. Guiteras doesn't seem to know yet that he is licked. The radicals have split into a dozen pieces over Hevia's appointment and Guiteras is left without a following.

January 18: President Hevia resigned this morning. He was President about thirty-two hours. That is a record even for Cuba. Pointedly disregarding the disrupted Revolutionary Junta, Hevia addressed his resignation to the proper person —Colonel Batista.

Alex told me, "I was hanging around the palace as usual. It was after midnight. Nothing doing, nobody there. Canel of Associated Press got disgusted and said he was going out to Camp Columbia to see Batista. Canel hadn't more than gotten out the door when I saw the Secretary of Public Instruction come downstairs. I ran over and asked if there was any news. He showed me an envelope which he had in his hand. It was addressed to Colonel Fulgencio Batista, Chief of Staff, Camp Columbia. The Secretary said, 'Don't say I told you, but here is President Hevia's resignation.'

"Hevia came downstairs after a while and we all said good-bye to him. Only a few people were there. Phil and I were the only American correspondents. Hevia left and the palace was completely deserted. There were only five policemen downstairs and everything was so still you could hear a cricket.

"I asked a couple of Cuban reporters in the Reporters' Salón who was president. That started a discussion. Nobody knew who was president. We decided Cuba ought to have a president and we ought to hustle around and find one. One of the boys suggested we go out to the National Hotel and ask Dr. Marquez Sterling, Secretary of State, who had recently returned from Washington. When we got to Marquez Sterling's suite, he was walking up and down distractedly in a bathrobe and slippers, and the suite was crowded with people. There were politicians of all sorts, former cabinet members, revolutionists, *Nationalistas*, ABCs, OCRRs, everybody except the students and Batista. An argument was going on. They were trying to persuade Marquez Sterling that he was President, but he didn't seem to like the idea. I sat in a corner and listened.

"Someone suggested we ask Dr. Edelman, Chief Justice of the Supreme Court. It was four in the morning by then. I rode in a car accompanied by two marines with rifles. I don't know why the marines went; apparently they didn't either. The procession arrived at the home of Dr. Edelman in Vedado and someone pounded on the door. We had to wait until the maid got up and dressed. I guess she thought it was another revolution and couldn't seem to find her clothes, so it took some time. Then she told Dr. Edelman we wanted to see him. We must have waited an hour while explanations were made and the Chief Justice got dressed. Just as we started back to town the electric lights went out. The employees of the *Cia. Cubana de Electricidad* had struck again.

"We went back to the National Hotel through the blackest town you ever saw. The only light was the one on Morro Castle. When we got to the National they had a few candles in the lobby. They handed out candles to all of us. The procession went up the stairs with old man Edelman, who had to be helped, and who was half asleep.

"Finally we got to Sterling's suite. He was still in his bathrobe and slippers. Nearly everyone in the room had a candle. There we were trying to give Cuba a President. We were all worn out and it was decided to leave Cuba without a president until ten the next morning when everyone would meet in the palace. The joke was that here we were trying to find a President and Batista sitting calmly out in Camp Columbia, and everyone knowing that if they didn't decide on Mendieta, Batista would step in and overrule the selection and put Mendieta in anyway."

Colonel Carlos Mendieta became President at about eleven this morning. The public crowded around the palace for blocks, they cheered until they were hoarse. They cheered President Roosevelt, Ambassador Caffrey and Assistant Secretary of State Welles. In fact, Cuba has again recognized the United States.

Phil went to the palace early. In the afternoon he entered the office, looking a wreck. His white shoes were positively black; his trousers were wrinkled; his coat split under one arm; his hair standing straight up; his collar looked as if it had been worn at least a couple of days. He said President Mendieta looked worse than he did by the time the inauguration was over. Hamburg, the photographer, came rushing in. He had nearly fallen off the palace balcony, camera and all, trying to get a picture of Mendieta.

At twelve-thirty the presidential salute was fired. Then La Punta Navy Headquarters' guns fired a salute to show that the navy was in accord with the selection of Mendieta; boats in the harbor blew their whistles; soldiers fired their rifles; every individual with a revolver shot a few times; everybody yelled. Downstairs the bartenders could hardly serve the drinks fast enough. Other cafés had similar crowds. The merchants closed up to give their employees a holiday. The town is celebrating the removal of the student government with almost the same enthusiasm as when Machado fell. Tonight, crowds are getting noisier and more rowdy. The Capitolio is lit from top to bottom; the palace has flood lights trained on it; the city is ablaze with lights and every street is crowded with celebrators.

Alex came by. This is the story he told me: "I got to the palace, it was already crowded and more people arriving. I slid into the cabinet room where I figured all action would take place. All the sectors were there, the ABCs, the OCRRs, the PANs and the XYZs, Menocal's men, *Nationalistas*, Liberals, Conservatives, etc. Old man Miguel Coyula made a speech in favor of ex-president Menocal as the man who should assume the presidency. It didn't go over very well. Then Dr. Manuel de la Cruz spoke for half an hour about Mendieta, and everyone shouted: 'Viva Mendieta.' The *Menocalistas* said they wouldn't accept Mendieta without a program of government. A *Nationalista* got up and said the idea was first to select a President and then give him a vote of confidence.

"Mendieta arrived downstairs. The palace was surrounded for blocks by people and when they saw Mendieta they howled and cheered. It took Mendieta nearly forty-five minutes to get from the entrance into the cabinet room. When he appeared everybody shouted, 'Viva Mendieta,' and that was all there was to it.

"I saw the Judges of the Supreme Court in various places with their black togas but after Mendieta finally got into the cabinet room they couldn't get the Supreme Court together to swear him in as President. Every time they would push the Supreme Court Judges to the cabinet table the crowd would surge with another *viva* and the next thing you knew a couple of the Judges would be clear out in the adjoining Salón of Mirrors. It looked hopeless but I was determined to see Mendieta take oath of office so I grabbed hold of the toga of one old Judge and hung on. I knew that according to law the Court must all be together to swear in the President. Well, the old Judge and I went here and there; we were pushed out into the hall, back into the cabinet room; we visited the office of the Secretary of the Presidency and the Salón of Mirrors.

"Finally, I got to the stairway and met Haas in a head-on collision. He said, 'Where the hell have you been?' I said, 'I've been hanging on to a Supreme Court Judge so I could see the President sworn in.' He said, 'Dumbbell, they swore him in half an hour ago.'"

Labor is not pleased over the selection of Mendieta. In fact, it now appears that the first thing Mendieta will have to contend with is a general strike. Labor says Mendieta is reactionary, which undoubtedly he is. Because they were angry over the ousting of the student government, the employees of the *Cia. Cubana de Electricidad* walked out.

Colonel Batista has soldiers posted around the plant and asserted he was not going to permit the night shift to leave until the day shift came on. Nevertheless they walked out and left the plant flat after turning off the current all over town. The company gave out a statement that the army engineers were assisting in starting the plant. However, it was navy engineers off the United States cruiser Richmond and the American engineers of the company who got the power on again.

Mendieta has promised the American government that one of the first things he will do will be to reduce the size of the army. He can do so if he has the nerve, but I doubt if he has.

The American government has promised Mendieta recognition, cancellation of the Platt Amendment, a new reciprocity treaty and probably a loan—the original Santa Claus. I hope it works out all right. All foreigners are happy over the Mendieta administration, knowing of course that he has the approval of the United States.

January 19: Doctors of the island walked out on strike this morning. Drugstores are closing in sympathy. This means that all city and government hospitals are without doctors, all first aid stations, all private hospitals and clinics. Not only is a sick individual denied medical aid but also medicine. The strike is to force the government to ratify the decree of the Grau administration providing that no physician can practice in Cuba without belonging to the Federation. The strike even extends to veterinaries.

Some Cuban youngster with a sling shot drove a nail into the eye of Mrs. Garcia's cat. She is an American from Arkansas and has quite a temper. She took the cat to Camp Columbia and demanded that they treat it. I can picture the amazement of the soldiers at seeing her arrive there demanding a veterinary.

January 20: President Mendieta's cabinet contains Dr. Cosme de la Torriente, Secretary of State, Dr. Emeterio Santovenia, Secretary of the Presidency, Col. Roberto Mendez Peñate, Secretary of Justice, and Dr. Felix Granados, Secretary of National Defense.

There are four cabinet posts unfilled.

Former President Grau left Cuba today for Mexico. He was escorted to the docks and given a fond farewell. Then the crowd marched to Central Park shouting against the Mendieta administration. Youthful members, in their enthusiasm, assaulted cigar stands and carried off as much as they could.

Guiteras has disappeared. He is said to be in Oriente, his original hunting ground, bent on stirring up sufficient trouble among the sugar mill workers to prevent the grinding of the crop.

January 24: I have just returned from an exclusive interview. President Mendieta was wearing a light gray suit and a gray tie. He has a kind face. At first glance I would have judged him to be a *gentleman colono,* a cane planter, rather than a politician. His white hair is still thick and healthy looking. His manner is a little preoccupied. We went into the cabinet room where he sat at his customary place at the head of the long table. The President talks very rapidly, far too rapidly to take notes. He began with the usual statements about patriotism and what he hoped to do for Cuba. Every Cuban president seems to memorize that particular speech, as a sort of requirement for office, making only slight variations in the delivery. Finally I asked him if Cuba was going to pay the Chase National Bank loans. He pulled up with a start, forgot about patriotism, and we got along fine after that. He can talk sense and to the point.

All the time we were talking one of his aides fairly danced and pranced behind his chair and at the first possible moment stated that the Archbishop of Havana was waiting to see the President. I asked a few more questions and then asked the President if I could write the interview in the first person and put his name on it. He smiled and said I could. Suddenly there was a terrific din of shouting from somewhere outside the palace. I remember the peculiar feeling it gave me, and it gave me some idea of what the President's life must be, what must go through his mind each time he hears an uproar of the people, and not knowing what has caused the uproar. Mendieta, however, remained quite calm, continuing to give me his attention. I liked him particularly because he seemed to have respect for his office, and to have that native courtesy for which no amount of glad-handing or joviality can substitute.

The aide hurried out, returned quickly, and said there was a delegation of children demanding to see the President. Mendieta walked out through the Salón of Mirrors to the balcony. We went along to see what was happening. One of the children made a speech in which he demanded that the government order the Havana Electric Railway Company, which operates the streetcars in Havana and Marianao, to let school children ride the streetcars free of charge. I could hardly keep from laughing but the President gravely asked them to appoint a commission to see the Secretary of Public Instruction and said that the matter would be given consideration. We all walked gravely back into the Salón of Mirrors and bade the President goodbye.

January 25: The car was in the garage last night for repairs and Phil and I had to ride a bus, known as a *guagua.* It is a good idea to be sure one's life insurance policy is in full effect before riding *guaguas* here. They kill more people every year than the revolutions. Nearly every day the local papers carry headlines, "Five killed, ten wounded." No one in the government pays the slightest attention. These stories are always embellished by pictures of persons dead, dying, or blood covered. No bus company has any insurance and when you ride them you do so at your own risk.

We started home last night. I hoped our driver might be a conservative, but I saw by the way his cap perched on his head that if we got home alive it would be no fault of his. We raced down Neptuno Street, striving desperately to pass another bus. The seats are so close together that one's knees touch the seat in front. You brace your knees against the back of the seat in front and thus resist sudden, unexpected stops. Just as we made a left turn under the traffic lights at Infanta Street to start up University Hill the motor expired. There we were in the middle of the street blocking all traffic. The chauffeur didn't seem the least surprised. He asked another chauffeur who happened to be in the bus to get out and push and with the help of several passengers the bus was pushed over near the sidewalk.

Then the chauffeur motioned a couple of passengers in front to get up and he dug under their seat and brought out a gallon can. Unscrewing a tap in the floor back of his seat, he poured in the gallon of gasoline. Considering the size of the bus I had no idea a gallon would even start the engine. But the chauffeur stepped on the starter and we sped up University Hill.

As the bus went around the corner the tires shrieked and skidded and something bleated loudly, "Baa! Baa!" I turned around and saw a woman in the back seat with a small goat in her lap. The goat was frightened all the way.

February 2:   To call on Batista is something like trying to see the King of Siam. You drive up to one of the gates of Camp Columbia, only to be told that *today* the other gate is to be used. Then you find that all passes and credentials which you have are just so much paper. The next move is to drive around to headquarters which is outside the limits of the camp. The soldiers on guard seem to think you might walk off with the building.

Phil and I climbed the imposing flight of steps and wandered into the room on the right, where half the Cuban army was congregated, and looked in dismay at the number of civilians sitting around, waiting. We realized that an appointment meant little. We sat and smoked up all the cigarettes we had. Finally, an aide told Phil that the Colonel had gone to tea and that it would be much simpler if we went over to his house. We walked out in time to see the Colonel leaving.

The Colonel strode out. Behind him came the fattest, blackest negro I ever saw, with a machine gun in his hand. Batista walked diagonally across the end of the parade ground to the nearest barracks. The balance of the bodyguard piled into two large Lincoln cars with their miscellaneous collection of rifles and Tommy guns. While the Colonel walked almost a block the automobiles drove slowly around the corner and met him as he approached the barracks. They all jumped out of the cars and fell in behind him, guns ready. The Colonel had gone to tea.

Phil and I drove to the nearest gate, where the soldiers grudgingly let us through, although they cast suspicious glances at us. We drove up to the Colonel's house. He still lives in the same house he occupied as a sergeant. It is a low, one-story building with a tiny yard in front. A soldier with a rifle leaned on the gate.

We sat on the porch with several other visitors and the guard. It was comfortable there looking out over the huge parade ground laid out by the American forces during the occupation of the island. The entire camp was constructed by the Americans and the soldiers are still occupying the wooden barracks put up at that time.

During the time we sat there a corporal of the guard called the soldier at the gate and the following conversation took place:

"Were you on guard duty last night?"

The soldier stared at him a minute and said, "I don't remember."

"You don't remember?"

"No."

"Well, you stand guard tonight."

"I don't want to tonight. My sister is sick and I want to go see her."

"Your *sister?*"

Another soldier sauntered up. The corporal turned to him.

"Was this guy on duty last night?"

"I think he was," with a look at the first soldier.

"All right, then you can get off tonight."

I asked Phil if he didn't think it would be a good idea to have the soldiers keep a diary, but he frowned at me.

The Colonel arrived with his bodyguard, who immediately distributed themselves around the porch in various weary attitudes. An aide asked us to come inside. We sat in the small sala. On the other side of the room was a beautiful carved settee and two chairs. There was a rug on the floor. I haven't seen a rug for years in Cuba. In the center was a small table, apparently antique. It was beautifully carved, four legs were attached to a center piece resting on the floor and then came up to curve and hold the sunken top. Around the top were portraits of Colonial ladies in blue and gold set into the wood.

The Colonel came in. His face is that of an Indian. I was raised among North American Indians and the Asiatic cast of his face is Indian, not Chinese. However, the Colonel states firmly that his parents were Cubans.

The Colonel has a charming personality. One can see how he is holding his own in the present position and he will undoubtedly continue to do so. His mind works like lightning. He smiles readily, often, gives his complete attention to the person addressing him, and reaches a conclusion almost before the person has finished speaking. Cubans as a whole are plausible. The Colonel is plausible in the superlative degree. He can practically convince one that a thing is true and that he is logical, which is extraordinary in a country whose idea of logic leaves one gasping. I told Phil after the interview that were the Colonel sincere, the government might as well let him run the country.

The task faced by President Mendieta was a tremendous one. He had to straighten out the tangled financial affairs of a country which had been torn by revolution, a country whose treasury was empty and which had defaulted on its foreign obligations; to open up the trade channels between Cuba and the United States, dried up by the high tariff policies of both; hold elections for a Constituent Assembly to draw up a new constitution. To do this he must assuage the bitter feeling among the many opposition groups who were not yet ready to lay aside violence.

Mendieta brought to these tasks good will, honesty, and a kindly sympathetic personality. He abhorred the use of force and his stocky figure, dressed always in white linen suits, was to many a symbol of return to normalcy. His most remembered statement on entering the presidency was: "I shall never soil my white suit with the blood of the people." But Mendieta lacked strong leadership, the ability to dominate a situation immediately and with decision, and his suit was to bear many red stains before the end of his regime.

The United States recognized the government of President Mendieta on January 23rd. Recognition of a Cuban government is tantamount to approval. Jefferson Caffrey, President Roosevelt's personal representative, delivered to the Secretary of State, Dr. Cosme de la Torriente, the note of recognition. Crowds who had waited all day started celebrating. The *U.S.S. Wyoming,* then in harbor, fired a twenty-one gun salute. Cabañas Fortress across the bay replied. The gunboat *Cuba* fired a salute to the flag of Admiral Freeman. Crowds gathered around the Presidential Palace, cheering. The President and his wife appeared on the north balcony. The United States was "queen for a day."

The students of Havana University were angered by the deposing of Grau and refused to accept President Mendieta. They expressed their displeasure in demonstrations, riots and strikes. Batista countered by ordering his soldiers to break up all student demonstrations and to make widespread arrests. He was determined, once and for all, to break the power of the university students. The leader of the students was Dr. Antonio Guiteras, a slender boyish-looking man, whose mother was an American. Guiteras, as Secretary of Interior, had put into effect the tremendous gains of labor during the Grau administration, thereby giving Cuba one of the most modern labor codes in the Western Hemisphere. Guiteras was decidedly anti-American. He was a dedicated anti-imperialist and talked strongly against the American State Department. He had courage. His escapes from traps which Batista's soldiers used to try to capture him became almost legendary.

President Roosevelt invited Cuba to begin negotiations to "modify the permanent treaty between the United States and Cuba and to revise the commercial conventions between the two countries." In other words, the United States was willing to abrogate the controversial Platt Amendment, which provided for American intervention in Cuba under certain conditions. Conservative Cubans informed me that the worst thing that could happen in Cuba would be the abrogation of the Platt Amendment, leaving the island at the mercy of the politicians and the military. They pointed out that now Cuba was in the same category with all other Latin American countries. I told them that for years their politicians had been screaming about the Platt Amendment and their need to be free, and now, the amendment was going to be abrogated and Cuba would be entirely on her own, unable to blame the United States for her mistakes. They were much perturbed.

The tobacco workers, 30,000 strong, declared a strike. Bombs began to explode throughout the island. Students rioted; first one section of labor, then another went on strike. The sugar workers began to strike in the provinces. The radical students and revolutionists hoped to force the resignation of President Mendieta.

President Mendieta signed a decree on March 7th suspending constitutional guarantees and placing the army in control of the island. Then he signed a decree ordering the dissolution of all unions whose members struck in defiance of regulations governing strikes. The army moved in five hundred strike breakers to Havana docks, paralyzed by a walkout, and broke the dock strike. Workers returned to work all over the island. The army had won the first round.

President Mendieta declared a moratorium on foreign debt payments until such time as government revenue would reach sixty million dollars annually. The reason given was that the amortization of foreign indebtedness would amount to 20% of the entire national revenue. Later in June the loan of sixty million dollars made to the Machado government by American investors was declared illegal.

Colonel Roberto Mendez Penate, Secretary of Justice, committed suicide on April 4, 1934. His death shocked the nation. The suicide was attributed to despair over Cuba's situation and friction with President Mendieta, combined with ill health.

The American Embassy residence was attacked on the morning of May 27th as the Ambassador was preparing to leave his home. A blue automobile sped by, its occupants firing at the soldiers on guard there. Reports circulated that the life of the Ambassador was in danger. At any rate, Caffrey became the first American envoy here to have a bodyguard. Two cars filled with police and soldiers accompanied him wherever he went and maintained guard around the Embassy at all times.

On May 29th Cuba and the United States signed a new treaty which annulled the Platt Amendment. The abrogation of the Platt Amendment was hailed with great enthusiasm in Cuba. Church bells rang; sirens and whistles were blown; crowds gathered in front of the Presidential Palace where the municipal band played the national anthem. Ambassador Caffrey was cheered as he arrived at the palace to congratulate President Mendieta. The President broadcast the news over a nationwide radio hookup. Later on in June the island held a three-day celebration of the termination of the Platt Amendment.

Meanwhile war between the civil and military authorities of the Island accelerated in pace. At the beginning of June several members of President Mendieta's cabinet threatened to resign unless civil authority was restored, while Colonel Fulgencio Batista, Chief of Staff, demanded that martial law be extended. Dr. Emeterio Santovenia, Secretary of the Presidency, resigned, stating he saw the country headed for a military dictatorship. "If the country wants to live under the heel of the military boot, it is all right with me, but the moment has arrived when the government must define itself. It must be either one thing or another—either military or civil," he said.

Colonel Batista won. Constitutional guarantees were suspended for another ninety days.

On June 15th an attempt was made to kill President Mendieta. A bomb exploded at a luncheon being given in honor of the President and his cabinet by Captain Rafael de la Paz, Chief of the Tenth Naval Station at Tiscornia. President Mendieta had just risen to address the luncheon guests when the bomb, planted under a stairway directly behind the President in the large dining hall, exploded. A sailor was killed, a naval lieutenant and five marines were injured. The Secretary of Communications, Gabriel Landa, was slightly hurt by bomb fragments. That night President Mendieta

signed one of the most drastic public order laws ever enacted
in Cuba. It provided the death penalty for those found guilty
of attacks upon persons or property by the use of explosive
mechanisms.

Two days later, fourteen people were killed and more than
sixty injured when gunmen attacked the parade of the ABC
Revolutionary Organization. The marchers, many of them
women, were proceeding happily along the Malecón Sea
Drive when a red sedan emerged from a side street and the
four occupants opened fire. Armed ABC men rushed the
automobile, fired at the tires, stopped it, and riddled the
attackers with bullets. Then the car was covered with gasoline and set afire. The attackers were identified as members
of a radical organization supporting the deposed President,
Grau San Martin.

The ABC Organization withdrew its support from the government and provoked a cabinet crisis. The Mendieta government had been supported by the *Nationalistas,* of which
President Mendieta was a member, the ABC Revolutionary
Organization, the *Menocalistas,* and the *Marianoistas,* adherents of Dr. Miguel Mariano Gómez. With the withdrawal of
the ABC, Colonel Batista became even more powerful.

The new trade treaty between Cuba and the United States
was signed on August 24th in Washington. The United States
reduced the duty on sugar, rum and tobacco from Cuba and
Cuba reciprocally lowered the duty on a list of products
which the island imports customarily from the United States,
including foodstuffs, textiles, automobiles, machinery, business appliances, iron, steel, copper, wood, paper and other
items.

American Ambassador Jefferson Caffrey told the press
there was improvement in Cuban conditions "all along the
line, economically, politically and financially." Horse racing
was resumed for the first time in several years at the famous
Oriental Park and the annual International Star Class Yacht
Regatta was held off the coast. The winter carnival was
scheduled. However, the government again suspended con-

stitutional guarantees and fixed a penalty of death for those convicted of setting fire to cane in the fields or other acts of sabotage.

Seven bombs exploded in various parts of Havana during the carnival on February 17th. The university students demanded suppression of military interference in political and civil affairs, dissolution of the Urgency Courts, guarantees of personal rights and other reforms. Bombings were so frequent in Havana that Phil was reporting them by groups.

We had moved to a house on Thirteenth Street in Vedado. The house had a small yard, a garage at the side and an outdoor patio that ended with a high wall. One night we returned home after midnight. Phil put the car in the garage while I opened the front door and turned our two small dogs, Sistie and Blackie, out into the yard. We sat on the steps, enjoying the cool night air. It was a quiet residential street and at that hour there was not a sound, not even of passing cars. Then there was a terrific explosion. The big tree in front of our gate protected us from falling masonry. The blast destroyed a portion of the garden wall of the house across the street. Sistie, sitting on the sidewalk near the gate, gave one startled yip and ran for our door. We started laughing but the neighbors who rushed into the street after the explosion didn't see anything funny in the situation.

At two A.M. the phone rang, and Phil's night man told me that forty bombs had exploded in Havana up to that moment that night. I woke Phil so he could send a dispatch. He was sitting on the edge of my bed dictating a dispatch, "Forty bombs exploded tonight in Havana . . ." An explosion rocked our house. A hot gust of air poured in through my big back window, rushed past us and down the stairway, shattering the glass entrance door. Phil simply dug his finger in his ear, shook his head to clear the ringing, and said, "Correction, forty-one bombs exploded tonight in Havana, and I think that was our garage."

However, it was not our garage. The bomb had been

thrown into the garden, landing near my window. There was no damage except to the garden wall.

President Mendieta's cabinet had to be reorganized when both the Secretary of State, Dr. Cosme de la Torriente, and the Secretary of Justice and Interior, Dr. Raul de Cardenas, resigned. Colonel Fulgencio Batista moved in to break the spreading strike which was to become known as the famous "Strike of 1935." Behind the scenes of this strike was, once again, Antonio Guiteras. On March 6th ten persons were wounded when five bombs exploded in the Customs House and Treasury Department. Soldiers and marines were ordered into barracks ready for emergencies. Guards at strategic points were strengthened. Soldiers and police armed with rifles began to appear throughout Havana. Batista declared that the strike was "a disgrace to Cuba as a civilized nation" and warned that the army was prepared to take drastic action to suppress any revolutionary attempts. Censorship was imposed on the newspapers and Havana University was occupied by soldiers. Leaders of the strike countered by ordering a walkout of workers in the departments of Treasury, Education, Labor, Justice, Communications, Agriculture and Commerce. Newspaper employees joined the strike.

At three-thirty A.M., March 5, 1935, Phil's night man telephoned and said that President Mendieta had "suspended all constitutional law." I asked if he meant the suspension of constitutional guarantees, which was customary in Cuba. He said, "No, suspension of *all* constitutional law."

That was dictatorship, plain and simple. Phil called the *New York Times* and told them that President Mendieta had just established a dictatorship. The night editor to whom he talked said, "The presses are rolling, but that must go in." There was immediate reaction, Ambassador Caffrey calling Phil and demanding to know why he had sent such a dispatch. However, after heated argument the Ambassador was forced to admit that when a government suspends all constitutional law the result is dictatorship. Mendieta had also established the death penalty for anti-government activity.

Immediately the situation in Havana became one of terror. The young revolutionists attacked army troops and police. On March 10th the President declared a state of siege in Havana. Phil and I, with the required military passes, drove through the streets and were stopped at almost every intersection by soldiers. Finally, I simply held the military pass out of the car door. After the commander of each group had read the pass by flashlight we were permitted to go ahead. I mention this to show how tight a control the military had clamped on Havana. Yet despite everything the authorities could do the sabotage and bombings continued. Hundreds of revolutionists were thrown in jail. Residents huddled in their homes at night as the bombs exploded and soldiers fired at real or imagined snipers. Searchlights from Cabañas Fortress swept the city.

A young revolutionist from the interior was brought to Havana and condemned to death before a firing squad. Since the crime had been committed prior to the establishment of the death penalty, we did not believe the government would dare to execute him. However, Louis Hamburg, of the American photographic services, came into the office and told me that the prisoner was going to be executed. Convinced of this, he had gone to Cabañas Fortress and had taken a picture of the youth eating his last meal and giving away his possessions to the guards. The guards had cooperated in order to get their pictures taken.

Later in the day we received news from government sources that the young man would be shot early the next morning. Phil immediately called Ambassador Caffrey, who was shocked, and said that he would call Colonel Batista. Louis Hamburg was upset, saying that if the execution did not take place his photographs were useless. Somewhat annoyed by his cold-blooded view of the situation, I remarked that the American people like a happy ending, and that if the prisoner was reprieved Louis could probably arrange to take a picture of the reprieve being read, with perhaps the firing squad standing in the background. It never occurred to me that Louis would take my remark seriously.

As the night wore on it became apparent that the prisoner would be executed. At four A.M. I drove Phil to the Fifth Police Station alongside the Almendares River Bridge. When Phil entered the firing squad was already there, wearing white gloves and leaning on their rifles. The prisoner was in an open cell with bars running from the floor to the ceiling. Dick Armstrong of the International News Service was among those waiting. He had a bottle of gin in his hip pocket, from which he frequently took a drink. He was standing in the doorway of a darkened office. He looked down and saw a rabbit which had hopped out of the office behind him. Dick turned to a correspondent near him and said in a hushed voice, "Do you see a rabbit?" The American correspondent said, "Rabbit? What rabbit?" For the rabbit had hopped back into the office. Dick looked down and could see no rabbit. Scratching his head, he took the bottle of gin from his pocket, stared at it, then threw the bottle out the window.

Meanwhile Ambassador Caffrey had called Colonel Batista again and insisted that there would be violent reactions if the young revolutionist were executed through retroactive application of the law. Batista agreed to stop the execution. Fifteen minutes before the hour of the execution, the prisoner was informed that a reprieve had been granted. But, Louis Hamburg, determined not to lose his picture story, in his very bad Spanish persuaded the officer in charge of the post that it would be more fitting and more dramatic if he were to take the prisoner out on the parade grounds where he was to be shot, and then read the reprieve. The officer marched the firing squad out to the area behind the station. The prisoner was taken from his cell, led outside the jail, and stood against the prepared post. He stood then, trembling, apparently thinking the soldiers had decided to kill him anyway. Then the reprieve was read again to the almost fainting prisoner. As soon as this was accomplished Louis waved his hand and said, "Thanks, boys!" The prisoner was marched back to his cell, still dazed.

President Mandieta by suspending all constitutional law, appointing Lieutenant Colonel José Pedraza as military supervisor of Havana Province and army men as supervisors of each of the other five provinces, had delivered Cuba into the hands of Colonel Fulgencio Batista. Batista's armed forces took complete control of the island. Traffic was halted; hotels, cafés and bars closed. Civilians went on trial before military courts and later several were executed. The President declared in a special statement to the *New York Times* that "the revolutionary strike being staged at present against my government is the work of a small minority who realize they would not obtain the support of the people in an election and wish to triumph through violence." The government began taking on new employees. Soldiers started operating streetcars and labor filtered back to work either voluntarily or under threats of the military forces. Leaders of the opposition went into hiding but the army continued to seek them.

Four political organizations agreed on holding general elections on November 1, 1935. This included the Nationalist Party, the National Democratic Party, the Republican Party and the Liberal Party. Then on May 8th the armed forces killed Dr. Antonio Guiteras. Guiteras and a Venezuelan adventurer, General Carlos Aponte, together with a group of followers of Guiteras, were trapped at a small ancient fort near Matanzas on the north coast, where they were waiting for a schooner to take them out of Cuba. Guiteras and Aponte held off several hundred soldiers and marines with machine guns in a spectacular battle which raged in the uneven terrain around the little fort. Both Guiteras and Aponte died fighting. Authorities captured twelve members of the Guiteras party, including two women, and it was believed some escaped. Guiteras became a hero of the leftist groups of Cuba and today a monument stands where he fell near the little Spanish fort.

There was a sequel to this killing of Guiteras. Almost every man who had anything to do with betraying Guiteras was killed off by the *Joven Cuba* revolutionary organization during the next two or three years. One officer of the Cuban Navy, who was considered responsible for betraying Guiteras, obtained a transfer to Cienfuegos. He became engaged to be married. One morning just before the wedding a group of packages containing wedding presents were put on his desk. When he opened one of them, there was an explosion. He, his aide, and another naval officer were killed. The *Joven Cuba* had completed its vengeance.

President Carlos Mendieta announced he would not be a presidential candidate in the elections set for December 15th. Cubans hoped that the rule of the armed forces was over but the power of Colonel Fulgencio Batista was to continue to grow.

Despite disorder, the economy of the island began to improve. The American Chamber of Commerce of Havana said, "Importers of American goods report considerable increase in sales throughout the island. The largest gain was in agricultural machinery. Steel products, automobiles and foodstuffs likewise increased." However, in August President Mendieta refused to discuss settlement of the public works bonds then in default with representatives of the American bondholders, United States Senators Gerald P. Nye of North Dakota and Burton K. Wheeler of Montana, on the grounds that the provisional government had no jurisdiction. The Senators demanded that the interest be paid, but nothing was done about the matter.

Colonel Batista celebrated the second anniversary of his coup on September 4th. He told the soldiers in a speech at Camp Columbia, which he renamed Military City, that if the army wanted to take over the government it could do so because of its power. "But," the Colonel said, "it has never wanted to nor tried to and we hope that the attitude of other elements will never force us to that extreme."

The first step to hold elections on December 15, 1935, was

taken in September with the election of delegates. The Democratic Party nominated General Mario G. Menocal as their presidential candidate and Dr. Pelayo Cuervo as candidate for the mayorship of Havana. Dr. Miguel Mariano Gómez was nominated presidential candidate of the Republican and Nationalist Parties. The Liberal Party nominated Dr. Manuel de la Cruz, but considered a coalition with the Nationalist and Republican Parties to support Dr. Miguel Mariano Gómez.

A one-hundred-twenty mile an hour hurricane swept the east central part of the island, killing twenty, injuring two hundred and rendering some five thousand homeless.

In November President Mendieta tried to conciliate the warring political parties. "The government cannot go against the wishes of the political parties and is making every effort to hold the elections as set for December 15th," he said. It was of no avail. On November 27th he indefinitely postponed the elections and invited Dr. Harold Willis Dodds, President of Princeton University, to come to Cuba to act as technical adviser to the government on modification of the electoral code. Professor Dodds arrived and by December 7th had worked out modifications which the government accepted. The Liberal, Republican and Nationalist Parties were satisfied; the Democratic Party considered the changes "unfair" and withdrew from elections. President Mendieta made a statement on December 9th that his government would go ahead and hold elections. He tried to get the political parties to agree on elections for January 10, 1936, but failed.

Discouraged and saddened, the President resigned on December 11, 1935. His statement read: "Cuba's welfare depends at present on holding general elections in which the public may freely and spontaneously choose governing officials to terminate the period of provisional administration . . . Since some political parties are now alleging my occupancy of the office of Chief Executive is their reason for not participating in elections, claiming a nonexistent partiality on my part, I believe that I am complying with my patriotic duty in presenting my resignation from my office."

The Cuban public was stunned by the sudden resignation. Colonel Mendieta and Mrs. Mendieta left the Presidential Palace at ten-thirty in the morning for their country estate.

The Liberal Party candidate, Carlos de la Cruz, blamed the entire affair on the United States and said the election plan of Professor Dodds "had the virtue of further entangling the political problem, precipitating the downfall of President Mendieta and demonstrating the outstanding failure of American diplomatic policy in Cuba." The Council of State and the cabinet, confirmed Secretary of State, José A. Barnet, as provisional President of Cuba.

José A. Barnet was sworn in as President on December 13, 1935. He was the fifth provisional President since the fall of the Machado regime. Once in office, President Barnet confirmed the members of the cabinet in their posts, promised elections on January 10, 1936, and announced a vague and generalized program.

The Cuban people gave little heed to the change of Presidents. The political parties squared off for the coming battle over the Presidency. Colonel Batista reiterated that the armed forces would remain neutral and act impartially in the elections.

Three candidates emerged from the political battle. Dr. Miguel Mariano Gómez, former President Mario G. Menocal, and Dr. Carlos Manuel de Céspedes, who had been removed from the Presidency by the sergeant's revolt headed by Colonel Fulgencio Batista.

It was a contest of personalities and the real fight was between Dr. Miguel Mariano Gómez and General Mario G. Menocal.

Meanwhile the Foreign Policy Association of the United States had taken the Roosevelt administration to task for meddling in Cuban affairs. In a report, "The Cuban Revolution," issued on January 5th, the association declared: "Unless a constitutional government in Cuba replaces the essentially military rule of Batista and Mendieta, it would appear that the United States has employed its influence to overthrow one dictatorship—that of Machado—only to have it succeeded by another."

On January 10th, Dr. Miguel Mariano Gómez y Arias was elected President of Cuba in an orderly election. Dr. Federico Laredo Bru, who was later to play a leading role in the political life of the nation, was elected Vice-President. Cuban women went to the polls for the first time in history. They had obtained the right of suffrage in the constitution approved June 12, 1935. Party leaders scoffed at the idea of the women exercising any decisive influence in election results, but they did not scoff a few years later.

But the atmosphere of the island was still uneasy. The election had been a contest between the Liberal and Conservative forces of the island and the radical element, forced into the background, heartily disapproved of both. On election day a series of bombs exploded in Santiago de Cuba, second largest city of the island, injuring several and causing some damage.

President Barnet fixed the island's 1936 sugar crop at 2,515,000 long tons under a new six-year restriction plan which the government approved. Cuba's sugar crop, long under restriction, was to continue under control until World War II brought unprecedented demand. The United States, Cuba's best customer, offered to buy 1,434,541 tons.

President-elect Dr. Miguel Mariano Gómez left for a trip to Panama, thence to Los Angeles and across the United States to visit President Roosevelt in Washington. He was accompanied by his wife and three daughters, his brother-in-law, Colonel Julio Morales Coello, and two secretaries.

Meanwhile, public attention focused on various happenings. The Count of Covadonga, former heir to the throne of Spain, who was in Havana with his Cuban wife, the former Edelmira Sampedro, daughter of a wealthy merchant for whom he had renounced his right to the nonexistent throne, fell ill. He suffered from hemophilia and his condition fluctuated.

George Bernard Shaw arrived in Havana on February 7th and declared that President Roosevelt was a Communist, but didn't know it.

A crowd of 14,000 Cuban baseball fans, including President José Barnet, saw the Havana team defeat the St. Louis Cardinals, 13-8, in an exhibition game.

Few people paid any attention to a decree approved by President José Barnet and his cabinet authorizing Colonel Fulgencio Batista to designate members of the army to serve as teachers in rural districts where no schools existed. However, this was the first link in a chain of events which was to oust a President and change the history of the island.

Although President-elect Gómez had not taken office, the Cuban Senate on April 30th unanimously resolved to call upon him "to exhaust all the means at his command to solve definitely the acts of bloodshed that newspapers report are shrouded in mystery and that are occurring with continuous frequency, and to secure the punishment of the guilty."

The explosion in the Senate was touched off by the mysterious death of Octavio Seiglie, prominent adherent of Grau San Martin, and Agustin Martinez, a commission merchant, whose charred bodies were found in an automobile near Havana. Colonel Fulgencio Batista immediately ordered an investigation.

The administration of President José Barnet drew to a close. He and Mrs. Barnet, a native of France, lived quietly in the Presidential Palace, entertaining with dinners which were culinary triumphs. He performed his traditional presidential duties with correctness and an eye to protocol. The public was hardly conscious that a president lived in the palace.

On May 20, 1936, Dr. Miguel Mariano Gómez y Arias was sworn in as the sixth constitutional President, thus ending the series of provisional administrations which had begun with the deposing of the Machado regime in August, 1933. Dr. Gómez had long been a favorite with the Cuban people. As son of General José Miguel Gómez, the island's second President, he had been in the public eye from his boyhood. He was short of stature, slender, with dark hair and eyes. Gómez was welcomed in the island's top society and cheered by the lower classes. He was affectionately known as "Eighty-Eight" due to his habit of carrying a very large revolver and his propensity to fight duels over politics. He was educated in the United States and Europe, as well as in Cuba. Political life attracted him and he was elected to the House of Representatives in his early twenties. During the last part of Machado's administration he was elected mayor of Havana. He held office four years despite the fact he openly opposed Machado. His efficient and economical administration of the mayorship of Havana added to his popularity. Later he organized the Republican Party which together with the Nationalist and Liberal Parties elected him President.

A crowd of some 25,000 jammed the streets around the palace and Misiones Park and cheered the new president. His wife, Mrs. Serafina Diago de Gómez, one of the most beautiful women of Cuba, watched the ceremony from the balcony in the Salón of Mirrors, crowded with diplomats, officials of the government and friends.

That night the President read a six thousand word message to a joint session of the Senate and House of Representatives in the National Capitolio. He recommended broad social, economic and agricultural legislation, cited the need for an ample political amnesty and a solution of the Havana University problem. He urged re-establishment of Cuba's foreign credit and the reduction of administrative expenses and respect for personal civil rights.

The first note of the coming bitter conflict with Colonel Fulgencio Batista was contained in a paragraph of the message, which read, "The army's moral support of the Republic and its material and practical aid are necessary for the defence of the state against disorders and disturbances. But force alone is precarious if it is not animated and authorized by reason and justice, without which firm and permanent peace cannot exist."

Assured of the protection of the new government, exiles began to return to Cuba. First to arrive was Dr. Joaquin Martinez Saenz, head of the ABC and former Secretary of Treasury under Mendieta. A mass meeting of five thousand demanded that the Gómez administration approve an amnesty to clear the prisons of all political prisoners.

Among the problems facing the new administration was the financial condition of the government. Although revenue collections had improved, governmental expenditures were still running beyond its income. The public works bonds, forty million dollars of which were in the hands of Americans, were in default. Total indebtedness was estimated at $247,934,000. The Supreme Court upheld the validity of the public works loans, amounting to eighty million dollars. President Gómez asked Congress for a budget of seventy-three million dollars for the 1936-37 fiscal year and obtained approval to increase silver coinage of forty-eight million *pesos* by another twenty million.

The first clash of civil and military power occurred at the end of June when President Gómez, pressured by the tri-party coalition to provide jobs for party adherents, dismissed three thousand government employees. The majority of these were military reservists, out of the twenty thousand reserve corps created by Colonel Batista. The reaction of Batista was immediate, and in an order to the heads of all regiments he stated that the dismissed reserves should be given "every attention which they merit by reason of their valiant and efficient conduct." The Chief of Staff warned governmental departments that he viewed the dismissals with great displeasure. "At the risk of their lives and with great loyalty, these reserves defended the spirit of civilization and our national institutions."

Acting on a message from President Gómez, the Cuban

Congress approved an amnesty for fifteen hundred political
prisoners, excluding however officials of the Machado regime.
Death sentences were commuted and the sentences imposed
for sabotage reduced. The revolutionary groups were not
satisfied with this partial amnesty. They also claimed that
it failed to guarantee the safety of political exiles if they returned. *Joven Cuba,* operating underground, continued its
fight with the military authorities who had killed their former
leader, Antonio Guiteras, in 1935. To obtain funds they re-
sorted to extortion and kidnappings. The civil war in Spain
was beginning to have repercussions on the island. Nearly a
hundred young Cubans left Havana to fight on the side
of the Spanish Republicans. The Spaniards in Cuba were
sharply divided and numerous incidents occurred. Then came
the bombing of *El Pais,* a newspaper which the radicals
accused of being pro-Fascist. On Sunday morning, September 20th, a truck loaded with dynamite which the police
estimated at fifteen hundred pounds, was parked beside the
El Pais building on Galiano Street. At six-ten A.M., shortly
after the hundreds of newsboys had scattered through the
city with the morning edition, the explosion occurred, killing
four and wounding twenty-seven. It wrecked the whole side
of the two-story building, cracked the walls and damaged
the interior of the Monserrate Catholic Church on the opposite side of the street, wrenched off doors and shutters of
adjoining buildings and smashed plate glass windows in mer-
cantile establishments within a radius of six blocks.

A shocked Congress immediately re-established the death
penalty. The bill provided that terrorists, kidnappers and
gangsters condemned by the Urgency Courts would be executed by a firing squad within twenty-four hours after sentence was imposed. This was the measure favored by the
military authorities. However, President Gómez intervened
and the bill was amended to provide for appeals to the Supreme Court.

Among those arrested by the military authorities was a
member of the House of Representatives, José Grau Aguero.

The House approved a motion calling on President Gómez to order an investigation and protested "methods of police repression." President Gómez ordered the Secretary of Justice, Dr. Estanislao Cartaña to "investigate the mistreatment of Representative José Grau Aguero and other citizens while under arrest."

The seeds of the conflict between President Gómez, determined to restore the supremacy of civil power in Cuba, and Chief of Staff Colonel Fulgencio Batista had been sown as far back as the nomination of President Gómez. Colonel Batista, who has proved himself a master politician time and time again, used his powerful influence to see that nominations for representatives and senators in all the parties went to those whom he could consider his adherents. Thus when Congress convened Colonel Batista could look with satisfaction on both houses, whereas only a few representatives and senators were staunch supporters of President Gómez' desire to restore civil power. At the same time, Colonel Batista, to insure the loyalty of the armed forces, created an *esprit de corps* which bordered on insolence. At Camp Columbia new masonry barracks were built for the enlisted men. Recreation clubs for officers and men were built and new houses for officers and their families. The entire camp had been beautified and the house which Batista constructed for himself would be a luxurious residence in any district. New military hospitals, even military orphan homes were under construction. The armed forces received new airplanes, the most modern rifles, machine guns, artillery and enormous shipments of ammunition. While the Gómez administration struggled with its problems, Colonel Batista staged one of the greatest publicity campaigns of island history to popularize himself and the armed forces. An unending stream of propaganda, through radio, moving pictures, books, pamphlets and speeches, condemned radicalism and eulogized the efficiency of a military government.

Batista announced his own plan of social reform, which included special schools for the children of workers and farmers, medical attention, old age pensions, as well as public works to provide employment for the working classes. The Colonel's popularity with the agrarian and working classes in the interior improved steadily. The armed forces meanwhile assumed many functions of the Public Works, Health, Education, Labor and Interior Departments. Batista was on the way to forming an unbeatable political force.

The climax came over a bill approved by the Senate to tax each bag of sugar produced in the island nine cents. It was a bill prepared and introduced by a member of Congress allied to the military authorities. The revenue, which was estimated at $1,500,000 yearly, would support the civic-military schools. Batista had opened seven hundred of these schools in districts where educational facilities were practically nonexistent and planned to establish twenty-three hundred more.

President Gómez took the view that the armed forces should not interfere in education. Secretary to the President, Dr. Domingo Macias, said: "The President sees the possibility of Cuba's future sons being educated in a Fascist manner."

Colonel Batista rallied support for the bill. The Association of Sugar Producers of Cuba adopted a resolution supporting the measure. Farmers and workers staged demonstrations throughout the country hailing Batista as "The Savior of Cuba."

Carlos Hevia, former President, living in exile in New York, issued a statement declaring that Batista was trying deliberately to bring about a showdown with President Miguel Mariano Gómez, for the purpose of forcing him out of office. "A military oligarchy has ruled Cuba for two years," Hevia said. "President Gómez has had no real power, but Colonel Batista seems to want to attain openly the power he has had all the time behind the scenes."

Finanzas Comercial in Havana bluntly stated: "The days of the present government are numbered. The President has no support among the people, Congress or the press."

The bill levying the nine cent tax on each bag of raw sugar passed the House of Representatives by a vote of 106 to 43. The measure was delivered to the Presidential Palace for signature or veto by President Gómez. Meanwhile a secret session of the House of Representatives under tutelage of Batista had been called to formulate accusations against President Gómez preliminary to impeachment. The charges were: Action endangering the stability of the nation; violation of the Constitution; coercion of representatives.

President Gómez vetoed the sugar tax. He stated that he regarded it as "unconstitutional and aiming at militarization of the nation's childhood."

The House of Representatives approved a petition of accusations against President Gómez to bring him before the Senate in an impeachment trial. At four P.M. on December 22nd the impeachment trial of President Miguel Mariano Gómez began. It ended on December 24th with the following verdict: "Dr. Miguel Mariano Gómez y Arias, President of the Republic, is hereby declared guilty of transgression against the free functioning of the legislative power and is removed from the Presidency of the Republic."

President Gómez issued a manifesto to the Cuban people stating his impeachment was a victory for the military forces which were determined to control the country. He said it would have been better if Colonel Fulgencio Batista, the Chief of Staff, had openly entered the Presidential Palace. The quick impeachment and removal of President Gómez stunned the public. They were aware of the friction between the military authorities and President Gómez but they had not expected the President to be ousted.

Colonel Fulgencio Batista and his military cohorts had gambled and won. Thus Colonel Batista consolidated his control of the island, which he held until 1944, when he voluntarily relinquished the reins of power to his political enemy, Dr. Ramon Grau San Martin.

Immediately after the impeachment, a Senate committee advised the Vice-President, Federico Laredo Bru, that he was now President of the island. A large crowd gathered at the Presidential Palace and cheered former President Gómez and his family as they left for their home on the Prado Promenade. Gómez did not remain long in the big Prado mansion where he had spent so much of his life, but retired to his cattle ranch in Sancti Spiritus, of Las Villas Province. During the Laredo Bru administration, Dr. Gómez organized the Republican Party and tried to make a come back. He ran for mayor in 1940, but was defeated by Dr. Raul Menocal, Batista's candidate. He then retired from politics. On October 26, 1950, he suffered a head injury in a jeep accident on his ranch. He underwent an operation in New York City but never recovered and died there.

9

In a drizzling rain Colonel Laredo Bru arrived at the Presidential Palace in an automobile escorted by the mounted Presidential Guard. Two companies of marines were drawn up to receive him. The public, busy with last minute Christmas shopping and preparations for the *Noche Buena* fiesta, were uninterested in the incoming President.

The ceremony held in the Salón of Mirrors was drab in comparison with the brilliant enthusiastic inauguration of former President Miguel Mariano Gómez. Chief Justice Juan Fédérico Edelman administered the oath. Across the bay the guns of Cabañas Fortress fired the twenty-one gun salute and the army band in the palace patio played the national anthem. Another President was seated in the uneasy presidential chair.

Laredo Bru was sixty-one years old. He had been born in the town of Los Remedios in Las Villas Province. At the age of twenty he had joined the Cubans fighting for independence against Spain. In 1900 he had been appointed to his first public office, the secretaryship of the Audiencia Court of Las Villas Province. Later he became assistant prosecuting attorney of the Cuban Supreme Court and prosecutor of the Audiencia court of Havana in 1910. He served as Secretary of Interior in the cabinet of President

José Miguel Gómez, the father of the deposed Miguel Mariano Gómez. In 1913 he had retired from politics to practice law in Cienfuegos. During the Zayas administration Laredo Bru and General Calixto Garcia Velez had launched the "Veterans and Patriots Revolution of Cienfuegos" in protest against the irregularities of the government of President Zayas. Laredo Bru had served three weeks in the cabinet of President Manuel de Céspedes. He had been one of the founders of the Nationalist Party which elected Miguel Mariano Gómez. Tall, austere in appearance, with a dry sense of humor, President Laredo Bru was to play a passive part in the island's turbulent history. He was married to Eleonora Montes and they had no children.

President Laredo Bru showed his awareness of the situation. The Secretary of State, General Rafael Montalvo, a friend of Batista, was the only holdover from the Gómez cabinet. Dr. Juan J. Remos, director of Batista's Civic-Military Institute, was appointed Secretary of National Defense. Dr. Zenon Zamara, a major in the military reserve, was chosen as Secretary of Health. The Secretary of Agriculture was Amadeo Lopez, a close friend of Colonel Batista, destined to play a major role.

President Laredo Bru issued a proclamation to the nation stating, "The constitutional crisis has been solved and a new era opens for the nation." The people, long enured to violence and political change, paid little attention. Business and industry hoped that their labor problems would ease off. Foreign companies, striving to hold their technical personnel and finding it necessary to fire their American employees as the 50% nationalization labor law had been progressively tightened, were anxious to see this legislation eased. They hoped that Batista would be more amenable to their pleas. They were doomed to disappointment. Batista, desiring the support of island labor, watched passively as the labor laws were tightened until it became impossible for an American to obtain employment. American firms were highly indignant when they learned that the British government had inserted a clause in the trade treaty signed with Cuba, authorizing British firms to "employ a reasonable number of nationals." The American government had made no provision to protect American firms.

Two days after the inauguration of President Laredo Bru, Colonel Batista, announced the program of the new government.

"Two things are imperative," Colonel Batista said, "the calling of a constituent assembly and approval of the educational law, which will be done by the government with the magnificent and patriotic approval of Congress. With the administration and Congress identified with these two promising proposals and with the armed forces complying with and enforcing the laws, the people of Cuba are to be congratulated."

International Sports Week opened. Jesse Owens outran a race horse. Villanova and Auburn University football teams played a game at the Tropical Stadium; Columbia University defeated the Vedado baseball team; and the Miami Club basketball team was defeated by the Hispano Club of Havana. Miss Katherine Rawls of Miami Beach, Florida, broke the world breast stroke record. The Giants were invited to train in Havana. Havana University was made an autonomous institution, and students prohibited from engaging in political activity. The army took over control of the national lottery.

Colonel Batista, on July 25, 1937, announced his three-year plan for the economic and social reconstruction of Cuba. The program was so extensive that some wag dubbed it, "the three hundred-year plan." Every phase of life was to be regimented. The sugar and tobacco industries were to be brought under tighter control; a new currency system created; the workers were to receive insurance, payment for holidays, hospitalization, and other benefits. Forest conservation, water supply development, distribution of state lands, organization of agricultural production and consumption, establishment of marketing and consumer cooperatives, regulation of mining and oil production, a vast health program, creation of a merchant marine, reform of the tax system, and a solution of the moratorium situation, were a few of his proposals.

On August 5, 1937, a registration tax of from $1.40 to $5.00 was imposed on all foreigners. This was not a revenue tax, but a means of keeping tab on all foreigners, motivated by the rising nationalistic spirit. Ambassador Jefferson Caffrey, who left Cuba in January, did not return and in June, J. Butler Wright was appointed Ambassador to Cuba. Wright came to Cuba from Czechoslovakia where he had served as Minister for three years.

The situation in Cuba was sufficiently quiet that Phil thought we could take a vacation. He wished to visit his parents in Los Angeles.

We took the ferry to Miami and then drove to California, having picked up our small daughter, Marta, and my sister, Irma, in Oklahoma. We spent a couple of weeks in Los Angeles and then started home. Early in the morning on August 23, 1937 we left Pomona, California, a small town just outside Los Angeles, having breakfasted there. A truck driver, who had driven all night and was dozing, turned straight into the path of our car. It was a four-lane highway and only two vehicles on the road. Our car turned over three times. My sister, who never lost consciousness, pulled me out from underneath the dashboard. I regained consciousness. I saw that Phil was lying in the road, unmoving. He was dead. Marta had been thrown just beyond him. She was gravely injured, having a broken leg and a six-inch skull fracture. The hospital at Pomona reported that she was dying when she was brought in. However, after months of suffering, she recovered.

The New York Times asked me to take over the position as correspondent in Cuba. I left Los Angeles after it had become certain that Marta would recover, and after my mother had arrived from Oklahoma to stay with her.

Phil had been widely known as the *Times* correspondent.

Added to that, he was one of those rare people with a real zest for living. I received cables from former Presidents, government officials, Cuban and American businessmen, and others who had been his friends. The worker who swept the street in front of our house in Vedado came to the house to present his condolences. It was difficult to come back to the same office where Phil and I had worked together so long and to take up the news coverage where he had left it. The presence of my sister, Irma, who abandoned her ballet studio in Oklahoma City, and of her husband, Gene Carrier, helped a great deal. I was given every consideration by the Cuban government as well as all our American and Cuban friends.

When Marta was able to travel I brought her to Havana. Several months later, my parents closed their home in Oklahoma City and came to live with us in Havana.

The anger of the students over failure of Congress to approve a political amnesty flared into open rioting in November. Six hundred students appeared at the Senate session and when that body, fearing trouble, suspended the session, the boys expressed their displeasure by rolling cuspidors down the marble stairs, breaking windows, and shouting criticism of the nation's lawmakers.

Finally, just before Christmas, Congress approved a general political amnesty. Offenders of various administrations, including former President General Gerardo Machado, whom the Cuban government had been trying to extradite from the United States, were included. Machado was desperately ill with cancer in Florida at the time. On March 29, 1938, he died. Also included was Machado's Secretary of Interior, Octavio Zubizarreta, who was in Cabañas Fortress under death sentence. President Laredo Bru signed the bill immediately. The amnesty was the most sweeping in the history of the nation, and by clearing the prisons Colonel Batista removed from the hands of the opposition a weapon of popular appeal.

After months of dickering with the American bondholders,

the Cuban government recognized the debt incurred by the Machado regime and made a new issue of eighty-five million dollars for its payment. The Manufacturers Trust Company of New York was appointed agent.

Elections for eighty-one members of the House of Representatives were approaching. People regarded the matter with extreme indifference. The Liberal and Nationalist parties, and the Democratic Party, had split into many factions. Only two important political leaders in Cuba had stayed off the Batista bandwagon—Mario G. Menocal and Miguel Mariano Gómez. When election day arrived on March 5, 1938, all the parties supported Batista so that there was really only the minor issue of local personalities. Less than half the voters went to the polls. In Havana only 20% voted. Hardly had the polls closed when Batista announced the breaking up of a revolutionary plot. Four men were killed in a clash with soldiers at Camarones, near Cabañas Fortress. Batista claimed that an attempt had been made to persuade high officials of the army and navy to revolt. He accused Dr. Guillermo Belt, former mayor of Havana, Dr. Alfredo Pequeño, a leader of the ABC, and Eduardo Martin, a lawyer, of planning the revolt. Also accused were Dr. Cosme de la Torriente, Communist leader Juan Marinello, Senator Octavio Rivero Partagas, Augusto Cuervo Rubio, and Dr. Alejandro Vargara, leader of the Agrarian Party. Batista declared that the American Embassy was involved in the conspiracy.

Ambassador J. Butler Wright indignantly denied this charge. "It is in our interest that Cuba enjoy complete tranquility and prosperity."

On March 27th, Batista distributed the first state lands to tenant farmers in Pinar del Rio Province. Two hundred fifty farmers each received fifty acres.

One month later Colonel Batista announced the suspension of his three-year plan until a constituent assembly could be chosen and draw up a new constitution. In a dramatic and unexpected statement, the strong man of the island told the people that he was sacrificing his plans for social and economic reconstruction of the Republic because of the clamor for a constituent assembly.

On May 4th four unidentified men kidnapped Felipe Rivero, publisher of the weekly magazine, *Jorobemos,* took him to the outskirts of Havana, and forced him to drink a large bottle of castor oil. *Jorobemos* had criticized the administration. *La Prensa,* official organ of the Republican Party, was closed by military authorities on September 1st. No explanation was given. But on the previous day *La Prensa* had stated that Colonel Batista planned to dissolve Congress and set up a provisional government. The Senate approved a motion to protest the closing of *La Prensa.* On September 9th President Laredo Bru signed a decree setting up legal procedure for closing *any* publication.

The history of the Communist Party in Cuba began in the twenties. The first small organization appeared in the town of Manzanillo, Oriente Province. In 1925 the Machado regime outlawed the party. The party, an underground organization, gained strength rapidly. Communists organized island labor into unions and then created the Confederation of Cuban Workers. Before long every labor organization in the island was in the hands of the Communists. Now the party applied for registration in order to participate in the constituent assembly. It was granted and the Communists were launched on a career which was to play a major role in Cuban affairs during the coming years.

Washington invited Batista to attend the Armistic Day ceremonies as a guest of the War Department. He accepted the invitation. Colonel Batista went sightseeing in Washington, attended, with President Roosevelt, the Armistice Day ceremonies at Arlington, and reviewed the West Point cadets. Snow fell in the North, the first snow Colonel Batista had ever seen.

Batista returned home to receive a huge welcome. As the Cruiser Cuba sailed past Morro Castle, the guns of Cabañas Fortress fired a salute. A crowd estimated at from fifty to seventy-five thousand lined the waterfront and jammed the streets up to the Presidential Palace. Despite the overcast sky, Havana wore a festive air with colored electric lights, flags and banners decorating the city. Disembarking at Caballeria Wharf, Colonel Batista was met by political leaders and high army and navy officers. He walked the several blocks to the Presidential Palace between long lines of police, soldiers and marines. President Laredo Bru, the cabinet and other high government officials were waiting to welcome the Colonel. From the palace balcony Batista reviewed a military parade of four regiments of the army, units of the marines, police, reserve corps, firemen, veterans, school children, representatives of labor, industry, agriculture and commerce. Banks and commercial and industrial establishments closed at noon and the President decreed a holiday for government employees. Batista told the people, over a national radio hookup, that the reciprocity treaty between Cuba and the United States would be modified in favor of certain Cuban products. He hinted that financial assistance would be given Cuba by the United States and that there would be military cooperation between the two countries. He said he had assured President Roosevelt that Cuba would not become a victim of totalitarian influences.

In an interview the following day, Batista explained that an oral agreement had been reached in Washington for reduction of the tariff on Cuban sugar entering the United States. In return Cuba would throw open her market to Louisiana rice and other North American products, manufactured and agricultural.

In February, 1939, Colonel Batista made a trip to Mexico to visit President Lazaro Cardenas. Commerce and industry openly disapproved of this visit since they looked on the Mexican President as being radical. On Batista's return President Laredo Bru decreed a holiday. This time, only labor gathered to cheer Batista, as he spoke from the balcony of the palace, praising President Lazaro Cardenas of Mexico as a "leader of democracy." Batista then promised labor to heed its demands. "Capital should not fear the spoliation of property, but if it does not wish to respect the desires and rights of the people, the resulting confusion will work against its own aspirations."

Congress approved a law on March 16th reducing rents to the level of July 1, 1937, and granting tax exemptions for from five to ten years to owners of newly constructed houses. Boarding houses were also ordered to cut their rates 25%. The law provided that water taxes would be reduced one-third to compensate for rent reductions. In Cuba, according to the old Spanish law, the landlord is forced to furnish water for his tenants without charge. There are no meters and the size of the pipe determines the water tax. To deny a tenant water is a criminal offense.

Former President Miguel Mariano Gómez opened the campaign of his Republican Party to elect delegates to the constituent assembly. In a radio address, Gómez placed the responsibility for the island's economic crisis and political confusion upon the shoulders of Colonel Batista and declared that the only remedy was in the restoration of civil power. He said Batista's three-year plan was "a fantastic panacea for our ills." He strongly approved the new electoral code. But he warned the people that a constituent assembly would be useless unless the election of delegates was carried out in an atmosphere of confidence and an attitude of impartiality.

President Laredo Bru vetoed the electoral code. Batista then recommended modification of the code to prevent a conflict between elections of the constituent assembly set for August 30th and general elections set for February 15, 1940. He pointed out that the two elections were too close together. The first indication that Batista might like to sit in the presidential chair was contained in this same statement, in which, in response to criticism by the opposition parties, he said: "If it is necessary for me to become President, I shall enter the campaign on an equal basis with other candidates and shall expect to win only by the vote of the people."

Fulgencio Batista, like many who seize and hold power by force of arms, wanted to believe he was popular with the people. Until the very last, when he finally fled the island, I am sure that Batista believed the majority of the people supported him and only a minority hated him. While he enjoyed power and its trappings—armored automobiles with many bodyguards, the roar of the saluting guns of his armed forces, the deference of foreign diplomats—Batista tried to put a "democratic face" on his regime and talked constantly of democracy. He once remarked, when he became irritated about the foreign press calling him a dictator, that at least he was a "democratic dictator."

Batista strove, not without some success, to overcome his lack of formal education, to learn how to fill efficiently the position he had created. He secretly employed instructors to teach him, his wife and children, in the social graces and faithfully followed the dictates of the long experienced members of his State Department. He read books of all kinds and at one time was an admirer of Mussolini.

The dark, good-looking Colonel was *simpatico,* an untranslatable Spanish word which means charming, personable, and having other attractive qualities. He fascinated all visitors, especially Americans. Even his enemies had to admit that the former sergeant was the outstanding personality in Cuba.

Just as Batista neared the presidential chair, there was a wave of divorces among the officers of his armed forces and his civilian officials. Machado had approved a divorce law designed to make Havana the second Las Vegas for Americans. Few Americans ever took advantage of this legislation. Ironically, Cubans began to see advantages in divorce. Hundreds of marriages were dissolved and new marriages contracted. This propensity for divorce has continued in Cuba and despite all the efforts of the Catholic Church, divorce has become an accepted institution. Even Batista and his wife Elisa were divorced in 1944, and he married his present wife, Martha, whom he met when he ran into her with his car as she was riding a bicycle along Fifth Avenue in Miramar suburb.

A few years ago when his oldest daughter, Mirta, decided to divorce her husband, Batista violently opposed the idea. Mirta told him the Spanish equivalent of, "Look who's talking," and went ahead with her plans. When she later married a young doctor at Batista's fabulous country estate *Kuquine* Batista, then President, refused to attend the wedding. Batista ruled Cuba with an iron hand but he had little success in ruling his eldest daughter, Mirta, and his eldest son, Fulgencio, or *Papo* as he was known.

The war clouds on the European horizon, to which Cuba had paid little attention, began to darken. Cubans suddenly became aware that the stream of Jewish refugees, who had been entering the island for several years, was becoming a flood. Sentiment against the entry of more refugees mounted rapidly. Secretary of Labor Juan Domenech Portuondo publicly advocated stoppage of all immigration. President Laredo Bru decreed that refugees must obtain authorization from the Departments of State, Labor and Treasury prior to embarking for Cuba. Steamship companies were made responsible for the expense of quartering and re-embarking passengers to whom permission to land might be refused.

Then came the famous case of the *S. S. St. Louis*, which arrived on May 27th, with 937 Jewish refugees. Authorities permitted twenty-nine to land but refused permission for the others, on the grounds their visas were not in order. A pressure campaign was launched by the American Jewish Relief Organization to persuade Cuba to accept these refugees. Lawyers and relatives of the refugees appeared overnight in Havana to present pleas. One refugee attempted to commit suicide by jumping into the bay, but he was picked up by a launch. Captain Gustav Shroeder of the *St. Louis* informed Cuban authorities he feared a wave of suicides, unless the refugees were permitted to land. However, President Laredo Bru was adamant. He ordered the *St. Louis* to depart immediately. The vessel sailed with the despairing refugees, while friends and relatives watched from the dock and the Malecón Sea Drive.

The *St. Louis* was reportedly lying off the Florida coast, when finally the Cuban government expressed willingness to consider a plan to permit the Jewish refugees to disembark in Cuba and remain in a provisional camp, until they could be re-embarked for another destination. But a bond of five hundred dollars must be posted for each refugee.

On June 6th the Secretary of Treasury, Joaquin Ochotorena, announced that since the bonds had not been posted by the Jewish relief committees, Cuba had decided not to admit the *St. Louis* refugees. The *St. Louis* set a course for home and the incident was closed.

However, during the next few years Cuba was to admit thousands of Jewish refugees. The Jewish Relief Organization of the United States poured money into Cuba to help the needy ones. Some few remained here, but almost all waited impatiently while the overworked American Embassy visa section strove to clear them for entry into the United States.

Cuba had never had a currency system. Only coins, forty cent pieces, twenty cent pieces known as *pesetas*, dimes known as *reales*, and nickels circulated. The Machado regime in 1929 had begun to issue silver certificates. Cuban coinage and certificates by 1939 reached ninety million dollars, as the various administrations issued more certificates. These certificates were valueless outside Cuba, but were legal tender in the island. Naturally, United States currency continued to be legal tender and the currency in which international transactions had to be carried out. The economic crisis caused the Cuban money to drop in value. To counteract this, President Laredo Bru created a stabilization fund to prevent fluctuation of the Cuban silver *peso*. The decree ordered all sugar exporters to deliver 20% of the price obtained for sugar to the Cuban treasury in American currency and receive in return this amount in Cuban silver certificates. Exporters of other products were ordered to exchange 10% of the purchase price of products sold. In September, when war broke out in Europe, the President raised the percentages to 30% and 15% respectively.

On September 9th Cuba took the first step to protect the shipping of the Allied countries. President Laredo Bru signed a decree prohibiting radio stations from broadcasting news concerning the movement of ships entering or leaving Cuban harbors. Already there were reports of the presence of German submarines in the Caribbean.

After the long lean years of the thirties, Cuba looked hopefully at the war in Europe and envisioned a wave of prosperity with the rising demand for sugar. However, two months after war broke out, the sugar industry and the government were still hesitating about whether to restrict the crop or to grind a free crop. Most of the demands for a free crop were political in origin since the industry hesitated to invest money in sugar which might be left on its hands. Expectations of a quick heavy demand for sugar had not been realized. The United States on September 11th suspended the sugar quota system under which Cuba had been marketing her sugar in the United States. This brought an automatic increase in the tariff from ninety cents to $1.50 per hundredweight. The sugar industry regarded the situation with gloom. The 1939 sugar crop had been fixed at 2,696,517 long tons and there was sufficient cane in the fields to produce 25% more in 1940 if a free crop was decreed.

Elections for delegates to the constituent assembly, which was to draw up Cuba's new constitution, were held on November 15, 1939. Voters were faced with a list of 916 candidates from which they were to elect seventy-six delegates. Four days later, on Sunday, I told Raul, my assistant, to go to the Superior Electoral Tribunal. He returned with a list of most of the precincts of the island. After considerable calculation, I was surprised to see that Batista's candidates had lost. The opposition had won forty-one delegates to the government's thirty-five. This story appeared on the front page of the *New York Times*.

The reaction from the local press and even the foreign news services was a unanimous cry that I was mistaken. Sr. Arroyo Maldonado, a Cuban employee of the Associated Press, told the local press on Monday morning that I was in error. It took the news services two days to acknowledge the truth. The opposition had won the constituent assembly elections. The victory of the opposition brought to the fore the old question of military versus civil power. The oppositionists hoped they would be able to return the army to its barracks and eliminate its interference in governmental affairs. Colonel Batista was determined this should not happen. He was bitterly disappointed by the results of the elections.

The Second Inter-American Labor Conference opened in Havana on December 1st. Delegates from all the American countries were present. John G. Winant, director of the ILO, was Secretary General of the conference. Cuba went into the conference as one of the nations with the most advanced labor legislation in Latin America. During the period from 1933 on, Cuba had enacted a mass of social legislation, including the eight-hour day, minimum wages, maternity tax and workmen's accident liability. Also, paid vacations had been established, and pensions in almost every industry and commercial establishment. Backed by such legislation, the labor unions, dominated by the Communists, had become the most powerful group in the island.

The conference was held in the auditorium of the Ministry of Education in old Havana near the waterfront. The Communists, represented by Vicente Lombardo Toledano, workers' delegate from Mexico, and Lazaro Peña, Cuban delegate, launched various attacks on the United States, urged the Latin American countries to refuse to contribute to continuation of the European conflict by furnishing supplies. Toledano declared the "Good Neighbor Policy was dead," and called on the workers to support the "peace policies of the Soviet Union." Russia had made a pact with Germany and had not yet become involved in the European conflict. James B. Carey, secretary of the Congress of Industrial Organization (CIO) of the United States, told a cheering group of workers in Havana that one of the principal aims of the CIO was to keep out of the European conflict. Neither he, nor Kathryn Lewis, daughter of John L. Lewis, who sat on the platform, listening to the attacks on the United States, said one word in defense of their country.

Finally the Declaration of Havana was approved. In this document, the delegates proclaimed their "unshaken faith in the promotion of international cooperation and in the imperative need for achieving international peace and security by the elimination of war as an instrument of national policy."

On December 6th Colonel Fulgencio Batista retired from the position of Chief of Staff of the Cuban army to run for President in the coming election. Colonel José Pedraza, Chief of the National Police and Inspector General of the army, took over command. The government political parties— Nationalist, Liberal, National Democrat and Communist— held conventions and nominated the Colonel as a coalition candidate. Most of the Colonel's staff followed him into retirement. Major Jaime Marine, who was promoted to Lieutenant Colonel before leaving the army, his bodyguards, publicity men, secretaries, photographers and servants moved over to the campaign headquarters established in Vedado suburb to help him in one of the most elaborate campaigns ever staged by a presidential candidate in the island.

Colonel Batista announced his platform. It contained all the points of his famous three-year plan for the economic and social reconstruction of the island, which he had launched in 1937. In addition, he pledged the maintenance of the sovereignty of the nation and strict neutrality. He also proposed to reorganize the tax system, stabilize the Cuban *peso* on a par with the American dollar, regulate the operations of banks, insurance companies and corporations, to create a national bank and to liquidate the floating indebtedness.

Elections were again postponed to July 14th by agreement between the government and the opposition parties. This was to give the constituent assembly sufficient time to draw up a new constitution before the elections took place. Former President Ramon Grau San Martin was elected to preside over the Assembly. On January 15th President Federico Laredo Bru signed a decree fixing the 1940 sugar crop at 2,753,903 long tons. Cuban sugar continued under control.

The Confederation of Cuban Workers had during the past year managed to organize the sugar workers into a Federation of Sugar Mill Workers. Now they demanded labor contracts and a 25% wage increase. The workers of sixty large printing firms in Havana struck for higher wages and textile workers also walked out. Employees of moving picture theaters struck. Everyone wanted higher wages. Cuba lost her largest cigar market. Great Britain banned cigars as a luxury not required in wartime. Out of twenty-seven cigar factories in Cuba, eighteen had been selling their production to Great Britain. It was a serious economic blow.

Ever since 1933 members of the former Machado government had been assassinated by groups who were still on a vengeance vendetta. Most of the victims had been relatively unknown figures. Little attention was paid either by the government or military authorities. However, on March 1st, Dr. Orestes Ferrara, former Ambassador to Washington and Secretary of State, was gravely wounded in midtown Havana. The driver of the taxi in which Ferrara was riding was killed instantly. The police said the assailants fired from an automobile with a sawed-off shotgun. His bodyguard, Miguel Balmaseda, had been murdered the previous November in front of Ferrara's home. Three days after Ferrara was wounded, the police killed Carlos Marti Borgus, of the National Police during the Grau San Martin regime, and wounded his seventeen-year-old brother-in-law. Police said Marti opened fire on them when they tried to arrest him as a suspect in the Ferrara shooting. A protest was immediately presented to the constituent assembly and the university students called a twenty-four hour strike in protest of the killing of Marti.

The Democratic Party decided to support Colonel Batista in the presidential race. The backing of the conservative element of Menocal improved Batista's already powerful position. The opposition was thrown into confusion by the Menocal-Batista deal. Former President Grau San Martin resigned as president of the constituent assembly. The remaining opposition parties, the Cuban Revolutionary Party (*Autenticos*), the ABC and the Republican Party, became the minority.

These three groups nominated Dr. Ramon Grau San Martin for president on March 18th.

As the war accelerated in Europe, a Nazi propaganda campaign got under way in Cuba to discredit the cause of the Allies and arouse suspicion toward the policy of the United States in Latin America. Every media of propaganda was utilized, radical publications and radio programs. Advantage was taken of the alliance between Germany and Russia. The Communists disseminated German propaganda as well as their own. The Nazi propaganda fell on a fertile field. Cuba was already divided. There were thousands of fascist-minded Spaniards in Cuba who had been followers of General Francisco Franco and were sympathetic toward Germany. The Communists were eager to help in the campaign as a means of diffusing anti-American propaganda, which was to become their major campaign in Latin America. On May 13th President Laredo Bru issued a neutrality proclamation. However on May 23rd Colonel Batista pledged Cuba's aid to the United States in case of war. "Cuba desires peace and hopes to maintain her neutrality," he said, "but the United States can count on us as a factor in its plans for the defense of the Caribbean." Then on May 24th President

Laredo Bru issued a decree barring Nazi and Communist propaganda.

At last the Cuban Constitution was completed by the assembly, changing the government to a semi-parliamentary form. The new constitution contained 318 articles. Business and capital were not at all satisfied, and termed it a group of codes rather than a basic charter under which the Republic could be governed. One of the most extensive sections embodied all the labor legislation up to that time, providing for supplementary laws to strengthen the rights of the workers. A moratorium was written into the constitution, despite protests of capital. This was to be the subject of controversy for years to come.

The Cuban people were ready to go to the polls. Colonel Batista had staged the most extensive and expensive campaign in the history of the Republic. Thousands of printed circulars, pamphlets, photographs, novelties, banners, electric signs, posters, sound trucks, moving pictures, campaign songs, speeches on the radio, telephone calls and other propaganda devices were utilized. Colonel Batista toured the island aboard a special train known as the "Train of Victory," making speeches in every town and village. Grau San Martin, lacking funds for an elaborate campaign, relied upon radio speeches, the personal work of his adherents, and his tours of the island during which it was claimed that his followers actually paid their own expenses.

The campaign ended on July 13th. 25,394 candidates were running for 2,342 offices. The battle was of course between Batista and Ramon Grau San Martin. Reinaldo Marquez, candidate of the small National Agrarian Party, was practically disregarded by the voters. It was a battle of personalities rather than platforms, as usual. Military headquarters ordered troops into quarters at midnight the day before elections. Eighteen hundred police armed with rifles were on duty in Havana. In the interior soldiers and marines took over the task of maintaining order. The sale of alcoholic drinks was suspended.

Polling was comparatively orderly. Only six persons were killed and forty wounded during the day. The opposition parties protested that the soldiers took an undue interest in the polling in various parts of the island. However, the elections, on the whole, were impartial and fair according to the best observers. Colonel Batista won in a sweeping triumph. He carried his entire party to victory both in the Senate and House of Representatives. In Havana, Raul Menocal, the government coalition candidate, won over former President Miguel Mariano Gómez. The majority of the people of the island favored Colonel Batista. There was no doubt of it.

Meanwhile, the war in Europe gave the Pan-American Union a new meaning. All the countries of the Americas, with the exception of Canada, which was already involved, wanted to be neutral. At the same time they wanted to sell as many of their products as possible. The closing of the normal European markets by the British blockade and by the exigencies of emergency finance was crushing the raw material producers of the Western Hemisphere. The United States, seeing war ahead, wanted the cooperation of Latin America to suppress fifth column activities, to supply the United States with raw materials, to take over part of the burden of defending the Western Hemisphere, and to reach an agreement concerning European possessions in this hemisphere. The United States was willing to extend economic cooperation, but was unwilling to be tied down to an exact formula. Thus the stage was set for the conference that was to weld the American nations into a bloc. The Pan-American Conference of Foreign Ministers opened in Havana on July 21, 1940. Cuba welcomed United States Secretary of State, Cordell Hull, father of the Good Neighbor Policy. The inaugural session of the conference was held in the House of Representatives' Chamber in the huge white National Capitolio. A detachment of soldiers was drawn up along the Prado and a double file guard of honor on the Capitolio steps, which were covered with an enormous red carpet. As the delegates mounted the steps, the guards pre-

sented arms. Inside the chamber, the delegates were seated
at desks. The galleries were crowded to capacity. President
Laredo Bru and his cabinet were dressed in white linen suits.
Tall, grey-haired Cordell Hull, dressed in a dark blue business suit, was given an ovation by the delegates and the
galleries. Mrs. Hull, attired in dark blue, with a white hat, sat
in an upper box.

One of the *Times* Washington correspondents, Harold
Hinton, was sent to Havana for the conference. He was a
close friend of Cordell Hull and he reported the conference
from the viewpoint of the American delegation. Harold was
a charming, likeable man, pleasant to work with. He was
such an admirer of the Secretary of State that sometimes to
annoy him when we were discussing politics I would ask,
"Who is talking, Cordell Hull or Harold Hinton?"

Evelio Rodriguez was covering the conference for his
newspaper and helped me a great deal with the Latin American delegations. One day I spoke to him about a controversial
resolution which was being approved that afternoon by one
of the committees. There was always a considerable delay
before the resolutions were released to the press. Evelio
thought he could arrange to get a copy, and several hours
later he brought me several sheets of new carbon paper
which had been the ones used to write the final resolution
which the committee had approved. I took it off the carbon
with only a little trouble, using a mirror. And two hours later
the Argentine delegate decided to release the resolution to
the press! It was July and hot—hot even for the Cubans. The
temper of the delegates flared and there were angry discussions. Argentina struck the main controversial notes, as
usual. It was several days before agreement was reached
on any of the more important issues. In the Havana Declaration, the American Republics decided to take over and administer territories held by European countries in any case
of an attempt to transfer control of such lands. Suppression
of fifth column activities was approved. The United States
agreed to set up commodity marketing rules, including loans

to producers. In regard to defense measures, the conference left this to be worked out by military agreements between the United States and each individual country. None of the Latin American countries was willing to take up the matter of concerted action to repel invasion. They were all continuing to dream of neutrality. However, the threat of being involved in the European war was sufficient to give the Pan-American Union more solidarity than it had ever had previously. For the first time in history, the American nations had been able to reach a unanimous decision of political importance.

The Declaration of Havana in reality was a substitute for the Monroe Doctrine, and an improvement, since *all* the American nations were pledged to defend any portion of the American continents which might be in danger of seizure by a European power. The declaration set up machinery to take over, under a collective administration, any European possession in the Western Hemisphere threatened with a transfer to another non-American power.

III Batista in Power

10

Colonel Fulgencio Batista was sworn in as president on October 10, a national holiday known as the *Grito de Yara*. Flags and banners decorated the midtown section of Havana. Commercial and industrial activities were suspended. Despite a drizzling rain, thousands jammed Misiones Park. Special police detachments were thrown about the palace and guarded the route over which the President-elect traveled.

Just before noon the automobile occupied by Colonel Batista approached the palace. The crowd cheered and shouted. The dark handsome face of the Colonel was wreathed in smiles. He had achieved his greatest ambition—to rule as a constitutional President. He, an uneducated man, a man of no wealth or consequential family background, had not only outmaneuvered all his political competitors, but had won the approval of the majority of the Cuban people. This is one of the great ironies of modern political history, not only in Cuba, but throughout the world. Batista rose to power and retained power through the military, but it was his personality that made his iron fist somehow more acceptable to the Cuban people than Machado's had been.

In the Salón of Mirrors Batista took the oath of office, administered by the Chief Justice of the Supreme Court, Dr.

Juan Federico Edelman, who had sworn in so many Presidents during the past ten years. "I swear to fulfill faithfully the duties of the office of President of the Republic, complying with and enforcing the Constitution and the laws," Batista declared.

A battery of artillery near the palace fired a salute. The palace and military bands played the national anthem. Señora de Batista watched the ceremony from a balcony of the Salón of Mirrors. The new President immediately stepped out on the palace balcony to address the cheering crowd. His words asking cooperation of all the people were carried throughout the island over a radio hookup. Later in the day the President spoke over the RHC-Cuban chain and the Columbia Broadcasting System in the United States. He greeted the American people, declared continental solidarity had been achieved, and urged closer economic cooperation. "The close relationship between international security and the normal economic development of our democratic peoples demands that Americanism cease to be a concept of protocol and become an understanding of economic, social and political need."

President Batista's cabinet was drawn from five of the seven parties which formed the Socialist-Democratic coalition. The Communist Party and the small Popular Party failed to obtain posts. He appointed Senator Carlos Saladrigas, a close friend and former head of the ABC revolutionary group, as Premier.

Cuba's budget for 1941 was fixed at $83,986,959 by President Batista. However, Congress failed to approve the budget. For some reason no budget was ever approved by Congress during Batista's term of office and the President simply signed decrees allotting money for government expenses.

Under leadership of the Secretary General of the Confederation of Cuban Workers, frog-voiced Lazaro Peña, a Communist, twenty-five thousand workers marched to the Presidential Palace, demanding that the confederation be granted

a legal charter. The marchers carried placards condemning
the imperialistic war. The Communist Party had expected to
obtain recognition of the confederation immediately after
Batista became President. The confederation was already
affiliated with the Latin American Federation of Workers
headed by the Communist Vicente Lombardo Toledano of
Mexico City.

Although the war in Europe was more than a year old,
there had been no great increase in the demand for sugar.
Now the sugar grinding season, always beginning in January,
was approaching. With the European market closed, and
some million tons of sugar already on hand, producers
wanted to reduce the crop to about two million tons, one-
third less than the year previous. At the same time, the producers wanted the United States government to finance an
extra 500,000 tons over the basic crop. The matter was under
discussion with the Export-Import Bank in Washington.
Meanwhile, the industry itself had internal difficulties. Small
mill owners were demanding a larger grinding quota. American-owned mills, which had ground 65% of the annual production for many years, wanted to continue their assign-
ments. The producers wanted to reduce wages since the
price of sugar had declined, in accordance with a law approved the year previous that pegged wages to the price of
sugar. But the sugar mill workers threatened to strike and
not work the harvest unless they received the same wages as
the year previous. President Batista signed a decree on January 18, 1941, fixing the wages at the same level as the previous year.

At the end of March the Export-Import Bank of Washington loaned Cuba eleven million dollars with which to
produce an additional 400,000 tons of sugar.

On January 29, 1941, Batista ordered suppression of all
totalitarian propaganda in Cuba. The Communist Party,
which had supported Batista for President, was exempt from
this order, so that the measure really referred to propaganda
by the Germans, Italians or Spanish Fascists. Propaganda

agents were ordered arrested and legal machinery created for the deportation of foreigners convicted of such activities.

The Cuban tourist season opened but with the war in Europe, which was already causing great uneasiness in the United States, tourist traffic began to decline. This was to be the last tourist season for several years.

In February, four months after President Batista had taken office, an incident occurred which showed that the Chief Executive, although sitting in the presidential chair, was still the island's strongman. Reports of dissention between the President and Colonel José Pedraza, Chief of Staff of the Army, had circulated for several days in Havana. Then on the night of February 3rd the climax was reached. According to the President the difficulty had been precipitated by his action in returning to civil authority certain departments, including port police, fishing and lighthouses, and by his dismissal of the Chief of Police, Bernardo Garcia. "This," Batista said, "provoked an attitude of sedition on the part of the chiefs of the army and navy, which I was forced energetically to curb, and to take over the command of the armed forces." According to other reports, Colonel Pedraza and Colonel Angel A. Gonzalez, Chief of Staff of the Navy, had decided to depose the President and take control of the island.

On the night of February 3rd the Presidential Palace guard was reinforced, sandbags placed at entrances and machine guns mounted. Reporters were ordered out of the Presidential Palace. President Batista, dressed in a leather jacket, dark trousers and a white shirt open at the throat, left the palace in company with Colonels Manuel Benitez and Galindez for Camp Columbia Military Headquarters. Upon arrival there, Batista called together the colonels, members of the group so long in control of the island, and demanded a pledge of loyalty from them. All of them supported him. Both Pedraza and Gonzalez were forced to resign and were placed under arrest. They left Havana for Miami the next day together with their wives and aides.

President Batista then appointed Colonel Manuel Lopez Migoya, as Chief of Staff, Colonel Manuel Benitez, Chief of National Police, and Lieutenant Colonel Jesus Gomez Casas, Chief of Staff of the Navy. The next day the President told the public that the officers removed had tried to make him a "puppet President."

On May 27th President Roosevelt made a speech which was termed the "last call" to the Americas for a joint defense of democracy. Cubans gathered in public places to hear the address which was translated into Spanish by local radio stations.

Batista's entire cabinet resigned as a result of friction between the Cabinet and Congress over patronage in the various departments. Three weeks later a Senate meeting ended in numerous fist fights. The controversy started when the opposition demanded the Senate approve a resolution asking the government for an explanation of the closing down of the *Voz del Aire* Radio Station. Several senators were sent to the hospital.

The fist fights surprised me, since the custom is to challenge one's adversary to a duel. Dueling is prohibited by law in Cuba, but that had never previously prevented members of Congress, newspapermen and politicians from defending their honor with swords or pistols. The duels were usually held at a country estate near Havana. The news of the duels always appeared on the front pages of the local newspapers, telling the names of the seconds and cause of the quarrel. The newspaper reports always stated that the loser of the duel had been "wounded while examining the weapons."

In the National Capitolio was a big room where the senators and representatives practiced fencing. With its high windows, its medieval décor and display of foils, it had the atmosphere of an old castle. However, adjoining this room were modern showers, lockers and dressing rooms for the fencers. This part of the Capitolio, which few Americans ever knew existed, was in charge of Professor José Maria Rivas, who presided over hundreds of duels. Two men were fenc-

ing the day I visited. I stayed to watch the skill and grace of
the art which fascinates me. Set to music it would be ballet.
Except that I cannot forget that it was once a deadly art.

The Cuban government opened negotiations through
diplomatic channels with the United States seeking "a satis-
factory solution to the grave situation" facing Cuba's sugar
industry as a result of the price ceiling fixed on raw sugar by
the Office of Price Administration of the United States. The
sugar industry denounced the price as "totally unfair." Food
began to skyrocket in price. President Batista on August 16th
signed a decree fixing a maximum profit of 10% for wholesalers and 20% for retailers. He also set up a commission to
control the importation into Cuba of all products subject to
priorities in the United States. Batista next obtained authorization from Congress to borrow twenty-five million dollars
from the Export-Import Bank in Washington for public
works, agricultural development and other projects.

On November 5th negotiations were opened for the purchase of Cuba's entire 1942 sugar crop by the United States
and Great Britain. The sugar industry was favorable to the
sale, but wanted more money than the ceiling price imposed
by the United States. Cane planters were highly dissatisfied.
They said that not more than 3,400,000 long tons could be
produced in 1942 owing to past restrictions, which had prevented any new cane plantings. They believed they would
get a better price by selling to various buyers.

December 7, 1941 was a mourning day in Cuba, com-
memorating the death of General Antonio Maceo and other
heroes of the struggle for independence.

The equestrian statue of General Maceo, in Maceo Park on
the Malecón Sea Drive, has always been my favorite. The
rearing bronze horse with the General astride it has only its
two back hoofs on the pedestal, but it is so perfectly
balanced that the statue has withstood hurricane winds of
160 miles per hour. My father listens to news broadcasts from
the United States almost every hour. With a majority of the
Cuban radio stations closed on account of mourning, my

father was listening to the newscasts with rare pleasure, since usually some Cuban radio station interferes. About three o'clock he called me to say that Japan had attacked Pearl Harbor. The American participation in the Second World War had begun.

The Cuban Congress on December 9th approved a declaration of war against Japan. Three thousand university students demonstrated outside the Capitolio, demanding organization of armed forces and deportation of fifth columnists or their imprisonment in concentration camps. Gene Carrier, my brother-in-law, went to the Capitolio to take a picture of the demonstration. For a long time he had been wearing his hair in a crew cut and we had laughed about him looking like a German officer. Even the German consul in our building had always seemed to treat him with a special politeness. That afternoon when Gene was taking pictures of the students, some of them surrounded him and demanded to know if he were a Nazi. Gene got his pictures and retreated rapidly.

The authorities appealed for calm. Soldiers and rural guards were ordered to protect foreigners and their property throughout Cuba. On December 10th Cuba forbade the entry of European nationals with exception of those of the British Empire into Cuba. The measure was directed at European refugees, who were continuing to arrive in droves from Spain and Portugal. On December 11th President Batista signed a declaration of war against Germany and Italy. He ordered immediate confiscation of Italian, German and Japanese holdings and the internment of Axis nationals on the Isle of Pines, located south of Havana Province.

On December 19th President Batista was granted emergency powers. This measure declared a state of national emergency in Cuba and granted the President such ample powers that Congress actually became unnecessary. He received authority to take any necessary defense steps, including the calling up of an armed force, making military pacts with the United States and other nations fighting the Axis powers, regulating trade, industry and labor, combating espionage and profiteering and levying war taxes.

The President immediately signed a decree establishing a concentration camp for enemy aliens at Torrens Farm, 25 miles from Havana. Within a few days 1,370 Italians were detained and the President ordered the detention of three thousand Germans who were registered as being residents of Cuba. The Spanish flag was banned from Cuba. Authorities began a roundup of Japanese residents.

At the end of December the President, taking advantage of the new emergency powers granted him, imposed higher taxes of all kinds, created an income tax, luxury taxes, and approved a 20% surcharge on all existing taxes. He approved taxes on registrations of foreigners which ran from twelve dollars to one hundred forty dollars annually according to income. There was immediate protest. This tax was considered unconstitutional, since it was a tax on income already taxed by the new income tax law. Later the tax was reduced to a scale from three dollars and fifty cents to fifteen dollars yearly, according to income. Foreigners were given *carnets* and fingerprinted.

On January 28th the President signed a decree authorizing the sale of the entire 1942 sugar crop to the United States. The contract provided an increase in price to 2.65¢ per pound. On February 17th the President fixed the crop at 3,600,000 long tons. Later it was raised to 3,950,000 tons, when it became apparent the island had sufficient cane to produce that amount.

Cuba began to feel the loss of the tourist trade. The first indication of this came with the closing of Sloppy Joe's Bar, famous among visitors. It closed after an operation of twenty-five years.

The attraction of Sloppy Joe's for Americans was always a mystery to the Cubans. I once heard two old Cubans, dressed in their white starched suits, discussing Sloppy Joe's. They could not understand why anyone would go to a place which provided only stools to sit at a bar. "It must be de-

cidedly uncomfortable," one remarked. "Ah," said the other.
"I think it is to keep from paying the waiter a tip."

On February 12th Batista curbed beef exports to 24% of
national consumption. During the thirties, Cuba had become
a beef exporting nation. High prices in the United States
caused a tremendous increase in exports. The President fixed
the price of 3.8¢ per pound on the hoof. The retail price was
raised two cents on first class, one cent on second class beef.
Cattle producers and butchers protested these prices and
beef vanished. Five months passed in Havana without any
beef being put on sale except on the black market, which
began to flourish.

For years I had sent to the *Times* a daily weather report
for the record they carried of temperatures and weather
conditions in cities all over the world. Through this I had
become acquainted with Major Millas, head of the National
Observatory, which sits on a high hill across the bay from
Havana. Now the Major called me to say that all weather
reports were prohibited as a war measure. Also, radio
stations and newspapers were prohibited from giving news
on the movements of ships.

Meanwhile, the Nazi submarine campaign in the Carib-
bean was stepping up. Ships loaded with sugar were being
torpedoed with increasing frequency off the north coast of
Cuba. This submarine campaign was to cost the United
States and its allies fifteen hundred vessels in the Caribbean.
Many oil tankers went down.

Submarines were lying off the north coast waiting for
vessels to leave the island. There were no convoys as yet.
Stories were told by surviving sailors reaching Havana about
desperate fights with sharks, after their ships were torpedoed.

One such incident was told to me by the cook on a ship
which had been sunk off the north coast of Cuba near Nuevitas in Camagüey Province. The cook said they had cleared
port that afternoon and were steaming along sometime after
midnight. They never saw the submarine which fired the

torpedo. The vessel sank within fifteen minutes after it had
been hit. It was a cargo vessel and had some lumber on
board. The cook said he jumped into the water and found
a plank to hang onto. Another crew member held to the
same plank until they found a bigger one. The boilers burst
when the vessel sank, coating the sea with oil, which the
cook claimed sharks do not like. But by the time daylight
came the oil had drifted away and the sharks were all
around them. One lifeboat was floating, with several of the
crew members in it. The cook and his companion were pulled
into the lifeboat. He told how they beat off the sharks with
their oars when they got too close. They rowed all day without spotting land, but at night they saw the lights on the
coast and reached the shore.

President Batista ordered a blackout of all coastal towns,
including Havana. However, the blackout in Havana was
doomed to failure. It lasted only a week. The entire Malecón
section protested bitterly including residents, merchants and
café owners. Only four blocks deep along the shore were
blacked out, a measure completely ineffective, since the
lights from the rest of the city silhouetted any vessel near the
coast. The blackout was soon abandoned. Some submarines
were seen off Havana and residents at various times found
the Malecón ankle deep in petroleum which had been
washed ashore from sinking tankers. Cuba's radio communications in coastal areas were admittedly inadequate.
The government had only ten stations scattered along a
coastline of twenty-five hundred miles. The radio apparatus
used by the navy and army posts was antiquated and long
stretches of the coast were without communication facilities
of any kind. One hundred fifty amateur stations were in-
corporated into an Auxiliary Radio Corps to help out.

On May 4th a Nazi broadcast from Berlin warned President Batista that the palace might be shelled by Axis war
craft. Berlin was annoyed with Batista for cooperating with
President Roosevelt. "President Batista of Cuba, close friend
of War Promoter Roosevelt, said we Germans were vile

animals that must be attacked in our dens. Friend Batista, remember you live only a few meters from the waterfront."

Shipping difficulties increased, handicapping foreign trade. Economic conditions in Cuba grew steadily worse. Fruit and vegetable growers were able to export only about two-thirds of their customary tonnage to the United States, owing to the lack of vessels. Raw material supplies of industries began to run low. The United States system of priorities made it almost impossible to obtain materials. Stocks of merchandise were being depleted and prices rose beyond the purchasing power of the average Cuban. Lack of steel and iron threatened to paralyze the construction industry, with resulting unemployment. Cuba had no war industries to take up the slack in labor.

The government rationed gasoline and tires. Gene bought a fifty gallon drum and when I got my supply I always saved a gallon or two, which came in handy when, for fifteen days, there was no gasoline available due to the submarine campaign. To save gasoline Gene and I frequently walked home, some three miles. Most of the way was along the Malecón Sea Drive, which made a pleasant walk at midnight when traffic had almost ceased. Several times we found the Malecón covered with thick black oil from some torpedoed tanker. The tide brought it in, particularly in the section of the Malecón near the mouth of the bay.

The tobacco industry suffered severely from the loss of the European market. Cigar factories began to close. Shipments of leaf tobacco to the United States increased and was the one bright spot in the tobacco industry picture. Another bright spot in the economic picture was the mining industry centered in Oriente Province where thousands of men worked in the manganese mines. Also, the railroads added workers, since they were now hauling all sugar to Havana for shipment under convoy. However, the other ports from which sugar had formerly been shipped were paralyzed by the submarine campaign and thousands of dock workers were idle.

Wages were higher in Cuba than for many years but the cost of living was advancing faster than wages. Also, the government had imposed heavier and heavier taxes.

Cuba granted bases to the United States armed forces, on a temporary basis, since the agreement stated, "after termination of the emergency it is understood that the facilities will become a training center of the Cuban Air Force." The agreement of military cooperation between Cuba and the United States was signed on June 19th at the Cuban Ministry of State. Dr. José Manuel Cortina, Minister of State, signed for Cuba and American Ambassador Spruille Braden for the United States. The first base was built at San Antonio de los Baños, twenty-five miles from Havana. At San Julian, in Pinar del Rio Province, a smaller base was constructed, strategically located at the western tip of the island. From there, bombers could patrol the waters of the Gulf of Mexico and the Caribbean between Cuba and Mexico.

In August, 1942, Cuba lost two ships between Key West and Havana. The two ships, moving in a large convoy, were torpedoed. They were small freighters, the *Santiago de Cuba* and the *Manzanillo*. The bodies of the crew were recovered and brought to Havana by a United States destroyer on August 19, 1942. Thousands crowded the docks and lined the streets as the coffins were unloaded and borne to the Capitolio where they lay in state until the burial next day in Colon cemetery. President Batista decreed a state of mourning. Public offices and theaters were closed. Radios suspended all commercial programs. Throughout the entire island services were held in honor of the sailors. "The first Cuban victims of Nazi-Fascist fury have had the sad privilege of awakening the war consciousness of our people," said the Minister of Communications, Marino Lopez Blanco.

On August 24th the Senate authorized five Cubans to join the American armed forces. Later, many Cubans living in the United States were drafted by the United States government. On September 5th the Cuban police arrested Augusto Luning, who was to be the only spy executed in the whole of

Latin America during the Second World War. Luning had arrived in Havana in September, 1941, under the name of Enrique Augusto Luni, using a Honduran passport. He opened a commission agent's business and later bought into a woman's dress shop. He made two trips to the Dominican Republic and one trip to New York, where he stayed three months. Luning was captured through the combined efforts of the British Intelligence Service and the U.S. Federal Bureau of Investigation. Letters sent by Luning to Spain, ostensibly about commercial transactions, were found by the British censors to contain messages in invisible ink. Luning lived in midtown Havana in a small apartment. He had many beautiful canaries, whose lilting songs covered the noise of the radio transmitter with which he sent messages to the German submarines in the Caribbean. He frequented the port dives and bars and obtained information about ship movements, as well as information on the construction of military and air bases by the United States.

Although it was reported that Cuban authorities offered Luning clemency if he would reveal his connections with other agents in Latin America, he refused to give information. The night before he was executed, Luning was visited by a woman. The Cuban press speculated as to the identity of the woman, but the Cuban authorities never revealed her name. One columnist said that Luning played solitaire during the night before he faced the firing squad.

Each newspaper was permitted to have one representative witness the execution. Luning was shot in the old moat of Principe Fortress Prison. The press watched the execution from the top of the moat. Just as the sun slipped above the edge of the horizon Luning walked out of the prison accompanied by a priest and two soldiers. The firing squad was already in position. Luning was tied to a post near an angle in the wall of the moat. He refused to be blindfolded and stood erect as the orders were given: *"Atención, Apunten, Fuego."*

Material shortages became acute. Gasoline was so scarce

that garages were ordered to mix alcohol produced locally with the gasoline. Sales to private cars were stopped. Only those granted ration cards were permitted to purchase gasoline. On November 1st the government probibited the sale of gasoline for fifteen days. A black market in gasoline had developed and much imported gasoline was finding its way into that market, where it sold for one dollar a gallon. President Batista also set up a compulsory military law, but the results were not encouraging. On October 15th the thirty day period of registration expired and it was necessary to extend the period by reason of the few who had registered. The university students had refused to register because they did not approve of the service law. Later Congress modified the bill and Batista tried again to register all male citizens between eighteen and fifty.

Mail to Cuba became more and more irregular. Letters were long in arriving, except by air mail. Newspapers, magazines, and fourth class mail piled up in Florida ports. The people protested.

Batista sent to Congress a message recommending a budget of $89,993,595 for 1943. Twenty-two million dollars was for the armed forces, seventeen million dollars for education and seven million dollars for health. The 1942 budget closed with a deficit estimated at some ten million dollars.

On November 16th some fifteen hundred Cubans crowded into the Ministry of National Defense to volunteer for foreign military service against the Axis. The Ministry ordered 127 registration centers opened in the island and the number expected to volunteer at that time was between ten thousand and fifty thousand. Nothing ever came of this because the United States did not ask Cuba for soldiers.

Cuba began the organization of a Cuban F.B.I. and American members of the United States F.B.I. were contracted to train this corps. Hundreds of Cubans visited the American Embassy in an effort to get to the United States to work in war industries and the two countries opened negotiations for special regulations which resulted in the entry into the United States of thousands of skilled Cuban workers.

José Fernandez Pelaez, a former police lieutenant during the Machado regime, was shot and killed near his home on University Street early one morning in February. His assailants left a card beside the dying man accusing him of being one of the officials who had participated in the August, 1933 massacre by Machado officials. Cubans, it seems, never forgive or forget.

On March 6th President Fulgencio Batista appointed several new cabinet members. For the first time he gave the Communists representation. Dr. Juan Marinello, Communist leader and member of the House of Representatives, was appointed Minister without Portfolio. Then on April 7th Cuba recognized the Soviet Republic. Maxim M. Litvinoff, Soviet Ambassador to Washington, came to Havana and presented his credentials on April 9th. The same day President Batista gave the Communist controlled Confederation of Cuban Workers, which dominated all island labor, official status, thus tightening the hold of the Communists on labor.

In June the Cuban navy bagged its only German submarine, after a battle which took place off the north coast. The United States had transferred to Cuba ten submarine chasers. It was one of these which sunk the submarine.

On July 4th Cuba for the first time celebrated the United States Fourth of July. Some eighty thousand Cubans from all walks of life paraded. President Batista attended ceremonies held at the Maine Monument. Four Havana newspapers published special editions. Eight radio stations broadcast special programs in honor of the United States. The Rotary Club sent American troops on Guadalcanal ten tons of candy.

American Ambassador Spruille Braden sternly and publicly warned the Americans in Cuba that they should take no part in political affairs of the island. "I am sure that I express the sentiment of every patriotic citizen of the United

States when I declare that no single American should participate in any way directly or indirectly in the domestic political affairs of Cuba," Ambassador Braden said. Many Americans and Cubans stored away this statement for future use.

President Fulgencio Batista signed a decree fixing the 1944 sugar crop at 4,250,000 long tons of which 178,084 tons were reserved for local consumption. The entire crop had been sold to the United States. A month later the President upped sugar workers wages 10%. The growing nationalistic spirit was illustrated on January 20th by a public manifesto launched by a group calling itself "Cuban Front." This group demanded the employment of 90% native Cuban workers, the cancellation of all citizenships granted since 1933, and the closing of the doors to immigration. The petition was presented to Congress with twenty-five thousand signatures. A university professor was said to be the head of this group. However, after the first sensational demand, the group faded into the background.

The Cuban Communist Party changed its name on January 22nd to Popular Socialist Party, in line with the new Communist international policy being prepared for the postwar period. According to the Superior Electoral Tribunal, the Cuban Communist Party had 122,000 members. On March 14th President Batista appointed Carlos Rodriguez, Communist leader, as Minister without Portfolio.

Political parties began to make nominations for general elections to be held in June. The government coalition composed of four parties: Liberal, Democratic, ABC, and Popular Socialist nominated Dr. Carlos Saladrigas. The opposition nominated Dr. Ramon Grau San Martin who was supported by Vice-President Gustavo Cuervo Rubio who had quarreled with President Batista several months previously.

The government coalition claimed a registration of 1,218,-000, the opposition, 650,000. Some three hundred thousand voters failed to register. Since voting is obligatory in Cuba according to the constitution, the three hundred thousand voters, known as the neutral mass, were to play a prominent role in the elections. This was to be the first election in Cuba with a direct vote for the President. Any voter could split his ticket, voting for either presidential candidate he favored, and then could vote for congressional, provincial and municipal candidates within his party. This clause was to change the political history of Cuba.

I decided to see Dr. Grau San Martin. Dr. Guillermo Belt, who later became Ambassador to Washington, arranged the interview and accompanied me. We went to Dr. Grau's old Spanish house. While we were waiting I noticed that lined up on each side of the salon were heavy native rocking chairs. There was practically nothing else in the room. The man who asked us to wait, evidently an aide to Grau, was a big fat man with a round baby face. Dr. Belt told me he was Major Genovevo Perez Damera. Damera was destined to become Chief of Staff of the Cuban army.

I told Dr. Grau that I had only one question—what was his attitude toward the United States air bases constructed in Cuba during the Second World War. It was a difficult question for Grau, because of his extreme nationalistic stand. After more than an hour of conversation during which I returned again and again to this one question, he gave me an answer. Then to be perfectly sure about the interview I had Grau read and sign it. Dr. Grau stated, without qualification, "The United States military air bases in Cuba should become a permanent part of the defense system of the Americas. It will undoubtedly be necessary in view of the postwar plans for maintenance of world peace now being formulated by the Allies for Cuba to indefinitely extend military cooperation to the United States."

That was a bombshell. Many a follower of the Autentico Party wondered what had possessed Grau, long a severe critic of the United States, to make such a statement. The War Department of the United States was highly pleased. The United States had been angling for some time to find out what Grau's attitude would be concerning the air bases.

Later, one of Dr. Grau's followers wrote in *Bohemia* magazine that I was an unscrupulous correspondent. He was sure that Dr. Grau had never made such a statement. Other Cuban newspapers regarded my report with suspicion.

Then Eddie Chibas, one of Dr. Grau's greatest supporters, wrote an article in *Bohemia* stating that the interview was accurate and that the presidential candidate had meant exactly what he said. The controversy terminated.

Elections were held on June 1, 1944. President Fulgencio Batista had refused to run and had backed the campaign of Dr. Carlos Saladrigas. Dr. Saladrigas was tall, slender, charming in personality, but he had none of the rabble rousing qualities which seem so necessary in Cuban politics. Dr. Grau, on the other hand, during the years since he had headed the student government in 1933, had associated himself with those who advocated benefits for the workers, redistribution of wealth, and the restoration of full civil authority. He had a long lantern-shaped face and prominent teeth. He spoke, hour after hour, on any and every subject, promising everyone a pot of gold and an easy chair. The masses adored him.

Dr. Ramon Grau San Martin was elected. It was an overwhelming victory. For eleven long years the followers of Grau had persisted, in spite of defeat after defeat, and their persistence had finally obtained results. Hysteria gripped the nation. Even before the election returns had come in from the interior, Grau's followers, who had maintained a private count on votes throughout the day, staged spontaneous demonstrations. Cars filled with shouting adherents raced through the streets, flags and banners flying. Thousands gathered outside Dr. Grau's home in the Vedado residential district.

The election of Dr. Grau San Martin unleashed a new wave of nationalism. Dr. Grau had coined the phrase "Cuba for the Cubans." Now his followers announced their determination to make Cuba "economically independent." Such an achievement is virtually impossible, since the United

States continues to buy the bulk of the sugar on which the Cuban economy depends. Economic independence is impossible for most of the Latin American countries as long as the United States remains their only major consumer. European trade is not especially desirable since most of Europe and all of Asia is short on dollars, which Cuba must have to buy imports. Cuba has never even been able to raise sufficient food for her population. The Cuban *peso* is worth nothing outside of the island and is not quoted on any international exchange. Ever since the National Bank of Cuba was established and the Cuban *peso* given obligatory circulation in Cuba every importer has to buy American dollars for his imports and every exporter demands American dollars for his goods. With this trade and currency situation Cuba is economically dependent on the United States and will continue to be so. True, Cuba could raise more food, could manufacture more goods, could diversify and increase her native production, and doing this would benefit Cuba. But "economic independence" is not merely a dream without substance, but a fallacy of such profundity that any serious effort to make the island "independent" would result in economic disaster. Added to this, Cuba is the key to the Gulf of Mexico. The United States will, regardless of the rights of Cuba, in self-defense see to it that no other power or unfriendly administration rules the island. Whether in health or in sickness, or for richer or poorer, in that sense Cuba is wedded to the United States—and until death do them part.

The government coalition parties were stunned. As the returns came in, Dr. Grau found that although he had been elected President, the government coalition parties had put into office a majority in Congress, and in provincial and municipal governments. Grau's administration was to be a government by a minority. But that did not handicap the new President in view of the tremendous powers which Batista had obtained from Congress during his term of office.

Batista was being praised in all quarters for the free and honest elections, which had swept his political opponent into

office. The *New York Times* editorially called it "one of the
few free elections in Cuba's history." Thus Batista went out
of office amid the praise and good wishes of a great percentage of the public.

Dr. Ramón Grau San Martin, returned to the Presidential
Palace on October 10, 1944, amid a wild celebration which
lasted three days. He had been forced out of the Presidency
in 1933, defeated for the office of President in 1940, and his
triumph was sweet indeed. Havana was lavishly decorated
with banners, flags, palm fronds and electric lights. Thousands poured into the city from the interior. The island hailed
Grau as a great democrat and the "savior" of the nation. On
the morning of his inauguration crowds began to gather at
daybreak around the Presidential Palace.

A chorus of one thousand male voices sang the *Autentico*
hymn. Automobiles and trucks raced through the streets,
blowing horns. Boats and harbor industries blew their whistles, church bells rang and firecrackers exploded. Bars and
cafés were crowded.

President Grau spoke to the cheering throngs, promising
to continue the work of the 1933 revolution. "It is not I who
have taken office today," he said, "but the people."

Hardly had the inauguration celebration ended when
Havana was struck by the worst hurricane in many years.
For several days we had received reports from the National
Observatory in Havana, and particularly from the Weather
Bureau of Miami, on which most of the Caribbean islands
depend for weather reports, that the hurricane was moving
northward over the Caribbean and would strike the island
in the western part.

We lived in a huge old Spanish house, one that had withstood its share of storm and wind. I asked my father to see
that the catches and bolts on the doors and windows, which
we rarely closed, were in order. Dad, accustomed to the swift
moving, violent cyclones of Oklahoma and Texas, could
hardly believe that a straight wind would do much damage.
He considered a hurricane scarcely more than a "good, health-

blowing, everyday Texas wind." Not until the day before the hurricane did he comply with my request.

As a hurricane approaches, one becomes conscious of the low pressure. There is a strange stillness, a different quality to sound that makes one's voice seem changed in tone, an acute awareness of the silence of unmoving things. The clouds race across the sky high above the earth and the wind blows in gusts. But the wind one feels and the clouds swooping past above seem unrelated to each other. People become irritable and a sense of fear seems to pervade the atmosphere.

When Gene and I came home that night, the town had been boarded up and battened down for the blow. Plate glass windows were either boarded or taped to withstand the pressure; trees in the parks had been staked down with ropes. The radios had been broadcasting warnings all day. At about two o'clock in the morning I was awakened by Honey Girl, Dad's big police dog. Honey Girl had been raised in Oklahoma City and had never been through a hurricane and she was frightened. The wind was howling around the corners of the house, and the windows and doors, which never fit tightly in Cuba, were shuddering from the blasts.

I got up and found that my housekeeper, a girl from Oklahoma, and Anisa, the cook, were up and dressed. Anisa had been raised in Gran Caiman and in the Isle of Pines, where hurricanes are greatly feared and where the damage they do is tremendous. They had hot coffee and sandwiches ready. My sister and her husband got up, but my mother and father slept peacefully. Dad had gone to bed highly skeptical about the hurricane.

The electric lights had already been turned off by the power plant. We groped about using a couple of hurricane lamps and candles which threw long shadows on the high ceilings. The force of the wind increased as daylight approached and the hurricane moved in from Batabano on the south coast.

We watched the hurricane through the glass doors of the salon of the house which Irma used as a ballet studio. To my amazement the glass doors held. Fortunately the wind only hit them glancingly. The trees along the street and our palms inside the yard gave way and toppled one by one, some pulling their roots out of the ground, others snapping their trunks. The noise of the wind was terrific. There is something frightful about the roar of a hurricane wind.

About noon the wind lessened. Dad remarked that it was all over. "But the wind down here knows her business," he admitted. Gene and I plotted the hurricane on the map and we told him we thought the eye of the hurricane, where there is complete calm, was going to pass over Havana. It did and the wind died. There was a strange hush. The people of Havana knew what it was and no one ventured outside. When any of us talked, our voices sounded too loud. One was particularly aware of the distance between one person or one thing and another.

It wasn't long before the wind began to blow from the opposite direction. The strongest winds of the hurricane, blowing counterclockwise, struck the city. We watched the fallen trees as they were lifted and thrown to the other side of the street. The wind increased to 160 miles an hour, according to the recording equipment at the National Observatory. By four o'clock in the afternoon the hurricane had moved northward and the wind had dropped to about fifty or sixty miles an hour. Gene and I managed to get the car out of the garage. After Gene chopped the limb off a ceiba tree which was blocking the entrance to our driveway, we headed into Havana, choosing streets without trees, avoiding trailing wires, cornices of buildings, lumber, masonry and other debris. At the Manzana de Gomez, across from Central Park, all the trees were lying stretched across the pavement in spite of the ropes that had anchored them.

Electricity, which was off in all the suburbs, was still available in the downtown area where the power lines are subterranean. We started checking the damage in the harbor, where thirty small craft had been damaged, three vessels sunk, and four had broken their moorings and run aground.

The city was paralyzed. Electric wires were down all over town, debris covered the streets, and the lower sections of the city were flooded. It was some ten days before we had electricity out at the house and before normal life was restored in the city. Out in the country the damage was greater.

One of the freak accidents involved a schooner which had been tied up at the Regla docks. The captain and crew had taken refuge ashore. The schooner tore loose during the storm, sailed out of the narrow mouth of the harbor—a feat which no navigator would have relished attempting under storm conditions, with the huge rocks on both sides. Then it took off to the north. A United States coast guard ship found it several days later, tossing around in the sea, undamaged, with only the crew's pet dog aboard.

In November Cuba rejoiced over the reelection of President Franklin D. Roosevelt for the fourth time. Headlines in newspapers declared it was a great democratic victory. "Roosevelt's victory is our victory," *El Pais* declared. "He is the best guarantee of the permanency of the postulates of the Atlantic Charter." The House of Representatives approved a motion to send congratulations to President Roosevelt in the name of the Cuban people.

The sugar crop, always the most vital question of the island, loomed large on the horizon. In January the size of the crop would have to be decided. Sugar producers declared they would not accept less than 3.25 cents per pound from the United States as compared to the 2.65 cents they had accepted all during the war. They pointed out that with workers clamoring for higher wages and other increased production costs it would be impossible to sell future crops at the price offered by the U.S. Commodity Credits Corporation.

The people waited impatiently to see what Grau's policy would be in regard to the armed forces, which had been dominant since Batista had taken over the island in 1933. On November 4th President Grau began the shakeup of the army. He appointed Lieutenant Colonel Pino Donoso, a retired army officer, Chief of National Police. Brigadier General Ignacio Galindez, one of the original group who had gone into power with Batista, was removed from command of Camp Columbia. Military chiefs in all six provinces were shifted and some retired. On December 30th Chief of Staff General Manuel Lopez Migoya announced the dismissal of five army officers, including the commander of Cabañas Fortress, Francisco Tabernilla y Dolz. Tabernilla was a close friend of Batista. Several months later Lopez Migoya was forced to resign by President Grau, who appointed Major Genovevo Perez Damera, a huge balloon-shaped man, as the new Chief of Staff. Perez Damera had accompanied Grau into exile in Mexico in 1933.

The shakeup of the armed forces continued. Within a few months the majority of the officers who had supported Batista were no longer members of the armed forces. President Grau ordered the "Fourth of September" flag, which Batista had created, withdrawn from all military posts and installations. He annulled that military holiday and created his own "Soldier's Day" on December 15th. Piece by piece Grau broke the hold of the army on Cuba. While the people suffered many disillusions during his administration, they were almost unanimous in praising Grau for placing civil power once more in its rightful place.

The Cuban worker in almost every commerce and industry already had pension funds to take care of his retirement. Nevertheless, in December a bill was passed setting up a pension fund for dentists. This fund was obtained by means of a tax on toothpaste, dental products and equipment. This was the beginning of a trend. During the next ten years consumers were to find themselves paying a tax on almost every product purchased in order to support doctors, lawyers, druggists, architects, barbers, manicurists and other professions. The United States, under the New Deal, never achieved such a degree of socialization.

On January 22nd a bomb exploded in the home of Professor José Brower. Early in February another exploded in a Havana theatre. Then one exploded in the hospital of the Spanish Regional Society, *Centro Gallego*. A revolutionary plot was uncovered, an intended assassination of President Grau and the Chief of Staff. Grau announced that the conspirators were "capitalists" who had had business dealings with Fulgencio Batista. Many were arrested, including José Pedraza, former Chief of Staff. Pedraza and five others were sentenced to one year in prison. The public believed that the case against Pedraza lacked evidence for a conviction, but they were surprised at the light sentence imposed.

The Communist Party reversed its policy and decided to support President Grau. Prior to his inauguration, Grau had informed the foreign press that he intended to deal severely with the Communists and break their hold on labor. But now he decided to accept their support. Senator Juan Marinello and Representative Blas Rocas visited President Grau and emerged with smiling faces. Then on March 7th President Grau gave to the Communist dominated Confederation of Cuban Workers $750,000 with which to convert the Havana *Fronton, Jai Alai* building, into a Workers' Palace.

I had been following the activities of the Communists in Cuba for a long time. In March, 1945 I wrote an article stating that Russia's "bid for influence in Latin America had made Cuba one of the focal points of Communist propaganda in the Western Hemisphere." It was commented on in the United States with considerable surprise.

Edwin L. James, at that time the Managing Editor of the *New York Times,* sent me a cable saying that the magazine *American Mercury* wanted me to write a piece on the subject and giving me permission to do so. I described how the Communists were using Cuba as a center for Soviet propaganda in an effort to bring Latin America within the orbit of Soviet influence. I described the luxurious Soviet Legation where elaborate fiestas were attended by Cuban society, attracted by the flow of vodka and the delicious buffets. I mentioned a hitherto unknown key figure in the Communist plan, Fabio Grobart, born in Poland, but now a Cuban citizen. He was later withdrawn by the Soviet foreign department when the spotlights of many publications in the United States were turned on him. Unfortunately, identifying the personalities of the Communist propaganda machine does not halt the Communists. This is something Americans have difficulty in understanding, the flexibility and mobility of the Communists, which allows them to follow a single purpose with a variety of means, and thus to shift and replace their representatives with ease and a minimum of diplomatic embarrassment. Exactly as Americans tended to believe during these years that once Stalin was gone, everything would be fine, so they believed that the Communist threat in Latin America could be removed by merely putting pressure on a few men.

As soon as the story was published in the *American Mercury*, the Associated Press cabled the text to Havana and it appeared in all the newspapers. The Soviet Legation was much perturbed and the *Chargé d'affaires* at that time, Dimitri Zaikin, gave a press conference in which he stated that I was an irresponsible trouble maker and an agent of Yankee imperialism. Later, Pravda called me a liar and the local Communist newspaper *Hoy* published front page editorials criticizing me. A broadcast from the Communist radio described me as being six foot tall, with freckles all over my face, thin and decidedly unattractive. I thought that was amusing. But I was not amused to see how promptly the Communists rallied to defend one of their own, while in the United States (in June, 1945) many people seemed to feel that it was rather vulgar and in bad taste to even mention the Communists.

In April the death of President Roosevelt shocked and saddened Cuba. Dr. Raul Menocal, Mayor of Havana, ordered all public spectacles closed. The Minister of Education, Luis Perez Espinos, suspended classes in schools. Flags throughout the island were lowered as a tribute to the late American President.

When Grau ran for President, the revolutionary groups, which had long been secret organizations, emerged to help him in his campaign. After the inauguration, these groups, particularly the nine most powerful organizations, moved in on various government ministries. In time they became almost an invisible government, imposing their decisions on cabinet ministers, government officials and sometimes even the President himself. An example of this occurred on April 24, 1945. Grau had promised to pardon several revolutionists sentenced to prison in Principe Fortress by the Batista administration. Several months after Grau's inauguration, when no pardon was given, one of these revolutionists tried to escape and was shot by the guards. The group to which this revolutionist belonged demanded to see Grau and find out why he had not complied with his promise to pardon those in jail. The interview was not granted. The revolutionaries blamed the Chief of the Secret Service, Enrique Enriquez. On the morning of April 24th, Enriquez, riding in his automobile toward the Presidential Palace, drove through Fraternity Park near the National Capitolio. An automobile drew alongside and its occupants fired at Enriquez with a machine gun. Enriquez was severely wounded and died on the operating table of the hospital. The killers were never apprehended. Sometime later various revolutionists in Principe Fortress were pardoned.

The surrender of Germany on May 7, 1945 caused no celebration in Cuba. The island had no soldiers fighting, except the small number with the United States forces. On May 16th the Cabinet decided to release the Germans in concentration camps.

On August 14th the Cubans rejoiced over the news of the surrender of Japan. Celebrating crowds gathered in Central Park. Firecrackers exploded and flags and banners were in profusion. Buildings were floodlighted and the searchlights in the Capitolio and Cabañas Fortress were turned on. On September 3, 1945, President Grau San Martin declared a two-day official holiday in celebration of V-J day. The President set the 1946 budget at $163,880,000, twice the revenue of the government when war began.

On February 26, 1946, Grau fixed the sugar crop at a minimum of 4,250,000 long tons. Local consumption was estimated at 350,000 tons, 250,000 tons were to be held by the National Sugar Stabilization Institute, 20,000 tons were alloted to UNRRA and the balance sold to the United States.

The President had requested sugar producers to turn over to the government the difference in price to be paid by the United States for the 1946 sugar crop and the price obtained from other countries. The world price was considerably above that paid by the United States and the difference was estimated at some twenty million dollars. This became known as the sugar "differential" and caused much protest from sugar producers and cane planters, and was one of the greatest grievances against President Grau's administration. The President failed to announce just what the government intended to do with this "differential."

On March 6, 1946 the Education Association of Cuba sounded the first alarm against Communistic influence in schools of the nation. In an open letter to government authorities, teachers and public members of the Association declared Communists were gaining control of all teachers associations in order to spread Communist doctrine. The Communists had grown steadily in power since former President Batista had established diplomatic relations with the Soviet Union. Cuba had become one of the focal points of Communist propaganda in the Western Hemisphere and a center from which orders went out to other countries. Conferences were being held in Havana between Moscow chiefs and Latin American communist leaders. Schools for agitators were being operated, and anti-American propaganda programs were being initiated. In Vedado the Soviet had taken over a beautiful mansion with luxurious furnishings and spacious grounds. Fifty staff members, including a press attaché, were installed. At that time no other diplomatic representation in Cuba had a press attaché. There were only a few Russians in Cuba and no business was transacted with that nation, so that it could easily be deduced that this big staff was part of an elaborate propaganda establishment, as it proved to be during the next few years. The Legation gave lavish parties. Meetings, radio broadcasts, exhibitions of paintings and sculpture, publications and other media were utilized by the Soviets to sell communism to the masses of Cuba. The Confederation of Cuban Workers, which controlled all island unions, was headed by Lazaro Peña. Every one of the unions was headed by Communists. The Communists controlled the powerful radio station *Mil Diez*, Cuba's only free channel station, and the daily paper *Hoy*, which published direct propaganda cables from Moscow.

Before Russia entered the war against Germany, the Communists had bitterly criticized the United States for its aid to Great Britain and France. Then, overnight, the war became the "peoples' war" against Nazism and Fascism. With the death of Roosevelt the Party line changed; the Communists began the greatest anti-American campaign ever launched in Latin America. By September 1946 the campaign against the United States was extremely violent. The old cry of Yankee imperialism had been revived with new vigor. The United States was accused of seeking not only to exploit the Latin American nations and to infringe upon their sovereignty, but of trying, with the atomic bomb, to bring on another war and control the entire world. Only the Soviet Union stood between the small nations and the greedy United States, according to the Communists.

The campaign served its purpose of arousing animosity against the United States in a long range plan to destroy the United States influence in Latin America. One of the propaganda media was the official bulletin of the Soviet Legation, which extolled the virtues of Soviet institutions and depicted Russia as a paradise for workers. At intervals it printed attacks on the United States press, and reprints of speeches made by Soviet leaders attacking the United States. The Communist propaganda effort was designed for the masses.

It was clever in its psychological appeal, particularly in its distortion of facts and figures.

American propaganda has always been woefully deficient. It is even today misdirected and ineffective. It is reasonable to say that we have been defeated in the "cold war" by the Russians on every count. During the war the propaganda was handled in Latin America by the Office of Coordinator of Inter-American Affairs, which had subsidiary offices operating in all Latin American countries, with the exception of Argentina. Later, propaganda was taken over by the United States State Department, but it has never been effective. In Cuba the American campaign has consisted largely of the distribution of literature illustrating and describing the war effort of all the allies including Russia. Later the greater part of the propaganda was directed toward telling about "the American way of life." Educational films were shown, news was broadcast, but without any comment to explain the United States point of view; a Cuban-American Cultural Institute was sponsored; scholarships in American schools were and are still granted; visits of journalists and educators to the United States were arranged.

Little or no advantage has ever been taken of channels already existing through which various sectors of national life could be reached. Local organizations endeavoring to promote friendship between Cuba and the United States receive little cooperation. The propaganda has been directly almost exclusively to the upper and educated class. One of the great stumbling blocks to American propaganda has been the Communist cleverness in seizing upon the word "democracy," giving the masses of Latin America an entirely new and erroneous definition of democracy, one calculated to draw them away from friendly relations with the United States.

The fear of the American people of the word "propaganda," which in Spanish means any kind of publicity or advertising, has contributed much to the American failure in the cold war. Just why the United States does not attack the Soviet Union at every weak point, reveal actual working conditions in Russia, the truth of the purges, the concentration camps and slave labor, and do this by radio, newspaper, by every possible means, is something which will always remain a mystery. Had the United States followed this aggressive policy throughout the world, there would be a different picture in international relations today. No nation can win the respect of Latin America by being apologetic for its own way of life, which is exactly what the United States has been doing.

On March 25, 1946 the diamond embedded in the floor of the Salón of Lost Steps of the National Capitolio was stolen. Just how this could have been accomplished in a building guarded by the police amused and intrigued the Cuban public. It was a 23-carat yellow diamond worth only $9500, but it had been literally pried and chiseled out of its setting. The theft created a minor sensation. There was speculation about a band of foreign diamond thieves and about enemies of the government. All clues proved false and the authorities confessed the diamond had simply disappeared. Weeks later President Grau announced that he had found the diamond on his desk. He refused to explain how it got there, although it was reportedly sent to him through the mail.

The theft of the diamond became the basis for jokes and cartoons. One cartoon showed an official of the United Railways arriving at the palace to ask President Grau if by chance the two locomotives stolen from the railway several weeks previously had as yet appeared on his desk.

A new revolutionary plot was discovered on May 17th. Early in the morning, people living near Camp Columbia military headquarters were awakened by rifle and machine gun fire. It went on for some thirty minutes. Later in the day General Perez Damera announced that an attempt to seize Camp Columbia had failed. Captain Jorge Agostini, Chief of the palace Secret Service, said the government believed it was an attempt to cause alarm and disturb public order just before elections. No one was arrested, strangely enough.

In June, Army Headquarters announced the retirement of thirty-nine soldiers and discharged sixteen others. It was said that they were involved in the conspiracy.

There were no disorders in the partial elections which took place on June 1st. President Grau won a sweeping victory. Dr. Manuel Fernandez Supervielle, Grau's candidate for the mayorship of Havana, was elected.

After months of negotiation, it was decided to sell the 1946 sugar crop at the basic price of 3.675 cents per pound to the United States plus an increase for shipments in the third and fourth quarter of the year in proportion to any price rise of goods Cuba imported from the United States. The contract covered two years. The United States also agreed to buy a minimum of one hundred fifteen million gallons of blackstrap molasses in 1946 and one hundred sixty-five million gallons in 1947. Over a two year period, the United States agreed to buy forty million gallons of alcohol, a transaction involving one billion dollars. Cuba was started on the dizzy period of prosperity that had been denied to her during the war, but inflation was to nullify the higher wages of the workers. It became apparent that Cuba faced meat rationing. Severe droughts and the tremendous wartime exports had depleted the cattle herds of the island.

The United States decided to turn over to Cuba the air bases constructed during the war. Gene and I went out to San Antonio de los Banos, the airfield from which American planes had patrolled the Caribbean and which had been an important link in the southern route of military air transports flying between the United States and Africa. We passed a long line of artillery and infantry going to the base for the parade that was to be held after San Antonio had been transferred into Cuban hands. The airfield with its mile long runways had been built by the United States at a cost of twenty million dollars, amid scandals, graft and general difficulties. It is located twenty miles from Havana and in the middle of good tobacco land. The expropriation of this land by the Cuban government had aroused much resentment among the farmers in the district. Most of the buildings, particularly the barracks, were of wood, which does not last long in this country because of the *comejenes* or termites.

It was a simple but impressive ceremony. In the small reviewing stand built for the occasion was the Chief of Staff, Genovevo Perez Damera. Brig. General William W. Bassal, U.S. Commander of the Antilles Defence Area, spoke briefly. Damera spoke less briefly. Then the United States troops marched past the reviewing stand to the air transports drawn up on the field, with their engines roaring. The American officers took leave of the Cuban officials and followed the troops into the planes. Within five minutes the transports roared into the air and not a single American remained on the base.

Knowing there would be a considerable delay before the military parade, which was to be reviewed by President Grau, Gene and I and three Cuban reporters went to the Officers' Club. It was a strange feeling to see it empty. Americans build so rapidly and then leave so quickly. A radio was still playing softly in the salon. We found cups and drank coffee. One of the Cuban reporters complained about the American troops going off and leaving the breakfast dishes unwashed. I thought that was exceedingly funny. The United States had just presented Cuba with a twenty million dollar air base, and Cuban gratitude was a complaint about the dirty dishes.

President Grau San Martin decided that since the price of sugar had risen due to the clause in the contract with the United States, he would seize the increase for the government. The sugar producers and cane planters protested. After considerable discussion it was agreed that the producers would turn over 300,000 tons of sugar of the 1947 crop for resale to countries other than the United States, on which the government would collect the differential in price. Meanwhile, every worker in the island was demanding a raise. In November, 1945, Grau had seized the American owned Havana Electric Railway. This had been done to enforce wage increases which the company claimed it could not afford. The practice of seizing businesses and industries to enforce workers' demands became the established custom of the government. The President could put such measures into effect by reason of the extensive wartime powers which had been given to Batista and never repealed. In 1946 President Grau had signed more than 3,000 decrees, while Congress approved fewer than twenty laws. Government revenue had reached a new high during the Grau administration, some two hundred forty million dollars being collected in 1946. Grau's public works program had failed to materialize; only a few streets in Havana had been paved; many projects were started but none ever seemed to be finished. Towns in the interior began to stage mass protest meetings against the waste of money and failure of the government to carry out announced projects.

Even the revolutionary organizations, which had so enthusiastically supported Grau, began to grow restive. On October 12, 1946, six of the big nine announced withdrawal of support from President Grau. They pointed out that graft was rampant in governmental departments, black markets flourished, and the public works program had broken down. Beef shortages reached such a point that the army was ordered to seize sufficient beef to supply Havana. The cattlemen were refusing to sell because of the government price of eight cents on the hoof. Even this measure failed to solve the problem and Havana continued meatless.

On February 1, 1947 the government seized the American and British owned United Railways of Havana. This railway had hired many employees during the war, when sugar was being shipped from all parts of the island to Havana. Now the other ports were open and sugar had resumed normal shipping routes. However, owing to the labor legislation, the Railways were unable to dismiss any workers and operations were being carried on at a huge annual loss.

As the year 1947 began, it was plain that although Cuba was enjoying a period of great prosperity, the people were becoming more and more critical of the Grau San Martin government. Commerce and industry, as well as the general public, were dissatisfied. Strangely enough, although the war had ended and shipping resumed, food was scarce. Prices continued to rise despite government control. "Whenever the government fixes a price on an article, that article disappears from the market and can only be found on the black market at a much higher price," was the way the man in the street summed up the situation.

President Grau's support of Communist labor leaders, instead of his own *Autentico* labor leaders, had almost destroyed the once sizable *Autentico* labor movement. Now, the *Autentico* labor chiefs prepared to battle the Communists over control of the Confederation of Cuban Workers. Led by Eusebio Mujal, the *Autenticos* marshaled their forces, as the Fifth National Labor Congress opened. The Communists won the battle before it started. In a dispute over credentials, the Communists having packed the Congress with "pocket unions," the *Autenticos* walked out. It was the beginning of a struggle in which both Communist and *Autentico* leaders were to die.

On May 4, 1947 Cuba was shocked by the suicide of the Mayor of Havana. Dr. Manuel F. Supervielle, fifty-three years old, was dean of the Havana Bar Association and the first President of the Inter-American Bar Association. His experience in politics had been very little prior to his election as Mayor. Supervielle shot himself in his garage with a revolver borrowed from the patrolman Sergio Alvarez who was on duty in front of the Mayor's home that morning. He left a note reading: "Owing to insurmountable obstacles which prevent me from complying with my promise to the people of Havana and facing the idea of failure, a thing which I cannot bear, I make this determination. As a man with a conscience I prefer suicide."

Supervielle had been elected on the campaign promise to

provide Havana, which for twenty years had suffered from a scarcity of water, with an ample supply. He had attempted to have a plan drawn up for improvement and amplification of the water system, but had been blocked at every turn by politicians bent on collecting graft, and by the negligence of President Grau in providing money from the national treasury. Thousands turned out for his funeral and the popularity of the government declined another degree.

On July 4, 1947 an attempt was made to destroy the Havana Produce Building. Police captured five hundred pounds of dynamite and two thousand feet of fuse. Police and soldiers searched all automobiles entering and leaving the city in an attempt to find arms.

On April 30, 1947, President Grau appointed Dr. Carlos Prio Socarras as Minister of Labor. Dr. Prio Socarras, forty-two years old, had a long history as a revolutionist. He had been Secretary General of the famous 1930 Students' Directorate of Havana University which led the fight against the Machado dictatorship. He had spent three years in prison at that time. He presided over the Revolutionary Junta of Camp Columbia the night Batista took control of the island. He was one of the founders of the Cuban Revolutionary Party (*Autenticos*). He had helped write the 1940 constitution and served under President Grau as Prime Minister.

Minister of Labor Prio Socarras saw the handwriting on the wall. His first efforts were toward breaking the hold of the Communists on island labor and putting the labor leaders of his own *Autentico* Party in control of the Confederation of Cuban Workers. The fight for control of labor between the *Autenticos* and the Communists began in earnest. Disorders and armed clashes occurred with growing frequency. On July 17th the government was forced to send special detachments of troops to the Havana docks when Communist stevedores struck.

Minister of Labor Prio Socarras ordered the Communists evicted from the Labor Palace, on the grounds that the building belonged to the Confederation of Cuban Workers and had been taken over by the Communists. *Autentico* labor and other anti-Communist elements of labor demanded that the government force the Communists to turn over to them the funds and books of the Confederation and to investigate past expenditures. They claimed the Communists had used dues and money collected from labor to pay for Communist Party propaganda.

On August 1, 1947, Senator Eduardo Chibas presented a petition for registration of the new Cuban Peoples' Party. In a weekly Sunday night broadcast, rated as having the highest listening record of any program on the island, Chibas criticized the graft and inefficiency of the Grau administration, naming names and citing facts and figures. Chibas announced his candidacy for President in the 1948 elections. The Cuban Peoples' Party was soon to acquire the name of *Ortodoxos* (orthodox *Autenticos*) and to become a powerful organization.

Gang warfare came to a climax on September 15, 1947, when a gun battle between two rival revolutionary groups within the National Police itself made it necessary to call out army troops. The battle took place in Marianao, a suburb of Havana, across the Almendares River. A group headed by Major Mario Salabarrias, Chief of Secret Police, attacked the home of Police Major Morin Dopico where several of the group headed by Police Major Emilio Tro were barricaded. Six were killed; Major Emilio Tro, the wife of Police Major Morin Dopico, Lt. Mariano Puerta, Policeman Luis Padierne and Jesus Dieguez, secretary of the revolutionary group known as Union Insurreccional Revolutionario (UIR). Twelve were wounded, including the baby of Major Dopico. Major Salabarrias and several others were tried and sentenced to thirty years imprisonment.

For several months various revolutionary groups together with the Dominican exiles and other Latin Americans had planned an armed expedition against Generalissimo Rafael L. Trujillo of the Dominican Republic. Trujillo has held Santo Domingo in an iron grip for a quarter of a century.

Strangely enough, the United States State Department had supported Trujillo throughout this entire period. Americans seem to be "economic missionaries"—show them a few roads, water works and modern public buildings and they are inclined to believe that dictatorship is good for the country. Perhaps Americans are too squeamish to look behind the scenes in Latin America and see the blood and suffering caused by these so-called "benefactors."

I first became aware of this group when people started telephoning my house and asking for General Juan Rodriguez and General Miguel Angel Ramirez, Dominican exiles who were the organizers of this movement. My telephone number in Vedado was only one number different from the José Marti Childrens' Park and many people made the mistake of dialing my number. Recruits for the expedition were being trained in *Parque Marti*.

For months President Grau San Martin ignored the preparations and his Minister of Education, José Aleman, helped the revolutionists buy arms and equipment with money from the Ministry. Fifteen hundred youths had been recruited and trained. They were taken to Cayo Confites off the north coast, near Nuevitas, a tiny sandy island, from which they were to embark for the Dominican Republic. Two million dollars worth of ships, planes, arms and equipment had been accumulated for the expedition.

Meanwhile, Trujillo, informed of the proposed expedition by his Cuban spies, appealed to the United States to save him. The United States, following the policy of status quo, not wanting the peace of the Caribbean disturbed, urged the Grau government to break up the expedition. The President finally yielded to pressure and the Cuban army and navy surrounded Cayo Confites and captured 850 members of the expedition. Eleven bombers, hundreds of rifles, two ships, and supplies and ammunition were confiscated. Other members of the expedition, including the leaders, escaped from Cayo Confites. Among these was Fidel Castro, then a student at Havana University who swam the shark-infested

Nipe Bay with a machine gun and ammunition belt strapped to his back and thus escaped arrest.

The failure of the Cayo Confites expedition marked the end of the political career of José Aleman. The Cuban Senate approved a motion expressing lack of confidence in Minister of Education Aleman who was in Miami, on leave of absence. Reports had circulated for months of a fortune being amassed by Aleman. These reports were confirmed several years later when he died, leaving millions of dollars, represented largely by property in Miami.

The Navy brought the captured members of the Cayo Confites expedition to Havana and held them at Camp Columbia Army Headquarters. The press was advised. I went out to the Camp with Gene Carrier and several Cuban reporters. We saw the prisoners that afternoon—sunburned and unshaved youths—held in the prison compound. Unexplainably, the press was prevented from leaving until about eight that night. Apparently the military authorities were writing up their report, although the information released to us was not extensive. Some one had given orders to tell the press very little. Three American pilots and several other Americans were in the group. One hundred and fifty prisoners, including the Americans, were released. Others were freed within a few days.

This was the beginning of the Caribbean Legion, sometimes called the "Phantom Army of the Caribbean." The following year Dr. Carlos Prio Socarras, who had been helping the Cayo Confites expedition and was a friend of the Dominican exiles, became President of Cuba. José Figueres, a young coffee planter in Costa Rica, rose in revolt against the government of Teodoro Picado and Dr. Rafael Angel Calderon who, backed by the Communists, had refused to turn over power to the duly elected President Otilio Ulate, publisher of *Diario de Costa Rica*. Members of the abortive Cayo Confites expedition rushed to Costa Rica to help Figueres. President Carlos Prio Socarras sent him arms and ammunition which had been seized at Cayo Confites and which were still stored in the Cuban army munition deposits. The principal source of weapons for the Nicaraguan revolution, however, was the Caribbean Legion's reserve arsenals in Guatemala. These weapons too had been originally intended for the expedition against Trujillo.

Figueres, with his small group of young Costa Rican lawyers, doctors, engineers and planters killed twenty-five hundred American trained government troops, suffering less than a hundred casualties. It was the first shooting war against the Communists in the Western Hemisphere.

Horacio Ornes, former Dominican diplomat and brother of German Ornes, once publisher of Trujillo's official newspaper *El Caribe*, led a successful expedition against Puerto Limón on the Caribbean coast of Costa Rica. Ornes and the sixty-one Costa Ricans who accompanied him in the attack became the military heart of the Caribbean Legion.

After the successful Figueres revolution, a number of Dominicans, Nicaraguans, Hondurans and other exiles remained in Costa Rica to prepare to fight for the liberation of other Caribbean countries. Jerry Hannifin, correspondent of *Time* magazine, suggested that this revolutionary group should inherit the name of the Caribbean Legion. Ever since this basic organization, which is pledged to the overthrow of the Latin American dictators, has been known as the Caribbean Legion. The Legion again attempted to overthrow Trujillo and failed, due to penetration of its ranks by Trujillo agents. Four Americans died in the landing on the beach at Luperon in Santo Domingo. Trujillo remained strong in his island empire. Then, in 1952, Batista seized control of Cuba. Perez Jimenez held Venezuela with an iron fist. The efforts of the Legion to overthrow dictators were useless. They could not assemble sufficient arms, transportation, or financial support. Finally the Legion disappeared.

In March, 1959, there was a rebirth of the Legion. Fidel Castro's victory in Cuba caused a resurgence of hope and belief in the hearts of men who had begun to consider their cause hopeless. Familiar faces were seen around Havana.

The revolutionary forces of the Caribbean gathered strength to make another attempt to overthrow Trujillo, the Somozas in Nicaragua, and the regime of Duvalier in Haiti. Even Paraguay and Spain were mentioned as objectives.

Minister of Labor Prio Socarras continued his fight to break the hold of the Communists on labor. He declared the congress held by the Communists illegal and that the congress held by the anti-Communist groups was the true labor congress. The Communists called a four hour protest strike. The government retaliated by arresting Lazaro Pena, Communist leader, and 125 others. Leaders of the Communists who were not caught in the roundup went into hiding. Arrests continued until seven hundred had been jailed.

Jesus Menendez, Communist member of the House of Representatives and head of the Sugar Federation, was shot and killed by a Captain of the army in Manzanillo, Oriente Province. The Communists called it murder. The army declared Menendez had fired the first shot. Other killings followed.

High school students in Guantanamo rioted in demand for a new building and in a clash with army troops several were shot and wounded. In Havana, on February 10, 1948 the students of the high school located across from Central Park, staged a riot in which dozens of streetcars were badly damaged, and school furniture was thrown into the street. It was necessary to call out police reserves. The cabinet immediately appropriated one hundred thousand dollars to build a new high school in Guantanamo. Later four students were hurt in a riot at the Arts and Crafts School of Havana, but the reasons for this disturbance were vague.

Elections were to be held on June 1, 1948. Parties began selecting candidates.

Dr. Prio Socarras, candidate of the *Autenticos,* based his bid on destroying Communist influence in Cuba. "The first step is to remove the mask of the Communists and expose their ultimate aims of world domination," he said. "My idea is to destroy the Communist party in Cuba."

On May 6, 1948 the government seized and confiscated *Mil Diez*. This had been one of the principal propaganda media of the Communists in the Caribbean and its loss was a severe blow.

Dr. Eduardo Chibas, candidate of the Cuban Peoples' Party (*Ortodoxos*), based his campaign on promise of honesty in government. He won many followers. Don Ricardo Nuñez Portuondo, candidate of the Liberal Party, and one of Cuba's best known surgeons, was running for office for the first time. This fifty-four year old physician had been born in Philadelphia. He was backed by the conservative element in the Liberal-Democratic coalition.

Dr. Juan Marinello was the head of the Communist Party. It can hardly be possible that he expected to win.

Dr. Carlos Prio Socarras was elected on June 1, 1948. Chibas made a good showing and proved that his party would be a threat in the next election. Dr. Ricardo Nuñez Portuondo, disillusioned by the small vote, returned to his profession as a surgeon.

Fulgencio Batista, although living in the United States since he left the presidency, was elected senator on the Liberal-Democratic ticket, in absentia. His brother, Francisco Batista, candidate for Governor of Havana Province, also won.

11

Dr. Carlos Prio Socarras was inaugurated on October 10, 1948. The forty-five year old President and his beautiful wife moved into the palace in a round of inaugural festivities, but his problems were pressing and numerous. Spiraling inflation, labor unrest, declining revenue, financial crisis, and unrestrained gang warfare confronted him.

Despite the record revenue collected during the Grau administration, the government at the time Prio took office was unable to pay its bills. The money had been drained off in extravagance, over-ambitious public works programs, and in graft. Public employees of various departments claimed they had not been paid for months. Hospitals and prisons were without supplies. Investments were drying up as capital, angered by Grau's arbitrary methods of raising wages, seizing industries to enforce workers demands, and increasing taxes, had resolved to invest no further money in the island.

The bright spot in the picture was the financial situation. Revenue was pouring in at a high level. In 1947 the government had collected an all time high of $244,462,071. Sugar, the economic index of Cuba, still commanded a good price, but increasing world production was causing producers to view the picture with some concern.

As the year 1949 began, President Prio tried to form a

democratic bloc against the dictatorial regimes of Latin America. He sent personal representatives to various countries, but was forced to abandon the plan since those countries were completely lacking in enthusiasm. However, reaction from the Latin American dictators was not long in coming. General Somoza, President of Nicaragua, accused Cuba's new President of planning to furnish arms for a Central American revolution. The Cuban Ministry of State denied the charge, stating, "The democratic government of Cuba naturally feels sympathy for oppressed peoples, but arms in Cuba cannot be furnished for revolutions."

Despite this denial, arms could be purchased in Cuba. Moreover, President Prio sympathized with the political exiles of Latin America who were plotting against dictatorial governments at home. Exiles from Venezuela, Nicaragua and Santo Domingo found a welcome in Cuba. Many were given monetary assistance. Among the most prominent exiles were former Presidents of Venezuela, Dr. Romulo Betancourt and Romulo Gallegos. Members of the Caribbean Legion were made welcome and given facilities by the authorities.

President Prio returned the American owned Coca-Cola plant, which had been seized by the Grau administration, and ordered beef imported free of duty to relieve the shortage. He ordered cancellation of the decree under which the luggage of all persons leaving Cuba was searched in an effort to prevent American currency from being taken out of the island.

Former President Fulgencio Batista returned to Cuba on November 20th. He established himself and family at a country estate called *Kuquine*. Soldiers were detailed by army headquarters for a twenty-four hour guard at *Kuquine*. It was from this beautiful country estate that Batista was to run for President and to stage the military coup which put him again in control of the island.

The Cuban Congress enacted a law to force land owners to lease tillable land and regulated sharecropping. Owners of more than fifty acres of tillable land were ordered to rent it in maximum lots of 167 acres to the first farmer or collective group of farmers who applied, unless the land was being farmed personally or by tenants. Cane land was exempted, as well as grazing land, if sufficient cattle were being raised in the opinion of the government. Taxes were increased on owners who refused to rent land. The law was considered a forward step in the attempt to create a more stable farming class. Thousands and thousands of acres of land in Cuba are in the hands of a few who neither till it nor permit others to do so. At the same time, land values have always been and are still kept at excessive levels by these few, so that farmers are unable to buy land for their own use.

President Prio Socarras signed the law establishing a national bank of issue on December 23, 1948, thus finally putting into effect the dream of the island for many years. Batista had talked constantly about the national bank. Dr. Ramon Grau San Martin had talked about establishing such a bank during all of his four years. Now, after the island had purchased gold for a number of years and accumulated sufficient reserve during the prosperous years of the war, the bank was at last a reality. Banking experts from the United States Federal Reserve and from private institutions cooperated in drawing up the law and the private banks of the island, the most powerful of which were American and Canadian, took stock in the bank. The bank opened on April 27, 1950. The dual currency system of American dollars and Cuban *pesos* was to continue until June 30, 1951, when the dollar was no longer legal tender in Cuba. All bank accounts, with the exception of some savings accounts, were converted into Cuban *pesos*, which were at par with the American dollar.

Reports began to circulate concerning differences between Prio Socarras and former President Grau San Martin. On January 15, 1949, Dr. Grau San Martin publicly demanded that President Prio "clear up the responsibilities" of an eighty-four million dollar government deficit. Minister of

Treasury, Antonio Prio Socarras, the President's brother, had told the press the deficit of the government at the time President Prio took office would run at least eighty-four million dollars. Cabinet ministers had been complaining ever since they took office that they had no money to run their departments.

Auditors of the government continued to dig into the records. Within a month Dr. Grau was forced to appear before the Audiencia Court of Havana to hear charges that his government had misappropriated $174,000,000. He pleaded not guilty, alleging that all spending had been carried out legally.

The *Autentico* Party began to divide when some of the members supported Grau against Prio. In Camp Columbia, Major General Genevevo Perez Damera, close friend of former President Grau, was still Chief of Staff of the Cuban army. Rumors circulated that he was preparing to stage a coup d'état and put Grau back into the Presidency. The American Ambassador, Robert Butler, chose that moment to issue a statement praising Dr. Carlos Hevia, Minister of State, and the policies of the government.

The Communists were stepping up their campaign in Latin America against the United States. The peace movement which was to snowball into a world-wide movement began in Latin America. It was designed to keep Latin American countries neutral and to cut off the supply of vital raw materials to the United States, in case of war with Russia. In Cuba the Communists began to prepare for the American Congress for Peace and Democracy. Dr. Juan Marinello declared: "The democratic union of the peoples of the continent is indispensable for their liberation. Each day, each minute that passes, makes it more evident that United States imperialism, the most powerful and bold on earth, has the principal aim of using the products and men of Latin America to carry out their plans of slavery and conquest."

On March 6th the Cuban Communist party called on

Cubans to "free themselves from Yankee imperialism" and fight on the side of "Soviet democracy" in case of a war between the United States and Russia. Then on March 12th an incident rocked the Cuban nation and engendered ill feeling against the United States among many Cubans. Three American sailors desecrated the statue of Cuba's most beloved patriot, José Marti, located in Central Park. An angry crowd threatened to lynch the drunken American sailors. Police intervened, firing into the air, and rescued the sailors, taking them off to jail. The next day they were turned over to the United States Navy officials.

American Ambassador Robert Butler apologized formally to the Cuban government. Ambassador Butler went to Central Park and placed a wreath on Marti's statue. He expressed his "very profound regret at the unfortunate conduct of several sailors of the United States Navy."

Two hundred university students demonstrated in front of the American Embassy in downtown Havana shouting "Fuera Yanquis!" (Get out Yankees). Two stones were hurled through a window at the entrance. A crowd destroyed the wreath which Ambassador Butler had put on the statue.

Using radio broadcasts and the newspaper, *Hoy,* the Communists exploited the incident as proof of the insolence and contempt of the United States for Cuba. However, despite these efforts to keep the incident alive, public interest soon faded, leaving no permanent scar on the relations between the two countries. The United States Navy promptly forbade all ships to enter Cuban ports, which made the merchants and entertainers and "ladies-of-the-night" unhappy. Many months passed before a member of the United States armed forces appeared on the streets of Havana.

On March 31, 1949 the government seized the British and American owned United Railways of Havana. The railroad had taken on many extra workers during the war. Now, the railroad company was not permitted to dismiss these extra workers. The railroad was to become more and more of a burden on the government. Administrator after administrator confessed inability to run the railroad on anything approaching a businesslike basis.

Once again the exiled Dominicans in Cuba, aided by Eufemio Fernandez, former Chief of Secret Police of Cuba, attempted a revolution against Dictator Rafael Trujillo of Santo Domingo. Four Americans hired to fly planes loaded with arms into the Dominican Republic were shot by Dominican troops when they landed their planes at Luperon on the north coast of Santo Domingo. The Dominican Republic, which is no republic, immediately accused the Cuban government of cooperating in the new revolutionary attempt. Trujillo threatened to bomb Havana but no one took the threat seriously.

On August 24, 1949, the smoldering strife between the President and former President Grau San Martin flared. President Prio left the Presidential Palace at one A.M. and went to Camp Columbia military headquarters where he had called the top officers of the armed forces together, and advised them he was making a sweeping reorganization. Chief of Staff, General Perez Damera, absent in Camagüey, was advised by telephone that he had been removed. General Ruperto Cabrera, second in command, was promoted to Chief of Staff. Various officers were forced into retirement and others shifted in command. President Prio broadcast a message to the Cuban people explaining that he had been forced to dismiss the Chief of Staff because General Perez Damera had "attempted to raise a wall of isolation between the President and the Republic, which was an irregular and intolerable situation, since the President is commander in chief of the armed forces."

The university, long the center of strife, was torn with dissension and rivalry. The public had lost patience with all the revolutionary groups and demanded that the government dissolve them. However, powerful political figures of both the Grau and Prio administrations protected and abetted them in exchange for help in obtaining votes and con-

trolling certain portions of the political field. The President
kept trying. He dismissed the Chief of Police and appointed
a new man, reorganized the police force and urged that
gang killings be suppressed.

At the beginning of 1950 it was apparent that the Prio
administration was doing well. The island began the year
in a sound financial condition with the prospects of a fair
sugar market. The trade balance was favorable to Cuba. The
1949 sugar crop of 5,074,703 long tons had been sold, net-
ting the island about five hundred million dollars. United
States owned mills produced 51% of this crop. The United
States was not only Cuba's best customer but also her supplier.

President Prio's sympathy with democratic principles led
him to invite the Inter-American Conference for Democracy
and Freedom to hold its conference in Havana, and on May
12, 1950, the delegates from the United States and various
of the American nations opened the conference. The policy
of the United States, particularly that of the late President
Franklin D. Roosevelt, "of helping dictators in the Americas," came under attack. After three days of discussion the
conference created an organization called the Inter-American Association for Democracy and Freedom. This association pledged an active vigilance and fight against all totalitarian forces on the continent. No one seems to know what
happened to the association, but it is apparent that the rise
of dictatorships in Latin America during the next few years
completely obscured any action which the organization
might have taken.

On June 1, 1950 the Cuban people went to the polls to
elect half the House of Representatives. The *Autentico* Party
elected a majority throughout the island but in Havana the
opposition elected Nicolas Castellanos, who ran against Antonio Prio, brother of the President. The Communists supported Castellanos.

On July 4th a group of gunmen invaded the court where
the case against former President Grau San Martin for mis-

appropriation of $174,000,000 was being investigated and stole all the documents of the proceedings. This was to become the famous Case No. 82 against Grau but it never came to trial and did not deter Grau from running for President in 1954. No one was ever arrested for the stealing of the documents and none of the documents was ever found.

On August 24th the Communist newspaper *Hoy* was ordered suspended and the *America Deportiva* was ordered closed. A Communist Party radio broadcast over Station COCO was suspended. In Oriente Province the Chinese Communist publication *Kwong Was Po* was closed and the daily broadcast of Workers' Party banned.

On December 20th, Gregorio Simonovich, the kingpin of all smuggling activities in the Caribbean, was arrested. He was accused of smuggling Chinese and European aliens into the United States. Simonovich was a Russian who had long been known in Cuba. Reportedly, he had been a Communist agent, a smuggler of aliens and an informer for the American government. He arranged the illegal smuggling of aliens into the United States, but now and then reported these same aliens to the American government, so that, upon arrival in the keys near Key West, Florida, or in the airports near Miami, United States Federal men awaited them. It was a well paying enterprise. He was arrested by Cuba at the request of the United States government, according to reports. But Gregorio was freed by the court, which ruled there was insufficient evidence of a "crime against the stability of the Republic." There was no penalty in Cuba apparently for smuggling aliens into another country.

The next time Cuba heard of Simonovich he was under arrest in Miami. He claimed he had been kidnapped in Havana by United States agents and forcibly taken to Florida, but was never able to prove that. He was sent to a federal penitentiary for smuggling aliens.

The war in Korea stopped the recession which had begun in 1948. The 1950 sugar crop was sold at a good price, bringing the island $381,200,000. Cuba was again off on a wave of inflation. In February, President Prio sent a message to Congress asking authorization to send a battalion of one thousand men to fight in Korea as Cuba's contribution to the United Nations. However, no troops were ever sent, due to the unpopularity of the idea among the public. The Cuban people considered the fighting in Korea a misadventure and marveled that the Americans could not win against the North Koreans. United States prestige in Cuba reached a new low by the time the armistice was signed in 1953. The Cuban people considered the United States soundly whipped by the Asiatics. They could not imagine how any nation could restrain their armed forces from attempting to win total victory and permit the slaughter of their men, as was done by the United States. The Cubans therefore could only believe that the United States had been defeated, both on the battlefield and in the field of honor.

The Cuban Peoples' Party, the *Ortodoxos,* headed by Dr. Eduardo Chibás, was becoming a major political party. This reform party was almost a one man show. "Eddie" Chibás was affectionately known throughout the island. With a Sunday night radio program, Eddie bitterly criticized the administration of President Prio. Chibás broadcast the evidences of graft which he found in the Prio government. People all over the island poured information concerning government officials into his office. This made him a sure presidential candidate for 1952.

Then, on August 5th, Eddie committed suicide just as he finished his usual Sunday night broadcast. He pulled his revolver out of his pocket and fired, the bullet passing through his stomach. He died in the hospital on August 16th. The reason for his suicide, according to reports, was his feeling of frustration and despair over a quarrel he was carrying on with Dr. Aurelio Sanchez Arango, Minister of Education. He had accused Sanchez Arango of graft and of having invested much of the money in Guatemalan real estate. He went so far as to broadcast that he had proof which he would present to the public. He was unable to present his proof since the persons who promised it, failed to deliver it. Persons close to him said that the necessity of retracting a charge of graft he was certain was true, and his despair of ever awakening the people of the island to demand honest government, brought him to the decision to commit suicide. Thousands attended his funeral. He is still the symbol around which the *Ortodoxo* Party is organized.

Dr. Roberto Agramonte, Professor of Psychology, Sociology, and Philosophy of Havana University, took over the *Ortodoxo* Party and was named its presidential candidate for the 1952 elections. Agramonte, a calm-mannered, soft spoken, forty-eight year old professor, was the exact opposite of rabble rousing Eddie. He had been Ambassador to Mexico during the regime of Grau San Martin and the running mate of Chibás in 1948 when Chibás was defeated for the presidency by President Carlos Prio Socarras. However, the lack of political personality of Dr. Agramonte failed to hinder him. The wave of emotion which followed the death of Eddie made the *Ortodoxo* candidate a favorite. As one official expressed it, "The ghost of Chibas ran for President with Agramonte as a stand-in."

President Prio Socarras was supporting the *Autentico* candidate, Carlos Hevia, an Annapolis graduate. Hevia had served as Minister of State. Although he lacked the usual jovial, glad handing political personality, he was known throughout the island as an honest and upright man. He spoke English, was well known abroad, and considered by the public as an excellent choice for a candidate.

It was a three-cornered race. Former President Fulgencio Batista, who had returned to Cuba in November of 1948, had organized the Unitary Action Party, gathered together all of his former followers and staged a costly campaign to win the votes of the public. Both of the presidential candidates, Batista and Agramonte, trained their guns on the Prio administration.

Then, without warning, came the military coup of March 10, 1952.

The yachts of the St. Petersburg-Havana Race were coming in on Sunday night, March 9th. Gene Carrier, the photographer for International News Service and Acme News Pictures, and I were on the Yacht Club waterfront where the boats tied up after they finished the race. It was three in the morning. The Yacht Club was full of local yachtsmen and the crews of the racing boats who were drinking at the bar and relaxing after the arduous voyage from St. Petersburg. The Yacht Club is built out into the bay and is a pleasant place. Small motorboats putted around the black harbor. Across the bay Cabañas Fortress stood high above the harbor, on a point of land which thrusts out into the Gulf of Mexico. Further out on the point is ancient Morro Castle with its lighthouse.

Later, Gene and I drove along the wide Avenida del Puerto. We passed the palace, only a few lights showing at that time of morning. I told Gene to drop me at the office because I was too tired to drive home. I stretched out on the couch, reading a little. At six o'clock the telephone rang. Evilio Rodriguez, chief of publicity at the palace, told me that General Fulgencio Batista had seized Camp Columbia army headquarters and that President Carlos Prio Socarras wanted to see the foreign press. I said I would go immediately to the palace.

Then the telephone rang again. It was Carlos Tellez of International News Service. He said he would come by for me on his way to the palace. I started dressing, but before I had finished the bell sounded. I had to go downstairs to open the door. I told Tellez he would have to wait a minute until I put on lipstick as I had no intention of going even to a revolution without lipstick. He laughed and said he would wait. Those few minutes probably saved the lives of Tellez, Antonio Apud, who was with him, and myself. As we drove past the Bock Tobacco company, Antonio failed to make the

turn into Colon Street, which I always used whenever I was
in a hurry to get to the palace. I asked Antonio why he did
not use Colon Street, but he pointed out that it was a one-
way street. Tellez and I laughed at him for obeying traffic
regulations in the midst of a revolution. There was not a
single vehicle except ours in that section of town and daylight had come swiftly and completely. As we turned the
corner to come back to the palace machine gun fire broke
out at the Colon Street entrance. Having had considerable
experience in revolutions, Antonio stopped the car and the
three of us jumped out and ran behind the big stone columns
of an old building there.

Between us and the palace was Zayas Park and the half-
finished Museum of Fine Arts, then under construction. The
workmen gathered at the museum ran in every direction.
Across the street from us was the Ministry of Defence and I
saw soldiers armed with machine guns peering out the doors
and windows. I told Tellez and Antonio that if the soldiers
started shooting our position was precarious. We took the
risk of running back to the car. The shooting continued. We
learned later that several cars filled with soldiers had driven
up to the palace entrance, and the Palace Guard had
opened fire on them. We got out of the district as fast as
possible.

Before I had left the office, I had called Gene, telling him
to come to the palace. I also left a note on my desk saying:
"I have gone to the palace." Gene, arriving opposite the
palace shortly after the firing broke out, maneuvered his car
behind the Bock Tobacco Company and went to my office.
Seeing my note, he got his camera and went to the palace.
By that time the shooting had ended. He said there were
several dead soldiers and a doctor was taking care of the
wounded. Everything was in a state of confusion. He walked
in without anyone even looking at him. He went to the
second floor to see if President Prio was there. Gene took
pictures of Prio with a delegation of students who were

urging him not to resign the Presidency. However, Prio decided that it was futile to resist and Gene took pictures of his departure. Prio, his family and several cabinet officials obtained refuge at the Mexican Embassy and left Cuba several days later.

The coup had been practically bloodless. Batista, supported by a group of army officers, had taken over Camp Columbia. Other Batista men had seized Cabañas Fortress. In the interior, military posts had been taken over by the younger elements of the army. Within two hours Batista had made himself ruler of Cuba. Though he had support in other quarters, it was his popularity with the military that had made such a lightning coup possible. Thus it came as a complete surprise to the people of Havana when the radio stations began broadcasting that General Fulgencio Batista had taken control of the government "in order to save the country from chaotic conditions which endangered lives and property." In a nationwide broadcast from Camp Columbia, Batista told the people that President Prio Socarras had planned to suspend the presidential elections and make himself a dictator. He said, "I have been forced to carry out this coup because of my love for the people. I shall re-establish public order. I ask the cooperation of all the people in Cuba in this task of peace and cordiality. Shoulder to shoulder we must work for the spiritual harmony of the great Cuban family."

The streets of Havana, which had been filled with carnival merrymakers the night before, were deserted. Detachments of police and soldiers appeared in all sectors of the city and tanks moved in to surround the Presidential Palace. Batista suspended constitutional guarantees and canceled the elections scheduled for June. He announced that all international treaties and pacts, as well as obligations assumed by Cuba with the United States, would be respected and fulfilled. He said that if the United States were attacked by or involved in a war with the Soviet Union, Cuba would fight on the side of the Americans. He promised protection to all United States investments or such capital as might make future investments in Cuba.

Many businessmen and merchants were pleased by the Batista coup, feeling that he would bring law and order to the country, stability that meant prosperity and a sounder economy. Thoughtful Cubans pointed out that the democratic processes had been violated and that Cuba was once again in the hands of the military. *The New York Times*, commenting on the reaction of the people, said, "The attitude of the majority of the Cubans toward Major General Fulgencio Batista's coup of March 10 seems to be a mixture of confusion, resentment and hope." Carlos Hevia accused Batista of "putting ambition for power above the supreme interests of the nation." Dr. Roberto Agramonte, the *Ortodoxo* Party presidential candidate, condemned "this attack against peace and juridical order."

Batista made his first appearance at the Presidential Palace a few days after the coup. He called a press conference for the newsmen and photographers from American publications who had been rushed to Havana. All the furniture had been removed from the office of the President to make room for the television cameras, radio apparatus and a large gathering of the press. An aide opened a side door and General Batista, dressed in a white suit, his favorite attire, strode into the room like a conqueror. He paused as the photographic bulbs flashed, then strode over to me with outstretched hand. "Mrs. Phillips," he said, "I haven't seen you for years but you look just the same as ever, not one bit different." It was a spontaneous, friendly greeting. One of the finest qualities of Batista is a natural warmth that is quite independent of his political status or his political strategy. His friendliness was absolutely sincere, not only to me, but to everyone he spoke with. For exactly this reason few people could resist his charm. Foreigners, especially Americans, always left his presence favorably impressed and convinced that he was doing everything possible for his country. He must have believed this himself.

I had known Batista since 1933 and he had always shown the utmost consideration for me in every way. Even though I had written strong criticism of him, he never changed, never spoke a harsh or disapproving word. He maintained that attitude even in those troubled last days before his government was overthrown by Fidel Castro, when he received me with a show of pleasure as one would a long-time friend. The tides of political fortune might cause him to use severe and even brutal repressive measures, but his personality was never altered by misfortune. He was a born politician, using that word to mean skill in handling the conflicting interests of a nation. Although backed by military force, he strove in every way too placate the vested interests of the nation, to put on a democratic front where no democracy had ever really existed. He managed Cuba by means of counterpoint, sometimes in the interest of the nation, and sometimes to perpetuate his own regime. He was a master at playing his enemies against each other, keeping them busy quarreling among themselves. During his regime, despite the tremendous opposition that grew up against him, the opposing political parties could never unite into a solid front against him. Only an armed rebellion could have ever overthrown Batista.

Within a few days after the coup Batista had obtained the support of business and industry. He had assured them that he would keep the island's populace quiet and orderly and had hinted that he would control labor. And there was a cessation of strikes. However, Batista failed to enact the legislation so long demanded by business and industry, that is, some regulation under which an employer could dismiss a worker with severance pay. Even today it is almost impossible to dismiss an employee on any grounds, and this remains one of the greatest deterrents to new investments.

Labor accepted the coup with philosophical calm. Senator

Eusebio Mujal, Secretary General of the Confederation of Cuban Workers, attempted to remain loyal to President Carlos Prio Socarras. Mujal called for a general strike on March 10th in protest of the coup, but there was no response from labor. Batista prohibited all strikes for forty-five days, arrested Mujal, and prepared to take over the Confederation. However, Mujal quickly made his peace with Batista.

The students of Havana University protested angrily over the coup. In April, after a four day "wake" in a spectacular ceremony, they buried the 1940 constitution of Cuba.

On March 11th Batista's cabinet was sworn in. Dr. Miguel A. Campa was appointed Minister of State; Marino Lopez Blanco, Minister of Treasury; Alfredo Jacomino, Minister of Agriculture; Dr. Pablo Carrera Justiz, Minister of Communications; Dr. Enrique Saladrigas, Minister of Health; Dr. Andres Rivero Aguero, Minister of Education; Dr. Ramon O. Hermida, Minister of Interior; Dr. José A. Mendiguita, Minister of Public Works; Dr. Miguel Angel Céspedes, Minister of Justice; Jesus Portocarrero, Minister of Labor; Oscar de la Torre, Minister of Commerce, Dr. Andres Domingo Morales del Castillo, Secretary of the Presidency; Nicolas Perez Hernández, Minister of Defense.

A new constitution was approved and Batista became the "Provisional President." He suspended Congress but did not take away their salaries. The law making powers were placed in the hands of General Batista and his cabinet, although an eighty member Advisory Council was created to make suggestions on legislation. Batista named General Francisco Tabernilla Chief of Staff of the Cuban Army. Lieutenant Rafael Salas, soon to be a General, was made Chief of the National Police. All of the top officers of the armed forces were removed or forced into retirement. One of Batista's first administrative acts was to increase the salary of all members of the armed forces.

On March 27th the United States government recognized the Batista administration.

On March 21, 1952, two Soviet couriers arrived at the

Rancho Boyeros Airport. A young lieutenant decided the luggage of the couriers must be searched, despite the existing diplomatic immunity. The couriers, Fedor Zaikog and Alex Selatoz, refused to permit this, and returned with their luggage to Mexico. On April 3rd the Soviet Union broke off diplomatic relations with Cuba and announced the closing of the Soviet Legation in the island.

Only a few people in Cuba at that time knew that the breaking off of relations with Cuba, which had long been a center for the distribution of Communist propaganda throughout Latin America, was the first step in a change of policy by Moscow. In line with this, the clandestine headquarters of the Communist International in Havana was closed. Five top members of the Cominform were ordered to return to Russia. The Cuban Communist Party, then numbering 150,000, was ordered to go underground and to reduce its membership to a hard core of faithfuls who were willing to remain anonymous and to await future instructions from Moscow. The party was told not to provoke public disorders, to reduce propaganda, and to stop the anti-American campaign. The well known leaders, such as Juan Marinello, Blas Roca, and hoarse voiced Lazaro Peña, were ruthlessly sacrificed. They became a species of clay pigeon at which Batista could shoot. They were jailed at various times and within a few months had fled the island.

President Batista was forced to turn his attention to the sugar industry. During 1952 Cuba produced an all time record crop of 7,011,393 long tons. There was mounting world production and prices were declining. In agreement with the Cuban sugar industry, Batista in June, 1952, withdrew from the market 1,750,000 long tons of sugar. This eased the market and the price of sugar steadied.

Complaining that the Prio administration had left the Treasury empty, Batista began raising taxes. Postal rates were upped; taxes were imposed on beer; income, profits and capital taxes were increased. On July 1st the 1952-53 budget was fixed by President Batista at $314,285,931.

People became increasingly impatient with the slowness of the government to resolve problems which had accumulated over the years. The Prio government had started improvements in Havana but nothing had been terminated. Havana looked like a bombed-out city of Europe. Streets were torn up. Low lying sections of the city were flooded every time it rained due to lack of drainage. Mosquitoes and flies swarmed over the city and suburbs. Public works projects were started and stopped, leaving Havana more ugly and more in ruins than before the projects had been undertaken. The Grau administration spent four years on one mile of the important highway stretching between Havana and the José Marti International Airport. The Prio government finally did complete this.

At last, in 1953, work began on projects in Havana. Batista began the deficit financing which was to continue throughout his administration. The policy of selling internal bond issues, which had begun during the Prio administration, continued.

The 1953 sugar crop was sold at an average price of 4.1¢ per pound and brought the Island $450,000,000. An unexpected sale to Great Britain of one million tons helped to dispose of the entire 1953 crop. The fiscal year of 1952-53, ending on June 30th, showed a deficit of some $30,000,000. President Batista and his cabinet decided to reduce the budget for the coming year. The salaries of government employees were cut ten per cent. Nevertheless, the financial situation of the government was regarded as favorable. All interests and amortization payments on foreign and internal indebtedness had been paid. Reserves in foreign exchange were 4.6% higher than in 1952. Commercial agreements had been made with West Germany, Spain and Great Britain through which Cuba expected to sell more sugar and tobacco during the coming years. The Agricultural and Industrial Bank of Cuba (BANFAIC), established by the Prio administration, got into stride during the Batista regime. For the first time, agriculture and industry found financial assistance and were able to expand considerably. The Bank also created as an autonomous division a counterpart of the Federal Housing Administration in the United States, and for the first time it became possible for the wage earner of Cuba to own his own home. The Cuban F.H.A. brought about a tremendous increase in construction of homes in Havana, particularly low priced homes, and gradually spread throughout the island. With the establishment of agricultural cooperatives the BANFAIC greatly assisted the small farmers, who never had the slightest encouragement in Cuba. These cooperatives are now proving to be a major factor in Cuban economy. Mineral activities in Cuba increased. Manganese, iron and copper exports rose. The Nicaro Nickel Company owned by the United States government, increased its production. Today Nicaro is considered one of the chief sources of nickel for the United States.

Despite all this, however, unemployment plagued the government. With a population of six million, the unemployment figure was estimated at one million. President Batista decreed important tax exemptions for new industries as a means of stimulating the investment of foreign capital in Cuba. However, the labor legislation continued to be one of the chief obstacles to investment.

The United Railways of Havana, burdened with antiquated equipment, with far too many employees it could not dismiss under the existing labor legislation, and with various other problems, had become an insupportable burden on Prio's government. President Batista decided to purchase the railway from the British and American stockholders. He reorganized the railway under the name of *Ferrocarriles Occidentales de Cuba,* S.A., retaining 50% of the stock and offering the other 50% to the public. The stock was not purchased by the public. The government later found it necessary to force all commercial and industrial firms of Havana to buy stock through the imposition of taxes.

Rumors of conspiracies circulated throughout Cuba almost from the beginning of the Batista regime. Not a month passed but the authorities announced the discovery of a new plot. Arrests and wholesale roundups of oppositionists were frequent. Continual targets for accusations were Carlos Prio Socarras, Dr. Aurelio Sanchez Arango, Carlos Hevia, and revolutionaries living in exile in the United States and Mexico. These leaders were openly conspiring, buying arms and ammunition. Their none-too-secret aims kept the Batista regime in a state of nerves.

On July 26, 1953—a memorable date in Cuban history—the revolt came to Santiago de Cuba. Dr. Fidel Castro, a 27 year old lawyer of Havana, and 165 young revolutionists from Havana and elsewhere attacked the Moncada Army Post with its garrison of one thousand soldiers.

It was one of those suicidal attempts which Cubans make so often. Just how 165 youths believed they could take an army post of this size is something I cannot understand. Fidel Castro said later that it had been well planned, that their hopes were based on the elements of surprise and split-second timing, but that forty-five of the men took the wrong street in approaching Moncada and failed to arrive on time. Perhaps. But it is my personal opinion that Cubans simply do not measure the odds against success, that, indeed, they tend to deliberately defy overwhelming odds.

Two girls were in the rebel group, Melba Hernandez and Haydee Santamaria. The latter is now the wife of Dr. Armando Hart, Minister of Education. Within the first hour of battle, the tide had turned against the attackers. They seized one section of the post and the nearby Palace of Justice but were beaten off in the ensuing battle. No official figures of the dead and wounded were ever issued. The best figure I could obtain was "over 100 soldiers and rebels killed." Fidel Castro claimed that the army had three times as many casualties as did his group. But the army captured and executed seventy of his followers and killed many townspeople. Most of the rebels were captured in the hills outside of Santiago, where they had fled after the attack.

The Archbishop of Santiago, Enrique Perez Servantes, arranged the surrender of the remaining rebels, including Fidel Castro.

Vague rumors of the battle reached Havana Sunday morning but all the newspapers were closed, except *El Crisol* and *Alerta*. I made numerous telephone calls to Santiago de Cuba and between the information I obtained and the reports being received by *El Crisol* we pieced the story together. Then Press Wireless informed me that censors had appeared there and had declared that no news about the revolt in Santiago could be sent out of the island. I called the All America Cable & Radio Company and discovered that, strangely, no censor had been sent to their office. I sent my dispatches immediately through All America. That was the first time since Batista had seized power in March, 1952, that censorship had been imposed. However, late that afternoon, when it became certain that government troops had emerged victorious, censorship was lifted.

Months later, the rebels were tried in the Urgency Court of Santiago de Cuba. All except Fidel Castro. After being held seventy-six days incommunicado in a cell, he was secretly brought to trial at the Civil Hospital. No defense witnesses were permitted. The press was barred. Fidel Castro, however, speaking in his own defense, made one of the most audacious speeches ever to be heard in a courtroom. Why the court permitted him to do this is strange. Perhaps—and this will make sense to Latin Americans, whose concept of justice includes not merely the question of guilt or innocence, but the personality and human value of the accused—the judges were curious about this tall, fearless and defiant young man who had won the respect of the university students and professors. At any rate, after Fidel Castro began speaking, he soon had the courtroom fascinated by his daring flow of oratory. Castro defended the revolt on the grounds that "Cuba is suffering the most cruel and shameful despotism." He described the tortures and killings by the army of the captured revolutionists, giving the names of the officers and men who had been guilty of this. At one point in his speech he said: "Moncada was converted into a place of death and torture. The walls were stained with blood. The walls were splattered with parts and particles of human bodies; skin, brains, human hair—not the marks of honorable death, but of bullets fired only a few inches from human bodies. This cruel and brutal indignity was the only mercy the prisoners received, and the grass was covered with their dark and sticky blood."

He declared that Batista was one of the most cruel and despicable dictators of the Americas. He recounted how Batista's soldiers had mowed down the officers who had surrendered after the battle of the National Hotel in Havana and also after the fight at the Atáres Fortress in 1933. "Will Cuba ever have justice or freedom under a tyrant who commits and permits such atrocities? Never!" Fidel Castro told the whole story of why and how the new revolution had been organized. He gave a list of reforms which he intended to put into effect just as soon as he and the youths of the island overthrew the Batista regime. The audacity of Fidel Castro approached a climax as he stood before the court, knowing that he was at their mercy, yet protesting not his innocence of the crime for which he was accused, but commanding them to accept him as the liberator of the Cuban Republic. He spoke of his reforms, not with the sad and regretful voice of a man defeated, but with the determination of a man who believed he would someday succeed. The reforms, which today his revolutionary government is enacting, were outlined by Castro in his defense as follows:

1. Revolutionary law—give back to the people the sovereignty proclaimed in the 1940 constitution; punish all those guilty of crimes against the republic and crimes against humanity; the revolutionary government would assume all powers to legislate, to judge and to execute.
2. Give ownership of all lands owned by Batista and his supporters to the cane planters, and to those who rented the

lands on which they raised crops, and to those whose lands had been confiscated by the military.

3. Grant the workers and employees the right of 30% of the profits of all large enterprises, industries, mines, and commercial firms, including the sugar mills.

4. Give all cane planters the right to get 55% of their sugar yield and a minimum quota of 40,000 *arrobas* for all small cane planters.

5. Confiscate all property of those who had robbed or otherwise misused government funds, and strip their heirs of the right to inherit these properties, through special courts which would have free access to all sources of investigation; investigate and intervene in all associations registered in the country; and also ask foreign governments for extradition of persons and property illegally removed from Cuba.

6. Nationalization of electric and telephone companies; return to the people all exorbitant amounts paid for electricity and telephones; reform the educational system; agrarian reform and reduction of rents by 50%.

Castro ended his historic "defense" by declaring that he felt grave sorrow for the judiciary in Cuba, which was compelled to take orders from Fulgencio Batista. "I know that you have already decided on my sentence," he said. "I will not shame good men by asking for justice where there is none to be given." Fidel Castro, his younger brother, Raul, and twenty-seven others were sentenced to fifteen years in prison. They were sent to the Isle of Pines Penitentiary.

In May, 1955, Congress declared an amnesty for all political prisoners. This amnesty was eventually to prove the downfall of Batista. For Fidel Castro walked out of prison a free man, having made no bargain or compromise to obtain his freedom. He was more than ever before determined to overthrow Batista. He and Raul went to Mexico, where other Cuban exiles were plotting against the dictator. There, in the rugged mountains of Mexico, with arms furnished by Carlos Prio Socarras and other exiles, they began training in guerrilla warfare under the tutelage of General Alberto Bayo, who had fought the Rifs in Africa, and who had fought with the Republican Army during the Spanish Civil War. This was the nucleus of the expedition which was to land on the south coast of Oriente Province on December 1, 1956.

Batista and the Council of Ministers approved a public order law which silenced the island. For centuries in Cuba the public has discussed politics in cafés, bars, buses and on the streets, but now no one dared talk. The law provided stiff penalties for "propaganda" against the government. Fines and jail sentences were imposed for *desacato*, the elastic offense of "disrespect" for the government, which had been made famous by Peron of Argentina. Batista was gradually accumulating all the evils that inevitably follow the primary evil of destroying a democratic process.

The principal newspapers of Havana eliminated editorials and printed no comments about the government. The public order law came under heavy fire at the Inter-American Press Association in Mexico City in October, 1953.

On October 24, 1953, Batista lifted censorship and restored some personal rights. But the law of public order remained in effect. Not until May 4, 1954, when election campaigns were about to get under way, did Batista repeal part of this law. However, the public continued to hesitate to discuss politics in public.

In March, 1952, Batista had dissolved all political parties, including his own Progressive Action Party. Later, he had announced that general elections would be held in November, 1953. The opposition refused to participate. Former President Ramon Grau San Martin registered his small section of the *Autentico* Party, but the majority of the organization held aloof. The *Ortodoxo* Party, which had been given the best chance of victory in the June 1, 1952 elections canceled by Batista, refused to register. Elections could not be held.

Batista then stated that elections would be held in June, 1954, but only to choose a Congress. On October 16, 1953,

Batista announced general elections would be held on November 1, 1954. All the parties would have until February, 1954 to reorganize and register. On October 31st, 1953, Batista outlawed the Communist Party. As the period granted for reorganization and registration closed, the lineup of the political parties for the election was: Batista's own Progressive Action Party, the Liberal Party, the Democratic Party and the newly organized Union Radical Party. The opposition was represented by a small faction of the *Autenticos* under the leadership of former President Grau San Martin, and a small faction of the *Ortodoxo* Party which had been registered by Federico Casas. The majority of the opposition refused to accept the legality of the polls.

The government rejected the demand of Grau San Martin that voters be permitted to split their ticket. Batista remembered well that it was the split ticket provision, established in 1944, which had given Grau San Martin the presidency. Batista wished no repetition of that experience.

In April, 1954, Dr. Carlos Saladrigas, Minister of Labor, announced that the right to dismiss workers, long denied the Cuban employer, would be restored. This caused a storm of protest from labor. The government backed down.

Meanwhile, Batista was attempting to keep the island on an even keel economically. A decline in the national economy due to the reduced sugar crops and the tightening of money in the island, partly a psychological reaction to the disturbed political situation, faced Batista with the necessity of spending more money in public works. On June 11, 1954, he announced that bonds in the amount of $350,000,000 would be issued to finance a huge public works program. These bonds were to bear interest of 4% and were payable within thirty years. The program included roads, aqueducts, public buildings, hospitals, modernization and expansion of civil and military communications, and agricultural and industrial projects.

In July, Batista announced he would run for president and was quickly nominated by the government coalition parties. According to the electoral code, Batista was forced to resign in August, in order to carry on his campaign for the presidency. Grau San Martin was Batista's only opponent. Grau began to gather strength as prominent *Autenticos*, followers of former President Prio Socarras, announced their support. Grau was not popular with commerce, industry or the middle class, who remembered his previous administration. However Grau's party would automatically receive the minority representation in the Senate, three senatorships in each province, as compared to the majority representation of six senatorships in each province.

The *Ortodoxo* Party refused to participate in the elections. The *Autenticos*, who continued to regard former President Prio Socarras as their leader, considered the elections illegal.

On August 14th, Batista turned over the presidency to Dr. Andres Domingo Morales del Castillo. Morales del Castillo fulfilled his temporary duties quietly and unobtrusively and the public continued to regard Batista as the real head of the government.

Batista staged a lavish political campaign. He traveled through the island, visiting every town of any size. He spoke to thousands, shook thousands of hands. A crane, called *La Grulla* in Spanish, was injected into the campaign by Batista when he told the story of how in 1939, a crane was struck by an automobile on his farm at Ceiba de Agua. Batista caught the crane, its leg broken and dangling, swiftly cut off the leg and applied first aid. When the leg healed the General whittled a wooden leg for the crane and attached it with tape. The bird learned to walk with the wooden leg and became a pet on the farm. After the departure of Batista from the island, the crane languished and later died during a hurricane. The General likened the crane to Cuba. Batista claimed that he had found Cuba wounded and broken. He had given the country a good administration, but neglect by succeeding administrations had brought Cuba to such grief that he was forced once again to seize power. Or Cuba, like the crane, would die.

The story of the crane caught the imagination of the masses. *Viva la Grulla* was shouted at all political meetings. Newspapers talked of the crane, cartoonists featured the bird with its wooden leg, thousands of campaign buttons in the form of the crane were distributed. It is no tribute to the Cuban people to admit that *La Grulla* influenced them more than any profound study of economy or law could possibly have done. But if the Cuban masses are to be understood, if Cuban politics are to be understood, the appeal of such symbols must be recognized.

On October 27th the largest cache of arms and ammunition found up to that time was discovered in the cellar of the home of a former member of the House of Representatives, Francisco Cairol, who was already in the Isle of Pines prison serving a sentence for conspiracy. The government immediately began to round up all opposition elements. Bombs began to explode throughout the island and the government prepared for the outbreak of a revolution.

Grau San Martin threatened to withdraw from the elections. He declared the armed forces were being used by the government to coerce voters. He demanded the cessation of outrages against voters, complete freedom of the press, the return to voters of electoral registration cards allegedly in the hands of the government, and permission for the public to watch the counting of the votes. The government went ahead with preparations to hold elections as scheduled. Thousands of troops were distributed around the island to guard the polling precincts.

Herbert L. Matthews and I went to see Dr. Grau San Martin. The indomitable old man voiced his fears about the coming elections. He could not depend on the direct vote for president which had allowed him to win the elections once before. Batista, not likely to make the same mistake twice, had seen to it that the direct vote was abolished. We sat talking with Grau on the long porch which looks out onto a walled patio. Grau is a master at parrying questions and giving vague answers, but it was apparent that he did not believe he stood a chance. The wily old politician seemed to me merely to enjoy keeping his hat in the ring, and perhaps was basing his campaign on such slim possibilities as Batista dying unexpectedly, or on some sudden turn of events. Once during the discussion he looked at me and said, smiling, "I don't know why I am saying this. Mrs. Phillips knows the situation here just as well as I do."

Then, on October 31st, Dr. Grau withdrew from the elections. He said he could not be a candidate because of the "lack of guarantees for an impartial election."

Batista angrily announced that elections would be held despite the withdrawal of Grau. He accused Grau of adopting a conspiratorial attitude. He said Grau was withdrawing because he knew the people would all vote for Batista. Grau countered with the statement that it was true he knew he could not win a "rigged" election. He asked his adherents not to go to the polls. Dr. Roberto Agramonte, head of the *Ortodoxo* Party, which had refused to participate in the elections ever since they had been announced, approved and applauded Grau's act. Many people, however, including some Grau supporters, disapproved, feeling that they had been robbed of even a minor voice to represent them.

Batista was now without opposition for the presidency. The public washed its hands of the whole matter. On election day there was no excitement of any kind. Thousands of voters stayed away from the polls either on Grau's orders or through indifference. Even in the interior, where voting is always attended by some disorder, there was peace and tranquillity.

General Fulgencio Batista was elected President of Cuba. Returns showed that only 50% of the people had voted despite the fact that voting is obligatory under the law. However, it could hardly be expected that the courts could prosecute half the people. A few of Grau's party candidates won in their districts and the minority representation in the Senate went automatically to his party.

The New York Times, commenting editorially, called it

"Cuba's Strange Election." It said: "Cuba has just gone through one of the strangest and most potentially dangerous elections in her history."

General Fulgencio Batista was inaugurated on February 25, 1955. He took office in the Salón of Mirrors of the Presidential Palace, before a packed assembly of diplomats, members of Congress, government officials, and high-ranking army, navy and police officers. Outside thousands crowded around the palace and cheered.

A few hours before the inaugural ceremony police in the outskirts of Havana killed Orlando Leon Lemus, known as *El Colorado* and José Fernandez Rodriguez. The two were planning a campaign of violence against the government, according to the official statement.

The months between President Batista's election and his inauguration had been disturbed by bombings, which continued after the inauguration. Oppositionists at home and abroad smarted over his election and renewed their efforts to bring about a revolution. Capital, however, was pleased over Batista's election. Since he was now "constitutional president" they felt that the political and economic situation would improve. They had confidence in Batista's ability to bring stability to the island.

In July I went to Miami to buy a few clothes. Despite the fact that I was taking only a few days vacation, I decided to see Carlos Prio Socarras. I called his secretary and made an appointment. The taxi driver who took me out to the home of Dr. Prio looked at me curiously. At the gate an armed man came to see who had arrived. The driver remarked, "These Cubans seem to have lots of enemies. They must live a tough life."

There were several people in the living room when I went in. One of them was former President Carlos Hevia, whom I had not seen for some time. Prio was pleased to see me and told me he was going back to Havana to organize the opposition into a united front for elections. I wrote the story, which in some measure paved the way for his return.

When Dr. Prio returned to Cuba, he was met by a huge crowd at the airport. Ted Scott and I went to the Hotel National to see him. Ted wanted to tape an interview for NBC but we finally retreated to the bedroom since the living room was overflowing with friends, relatives, photographers and newsmen. Mrs. Prio, a very beautiful woman, seemed very happy to be back in Cuba. After the questions had been asked and Prio had dictated his answers to his secretary, he sat down on the bed and read them aloud a couple of times, laughing whenever he couldn't pronounce a word in English correctly. Then Ted made the tape recording. Prio declared that he would not participate in any future conspiracies against the Cuban government, but would organize the opposition parties into a solid bloc against the government and win the next elections. He was never able to do this. The opposition parties were split into many factions too bitterly opposed to one another to make agreement possible. Prio retreated to *La Chata,* his beautiful country estate, which President Batista had seized at the time of the coup, but later quietly turned back to Prio's lawyer in Havana.

I had visited this estate while Batista still had soldiers occupying it. The house is large and cost a considerable amount of money. But it was the swimming pool which attracted my attention. It is some distance from the house and has a Hollywood atmosphere, water pouring into the pool from a waterfall at one end, the whole lighted by hidden lights. There was a huge bathhouse with a pavilion where a hundred people could have danced, modern kitchen, pantries, dressing rooms. The only other thing unusual was a collection of jade which Prio kept in a special cabinet in the house.

The Cuban economic situation improved slightly during 1955. Russia purchased 500,000 long tons, but the island still had 1,268,000 long tons in reserve quotas. Batista embarked on a four-point program to ease the situation, particularly unemployment, with the three hundred fifty million dollar bond issue which he had authorized in 1954. The

program included public works, encouragement of new industries, and an increase of locally grown food products to
reduce imports.

In November, I decided to tour the island. Havana is so
much the focal point of everything that happens in Cuba
that one tends to have to force oneself to get away from it,
even for a few days. New Yorkers would probably understand this. Irma, Gene and I, one warm November morning,
drove down the Central Highway through hills and valleys
covered with Royal palms, to Matanzas. Matanzas, one of
the most magnificent harbors in the Western Hemisphere,
was founded in 1693. We stopped for *café con leche* and native bread, cut in strips, buttered and toasted, which is the
breakfast of most Cubans.

Across from the café was the Central Plaza, which in Colonial days had been the scene of many executions. I wanted
to see the Monserrate Hermitage. Perched on a hill, the old
church overlooks Yumuri Valley, one of the loveliest areas
of Cuba. There we saw, sitting on the wall, probably the
first red breasted robin arrived for the winter. Although I do
not like caves, just as I would never like a house with only
one window, we went a little way into the Bellamar Caves,
located near the shore. These Caves are famous the world
over. They are similar to the Mammoth Caves of Kentucky.

Leaving Matanzas, the country was level with miles of
cane on each side of the road. We passed through villages
strung like identical beads on a string. There were signs of
considerable prosperity—new homes, new filling stations,
new stores and a general air of improvement. Along the
highway the government was building small square houses
to replace the old picturesque—and undoubtedly unsani-
tary and unhealthy—*bohios* with their thatched roofs. My
sister complained that Batista was ruining the landscape.
We went then to Santa Clara, the capital of Las Villas Province, built around a central plaza, sprawling in every direction. It was here that the decisive battle of the "26th of July"
revolution was to be fought and won by the rebels. We

stayed at a new hotel which had been built with a hopeful eye toward tourists.

The next morning we drove to Sancti Spiritus, the center of the cattle industry. There we left the Central Highway, which goes on through Camagüey and Oriente Province and ends at Santiago de Cuba. We traveled southward through the Escambray Mountains towards Trinidad, the oldest town of the American continent. Along the way we saw men roasting a pig over a fire. Gene took a picture. It smelled good and the men invited us to join them, but it would have been hours until it was roasted. This is *lechon,* always eaten by the Cubans on *Noche Buena,* just as Americans always serve turkey on Thanksgiving Day. Trinidad has been declared a national monument. At Trinidad Hernan Cortes had gathered his expedition to set sail and conquer Mexico. Someone showed us an ancient ceiba tree near the mouth of a small river, where Cortes is said to have tied up his flagship when he arrived in the New World.

The government has prohibited changes in the central part of Trinidad. It stands just as it was centuries ago, with cobblestone streets never intended for automobiles. We visited the five churches and the palaces built by the Spanish *Hidalgos.* It was in this atmosphere that I sense how far removed modern Cuba is from its original culture. The centuries of Spanish domination were now no more than a tourist attraction—for Cubans as well as Americans. That night we stayed at a motel on a high hill. The cottage we occupied had a long living room, two bedrooms and a bath. From the terrace one had the impression of being able to reach out and touch the nearby mountains. We slept under woolen blankets with the wind whistling through the corridors of the mountains. Below were the lights of Trinidad, and off to the left the lights of the small port, Casilda, on the Caribbean Sea.

Underneath the hill on which we slept was one of the most fantastic caves imaginable. The owner of the motel had planned to establish a night club in it, and a great deal of work had been done. Broad stone steps led into a huge vaulted circular cavern. Natural air shafts running upward to the surface made the circulation of air so perfect that no ventilation was needed. Another huge recess had been adapted for dancing by installation of a tile floor. This had a natural stone platform for tables and the orchestra. On the other side was a cavern which was to be used for a gambling casino. Glittering stalactites and stalagmites and colored rock formations, lighted by floodlights, provided a décor which could never be artifically duplicated. It changed my opinion about caves.

We went to Cienfuegos over the new road which the Batista government was building, although we had been warned that in some places there was deep sand, since the road ran along the coast. It reminded me of Texas. During the entire trip we saw only one man on horseback, and one fisherman and his family. Heavy underbrush and trees crowded the highway on the land side, with only a few trails leading into seemingly impenetrable thicket.

We arrived in Cienfuegos in time for lunch. The seafood, for which the town is famous, lived up to its reputation. We returned to Havana along the southern route to Rodas, then northward through rice fields and cattle ranches to the Central Highway. Havana seemed strange to me, almost unreal, as if its swarming traffic and chaotic noise belonged to some other country, not to the agricultural provinces which I had visited.

A wave of disorders at the end of Nevember resulted in the death of several students and the jailing of more than a hundred. Oppositionists accused police of brutality and deliberate killings. President Batista declared the disorders "must and will stop." Not a week passed without announcement by authorities of the discovery of a conspiracy. Early in 1956, against a background of student disorders and bombings, President Batista opened discussions with the opposition to try to bring about political peace so that elections could be held. Batista had been successful for years in playing one group against another. Now, ironically, Batista discovered that he could not bring the factions together again. They could not even agree on what to demand from Batista. The only thing the opposition could agree on was that they wanted Batista out of the presidency. After several conferences between Dr. Torriente, "the grand old man of politics," and Batista it was decided that a committee should be appointed of both the opposition and government parties to discuss a possible settlement. These efforts were futile. The government would not agree to general elections.

The knife murder of a Dominican exile, "Pipi" Hernández, who had been living in Havana for several years resulted in a quarrel between Cuba and the Dominican Republic which strained relations to the breaking point. Hernández had been a foreman at the Habana Hilton Hotel, then under construction. Dominicans who had fled the vengeance of the Dominican Republic, and who had been given protection in Cuba, accused Trujillo of having Hernández assassinated. Evidence was uncovered which led Cuban authorities to believe that Trujillo was giving weapons to the Prio revolutionists and planned to help overthrow the Batista regime.

Trujillo had long feared and hated Cuba. The Grau San Martin administration had helped to arm the Cayo Confites expedition in 1947. The Prio administration had protected and aided Dominican exiles. When General Batista took over the Cuban government in 1952, he was cold to all offers of Trujillo's friendship. Dominican exiles continued to live in Cuba unmolested. Early in 1956 the Chief of Staff of the Dominican Republic army, General Felix Hermida, publicly accused Francisco Tabernilla, Chief of Staff of the Cuban Army, of giving arms to Dominican exiles. Cuba, angered by these charges, took the case before the Inter-American Peace Committee of the Organization of American States on Feb. 27, 1956. Cuba declared that the accusation of General Hermida was false and accused the Dominican Republic of sending spies to Cuba, in particular, Captain Ulises Sanchez Hinojosa of the Dominican army, who had entered Cuba in the guise of an exile. Cuba also accused secret agents of Trujillo of being involved in the murder of Hernández.

Minister of State, Dr. Gonzalo Guell, informed me about the appeal to the Organization of American States. I sent the story. The next day I received an indignant cable from the Dominican Minister of State claiming that Captain Sánchez was not a member of the Dominican army. That same day I obtained a clipping from the government owned Dominican newspaper *El Caribe* stating that Captain Sanchez Hinojosa had returned to the Dominican army after having been away on a secret military mission. I wrote a note to the Dominican Minister of State acknowledging his cable and attached the clipping. I haven't heard from him since.

The whole thing was a tempest in a teapot. Nothing ever came of it. Batista was having too much trouble on the home front to consider seriously an attack on the Dominican Republic. He may even have favored Trujillo, but considered it unwise to let this become known to the Cuban people.

In April, 1956 a conspiracy of young army officers, headed by Colonel Ramon Barquin Lopez, Military Attaché of the Cuban Embassy in Washington, was discovered by army intelligence. The officers were arrested and court-martialed. Thirteen, including Colonel Barquin, were sentenced to six years' imprisonment. Then came another revolt in Matanzas in which fifteen youths were killed. This was another suicidal attempt. Using trucks protected by sandbags, the small group attacked the Matanzas rural guard post on Sunday morning, April 29th. The soldiers shot them down with machine guns. Former President Prio was accused of fomenting the plot and was arrested but released almost immediately.

Several days later I went out to see Dr. Prio at *La Chata*. His public relations counsel, Sr. Rene Fiallo, drove me out since he said that undoubtedly the detachment of soldiers surrounding Prio's estate would think I was a friend or relative of his, and therefore allow us to enter the estate. Such a ruse was necessary because the government had imposed censorship on foreign correspondents. We passed the soldiers at the gate and drove in without incident. Sitting in one of the salons, Dr. Prio and I talked about the situation. He denied that he had anything to do with the attack on the Matanzas post. "I would not send boys to certain death," he said. He pointed out that only youths untrained in military tactics would have made such an attempt.

Apparently the government decided that Dr. Prio was too dangerous to be allowed to remain in Cuba. The day after my interview, he was put aboard a plane bound for Miami. When he arrived in Miami he said he had been told by President Batista to "either get out or go to jail."

Cuba was beginning to enter a period of prosperity. The sugar crop had been sold for $452,000,000. With the government pouring money into industry through its various banking institutions and into building construction through the F.H.A., a counterpart of the F.H.A. in the United States, the economy was rapidly expanding. Building construction had always been one of the bright spots of the economy and now a real boom started which changed the skyline of Havana within the next two years.

Many beautiful old colonial homes in Vedado, which begins just beyond the Maine Monument, were torn down and apartment houses built. Cooperative apartment houses are known in Cuba as *propriedad horizontal*. The largest of these was the Focsa. It is one of the largest in Latin America and dwarfed everything in the neighborhood, until the thirty-two-story Habana Hilton Hotel was completed. New apartment houses appeared in all the residential sections of Havana. All of the famous old restaurants were redecorated and air-conditioned. Hundreds of little clubs and bars opened—small, dark, with garish commercial-art murals, and so air-conditioned that it was a shock to enter them from the tropical night. The suburbs and highways around Havana were beginning to look like Florida. The big distributors of office equipment and household appliances moved out of Old Havana where streets are narrow and there is no parking space. New streets were paved and old streets patched. The Plaza de la Republica, beyond the Principe Fortress Prison, with its monument to José Marti, became like the hub of a huge wheel of new buildings; the Ministries of Communications and Justice, the Tribunal of Accounts, Ministry of Labor, National Library, National Theater, and City Hall.

President Batista had legalized gambling as a means of attracting tourists and to promote the construction of new hotels. The law permitted any hotel which represented an investment of one million dollars and any night club with an investment of two hundred thousand dollars to open casinos. Immediately, capital came to Cuba from the United States to build hotels.

The Habana Riviera and the Hotel Capri were the two largest hotels built by investors seeking gambling profits. The Habana Hilton was financed by the retirement fund of the Hotel and Restaurant Workers and was leased to the Hilton Hotels International Corporation. The Hotel National opened its casino in the 1955-56 winter season. Other casinos were opened at the Hotel Riviera, Hotel Capri, Hotel Sevilla Biltmore and the Comodoro Hotel. Three night clubs, the Montmartre, Sans Souci and Tropicana, had been operating casinos for several years with the tacit consent of the government. Tourism began to increase. Entertainment became more lavish. Name performers were brought from the United States and Europe for elaborate shows. Night life in Havana reached new peaks of gaiety and extravagance. Havana was making a bid for the title of "Riviera of the Caribbean."

Then in October violence again flared. Colonel Antonio Blanco Rico, chief of Cuba's military intelligence service, the SIM, and a group of friends were waiting for the elevator in the luxurious Montmartre night club. Two or three gunmen (the number was never clarified) killed Blanco, wounding also Lieutenant Colonel Marcelo Tabernillo, son of the Chief of Staff of the Cuban Army, his wife, and Senora Laura de Martinez, the wife of an army captain. The gunmen escaped down the automobile ramp which led from the ground to a second-story garage.

President Batista accused Carlos Prio Socarras during the Inter-American Press Association conference of having murdered Lieutenant Colonel Blanco Rico to convince foreign newsmen there was no peace and security in Cuba.

The afternoon following the killing, Brigadier General Rafael Salas Canizares, Chief of the National Police, sent a detachment of police to surround the Haitian Embassy, where nine Cuban youths had taken asylum several weeks before. The new Haitian Ambassador had gone out to lunch, leaving the embassy occupied only by the nine Cuban boys, the cook and a houseman. Canizares and several of his aides entered the Haitian Embassy. What actually occurred will probably never be known. Several of the boys were sitting in the salon. One was asleep upstairs. Another was taking a bath. Canizares and those accompanying him shot and killed the nine boys. One of the group, however, had a revolver. No political exile is permitted to be armed. The boy shot the Chief of Police in the lower abdomen. Some sources insist that the boy, dying from his wounds, drew his revolver and fired. Others claim that the boy fired the first shot and thereby enraged the police. Neither of these versions sounds quite true to me. But the police can scarcely be excused for violating the Haitian Embassy and killing eight unarmed youths. Ernestina Otero rushed out to Camp Columbia Hospital where she knew the General would be taken. Ernestina was there when they brought Canizares into the emergency section, which is just behind the hospital, separated from the main building. He was carried in, protesting that he was not badly injured. As she stood just outside the door of the emergency operating room, the General's brother arrived. Colonel José Maria Salas Canizares is a tall man with a brutal face and rough manner. He was later to become known in Oriente Province as the "Butcher."

He stormed toward the door, swearing at the top of his lungs. Suddenly he saw Ernestina. He shouted, "Get out of here," and gave her a shove.

Ernestina ran. But instead of leaving, she slipped into a small room adjacent to another operating room. Then she heard the siren of an ambulance. There was a window in the little room which permitted her to look into the operating room. It was the type of glass through which one can see without being seen from the other side. She watched as two boys were brought in, still alive, although riddled with bullets. They were dumped onto the operating tables like bags of flour. One lifted his head, stared around, then dropped back. The other was moving his lips. He lifted his hand and let it fall back. An officer came in. He consulted with one of the orderlies. "Get a doctor for them," he said. Just then Captain Moryon, an aide of Colonel Salas Canizares, burst in. He looked at the two wounded men, then shouted, "Never mind the doctor." He grabbed a knife from a table covered with instruments and cut the throats of both the boys. Ernestina said she would never forget the scene.

The Chief of Police died on October 31st. No one mourned him. He had been a killer all his life. Even at the time he helped Batista seize control of the government he had two charges pending against him in the police department for having killed without provocation.

IV _Fidel Castro_

12

On December 2, 1956, I arrived at the *New York Times* office early in the afternoon, as was my custom on Sundays. Immediately I received an inquiry about a report the United Press in Havana sent to New York stating that a revolutionary expedition headed by Fidel Castro, had landed on the south coast of Oriente Province, that it had been annihilated by the Cuban air force, and that Fidel Castro had been killed. Neither the Associated Press nor I knew anything about it. I was somewhat provoked that my sources had failed me. I quickly confirmed that an expedition had landed at Las Coloradas, sometimes known as Colorada de Belis, and had been attacked by air. But I could not confirm that Fidel Castro had been killed. I telephoned the newsman who helps me in Manzanillo, which has a large army post and an airfield. He told me that planes had been bombing the coast at Las Coloradas since the previous day and that troops were being moved from Manzanillo and Niquero into that district. He explained that Las Coloradas is not a sand beach, but a swampland which changes into jungle-like terrain further inland, and was practically uninhabited.

Sunday is a bad day to have a story. Government officials usually spend the weekends at their country estates. This was the second time Fidel Castro had started a revolution on Sunday, apparently figuring that it was the best time to catch the government troops napping. No source I had would confirm that Castro had been killed. But the *Times* foreign desk kept pressing me. We argued at various times during the night over the telephone. The editor on duty would not agree with me over the matter of confirmation, and the *Times* front-paged the death of Castro, in line with the report by Francis L. McCarthy, head of the United Press Bureau in Havana. A few days later McCarthy reported that Fidel Castro had been buried at Las Coloradas in the *flor de tierra*, that is, just beneath the surface of the ground, so his body could be easily exhumed. Not until Herbert L. Matthews talked with Fidel Castro in the Sierra Maestra mountains two months later was the McCarthy report finally proven false. Apparently McCarthy's information came from an officer in the Cuban air force, who had taken part in the air attack on the Castro expedition and who was enthusiastic about the accuracy of his bombing.

The report in *The New York Times* on the history-making interview between Fidel Castro and Herbert Matthews in February, 1957 was carried by the wire service and this prompted Edward (Ted) Scott of N.B.C. to write in his column in the Havana *Post* that Francis L. McCarthy and the U.P. had brought about a miracle of a kind that had not been seen since the son of man was born 2000 years previous.

The Matthews interview had tremendous impact, not only on Cuba, but on the entire hemisphere. Both the Batista government and the U.P. (now U.P.I.) had successfully convinced many people that Castro was dead. Matthews proved that Fidel was not only very much alive but was preparing to destroy the Batista regime. To that degree the meeting of Castro and Matthews was indeed a resurrection and the turning point of Castro's military fortunes.

Fidel Castro firmly believed that upon the arrival of his expedition the island would rise in revolt. But only his young followers in Santiago de Cuba made an attempt. On November 30th they attacked the strong army garrison at Moncada. The town echoed the sounds of rifles and machine guns. Many students were killed. The movement was crushed. General Diaz Tamaya, in charge of the military forces of Oriente Province, made an attempt to halt the bloodshed. This later cost him his post. One group of students barricaded themselves in a school. Surrounded by soldiers, they refused to surrender. General Diaz Tamayo called the parents of the youths together, told them he would withdraw his soldiers from one entrance of the school and permit them to go in and try to convince their sons to come out. Otherwise he would have to order the soldiers to take the school by force. The parents were able to persuade their protesting sons to leave the building.

President Batista immediately suspended constitutional guarantees in four of the six provinces of the island, maintaining them in Havana and Matanzas Provinces, apparently in the interst of the tourist season then in progress. However, in Havana, police and soldiers stood guard at public buildings, strategic points such as bridges, the harbor tunnel, and entrances to the city. The dreaded Military Intelligence Service, SIM, patroled the streets day and night and began a roundup of all revolutionary elements.

In Havana, news of the Castro expedition stirred little interest among the general public. It was considered merely another hare-brained scheme, like the suicidal attack on Moncada Post in 1953. Commerce and industry were prospering, the tourist season was good, the government was pouring millions into public works and new industry. Capital hoped the government would crush the tiny rebellion without loss of time.

Only the youth of the island was solidly behind Fidel Castro with his avowed intention of overthrowing the Batista regime. Only boys and girls from twelve to twenty-five believed it could be done, and they went into action. Terrorism flared. Bombs exploded; trains were derailed; towns were blacked out by sabotage of power lines; incendiary fires were started by the young revolutionists. Molotov cocktails, bottle of gasoline capped with a piece of waste and set afire, were hurled into trucks, government buildings and warehouses, the exploding gas scattering fire in every direction.

The Batista government issued statements claiming the rebels were being wiped out. The communiqués of Camp Columbia army headquarters announced skirmishes in which "many rebels were killed."

There were never accurate figures issued. Then one verified story reached Havana—fifteen youths had been captured and shot. This act prevented other rebels from surrendering in response to an offer by the army to spare their lives if they would lay down their arms. No one, not even the army, knew that the entire expedition had been killed or captured with the exception of Fidel Castro and eleven men.

Then the Batista government made its first major mistake. The bodies of youths began to appear on the streets and roads of town in the interior, particularly in Oriente Province. Once, I reported that the army had found twenty-one bodies in twenty-four hours around Holguin in the northern part of Oriente. The soldiers arrested the boys and killed them, then announced their bodies had been "found."

I looked in my files to get more information about Fidel Castro Ruz. He was born on August 13, 1926 on the Manacas Finca, in the district of Biaran, municipality of Mayari in Oriente Province. He was the third child of Señor Angel Castro Argo and Sra. Lina Ruz Gonzalez. He had a half brother and half sister, Lidia and Pedro, born of the first marriage of his father, the mother of these children having died; also two sisters and two brothers, Ramon and Angela, older than Fidel, and Raul and Juana, who were younger. Fidel was educated in Oriente Province, at a country school near the farm, then in La Salle School of Santiago de Cuba and later at the Dolores School. He had been an unusually active child, who spent all his available time riding horses about the countryside and hunting. A priest at the Dolores

School told me how he had taken Fidel and a group of boys into the Sierra Maestra Mountains on camping trips. These were Fidel Castro's revolutionary headquarters during the rebellion.

Later Señor Castro brought his children to Havana. Fidel entered Catholic Belen College for boys. His teachers reported that he was a brilliant scholar and a top athlete, his favorite sport being basketball. He was taller than the average Cuban, and possessed tremendous energy and determination in everything he did. Castro graduated from Belen in 1945 and entered Havana University to study law. He was an intense, idealistic youth who dominated his classmates on any question in which he was interested. One man who went to the university with him said recently that the students were a little in awe of Fidel. His remarkable ability at oratory usually resulted in the students giving him his way without opposition.

Fidel Castro interrupted his studies to take part in the Cayo Confites expedition against Trujillo of the Dominican Republic in 1947. From the beginning he revealed himself as an opponent of all forms of tyranny. When the Cuban armed forces broke up the Cayo Confites expedition and captured most of the young revolutionists, he escaped by swimming across the shark-filled bay, burdened with a machine gun and ammunition. Fidel, who had always been a leader in student affairs and intensely interested in politics, became a confirmed revolutionist. He returned to the university and resumed his studies. He became engaged and later married Señorita Mirtha Diaz Balart. They had one son, "Fidelito" (little Fidel), now nine. Several years before he embarked on the rebellion which overthrew the Batista regime Mirtha obtained a divorce. She did not approve of his revolutionary activities.

The year after the Cayo Confites effort, Fidel went to Bogota, Columbia, as a delegate of Havana University to a Latin American student congress. The student congress was scheduled to meet at the same time as the Ninth Conference of American States. The intention of the students was to protest against United States policies. A number of groups wished to break up the conference, including the Communists, who seem to have planned the matter efficiently. Jorge Elecier Gaitan, a leader of the Popular Party in Bogota, was killed. Riots broke out. Columbia has always had violence in politics. Many were killed in the rioting and millions of dollars worth of property was destroyed.

Castro became involved in this *Bogotazo* and finally had to take refuge in the Cuban Embassy. Dr. Guillermo Belt, head of Cuba's delegation to the Conference of American States, arranged to have Castro and several companions flown out of Bogota. Batista later made political use of this incident, stating that it proved Fidel Castro was a Communist. There can at least be no doubt that Castro did commit himself, if not to the Communists, to a Latin American group that had strong anti-United States sentiments.

Fidel graduated from Havana University in 1950 and began to practice law. He defended numerous people of the lower classes caught in the snares and technicalities of the law, and also took on a few criminal cases, but his main interest remained in politics. He was an admirer and follower of Eduardo Chibás, who founded the *Ortodoxo* Party and later committed suicide. When Batista overthrew the Prio administration in March, 1952 and seized the government, Castro presented a brief to the Urgency Court in Havana asking the court to declare the assumption of power by Batista unconstitutional. No attention was given to this petition. Castro then decided that he had no recourse except to try to overthrow Batista by force of arms. I have described previously the suicidal attack at Moncada and the trial and imprisonment of Castro which resulted.

The December, 1956 expedition marked the first time in the history of the Republic that an armed group had invaded Cuba for the purpose of overthrowing the government. This interested me. I admired the courage of this small group of

young men, but I was not convinced that such an attempt
had any real chance of success. All previous overthrows of
the government had been by military coups. Only the army,
or a political group supported by the army, had the power
to put presidents into office and to remove them at will.
Since 1933 the army had remained loyal to Batista. He had
increased the size of the army enormously and had established new military posts throughout the island. Camp Columbia had been rebuilt, with modern barracks, hundreds
of houses for soldiers, clubs for officers and enlisted men,
and the finest hospital facilities in Cuba. Batista had raised
the pay of the armed forces, provided uniforms that the
soldiers were proud to wear, and had made their living conditions pleasant for them. The army was not likely to falter
in its support of Batista, and for this reason I did not believe
that Castro could succeed.

This revolution had certain similarities with the 1933
movement against Machado. In both revolts terrorism and
sabotage were major instruments of resistance. But the terrorism of the Castro rebels was carried out by small groups,
while in 1933 it had been done by a vast network of student
engineers, chemists, and others with professional skills and
organizational abilities, and had been much more efficient
than the present group. On the other hand, sabotage was
used more effectively by the Castro rebels, whose targets
were military installations, supplies and transport, and whose
operations were island wide; whereas in 1933 sabotage had
been confined largely to Havana and Santiago de Cuba.

Terrorism spread through the island. Hundreds of bombs
exploded. It seems incredible how school children obtained
such enormous amounts of explosives. For this was the work
of children. They went about the dangerous business of making and exploding bombs with the same delight that American children have for Halloween, and yet with absolute
seriousness of purpose. They had practically no support
from older people, and quite often had to keep their work

secret from their parents and relatives. "Why the hell do these youngsters have to start a revolution?" one businessman complained to me. "I don't understand it!"

"They want to be free," I said.

"Free? What is this *free* business? Why, things have never been so good."

Christmas in Havana was gay. Hundreds of fiestas were held in private homes and the luxurious clubs. Tourists poured in by plane and by ship for the holidays. New tourist hotels were being constructed and others were in the blueprint stage. Everyone was optimistic. The Havana Riviera had opened with tremendous publicity and many guests.

I began to look around for contacts close to the movement. None of the political parties were involved with the rebellion. In fact, it seemed the rebel youths were just as angry with the old political parties as they were with the Batista government. One man, whom I had known since the days of the 1933 revolution, told me ruefully that his son had remarked that he, the boy's father, would have to be eliminated from the political life of the nation when Castro's revolution won.

The boys responded enthusiastically. Even those the police were searching for came to my office and those in hiding sent word for me to come to see them. I always hesitated to visit any place where a boy was in hiding because it meant that someone might follow me, or see and recognize me, and cause me inadvertently to betray the boy. I remember I saw Fructuoso Rodriguez, President of the Federation of Havana University Students, who was in hiding, two days before he and three companions were killed by the police.

It began to look as though the revolution was going to fail. The government announced mopping-up operations and set a forty-eight hour ultimatum for the rebels to surrender their arms or be killed. The government claimed that the rebels were surrendering in droves, but apparently that was not true.

Then I heard that Fidel Castro was obtaining recruits faster than he could supply them with weapons. I was told that Fidel demanded that every boy who wanted to join him must bring a rifle and some ammunition. The only way to get a rifle was to assault a soldier and take his rifle. This began to happen all over the island. In the provinces, a soldier risked his life walking the streets alone. Then Castro got his first feminine recruit, Celia Sanchez, who became the best known woman of the rebellion. She was the daughter of a physician who lived in El Pilon on the south coast of Oriente Province, at the edge of the Sierra Maestra Mountains. Her sister told Ted Scott that she took off into the mountains, despite family protests, and found Fidel and his small group of rebels. Celia Sanchez is a tiny girl. When I saw her in Havana, after the rebellion, she was at Camp Columbia army headquarters handling Castro's appointments, receiving delegations, giving orders concerning administrative matters, and working indefatigably. Her uniform was much too big for her. She seemed entirely devoid of feminine vanity, until I noticed a gold chain around the top of her heavy, bootlike shoes.

I reported in the special financial section of the *Times*, January 4, 1957, that Cuba was prospering and money pouring into the island for new industries. The government had pumped two hundred million dollars into the economy in public works and industrial projects and expected to spend the balance of the three hundred fifty million bond issue of 1954.

Simultaneously with the start of the sugar crop, President Batista suspended constitutional guarantees and appointed a censor for each newspaper. American publications came under the censorship and when anything they carried displeased the secret police, the publications were withdrawn from circulation. A wave of protest from the United States caused the government to hurriedly announce that the order had been a mistake. American publications were permitted to go on sale after that.

The Sierra Maestra Mountains are so rough and so much like a jungle that Batista's army did not want to go in after the rebels. The soldiers camped around the foothills, waiting for the rebels to come out. Castro decided to prove to the Cubans that he was alive. He decided to get a reputable foreign correspondent to go into the Sierra Maestra and interview him. Señor Felipe Pazos, first president of the National Bank of Cuba when it was established during the Prio Socarras regime, came to my office to see me. He asked me to go to his office in the Bacardi Company to see one of Fidel's rebels who had just come to Havana. Naturally I was delighted. At the appointed hour I went to the Bacardi building, near the Ministry of Defense, and was taken through various offices to a room where a group of boys and Señor Pazos were waiting. One of them was Faustino Perez, one of the best known figures of the rebellion, who is now heading a ministry created to recover money and property stolen by the Batista regime. We talked the matter over. They told me it would be difficult for me to go since an American woman would be conspicuous. Besides, upon my return, Bastista would have me deported. I thought it over a few moments and then promised I would get someone to go with them into the mountains. When I reached my office, I found Ted Scott. He had been in Latin America covering revolutions for years. He had been an adviser to Pepe Figueres, president of Costa Rica, during the successful revolt Figueres had staged in 1948. Ted Scott is the NBC correspondent in Cuba, a columnist and editorial writer for the *Havana Post*, and has been living in Cuba since before Batista came to power. He had just received a letter from Herbert Matthews of the *Times* in which Herbert had remarked that he and Mrs. Matthews were thinking of coming to Cuba. Matthews had been in Havana several times and had written numerous articles, none of which had pleased President Batista. Ted suggested that Matthews could go to the Sierra Maestra, since it was a "one-shot" job, and then leave Cuba.

I sent Mr. Emanuel Freedman, the *Times* foreign editor, a cable asking that Matthews come immediately. Then I arranged the details of the trip with Davier Pazos, the son of Felipe Pazos. This young revolutionist sat in a chair by my desk and we discussed the details while people came and went. My office at times has the appearance of Grand Central Station. Not even my assistant, Raul Casanas, or Doctora Sarita Rodriguez, a young woman who helps me at intervals, ever suspected what was going on.

Herbert and Nancy arrived and we talked the matter over with Davier. Herbert went out and bought some rough simple clothing, the kind Cuban villagers wear. To cross the island, however, Herbert dressed in New York fashion. It was decided to take Nancy so that she and Herbert would appear to be American tourists. They left Havana on a Friday night, accompanied by Davier, who spoke excellent English and looked like any American boy, by Faustino Perez, and a girl, Lilian Mesa, who drove the car.

They traveled along the Central Highway. Mrs. Matthews tells an amusing story about the trip. She said Lilian, who was using the name Marta, had no sense of direction. After daybreak they decided to stop for coffee in Santa Clara. Marta drove around and circled the same young policeman standing on a corner three times, asking him how to find a cafe and how to get out of town. They finally got to Bayamo and then to Manzanillo, where they rested at the home of a friend. That night Herbert, Davier, Faustino and two or three other youths left town in one of the jeeps which the American army uses. Cubans have bought many of them in recent years, mainly because of the poor condition of the highways.

The army had a road block and a soldier inspection on the road the group intended to use, so they had to take another route. Meanwhile it had rained and the roads were deep in mud. They had to pass through one army patrol, but the story that Herbert was a rich American who was going to look at a sugar plantation with the idea of buying it convinced the army guard, although he looked a little dubious. At any rate, they went on driving through rice plantations and roads that were merely trails. Finally at midnight they reached the place where they must leave the jeep and travel on foot. It was bright moonlight, cold and damp. They crossed a stream, wading up to their knees. Davier fell into a hole, getting soaking wet. They arrived at the appointed place, but there was no scout to meet them, so their guide left them in a thicket and went on. At last, through the use of the night birdcalls, they made contact with the scout and were led to the place where they were to meet Fidel Castro. They were in a thick jungle, Herbert said, and had to talk in whispers for fear of some wandering army patrol. Fidel Castro arrived at daybreak. He and Herbert sat talking for hours. Later, Herbert and Davier came down from the hills in broad daylight, keeping under cover of the heavy trees and undergrowth.

Herbert and Nancy returned to Havana. I had told everyone they had gone to Santiago de Cuba where Herbert wanted to look over the situation, which was perfectly normal. In a couple of days I took them to the airport and breathed a sigh of relief when I saw them step on the plane. Knowing Cuba and how practically nothing is secret I feared that someone who saw them on the trip might arrive in Havana and reveal that Herbert had been to Manzanillo. Several days went by before Herbert's series of three stories were published in the *Times*. The first article was published on Sunday, Feb. 24th. It was deleted from the *Times* which arrived in Havana. However, the New York edition was brought into Havana by travelers. It created a sensation. Within a few hours the story was all over Havana. The next day hundreds of copies were shipped in of that story and the two following ones.

The government reacted immediately, calling the article a fake. The Minister of Defense, Dr. Santiago Verdeja, in a cable to *The New York Herald Tribune* called the story a "chapter in a fantastic novel." The article had been published with a photograph of Fidel Castro and his famous telescopic-sighted rifle against a background of the Sierra Maestra jungle. The Minister commented: "It is noted that Matthews published a photograph, saying it was of Castro. It seems strange that, having had the opportunity to penetrate the mountains and having had an interview, Matthews did not have a photograph taken of himself standing beside the pro-Communist insurgent in order to prove what he says." The Minister went on to say that the government "does not know whether Fidel Castro is alive or dead, but the government takes full responsibility for stating that no such supporting forces as Matthews described actually exist, and with the same responsibility the government reiterates that at no time did the correspondent have an interview with the man to whom he ascribes so much force and so many nonexistent creeds."

The next day the *Times* published another article by Herbert with a picture of him and Fidel Castro in the mountains. The government called that a "composition" picture. The last *Times* article was entitled "Old Order in Cuba is Threatened by Forces of an Internal Revolt." In the meantime there had been so much protest by American and Cuban newspapers that Batista had given orders to lift censorship. The local press translated and published the three articles. Government officials were in a rage. I have been told that President Batista sincerely believed that Fidel Castro was dead, as had been reported to him by his army. A week later Dr. Joaquin Martinez Saenz, president of the National Bank of Cuba, told me that he had argued with Batista over the articles, which Batista firmly declared were fakes. Saenz pointed out that no newspaper of the reputation of the *Times* nor a writer of the reputation of Matthews would make up a fake interview. Finally, in exasperation, Saenz declared, "If it is published in *The New York Times*, it is true in New York, true in Berlin, true in London and true in Havana. You can depend on it that the story is believed by the entire world." Batista was very much annoyed.

The article became a national issue. General Martin Diaz Tamayo, military chief of Oriente Province, chimed in with a statement that it was an "imaginary interview because it was impossible for anyone to get through the lines of troops surrounding the sector in which Castro is operating." But despite these denials by the government, the interview had put the tiny rebellion of Castro on the front pages of newspapers throughout the world and revived the revolution, which had been making little progress. From that time on youths flocked to join the ranks of Castro's insurgents, money began to flow into the treasury of the revolutionary movement, and the "26th of July" revolution was on its way to final victory.

President Fulgencio Batista and his government never suspected I had anything to do with the interview. Even Edmund Chester, Batista's public relations counsel, who should have known better after knowing me all these years, overlooked me entirely in the "battle of the Matthews interview." Nor did my own office force think I was involved. I told Raul Casanas, my assistant, when he talked to me about it, that undoubtedly Matthews arranged the whole thing in New York before he came. When the officials of the Presidential Palace angrily demanded of Raul how Matthews had managed the "fake interview," Raul told them in all sincerity that in our opinion, his and mine, Matthews had arranged the entire matter in New York.

Later, when I began to hear rumors about the people who had been with Herbert and Nancy in Oriente Province, I went to see Sr. Felipe Pazos and told him I thought his son, Davier, should leave Cuba. Pazos was extremely worried. He said his son refused to go. The government arrested Faustino Perez, but since constitutional guarantees were back in effect, thus permitting the process of civil law, Perez was released by some legal maneuver.

The followers of Fidel Castro and the other revolutionary groups increased terrorism and sabotage. On March 2, 1957, constitutional guarantees were again suspended, nullifying all rights of free speech and assembly and of *habeas corpus* and other civil rights. Censorship was not imposed. Newspapers began to print stories of terrorism and sabotage. I wondered just how long this would last. From the United States Guantanamo naval base came the story that three American boys, whose fathers were members of the United States Navy, had gone into the mountains to join Fidel Castro. They were Victor J. Buehlman, seventeen, Michael L. Garvey, fifteen, and Charles E. Ryan, nineteen. It was an embarrassing situation for the Navy. About a month later, the two younger boys returned home, after their parents, the Navy, and the Embassy in Havana tried every channel to force them to return. However, Ryan stayed on, fighting with the rebels. His first battle was at El Macho, several weeks later, when the rebels swooped down from the mountains, killed and wounded a number of soldiers at the army post and made off with several truckloads of supplies.

On March 13, 1957, I decided to get my hair cut. That sounds commonplace enough. But invariably something happens when I am away from my office. Returning along the Malecón Sea Drive, I told the taxi driver to use the Prado Promenade, then turn into Refugio Street, where my office is, a block from the palace. I gave the driver these instructions because the direction of traffic had been recently changed in the one-way street. As we reached Refugio Street the driver stopped. Automobiles were roaring out of the street in the wrong direction. He turned around and said, reproachfully, "Señora, I thought you said the traffic had been changed." I said, "Never mind, I'll get out here."

I gave the driver his fare and started walking. Suddenly firing broke out. I hurried along, staying close to the wall, and hoped for the best. When I reached my door I found it locked. I opened the door to find Raul Casanas and Sarita standing at the top of the stairs. They shouted: "Where have you been? Didn't you know they have attacked the palace?" Cuban buildings are made with thick stone and concrete walls. I climbed the stairs. I felt much safer to be inside. I found we had two visitors, Gonzalo de Quesada and Dr. Alonzo Llinares, both of whom I have known for many years. They were forced to stay the entire afternoon. Soldiers and sailors moved into Refugio Street and started shooting at anything moving. In the big apartment opposite the palace, people were lying on the floor, with bullets smashing into their ceilings.

The firing increased. Tanks moved in to fire their guns, mostly at the tops of buildings, where they claimed snipers were lurking, but the only thing they did was knock off cornices. I called *The New York Times* to tell them of the attack and dictated the first dispatch, although it was difficult for them to hear me in New York with the crash of gunfire in the background. Then I found that although I could call New York I could not call anyone in town. That was a frustrating experience. I solved that problem by having people who called me tell others with whom I wanted to get in contact to call me. Apparently it was only the dial on my telephone which was out of order.

The attackers had driven up in a truck to the Colon Street entrance of the Presidential Palace while the Palace Guard were having lunch. They rushed the entrance, firing as they went, got inside the palace and onto the second floor. But there an iron grill stopped them. In the battle forty of the attackers and a number of the Palace Guard were killed. A few escaped. Strangely enough, they had bazookas available, which they did not use. They failed to get support from another group supposed to arrive just after they attacked. This apparently unnerved them. Bad planning and timing, which so often happens in Cuba, made the attack a complete failure. Had they used the bazookas, which they had available, and had they been prepared to blow out the big iron grill door with explosives, they might have succeeded in assassinating Batista, which was the purpose of the attack.

Meanwhile a group of university youths seized the control room of the CMQ radio station in Vedado and broadcast that the president had been killed and the government overthrown. The timing was wrong again, of course. When the group, headed by the President of the Havana University Student Federation, José Antonio Echevarria, left the station, they were shot down by police just outside the station.

Even after the attackers had been killed and order had been restored in the palace, soldiers, sailors, police and army tanks surrounding the palace kept right on firing. Bullets hit the walls of my office on opposite sides, which shows they were firing from all directions. My office is the second floor of an old Spanish building with thick walls, big shutter doors which open out onto a terrace, and high windows at the back. The only danger there was that soldiers in some other building nearby would make a target of my office or that a tank would start firing point blank at the walls and windows.

It is strange that more bystanders didn't get killed. A man walking in Zayas Park was one of the few civilian casualties. A man I know was driving beside the palace when the attack started. He tried to escape through Zulueta Street, but a bus blocked his way. The driver jumped out of the bus and ran. The driver of the car decided to lie flat in the bottom of his car. Why he was not killed is a mystery, because all the cars parked in and around Zayas Park were riddled with bullets. When the tanks moved in and started firing, he could stand no more. In desperation, he crawled out. The soldiers grabbed him, with every intention of killing him, thinking he was one of the attackers, but he managed to convince them with his identification cards that he was only an innocent bystander. A tourist, Peter Korenda of New Jersey, walked out on the small balcony of the hotel on Colon Street, and a soldier shot and killed him. It was reported that he had a camera and was intending to take pictures. He really should have known better. I wrote a

story for the travel section of the *Times,* advising tourists, at
the sound of the first shot, to get inside a building and stay
there and not look out.

The Museum of Fine Arts, just across Zayas Park from the
palace, had all kinds of holes in it. Edward Scott, NBC correspondent, had a room on the corner of the Sevilla Biltmore Hotel, just across the street from the museum. Two 20
mm. shells were fired into his room. One tore through his
wardrobe and all his suits making a big hole in each and
exploded against the far wall, tearing out the wall. Another
smashed his bookcase and everything around it. A third
failed to explode and he carried it around for several days
as proof that it was the army shooting into his room, not the
rebels.

By six o'clock the firing had died down. However, the
soldiers downstairs would not let us leave the office. I called
the Presidential Palace and got Dr. Andres Domingo Morales del Castillo, Secretary to the President, on the line. I
reminded him I had an appointment to see President Batista at seven-thirty. He seemed surprised that I should call,
in view of the situation, and said all appointments had been
canceled. I insisted that I wanted to see the President. Finally, he laughed a little, and said my appointment would
be honored. I asked him if he would send a policeman or
soldier after me, because the army wouldn't let me out of
my office. He promised he would.

About ten o'clock that night a policeman appeared to escort me to the palace. I took along Raul Casanas and Edward Scott, who had just arrived at the office. The policeman delivered us to the army tank corps alongside the Bock
Tobacco Company and said his authority ended there. Dr.
Domingo sent a man out from the palace to get us. We
walked across the street to the palace. On the sidewalk and
in the streets were pools of dried blood. Inside the patio an
attempt had been made to wash away the blood, but red
glistened here and there on the floor of the patio, which was
still wet. An automobile which had been parked in the patio

was full of bullet holes. We went to the second floor and found the President surrounded by members of his cabinet. Everyone was highly excited. Batista was flushed and animated as he told how he had directed the defense of the palace, a revolver in one hand and telephone in the other. Mrs. Batista and one of their four sons had been in the palace, on the third floor, which is living quarters of the President. The other children were in school.

The room of the palace reporters, who are kept on duty by their newspapers and radio stations almost around the clock, is located at the Colon entrance. Several of these reporters told me that when the attack started everyone ran to the bathroom, which offered the only protection in sight. The bathroom was much too small for the number of them, but they managed to get in and stayed there. They were very much upset and I don't blame them. One machine gun burst through the door and the press would have been nonexistent. The attackers were Havana University students of the *Directorio Revolucionario* and followers of Prio Socarras, the group known as the *Autenticos*. Batista's military intelligence service went out that night to round up revolutionaries. Dr. Pelayo Cuervo Navarro, head of the *Ortodoxo* Party, which had been the leading party when Batista had seized the government by military coup in March, 1952, was taken into custody. The SIM murdered him alongside the Country Club lake, where his body was found the next morning. He had nothing to do with the attack. He was an enemy of Grau San Martin and had kept pushing through the courts the charge against Grau for misappropriation of $174,000,000 during his administration.

The government circulated the story that friends of Grau San Martin had killed Dr. Cuervo. The murder remained a mystery until February, 1959, when the revolutionary government announced that Colonel Orlando Piedra, chief of the Police Bureau of Investigations, and several of his men were responsible. It soon became clear that Fidel Castro had no connection with the attack on the palace. It was a suicidal attempt, badly planned and executed, and never had a chance from the start. This happens so many times in Cuba where everyone is an individualist and wants to do everything on his own. The police, searching the houses of the relatives of the dead students, captured a lot of arms in Havana, but they never got all of them. How so many arms could be smuggled into one city seems amazing. Someone remarked that all one had to do was to shake a tree in the park and out would fall a rifle.

The opposition political parties began to try to find a solution to the situation, but it was hopeless from the start. The parties were unable to agree on what they wanted and Batista was in no mood to make concessions. The military intended to keep control of the island and they viewed any election with misgiving. Dr. Grau San Martin, wily old politician, sat in his luxurious Fifth Avenue home and spent his days conferring with other politicians.

Batista announced that Fidel Castro was no longer in the Sierra Maestra Mountains, that his forces had dispersed and either fled the country or returned to their homes. Batista succeeded in convincing many of the people in Havana that the rebellion was over. True, there had been few recent reports of rebel attacks. But I surmised that Castro was awaiting arms and trying to organize his growing army. At any rate, when I noticed that none of the soldiers had been withdrawn from Oriente Province, I decided the President was talking only for publication.

President Batista raised the average price of sugar 1.86¢ per pound. This gave the workers an extra $16,000,000 bonus. Havana was prosperous, tourists were pouring in, and life went on smoothly, on the surface. Government officials organized a big demonstration to show the world that all the people supported President Batista. Thousands marched to the palace. Public employees were told to go to the parade or lose their jobs. Labor was mobilized by Eusebio Mujal and officials of the Confederation of Cuban Workers. All government political parties got out their adherents and furnished free transportation and liquid nourishment. It was an official success. Ted Scott and I were in the palace. Dr. Gonzalo Guell, the Minister of State, took us around to one side of the palace offices to show us how really magnificent the demonstration was. But I had seen too many of these demonstrations not to know exactly how they were organized.

Eusebio Mujal, Secretary General of the CTC, began to have trouble with the Cuban Electric Company union. Mujal had been a labor leader of Dr. Grau San Martin's *Autentico* Party. When Batista seized the government Mujal made a deal and remained as head of the CTC. Angel Cofino, head of the electric power union, suddenly withdrew his union from the confederation. The fight was on. Of course Mujal, backed by the government, won. Cofino was expelled from the union and many employees were arrested.

Few reports came out of Oriente Province. Terrorism seemed to die down and when the forty-five day suspension of constitutional guarantees terminated on April 16th, Batista said they would not again be suspended. However, the police and military intelligence went on arresting, torturing and killing. Relatives came to my office to tell me of boys disappearing. One young lawyer was arrested because he was defending revolutionists in court. He happened to be a good friend of a man who had connections with Batista. This man went to Batista and demanded the young lawyer's release. Batista gave the order, but by the time they got him out of the police station, where Ventura, a professional killer in a police uniform, had been "interrogating" him, it was too late. He died a few days later. Ventura is a good-looking young man, affable, well mannered. Yet I have been told that his greatest pleasure is listening to the screams of torture victims. He was steadily promoted by President Batista and when he fled the island with the President he was a Lieutenant Colonel.

In April, 1957, the Cuban government invited the foreign correspondents and some local reporters to go to Oriente

Province and see the operations of the soldiers. This was just after a group of Castro's insurgents had slipped into the small army post at La Plata on the south coast and cut the throats of the sentries and of twelve soldiers, who were sleeping there. Gene Carrier and Ted Scott went on the trip. The army told me they had no facilities for a woman, so Ted covered for me. They were flown to Cabo Cruz or El Pilon sugar mill, belonging to Julio Lobo, then went by jeep to La Plata, where more than a hundred soldiers were encamped. They visited El Macho by jeep through the rough mountains. Gene said that Colonel Joaquin Casillas Lumpuy was in charge of showing the press around. Also Major Jesus Blanco and Major Morejon, both infamous war criminals who were later tried and shot in Havana. When the rebels captured Santa Clara on January 1, 1959, Colonel Casillas Lumpuy was shot for having ordered the bombing and strafing of civilians of the town.

The trip had been planned carefully to impress the foreign correspondents. As they went through a little settlement, El Ramon Portillo, they found a small store in which country people, dressed in their best, were dancing to an old phonograph. It was terribly hot, Gene said, but the people were dancing, apparently not too happy about it. The bar was serving them rum and sandwiches. Gene said he noticed that when they started to quit dancing Colonel Casillas ordered them to continue. Later they closed the bar and invited the people outside to answer any questions the reporters cared to ask. Colonel Castillas told them in a loud voice that they could tell the reporters anything they wanted. They all praised the government, particularly the army, for "protecting" them.

The reporters and correspondents spent the night at La Plata sleeping on the porch of the officers' barracks. Later that afternoon, when the officers were out on the range practicing, Colonel Barrera invited the reporters and correspondents to watch. Ted Scott was asked if he would like to try shooting with a pistol, if he knew anything about it.

Ted put on a demonstration of pistol, rifle and machine gun firing that astounded the officers. Colonel Barrera remarked that he thought it strange a foreign correspondent could shoot so well. Ted replied, "The army always forgets that they do not have a monopoly on using firearms. I have heard there are many civilians in these parts who are just as good shots or better." It was a pointed remark, and did not please Barrera, who lost a measure of his cordiality.

On May 11, 1957, Dr. Manuel Urrutia, presiding over the Urgency Court in Santiago de Cuba, which was trying a group of young revolutionists, including twenty-two members of the Castro expedition, issued his famous decision. Dr. Urrutia said it was his opinion that all the young revolutionists should be freed because he believed "that all people have a right to take up arms against a dictatorial government." That decision made him President of Cuba when the rebellion was won, but at that time it was only a brave gesture. He immediately fled abroad.

American Ambassador Arthur Gardner resigned on May 14, 1957. He was a *simpatico* person but woefully lacking in the knowledge of diplomacy. He had been a businessman all his life and knew nothing of diplomatic affairs. He liked President Batista and openly told everyone what a fine president he was. I think that at times he even embarrassed President Batista with his support.

Fidel Castro made an appeal to the United States to stop furnishing arms to Batista. Robert Taber and Wendell Hoffman of Columbia Broadcasting Company had gone into the Sierra Maestra Mountains to see Castro, taking with them photographic and sound recording equipment. They spent several weeks with Castro and came out with excellent pictures. The Batista government had conducted an extensive propaganda campaign designed to make the Cubans believe that Castro had left the Sierra Maestra and that the revolution was about over. Suddenly, Castro appeared on television screens throughout the United States, making an appeal for the United States to stop shipping arms. President Batista was much upset. He couldn't understand how all these reporters got through the "ring of steel" which his army claimed had been thrown around the Sierra Maestra.

The foreign press heard that arms and ammunition had been stolen from the United States naval base in Guantanamo. The American Embassy finally admitted that a small quantity had been stolen. My information from people who came from Guantanamo was that a considerable number of mortars, rifles and ammunition had vanished from the base. It had been done by Cuban employees at the base. The United States government never was very specific on this matter.

We had another upswing in terrorism throughout Cuba. Bombs exploded, fires started, power lines were cut. Havana was cut off from telephone and telegraph communication with the eastern provinces for several hours.

A bomb exploded in the Central Park area, blacking out Old Havana. According to the story which came out later, a group of youthful terrorists, including an employee or two of the Cuban Electric Company rented a house on Suarez Street. They tunneled from the kitchen down and out into the street to reach a central transformer. Then they placed a bomb at the transformer. The explosion occurred sometime after midnight. Most of the morning newspapers were getting ready to go to press. There were no newspapers the next morning. The district affected was around Central Park, the San Rafael Street shopping center, and the waterfront. Elevators in apartment houses stopped, and electric pumps, used to lift water from the ground to the tanks on the roof of every house, since there is no water pressure, were useless. The whole section was soon without water. It took almost three days for the company to complete emergency repairs. No one notices how necessary electric power is until it goes off. Fortunately I keep kerosene lamps and a lantern in case of hurricanes. There was a rush to buy kerosene in every *bodega*. However, I think most of the people simply went to bed when it got dark. This suddenly became the quietest section of town you could imagine. As soon as it was dark the *bodegas,* cafés and other stores closed. The streets were deserted, except for an occasional automobile, and the police and soldiers circling through the district. It was certainly not safe to be on the streets.

We were busy at the office. Sarita, who lived some distance away, decided she would remain in the office. I could not go to Miramar where I live—the situation was too uncertain. Raul Casanas decided he wasn't going to walk through the black streets with soldiers and police throwing flashlights in his face and pointing Tommy guns at him. Sarita found an army cot, Raul slept on a chaise longue. Sarita found ice which we put in the refrigerator in a big pan. We settled down for a state of siege. Out in the suburbs power was being maintained and lights glowed along the horizon, but downtown Havana was a dark, uncomfortable place. To add to our difficulties the telephones became deficient. The emergency power plant of the telephone company could not carry the load. During the day it was often easier to go to a place rather than telephone. At night the telephones worked a little better in our district. By the time the company got the power back on we were out of water. None of us had been able to take a bath for several days.

Meanwhile, we had reports of fighting from Oriente Province. In a commando raid on the military post at Ubico, on the south coast of Oriente Province, the Castro rebels killed eleven and wounded nineteen soldiers, confiscated arms, ammunition and supplies, and fled back to the hills. The government was highly indignant, calling the guerilla tactics cowardly. This just about convinced me that Batista's days were numbered, no matter how large an army he possessed. I heard later that the young American was in the group that attacked Uvero.

An expedition landed on the north coast of Oriente Province. Twenty-six youths aboard the yacht "Corinthia" sailed into Carbonico Bay about a mile from the Nicaro Nickel plant. They landed and headed immediately into the Sierra

Cristal Mountains. Gene Carrier says he has flown over the Sierra Cristal, which are very rocky, not jungle-covered like the Sierra Maestra. Gene enthused over the beautiful little valleys he saw and several waterfalls, which are highly unusual in Cuba.

On the 28th Camp Columbia army headquarters announced that sixteen of the expeditionaries had been killed in a battle with government troops. A few days later I learned that the sixteen rebels had been captured and executed. The leader of the rebels was Calixto Sanchez, who had headed the air transport workers' union at José Marti International Airport. He had fled from Cuba after the attack on the Presidential Palace and had organized the expedition. He and the others belonged to the *Organizacion Autentico.* Apparently Prio Socarras had furnished the yacht and the arms. This was one of the incidents that caused Prio to be always in trouble with the authorities in Miami, where he was living in exile. A police officer in Miami told me that State and Federal authorities in Florida knew that in spite of all the arms and ammunition they had confiscated, they managed to halt only about 10% of the revolutionary supplies flowing from Florida.

Months after this expedition the father of one of the sixteen rebels killed came to my office and told me what had actually happened. The twenty-six men landed at Cabonico Bay and brought their arms ashore without incident. They marched toward the Sierra Cristal which lay to the east. Their food gave out and the feet of several of the boys became festered. They could hardly walk. Five of the group turned back and surrendered to the authorities, revealing to them the direction taken by the others. Three members of the expedition got lost in the mountains and were never heard from again. The group, now reduced to eighteen, was forced to risk approaching the house of a *guajiro* and ask for food. The *guajiro* invited them into his house, was courteous and hospitable, but while his wife was preparing the food, he sent his son to the army post only a few miles away.

Just as the revolutionaries were sitting down to eat, soldiers arrived and surrounded the house. Only two members of the expedition escaped. The remaining sixteen were taken into custody. The prisoners were marched to Caimito, then put into trucks to be taken to Mayari, where they were to be held in prison. Enroute to Mayari, at the village of Levisa, the army captain received a radio message and the trucks turned back. In the early evening darkness, when the trucks halted beside a small grocery store at a crossroads, the prisoners heard a broadcast from Havana stating that sixteen rebels had been killed in a battle with government forces. They knew then what their fate would be. It is terrible to hear one's death announced, but how utterly horrible to know that the announcement is not a mistake, but a death sentence.

A mile or so further on, Captain Chirino stopped the trucks, ordered the prisoners out, had them lined up in front of an orange grove, with the trucks parked so that their headlights would shine into the faces of the prisoners. Then the soldiers mowed them down. Humberto Vinat, one of the group, either fainted or fell just as bullets struck the man next to him. Two of his companions, killed by the fusillade, fell on top of him. Perhaps because of the darkness, the soldiers, without checking to see if all of them were dead, climbed into the trucks and drove off. Humberto Vinat crawled out from under the dead men who were lying on top of him, and, using the orange grove as protection, ran until he was exhausted. In desperation, he knocked at the door of a house and the farmer fed him, gave him clothes, and urged him to remain hidden in the house until the soldiers had moved out of the area. But Humberto was afraid the soldiers would return in the morning, find one of the bodies missing, and begin a search. Perhaps too, after one betrayal, he did not trust the farmer. At any rate, having relatives in Mayari, and feeling he would be safer with them, he set out on foot. In the outskirts of Mayari he was captured by the army and shot.

I asked Humberto's father whether Captain Chirino had given the orders for the execution of the rebels. But he was certain that the orders had come from General Francisco Tabernilla, in reprisal for the attack the previous night by the Fidel Castro rebels on the army post at Uvero on the south coast of Oriente Province.

The government's first announced offensive started at the end of May, 1957. General Francisco Tabernilla said the warfare "will be waged in such a manner as to oblige the rebels to fight." It didn't work out that way. Castro's rebels kept right on hitting and running. Every communique of the army ended, "The army is pursuing the fleeing rebels." Yet the army sent more troops to Oriente Province.

Killings and torture were going on in every town on the island, but particularly in Oriente Province. The government forces were arresting every youth they could get their hands on. Every person under thirty was suspected of being a rebel or a sympathizer. In Oriente at least, this was absolutely true. Stories of torture and killings were brought into my office almost daily by relatives and friends of the victims. Sometimes they brought pictures—horrible pictures of mutilated bodies. It looked like the work of some savage tribe in the deepest part of Africa. It seems incredible that there could have been so many sadists in the Cuban army. The rebels and their friends tried to get these pictures to the United States. Eventually they presented documentary evidence to the United Nations and the Organization of American States. But these organizations were too busy protesting the atrocities in Hungary to pay attention. No doubt it would have been embarrassing for the United States to admit that it was giving implicit approval to the same brutal methods of enslavement that it protested against in Europe. Batista poured hundreds of thousands of dollars into his public relations and publicity campaign in the United States. He hired good writers, put out weekly letters about the great prosperity of Cuba, brought writers and newspapermen to Cuba on junket trips, and entertained prominent visitors. In short, he convinced American visitors that the rebels were exaggerating and lying about the actions of his government. Even Americans living permanently in Cuba did not believe the stories told by the rebels. I tried to tell an American businessman who had been living in Latin America for twenty years about the government methods. He refused to believe it. "Cubans are not that type of people; they would not torture and kill." I reminded him that this had occurred during the Machado regime, although on an insignificant scale compared to what was going on now, but he brushed that aside and refused to believe any of it.

The Archbishop of Santiago de Cuba, Enrique Perez Servantes, appealed for an end to the violence and killing in Oriente Province. Civic, professional, religious, patriotic and educational associations in Santiago de Cuba protested to President Batista against the reign of terror. Batista replied by accusing the people of Santiago de Cuba of "remaining silent when members of the armed forces are killed by the revolutionists and of failing to protest the bombings and sabotage by youthful rebels." Batista had no intention of restraining the effective methods of Colonel José Maria Salas Canizares, the *carnicero* (butcher) of Santiago de Cuba. When a group of women dressed in black marched the streets of Santiago de Cuba protesting against Colonel Salas Canizares, the police arrested and jailed them.

Herbert Matthews returned to Cuba. He wanted an interview with President Batista so I called Edmund Chester. The President agreed to see Matthews if I came along. President Batista received us in his office on the second floor of the palace. Matthews had been requested to present his questions the day before the interview and Chester had all the answers written out in English. The President had decided not to give any more informal interviews, as he complained he was always being misquoted. The President was his usual affable self although he disliked Matthews a great deal. Herbert asked the President about the torture of youths in Santiago de Cuba by the government armed forces. Batista looked startled, but said that the military did not use such methods. Herbert replied that he had been in Santiago and the mother of one of the boys had described what the police had done to her son. The President brushed that aside. He abruptly changed the subject.

Batista claimed that the trouble was being caused by Fidel Castro, a Communist, and by Prio Socarras, who was furnishing arms and ammunition. The solution to the situation was the holding of general elections, which he was determined to do. Elections were going to be held on June 1, 1958. The President stated that his government would not discuss political questions with a criminal like Castro, but was willing to meet with the "decent, legitimate opposition." He would never yield to the desire for political amnesty for the Castro rebels. In answer to my question, he declared that the murder of Dr. Pelayo Cuervo was being investigated.

Herbert Matthews went to Santiago de Cuba to see what was happening there. He wrote that Castro's rebels were growing stronger in the face of the government's offensive. Fidel Castro was worshipped in Oriente Province. He described Santiago de Cuba as a city in open revolt in which "virtually every man, woman and child . . . except police and army authorities . . . are struggling at all costs to overthrow the military dictatorship."

President Batista was furious. He ordered newspapers in Havana not to print the two articles Herbert wrote. But the underground translated the articles into Spanish and distributed thousands of copies over the island.

It was decided to hold general elections on June 1, 1958. A new electoral code, with a direct vote for president, was approved. Batista ordered the government coalition parties to start their campaigns and "leave the suppression of terroristic activities to the armed forces." Senator Rolando Masferrer, who published *El Tiempo,* decided to hold a mass meeting in Santiago de Cuba to start the political campaign. Masferrer had been elected in Oriente Province where he had first organized his Radical Union Party, one of the four-party government coalition. Senator Rolando Masferrer had always been a gangster. For years he had been accompanied by bodyguards, armed to the teeth. Now he was organizing his private army, reported to number fifteen hundred men, and the scourge of Oriente Province, robbing, killing, torturing and extorting money. Masferrer thought of Oriente Province as his stronghold.

The *Times* had asked me to cover this political convention. I took the night plane, a British airline which made the trip in one and a half hours instead of the usual four. Newspaper people have to budget their time as a miser does his money. It was crowded with members of the government, including a senator and a representative, all going to the meeting. When we arrived at the Santiago airport, five of us rode the airport station wagon into the city. As we reached the outskirts, a group of soldiers stepped forward with machine guns, and demanded to know who was in the car. The driver turned on the overhead light. The soldiers looked us over, then waved us on. Gene Carrier, TV correspondent for NBC, was at the Casa Grande Hotel, which was overflowing with politicians from Havana and the private army of Masferrer.

Santiago was an armed camp. Police and soldiers were stationed on every street corner. Patrol cars rumbled through the city. The streets were deserted. Despite all these precautions, fifteen bombs exploded and bottles of flaming gasoline were thrown at government buildings by youthful revolutionists that night.

I entered the hotel and registered. Masferrer's men were walking around with a machine gun in one hand and a drink in the other. They all wore *guayaberas,* and as a distinguishing mark, a blue and white ribbon pinned to their caps. They were about the toughest-looking crowd I had seen in a long time. Casa Grande is a big sprawling hotel with several floors and a tiny elevator. There is a terrace on the left as you enter which overlooks the street and is about the most comfortable place in the hotel. In the front part of the terrace are dozens of rocking chairs. The back is used as a dining room. Men and women were sitting in the chairs, talking at the top of their voices. They were putting on a great show of enthusiasm. I ate dinner at one of the tables on the terrace. The *papaya* was excellent. After dinner I went with a group of newsmen and photographers to police headquarters in the governor's mansion. We walked the deserted streets. The police headquarters looked as though Santiago was undergoing bombardment. Sandbags were piled in front of the entrance. Barricades protected the walls. Louis Hamburg, Batista's personal photographer, was heading our expedition. He knew many of the soldiers.

We went in and were introduced to Col. José Maria Salas Canizares, the "Butcher." He was a tall heavily built man with the air of a conqueror. He greeted us, slapped Louis on the back, and invited us to see his prisoners. He showed us a number of youths penned up in a small section of the patio. Poor youngsters! They didn't look over fourteen or fifteen. They were obviously afraid, some of them bewildered. But there was courage in them too and a terrible manliness and dignity. I asked one of the policemen standing nearby how long he had been in the police force. He told me twenty years. He looked at the prisoners and said, "How unfortunate! You know they are paid a couple of *pesetas* to throw these bombs." That was the constant story of the Batista authorities, that the terrorists had been hired. I looked at the policeman, trying to determine whether he really believed what he was saying. I couldn't tell. I wanted to talk with the rebel youths, but the authorities would not permit me. I left the governor's mansion with a haunting memory of young faces which I would never see again. The real horror of what was happening in Cuba became clear to me.

I had made a point of obtaining a room opening on Céspedes Park, the small square where the meeting was to be held. But I began to consider it a mistake, if I intended to get any sleep. Gene and Louis had the room next to mine.

On the other side were a politician and his wife from Havana. The speakers' stand in the park was in front of City Hall. The stand was being finished with a great deal of hammering and loud talking. It was very hot, so I had to leave the big shutter doors open. There was no balcony, but the whole front of the room was doors and a balustrade. It looked as though that part of the house had once been a big porch.

At five o'clock in the morning the whole hotel awoke. Out in the park there was a tremendous crash of bugles and drums. The noise was tremendous. The woman next door screamed at her husband. This concert continued for fifteen minutes. At six o'clock the bells in the Cathedral rang. I jumped out of bed. The ancient cathedral of Santiago looked so close that it seemed almost possible to reach out and touch it. Apparently the bells were being rung but it sounded as though someone was hitting them with a sledge-hammer, as was the custom long ago. I tried to order coffee from downstairs but they told me frankly the hotel was overflowing and the employees were overworked. I would have to come downstairs. I started dressing. There was a loud knock on my door. I put on a housecoat and opened the door. There were five men. I asked what was going on. They said with considerable arrogance they had come to search my room. They poured into the room and then hesitated. One of them demanded: "Are you alone in this room?" I said emphatically that I was Mrs. Phillips of *The New York Times*. They stood looking at me. Then one of them said: "I'm sorry, but we are searching all rooms in the hotel. Pardon us." They all rushed out again. I noticed that out in the hall, sitting in a chair with a machine gun across his knees, was one of Masferrer's men. I decided it was going to be a very enthusiastic convention.

Masferrer had predicted that thirty thousand people would attend. I saw automobile after automobile drive up to the hotel with Masferrer men, carrying a suitcase in one hand and a machine gun in the other. But there seemed to be no one except people from Havana. The Santiago streets were still empty. The meeting was scheduled for three P.M. At that hour the park was still practically empty and I began to wonder if they could muster enough people to start the meeting. About four P.M. people from the hotel went out and took seats in the speaker's stand. The announcer began to talk about the tremendous enthusiasm being shown at the meeting and now and then a few yells for Masferrer and for President Batista were heard. This was being broadcast throughout the island. The small park never filled, but soon groups of negroes appeared dancing the conga, sixteen abreast.

I estimated in my report that not over four thousand attended the meeting. The government was furious. Composition pictures appeared in Havana newspapers, declaring that one hundred thousand persons attended. Later, Gene and I took a walk and couldn't find crowds anywhere. It was probably the most magnificent failure any political party ever achieved in Cuba. Because if there is one thing easy to do in Cuba, it is to get a big crowd. Cuban people will watch almost anything. Even the government parties began to realize that they had few followers in that end of the island.

Toward the end of the meeting, police shot and killed four boys in a car. The police claimed the youths had attacked a patrol car. My information, however, was that there had been an attack on a patrol car on the outskirts of Santiago, but that the police not wanting it to be known that the rebels had escaped, killed the next group of youths they saw in a car. When news of this shooting reached the meeting, the orators stopped. In about ten minutes the park was deserted; the politicians were hurriedly leaving the hotel.

13

In July, 1957, the rebel groups began talking about making a united front. Castro was fighting in the Sierra Maestra Mountains, but apparently had no contact with the other young terroristic groups in the island, or the followers of former president Prio Socarras. A series of efforts were made to consolidate the rebel forces. Meetings were held in Miami and later in Caracas which culminated in a Caracas Pact. However, it was merely a loose liaison arrangement. There was never any close cooperation or organization.

Colonel Pedro A. Barrera, in command of government troops at the Estrada Palma sugar mill, in the foothills of the Sierra Maestra Mountains, told newsmen and photographers that he expected Fidel Castro to surrender. It was another trip of newsmen on invitation of the army. Ted Scott covered the story for me. Colonel Barrera kept on being optimistic until the government decided he was simply sitting there waiting for Fidel Castro to surrender, so he was removed and sent abroad as a military attaché. One of the youths who served under him told me that Colonel Barrera was actually removed because he refused to follow the orders of General Francisco Tabernilla, Chief of Staff. General Tabernilla had ordered him to kill all prisoners. Whenever Barrera took a prisoner he called in the newspapermen, so that the army could not report him "killed in battle." This young rebel said Barrera was a fine officer.

Senator Masferrer, seemingly not discouraged by his convention in Santiago de Cuba, announced that he was going to hold another political demonstration in the Sierra Maestra Mountains and dared the rebels to try to interfere. He held it at Chivirico, a tiny port on the south coast a few miles from Uvero where in May, 1957, Castro rebels had swooped down on the military post and carried off the post supplies and everything in the commissary of the Babon Lumber Company, using the company trucks. My brother-in-law, Gene, went by army plane to Santiago de Cuba and then on a navy vessel around to Chivirico to take pictures of the meeting. He said hundreds of countrymen came in on horseback to the meeting. It was, relatively speaking, a fair success. Just after the meeting, shooting broke out, but Gene was already aboard the Navy vessel. Two of Masferrer's men were killed and several wounded. They claimed rebels came down out of the mountains and attacked. However, it came out later that a group of Masferrer's men had quarrelled among themselves. The whole affair was never accurately explained. Even a judge in Santiago de Cuba, trying to unravel the incident, finally announced that it had been a "family" fight and not under his jurisdiction.

On July 26, 1957, the fourth anniversary of the Moncada attack by Fidel Castro, the black and red flag of the "26th of July" revolutionary movement appeared in Havana and in interior towns. In Havana the police spent the morning rushing from one place to another to get the flags down. The flags appeared in such unlikely places as the top of the Habana Hilton Hotel, on the Pan American Airways building radio tower and on the Mercedes Hospital. How the rebels managed this shows considerable ingenuity.

The new American Ambassador, Earl E. T. Smith, arrived and presented his credentials. He was replacing Mr. Arthur Gardner, who had been so pro-Batista that he had actually embarrassed the President. On one occasion Batista said, "I'm glad Ambassador Gardner approves of my government but I wish he wouldn't talk about it so much." With the arrival of Ambassador Smith, the opposition hoped for the best. The Ambassador gave a press conference and said he would be glad to hear about the political situation from all factions. However, most of the opposition representatives were afraid to go near the embassy. I arranged for some of them to get in contact with the political officers of the embassy. I thought someone should hear their story.

Fidel Castro and his rebels attacked the Estrada Palma sugar mill where some two hundred soldiers were stationed. The mill was close to the Sierra Maestra Mountains, an excellent place for a post, hampering the rebel communications and supply lines. It was attacked by the rebels many times. I heard the story of this attack from a photographer who was with Fidel Castro at that time. This photographer said the rebels marched down from the mountains, walking along the dry beds of small streams or *arroyos,* which was the only way to get out of the mountains since there were no roads and few paths. Some of these streams had considerable water, but most of them were dry, except during the rainy season. The photographer had hopes of getting pictures of the attack, even though it was to be carried out at night. They marched until dark, with big sturdy Castro at the head of the column. The photographer said that walking beside him was a boy from Iowa, an American who had in some mysterious manner gotten to Cuba and joined the rebels. The photographer said he never did find out how, when or why the young American had joined the Castro rebels. All during the march, the mountain people gathered on the banks of the *arroyos* and cheered the rebels.

About dark they reached a small *bohio* not far from the Estrada Palma sugar mill. They stopped to eat and waited until time for the attack. The photographer claims it was that night that the rebel officers under Castro told him he could no longer lead the attacks. A big argument followed, Castro declaring he was in command of the army. But the officers stubbornly insisted they would not attack Estrada Palma unless he would keep to the rear. "If you are killed," they told Castro, "the rebellion will split into many groups. The young men will not want to fight with us. We will lose."

The photographer described the plan of attack. The rebels were divided into three groups. One started early, circling around Estrada Palma, prepared to ambush the reinforcements which would undoubtedly be called for by the soldiers at the mill. One group was to come up on one side and another, smaller force, was to attack from an adjacent side. The photographer was instructed to keep close to three men who were to cover the retreat, after the raid was accomplished, by burning a wooden bridge.

The attack was a great surprise. The main encampment of soldiers were asleep, permitting the rebels to capture vantage points, but soon the firing was heavy on both sides. After an hour of fighting, the photographer got separated from the group he was supposed to accompany. It was time, according to the plan, to begin to withdraw. He wanted to get across the bridge before the three youths burned it. He managed to get back to the bridge, but as he started across a group of soldiers downstream caught him silhouetted against the sky and started shooting at him. He threw himself flat on the wooden bed of the bridge and crawled across, dragging his photographic equipment. When he reached the other side, he waited. He knew something was wrong. There were not supposed to be Batista soldiers that near the bridge. He saw the gasoline cans which had been left there. Leaves had been heaped at the proper places to set the bridge afire. He waited until he saw the Batista soldiers advancing toward the bridge. He looked at the gasoline cans and decided to burn the bridge. He put down his photographic equipment and went to work. Soon the bridge was burning, the flames rising to the sky. He retreated as fast as he could, and finally found the small *bohio* again where Fidel Castro was waiting.

The rebels all got back before daybreak. The group which

had attacked the mill reported that some soldiers had been killed but not as many as should have been. It had been a darker night than had been expected and the Batista soldiers had kept under cover. The rebels marched back into the mountains and then rested. One or two men were slightly wounded, but none had been killed. The army announced in Havana that many rebels had been killed in an encounter at Estrada Palma Sugar Mill and that the others had fled. The army was "pursuing the fleeing rebels." This was always the last line of any communiqué. The photographer said the withdrawal of the rebels was leisurely and that no soldiers pursued them. They had captured arms, ammunition and supplies, not in great quantity, but sufficient to have made the raid worthwhile.

Ambassador Smith decided to go down to Santiago de Cuba. Ted Scott and I were at a cocktail party the night before he left. We told one of the officers of the embassy that undoubtedly the rebel sympathizers would stage a demonstration, but he didn't seem to agree with us. When the Ambassador arrived in Santiago de Cuba on July 31, 1957, he went to the City Hall to receive the keys of the city. As the ceremony ended a group of about one hundred women dressed in black gathered in front of City Hall shouting, "Libertad! Libertad!" and carrying placards protesting the "reign of terror" in the city. The police broke up the demonstration with fire hose and roughed up the women, dragging thirty of them off to jail. Several thousand spectators gathered to see the demonstration which had been of course planned. The Ambassador, annoyed over the police methods which he saw there, issued a statement: "I deplore the excessive action of the police."

That afternoon Santiago de Cuba buried Frank Pais and a companion who had been killed "in a gun battle." Later however it was revealed they had been captured and tortured to death. Frank Pais was the son of a Presbyterian Minister and a leader of the "26th of July" revolutionary movement in Santiago. Almost every person in Santiago de

Cuba turned out for the funeral. Thousands marched to the cemetery. Youths hauled down the Cuban flag on the cemetery flagpole and ran up the black and red rebel flag. The army had been withdrawn from the streets by the military authorities, who feared a massacre, especially with Mr. Smith present to witness it.

Ambassador Smith's statement about excessive police action caused a furor in Havana. The press headlined the intention of the Cuban government to ask for the Ambassador's recall. Senator José Gonzalez Puente issued a statement that "The Republic of Cuba rejects and repudiates interference in matters of Cuban sovereignty . . ." The United States State Department hastily assured Batista that the United States "had no intention of interfering in Cuba's internal affairs." A motion was presented in the United States Congress asking for the immediate withdrawal of Ambassador Smith. Congress is never informed on what goes on in Latin American countries. Congress, time after time, has undermined the authority of our best diplomats.

President Batista suspended constitutional guarantees for the fourth time since Fidel Castro landed. Censorship was imposed. Foreign publications were censored also. *The New York Times* arrived at my office with a gaping hole on the front page. I usually obtained a copy uncensored since a minor government employee, who had to cut out the articles indicated by the secret police, always saved me an uncut copy which I claimed, to people who saw it in the office, had been brought to me from Miami.

On September 5, 1957, a revolution broke out in Cienfuegos, a port on the south coast of Las Villas Province about 150 miles from Havana. Cienfuegos is a pleasant town, famous for its wonderful seafood. I had passed through there the year before when I was writing a tourist article. The uprising had been planned as a coordinated effort of naval forces all over the island, together with the help of the "26th of July" movement. However, something went wrong. The date had been set but had to be postponed. The Cienfuegos navy men never got the word of the postponement. They started the revolt at daybreak. The naval post there, which is the second largest in Cuba, imprisoned their officers—those not in the plot—and took over. At eight A.M., with the help of rebels, they seized the police station and other points in the town. Batista's troops moved in from Santa Clara with tanks and planes.

The rebels probably numbered between three and four hundred. Army planes strafed the city. The slaughter which occurred was incredible. Houses were strafed, innocent people in the streets were killed. Several aviators ordered to bomb the city refused to do so and dropped their bombs in the bay. These aviators were court-martialed and sentenced to six years. Ground troops fought the rebels, who were almost wiped out. The army took no prisoners. Only a few navy officers escaped death. Three of these captive officers were later tortured to death, according to court records. No one ever knew how many people were killed. The army, in mopping up operations, went into houses and took out any young man they could find and shot him. In the cemetery the army used bulldozers to make ditches, while big trucks picked up the dead from the streets.

The government kept the news from getting out of Cienfuegos. All newsmen including American correspondents were arrested on arrival there and sent away immediately. Gene Carrier went down with Louis Hamburg, Batista's private photographer, to get pictures for NBC. Despite their credentials and Hamburg's position the army detained them for hours at the entrance of the city and finally turned them back. One NBC man was arrested in Santa Clara and held for forty-eight hours. Censorship was of course in effect. There was no way to get the news out by cable. We began sending dispatches over the telephone. Strangely enough we got the stories through and from that time on, during the two year rebellion, we filed all reports by telephone. The *New York Times* recording machines make it easy to dictate stories.

The official report from the army stated that sixty were killed, among them twelve soldiers, and that thirteen soldiers had been wounded. My correspondent in Cienfuegos, a highly conservative man, said that at least a hundred were killed. Other stories put the dead at three to four hundred. The army declared that the rebels came down from the nearby mountains to start the revolt. But this was propaganda to hide the truth that officers and enlisted personnel of the navy had staged the revolt. At that time there was no indication that Fidel Castro had any insurgents in the hills around Cienfuegos. There were a few young men of the *Directorio Revolucionario,* the Havana University group, just starting to gather in the Escambray Mountains to the north of Cienfuegos. It was probably a small part of this group that joined the naval forces.

President Batista was shaken by the Cienfuegos revolt. He knew it had been planned as a revolt of all the navy and he realized that the navy could not be trusted. Soldiers were put on guard at many naval posts. In Oriente navy men on patrol were always accompanied by soldiers. Batista was in power only because of the loyalty of his military forces and he knew it. The infiltration of the navy caused him to become suspicious even of some of his soldiers. Many navy officers were discharged even though they had nothing to do with the revolt. Thirty-one officers, non-commissioned officers and enlisted men of the navy were tried at a secret court-martial in Camp Columbia army headquarters. I managed to get the information from a young lawyer attached to the Justice Ministry. I sent a report to the *Times* that three were sentenced to execution by firing squad, eleven to thirty years, one to twenty years and twelve to six years. The Cuban government was forced to confirm it. There was an immediate outcry. No one had ever, by decree of law, been shot in Cuba for revolting since the establishment of the Republic in 1902. Batista, well aware of the danger of arousing the public against him, had the death sentences commuted to life imprisonment.

General elections had been scheduled for June 1, 1958, but no one paid any attention. It was becoming more and more apparent that the rebellion was too deeply rooted to be ended by any elections held under the Batista regime. President Batista issued a statement saying he would not run for reelection. The revolution was beginning to affect the economic situation of Cuba. Merchants complained that the people were not buying. Motion picture theaters, a favorite target for bombs, were empty, and many in the towns and villages were closing. In Havana times were still prosperous, business went on as usual, but the continual disorders and fighting was creating an uneasy atmosphere.

The government decided to launch another offensive against Castro. More troops were thrown into the Sierra Maestra, but it was like looking for a needle in a haystack. Castro was now reported to have one thousand men. His lightning raids on army posts in widely scattered areas kept the soldiers in a state of tension. They feared the telescopic rifles, of which the rebels were reported to have fifty, each carried by an expert marksman. It was nerve-wracking for the soldiers to come out of their military posts early in the morning, hear the distant crack of a rifle and see one of their group fall. The enemy was too far off in the hills to give chase, so there was nothing to do about it.

Two cases of the murder of defenseless civilians were protested by the Cuban Medical Association and presented to the World Medical Association. One was the killing of Dr. Jorge Ruiz Ramirez in the small town of Taguasco near Sancti Spiritus in Las Villas Province. The police of the town shot a young rebel, but he escaped. His brother took him to Dr. Ruiz, who saw that he must be operated on immediately. The boy had a bullet in his spine. Dr. Ruiz decided to take him to Sancti Spiritus, where there was a hospital. They hired a taxi. An army patrol stopped the taxi, killed the wounded man, his brother, the doctor and the chauffeur. The other case was in Havana, where the secret police arrested Dr. Antonio Pulido Humara. He was beaten to death and his body thrown on the road to the airport. The police announced he had been hit by a car and killed. The World Medical Association asked permission of Batista to send an investigator to Cuba. Batista never even answered the request.

Physicians began to leave the interior towns. Seven or eight of them had already joined the rebels. The rebels had excellent physicians, although their facilities were wholly inadequate. Boys and girls all over the island gathered medical supplies and managed to smuggle them into the Sierra Maestra. The girls carried supplies in their wide skirts, which were so fashionable. In Oriente the military authorities tried to prevent women from wearing these big skirts, but they had a hard time enforcing it. Most of the medical supplies came from Havana, and despite the fact that the government rounded up and interrogated doctors and lawyers, the supplies continued to flow. One of the girls who was a nurse in the Sierra Maestra told me recently that they needed so many supplies because they were treating hundreds of the country people who had never had doctors for all kinds of diseases, especially intestinal parasites.

The Star Class World Championship Yacht Race was held in November. The best skippers of the United States and other countries sail in these races. I cover all international yacht races, although, frankly, I am not a yachtswoman. I simply describe the races and try to give an accurate picture of what happens. It was beautiful weather. I found my launch and we went out to the starting line, some two miles off the coast from the Habana Yacht Club. Sometimes I am practically alone in the launch but this being the first race and a world event the yacht was crowded with reporters, correspondents and photographers. I heard the man next to me telling a friend that fifty soldiers had been killed in a battle with the rebels. I could hardly believe that. I asked him about the story and he said he had heard it just before he left the CMQ radio chain for which he worked. I then asked Kauffman of the Associated Press who said he had not heard the story. There was a delay in starting and I got more and more worried. Quite frankly, my heart was not in the yacht race anyway. It seemed unreal in a land bloodied with civil strife. Gene Carrier was taking pictures for NBC. I asked him to cover the race for me, then got a nearby motorboat to take me ashore. Kauffman of Associated Press decided to come also. When we got back to the club Kauffman called his office and asked if they had heard about the battle. They hadn't. It was a *bola,* as the Cubans call it. But there was another story. Colonel Fermin Cowley, military chief of Holguin, who had been murdering and butchering like a bushman out of Africa, had been assassinated.

Cowley had been one of the "A" cell of the ABC Revolutionary Organization of 1933. He had entered the army a few years later and rose to the rank of Colonel. The story was that Cowley had ordered some kind of a part or accessory for his car from a hardware store. Two boys came down from the Sierra Maestra Mountains for the specific purpose of killing him. They went to the store, telephoned Cowley, and told him the part had arrived. It is not known whether the owner of the store knew of the telephone call or was involved. At any rate, Cowley arrived with an aide, and walked into the store. He was machine gunned in the doorway. He and his aide. The rebel youths fled back to the Sierra. However, military authorities, in retaliation, took eight village youths and executed them.

One morning Manolo Nunez, the agent who sells the *Times* in Cuba, called me and asked me to come to see him. That was an unusual request. I went immediately. He introduced me to a young Baptist minister who had just come from the Sierra Maestra Mountains where he had been with the insurgents of Fidel Castro for three months.

Reverend Victor Toranzo was short, round-faced and looked younger than his twenty-five years. He had graduated from the Baptist Seminary in Santiago de Cuba. I don't think he had ever had a church and when Fidel Castro asked for a Protestant minister, since he had a number of Protestants among his insurgents, Reverend Toranza volunteered. He and a Catholic priest went into the Mountains together. He told me he carried a big pack of Bibles.

The Reverend had contracted a throat infection. Dr. Ché Guevara, the Argentine doctor with Fidel, advised Rev. Toranzo to come to Havana or go to Miami to have his throat treated. Someone guided him out of the Sierra to Santiago de Cuba where he took a bus to Havana. The American Embassy gave him a visa, never imagining he had been with Fidel Castro. The American Embassy had been refusing to give a visa to any relatives of political exiles. Even the SIM passed the young minister through without question and when I saw him he was just getting ready to leave for the airport. I held his story until one of the rebels called to tell me he had gone. Rev. Toranzo told me several amusing stories. I asked if the insurgents had any prisoners. He said they didn't take many, usually disarming the soldiers they captured and setting them free. However, one group he had traveled with had a single prisoner. No one seemed to know what to do with him. He shared their food and clothing and also their long marches. He was one of them. He didn't try to escape because he didn't know how to get out of the mountains. One day after the group had been marching many miles for a rendezvous with another group and had even climbed a cliff with the help of ropes, the tired soldier told the preacher, "I couldn't understand why the army didn't get you rebels out of the mountains. But now I know."

Christmas, 1957, the revolution was one year old. Out in Oriente Province the rebels were attacking the soldiers almost daily, entering towns, pinning down the soldiers in the military posts by machine gun fire while they loaded trucks with food and supplies. They always paid for everything they took from the small merchants. However, the property of friends of Batista suffered. They carried off trucks, tractors, equipment of all kinds, food, cattle, anything they happened to need. They burned buses, putting the passengers out and leaving them to walk home, attacked trains, derailed them, took merchandise off trucks and burned gasoline trucks or carried off the gasoline. Although the Castro rebels had not struck a major blow at the army, their tenacity and determination was beginning to undermine the morale of the soldiers. In Latin-American history, never had a group of men so young, so inexperienced, so lacking of arms and finances, held out against a large, modern army for an entire year. Castro was the first Cuban in history who was able to instill in his men an uncompromising purpose and a long-range plan of warfare. He was the forerunner of a new turn in Latin America, the first evidence of a new spirit of lasting defiance to tyranny. Governments can continue to rule without the consent of the people, the military can continue to dominate a country, but the tenure of such rule can no longer remain indefinite.

In Havana, Christmas was gay, but the prisons were full and the armed forces prowled the streets like big cats looking for someone to pounce on. Money was flowing freely in the western provinces. The sugar workers had been given a bonus, seventeen million dollars, which they promptly spent for Christmas. There were many tourists in the capital city and night life was lavish. Christmas trees, adopted by the Cubans during the past several years, appeared everywhere. In every house, from mansion to hovel, there was a Christmas tree and the stores were filled with shoppers. The new Havana Riviera opened with a gala fiesta. Tourists arriving in Havana asked where the revolution was and were told it was only a minor disturbance seven hundred miles away. American businessmen told me that I was contributing to the ruin of the economy by stories of the rebellion. Both American and Cuban businessmen were annoyed. With Cuba so prosperous and money so plentiful, they couldn't understand why anyone would support a revolution. They wanted Batista to crush the Fidel Castro rebellion so they could "get on with business."

The rebels were trying to burn the cane. Miles of it went up in flames in Oriente Province. The sugar mills, El Pilon and Niquero, owned by Julio Lobo, lost all their cane. The circle of mills around the Sierra Maestra suffered heavily from the activities of the rebels. Despite this, the attempts of the rebels to sabotage the cane and reduce the sugar crop failed. Too much of Cuba was planted in cane for any local action to affect the over-all produce.

I sent Raul, my assistant, to Oriente Province to make a survey of conditions. He knew various government military commanders. I told him to go to Santiago de Cuba, to Bayamo, and then to Manzanillo, and to talk not only with the army, but to see people he and I knew to be rebel sympathizers. At Bayamo he found General Rio Chaviano, who sent him to Manzanillo in an army car, where he talked with both sides. As he was returning from Manzanillo in the army car, accompanied by an officer, the chauffeur began driving at breakneck speed through the hills. Raul told the chauffeur to drive more carefully. The chauffeur replied that the whole district was full of rebel sharpshooters and that he was only sorry the car would not go faster. They stopped to have lunch with General Chaviano. Raul reminded the General that the day before he had told Raul that the rebels had been dispersed and there would be no more cane burning. "Yes," said the General. "That is true."

"But I saw smoke rising in the cane fields for miles around as we came back from Manzanillo."

General Rio Chaviano laughed. "Raul, yesterday I told you that, and yesterday it was true. But today is another day."

Raul said the soldiers were nervous. One of them told him it was really getting rough. No one got any sleep when they were sent out on patrol. The soldier said they would camp and eat. After dark a rebel on a hilltop nearby would fire a shot into the camp. Everyone would jump to their feet, thinking they were being attacked. Later, the soldiers would settle down to sleep, with the sentries on guard. Then another shot or two would be fired into camp. This happened about every hour or two during the night. Three nights of this would send the army patrol back to the barracks, reeling with fatigue and loss of sleep. Sometimes the rebels would attack such a patrol after the soldiers were exhausted.

Fidel Castro, from his Sierra Maestra headquarters, announced that Dr. Manuel Urrutia would be the provisional president when the revolution was won. Dr. Urrutia was the judge who had issued the famous opinion that people "had a right to take up arms against a dictatorship." The actual announcement that Urrutia would be president was made in Miami, Florida, through Mario Llerons. The fourteen-page letter making the announcement had been smuggled out of the Sierra Maestra Mountains. Fidel Castro was always voluble, even on paper. The army always complained that the rebels took typewriters and office supplies, even a mimeograph now and then, out of posts they attacked. The rebels really needed them for all their correspondence, their announcements, and their propaganda. Fidel Castro's publicity in the United States and other countries was excellent, much better than that of Batista, even with his highly paid public relations men. Of course, it is impossible even for the best public relations men to defend an impossible position and Batista was finding that out.

14

The English-speaking colony in Havana is made up of Americans, British and Canadians, usually referred to as the "ABC" colony. Owing to the stringent labor laws, designed to prevent foreigners from working in Cuba, most of this colony are executives of companies. This gives the lower classes in Havana the impression that all English-speaking people are wealthy. Also, since the Americans, British and Canadians have similar business and social interests, they tend to group together, admitting into their affairs only Cubans of similar interests and cultural standing. They live comfortably in beautiful houses, for which they pay high rent of course, employ one to three servants, and belong to one or two clubs, such as the American Club, the Rovers Club, the Country Club, Habana Yacht Club and Miramar Club. The number of clubs a man belongs to does not reflect his personal wealth as much as it does his company's expense accounts. There is of course a small group who settled in Cuba many years ago and built up industries or business firms. This group has a different interest in and attitude toward the Cubans, since their fate is tied to that of the island. But the average executive lives here a few years and is then transferred to some other Latin-American, European or Asian country. Conversely, it is easy to find someone who has lived in India, China, Lebanon, Egypt or France. This also applies to the diplomatic corps. It is easy to understand why the "ABC" colony favored Batista, who represented a degree of security for business and industry. They had little interest in the activities of the Castro rebels, except as a possible threat to the stability of their lives.

There is, however, a cooperative spirit among the three nationalities, especially in community service, in social life, and in business negotiations. Their social life is pleasant and gay. In addition to diplomatic parties, there are private fiestas, cocktail parties and dinners. There is a warmth and true friendliness not usually found in international atmospheres. The usual pretence of boredom and meaningless sophistication that seems to afflict the international set in most of the world's capital cities, is not much in evidence in Havana.

The greater part of the women of the "ABC" colony belong to the Women's Club, one of the largest and most active in Latin America. Many Cuban women are members. The meetings are held in the Community House, built by the Masons. Here too the Little Theater and the Choral Society present plays and musicals during the year. There is such a dearth of cultural activity in Cuba that even amateur productions represent important progress in this direction. Many families belong to the Mothers' Club, which, founded many years ago, is now located in a large new building in Biltmore suburb. Children are encouraged to participate in sports; a library is available; there are tea dances for children from twelve to sixteen. Cuban children attend these parties and the "ABC" children all speak Spanish, since they attend private schools in which the enrollment is mainly Cuban. No one has ever heard of a delinquent teenager in the "ABC" colony. Although the children are sent to colleges in the United States, Canada, England and France, a considerable number return to Cuba to enter business or to get married, frequently to Cubans.

The Masonic Lodge in Cuba is the largest in any Latin-American country, with a membership that includes thousands of Cubans. José Marti, General Antonio Maceo and Generalissimo José Miguel Gómez, outstanding leaders in the wars of independence, were Masons. Today there are Masonic Lodges in all the major towns in Cuba and they wield considerable influence in the economic and political life of the nation. The many Protestant churches in Cuba include a surprisingly large number of Cubans in their congregations, particularly considering the long reign of the Spanish crown. The Catholic Church is losing ground slowly, and has never had the power that can be found in other Latin countries. The Anglo-American Association operates a hospital and a home for old people. Funds for these projects are obtained by a Community Chest Drive among the "ABC" colony.

1958 promised little happiness for the Batista government. True, the mills were grinding and the sugar crop, on which the economy of the island depends, was in no danger. But money was beginning to be a little scarce; the expenses of the government were mounting daily due to the tremendous costs of keeping the army on a war footing and in the field. Opposition to the government was growing, particularly in the interior. Fidel Castro gradually extended his operations. From Chivirico, a small port on the south coast not far from Santiago de Cuba, northward to Palma Soriano on the Central Highway, westward to around Manzanillo, Niquero and even Bayamo, field headquarters of the government troops, the rebels were roaming at will. This area is about two thousand square miles. The rebels entered towns to make purchases, attacked army posts, destroyed cane and rice plantations, carried off equipment of all kinds, attacked transportation and derailed trains. They drove off cattle into the Sierra Maestra Mountains, dividing them among the people, and retaining a beef supply. These cattle belonged to advocates of the Batista regime, who had big ranches in that district. The rebels constructed an emergency airport near Manzanillo where they received various plane loads of arms and ammunition. Once a rebel aviator arrived with a twin-engined plane which required more runway than the terrain permitted. The pilot managed to land the plane, but despite repeated efforts could not get it off the ground, due partly to engine trouble. The rebels were forced to burn it. The army reported they had shot down a plane which burned and all the crew burned with it.

The number of rebels was growing steadily. Youths from every town and district of the island went into the Sierra Maestra. Arms were so scarce that Castro was demanding that every recruit bring his own weapon and some ammunition. The other day a boy came into my office. He is fifteen, wears his hair so long he looks like a girl. He has delicate hands and bones. His natural sense of dignity and of genuine pleasure in the act of living is a trait found in most of the people from Oriente Province. He joined Fidel Castro at thirteen and since he had no rifle, Fidel Castro told him to go out and take one away from some soldier. He was so successful in this assignment that this became his job. Dressed in the usual dress of the countryman—an old pair of pants and a shirt hanging outside his trousers—the boy, who is still very small, went into towns, villages, walked about until he found a soldier alone, stuck a knife against his chest and demanded the soldier's rifle and ammunition belt. It was easy for such a small child to get near soldiers, since they paid no attention to him. Most of the time the soldier was so startled, he meekly gave up his weapon. But sometimes not. This youngster admitted that he had killed six with his knife. After several months of this, during which he captured more than thirty firearms, Fidel let him keep a rifle and put him in the regular troops.

The reprisals by the Batista armed forces, arbitrarily murdering innocent youths, in an effort to make the youth of Cuba afraid to assist the revolutionaries, was having an opposite effect. Young men everywhere decided it was safer in the hills fighting than remaining defenseless in towns and cities where they could be picked up by the authorities. That was one of the reasons Fidel Castro obtained so many recruits. But by this time Fidel Castro had become a sign of hope and liberty. Every young man in Cuba and most of the girls worshipped him as the symbol of the revolution.

Then the second front opened in the Escambray Mountains of Las Villas Province. I sent in the story given me by one of the boys of the *Directorio Revolucionario*. This group was composed of the Havana University students and others. The government immediately denied there were any rebels in Las Villas Province. The story was that a group had gathered in the Escambray Mountains with only a few rifles and some ammunition. They waited for an expedition from Miami, headed by one of the federation, Faure Chamount, which arrived with enough weapons to equip about two hundred fifty men. The expedition left Miami on January 31, 1957, aboard the yacht "Escapade" captained by a Cuban, Alonso. The navigator was an aviation pilot, Eduardo Garcia. The yacht had a capacity of five persons, but it carried fifteen together with arms and ammunition. The story of this expedition reads like most of the others —difficulties of all kinds, including lack of food. They finally made contact with a boat at Racoon Cove in the Bahamas, but instead of the yacht they expected, it was a little schooner, "San Rafael." By that time there was no water and food. They landed, found water but not food, then finally managed to kill a wild sheep.

They sailed aboard the schooner, for Nuevitas Bay on the north coast of Cuba, the "Escapade" returning to Miami. They made rendezvous with another yacht, the "Yaloven." The Cuban frigate, "Antonio Maceo" steamed by them but apparently took no notice. Aboard the "Yaloven," having again transferred the weapons, they went into Nuevitas Bay and headed toward Santa Rita Beach. There was the "Antonio Maceo" again but they sailed safely past. At night they unloaded the arms on the beach, where a group of revolutionists were waiting in a milk truck.

They needed more arms and ammunition. These had to come from Havana where so many were hidden that it was amazing. The officials were always capturing a cache of arms, but they seemed inexhaustible. I told one of the reporters one day when the army showed us a big consignment of arms that we should carve our initials on one and see if the same rifle appeared the next time they showed us a captured cache. However, perhaps my many years in Cuba have made me unnecessarily skeptical.

One of the *Directorio Revolucionario* boys told me that his job was hauling arms and ammunition down the Central Highway, where only a few army patrols operated. On one of these trips, an automobile crashed into him, almost destroying his car. He was not hurt, but rifles and machine guns spilled out from under the seats. The trunk was also full of weapons. Farmers in a field nearby, attracted by the crash, rushed to the scene. One of the farmers ran to a nearby village and got another automobile, then everyone helped load the arms into the new car and the boy sped on his way. The man who had collided with the boy's car found that his car could still be driven, so he left, too much worried about being found by soldiers, who might not give him an opportunity to explain that he had no connection with the rebels, to care about the damage to his car.

There is more than a little irony in the fact that the rebels used the Central Highway, the main supply line for the army, to transport their much needed arms into the western provinces. Indeed, the rebel system of transportation operated with less losses than that of the government. All along the Central Highway boys reported on the movements of army patrols. In every town and village, strung along the highway like beads on a string, the driver of the rebel car stopped and telephoned the next town to find out if any army patrol was on the road. If the road was clear he drove on. If not, he drove into a garage, arranged previously, and waited until the patrol passed. The method was simple, but extremely effective. And the drivers of the cars were such carefree youths that they were seldom suspected, even if an army patrol did pass them.

The government tightened censorship in Oriente Province. It became almost impossible to get news. They placed soldiers in all commercial radio stations, at the telephone exchanges, and threatened any reporter who tried to get a story out. We began to have to depend on travelers and rebel sources. The rebels continued to send couriers back and forth, mostly girls.

President Batista was determined to hold elections. The four government coalition parties nominated Dr. Andres Rivero Aguero, the Prime Minister, as their presidential candidate. Actually none of the parties were very much pleased over his nomination. He was Batista's personal choice. Rivero Aguero was a man of the people, having been born in Oriente Province of a very poor family. He had obtained an education by working and going to school in Santiago de Cuba and later in Havana at the university. Batista probably hoped that a man of the people from Oriente Province might have a calming effect on that strife-torn area.

Old Dr. Ramón Grau San Martin decided he would run for president as the candidate of the *Autentico* Party. He still had a part of the party left, although it was split into various factions, some following Dr. Carlos Prio Socarras, and cooperating with the revolution. Dr. Carlos Marquez Sterling, a lawyer, was the candidate of the Free Peoples' Party, a faction of the once powerful *Ortodoxo* Party. Alberto Salas Amaro ran with a small unknown party called *Nacional Cubana.*

The people of the island were not interested in the elections. They considered elections a trick to keep the power inside the same group backed by the military forces.

On February 10th ten bombs exploded in Havana. During the next few days a number of policemen were killed.

Throughout the Republic sabotage and terrorism continued. I began to send in stories brought me by travelers of the harsh treatment of the civilian population in the foothills of the Sierra Maestra Mountains. In the small town of Minas de Bueycito and in San Yao, the people were being forced to leave. Government troops were burning their homes and confiscating their lands. Major Sanchez Mosquera at Bueycito was giving paraffin tests to those he caught on the roads. If the test was positive, showing traces of nitrate, he shot them on the grounds that they had fired a gun recently. Many innocent people died. This same Major arrested Josie Norman and his son, both British citizens, as they were returning from their coffee plantation in the Sierra. Norman's wife was the granddaughter of one of Cuba's greatest heroes of the wars of independence against Spain, General Calixto Garcia, known in the United States as the man to whom the message to Garcia was delivered. Major Sanchez gave the paraffin test to both Norman and his son. It was positive. Norman, a musician, composer and former orchestra leader in London, explained to the Major that any person handling coffee and the fertilizer used on that crop gets nitrate into his hands. Major Sanchez finally released them, with a stern warning. But he released them only because he hesitated to shoot British citizens.

The government continued to pour reinforcements into Oriente Province. The army called for more volunteers and claimed to have already inducted ten thousand. These volunteers were given two months training and then sent to the Sierra Maestra or other parts of Oriente to fight. The rebels called them *bocaditos* (tidbits), since they had no knowledge of guerilla warfare and many times ran away. An old sergeant who had been in the Cuban army for many years returned to Havana, having been wounded in the leg. He said that he had command of about fifty of these new soldiers and was marching them to an advance post, which needed reinforcements, when they were ambushed by rebels. The sergeant was hit in the leg by the first volley and fell. He said he looked around for his soldiers and found himself alone. They had run off in every direction, "Like guineas," he complained. The rebels picked him up, took him out to a road and left him there for the government troops to pick up.

A third front was opened in the hills around Baracoa, located on the extreme eastern tip of the island. This is a considerable distance from the Sierra Maestra Mountains and northeast of Santiago de Cuba and the United States Guantanamo naval base, which indicated that it was either a new group or that Fidel Castro had sent them from the Sierra.

On February 15, 1958, the Cuban people were shocked over the treatment by American authorities of Dr. Carlos Prio Socarras. Accused of revolutionary activities and buying arms, Dr. Prio was handcuffed and forced to walk to jail. What angered Cubans was that the United States were granting political asylum to General Marcos Perez Jiminez, one of the bloodiest dictators of Latin America, who had just been overthrown in Venezuela. The United States should use a *little* common sense. If they are going to grant asylum to Jiminez, then why humiliate Prio, who had never killed or tortured anyone, and who was deposed by Batista. That treatment of Prio irritated every Latin American. I am sorry to say that the United States authorities always seem to be highly successful in making enemies instead of friends throughout the whole of Latin America.

The Cuban army was now using small tanks, armored trucks and planes to fight the rebels in the Sierra Maestra. The tanks were not very useful in that kind of terrain and the planes were not effective. Gene Carrier had flown over the Sierra Maestra with the army several times. Gene said the Sierra Maestra was a green carpet that would hide anything except smoke from air reconnaissance. Also, by ten o'clock in the morning, the whole area was covered by a blue mist, so that even along the shore the aviators could not have spotted a rebel boat unloading arms in some cove.

The rebels had set up their own armory to make weapons. They had developed a type of hand grenade which was shot from a rifle. The boys told me it was very effective. Also they mined the roads with dynamite. Many of the bombs which the government planes dropped into the Sierra didn't explode. The rebels took these apart and used the explosives for their own weapons. They became highly proficient in the use of dynamite. Many an army patrol or reinforcement column found half a mountain coming down at them, burying trucks, making roads impassable, and effectively stopping their advance.

An international automobile race was planned in Havana for February 24th. Racing drivers known throughout the world attended, including Juan Manuel Fangio, Argentina's world auto-racing champion. The night before the race Fangio was standing in the lobby of the Hotel Lincol, located near the Malecón Sea Drive, along which the race was to be run. A young man walked up to Fangio as he was conversing with his mechanic and a couple of other people in the lobby of the hotel. He said, "Are you Fangio?" Fangio, thinking it was one of his fans, replied in the affirmative. The man shook his hand and said, "You don't know what it means to meet you, Fangio." He thrust a pistol against Fangio's side and said, "Not a word, come with me." The two walked out of the lobby and stepped into a waiting car. The revolutionists had kidnapped Fangio.

The story hit the front pages of newspapers all over the world. Fangio was kept until February 25th, the day after the race. There was additional misfortune at the race, since an oil slick on the street caused one of the cars to crash into the spectators, killing four and injuring fifty.

Ted Scott, Gene Carrier and I saw Fangio at the Argentine Embassy just after Ambassador Rear Admiral Raul Lynch had picked him up at a house on the outskirts of Havana. The youthful kidnappers had called the Ambassador and given him the address. Fangio told us he had been transferred three times during his period as a captive, in three different automobiles, to three different houses—all well furnished. He saw part of the race on television. He said his captors treated him nicely. He had been well fed and never felt he was in danger. In fact, he seemed to think the rebels were charming people.

Of course the Batista government was embarrassed and angry. They started picking up all youthful revolutionists. Perhaps someone talked. At any rate, they arrested the boy who had headed the kidnapping group. His wife and a man I know came to see me some forty-eight hours after he was arrested to ask that I help save his life. The young wife sat in my office and cried. Even as she sat there crying, it was too late. The police had tortured him to death. The only thing I could have done would have been to call the police and the Presidential Palace and tell them I knew the boy had been arrested and demand to know where he was being held. That at least would have prevented the government from announcing that he had been killed "in a gun battle."

The Catholic Church called for a "national union government" to end bloodshed and restore "normal political life." This statement was made by Manuel Cardinal Arteaga, Archbishop of Havana. President Batista was very much annoyed by this. It sounded to him as though he was being asked to resign or bring the opposition parties into his government. The night the statement was issued the palace propaganda department called in all the newspapers and asked them not to print it. The newspapers paid no attention and front-paged the appeal. The next day President Batista issued a statement. "I shall continue in office and hope that the public will freely choose their new officials in the scheduled elections."

The *Directorio Revolucionario* officials, hiding in Havana, declared, "President Batista must resign immediately and a provisional government be founded to return liberty and democracy to the people." The statement was given to me exclusively. But since the government and all opposition groups read *The New York Times,* soon everyone in town knew about it.

President Batista had recently appointed Dr. Emilio Nunez Portuondo, representing Cuba in the United Nations, as Premier. This was done in an effort to reach an understanding with the opposition political parties and open the way for elections. However, on March 12th, President Batista again suspended constitutional guarantees. Censorship again went into effect and foreign correspondents were notified that outgoing dispatches must first be submitted to censors. Premier Nunez Portunodo realized immediately that the atmosphere was not one in which elections could be held. He and all the ministers resigned in accordance with the semi-parliamentary system of Cuba. "Elections cannot be achieved under present circumstances," he said.

On March 17th Fidel Castro announced total war against Batista to start April 1st and said that he was going to call a general revolutionary strike. His manifesto was printed and circulated by the underground all over the island. "Revolutionary action must be carried out progressively from this instant until it ends in the strike that will be ordered at the proper moment." Castro gave every official, noncommissioned officer or enlisted man of the army, navy and police until April 5th to resign or lose his right to remain in the armed forces. He told the judiciary to resign if its members expected to keep their positions. Immediately, civic and professional associations demanded that President Batista resign and a provisional government take over to hold "impartial elections."

Batista called the total war declared by Castro a demonstration of "arrogance." On March 23rd, he suspended elections, postponing them from June 1st to November 3rd. Ambassador Earl E. T. Smith and the United States State Department were really "jolted," as someone expressed it. They had been depending on elections to settle the Cuban situation. Apparently they had erroneous information con-

cerning the situation. They continued to be hopeful however and later regarded the November 3rd elections as "the
solution to Cuba's problems."

The Cuban Police tried to track down members of the
Board of Directors of the Cuban Bar Association who had
endorsed the demand for a national unity government
made by the Catholic Church. Dr. José Miro Cardona, dean
of the Bar Association, had presented to the Board of Directors a report on the situation which had been quite uncom-
plimentary to President Batista and his government. Within
a few days Dr. Miro Cardona took political asylum in a
foreign embassy in Havana and later left the island.

Herbert Matthews came by on his way to Jamaica. He
stayed a few days and wrote some articles. However, I didn't
agree with him at all when he said, "Havana is ripe for rebellion." The young revolutionists had little support in this capital city, labor was not inclined to strike or to rebel, and I
was so sure that the entire "total war" in Havana would fail
that I told the Castro boys who came to see me that it was
premature and stupid. I told them the strike would fail and
many of them would get killed. Fidel Castro had set April
1st as the start of the total war against Batista, but he had
not fixed the date of the general strike. It became a war of
nerves. Every possible precaution was taken by the government. Guards were increased at all points, every young man
in sight was arrested. Congress declared a state of national
emergency which gave the President unlimited power over
every phase of national life.

I received a story that Batista had made a deal with
the Communists, who control certain powerful unions. Batista had announced many times that he had eradicated
the Communists from Cuba. The strange part of Batista's
war against Communists was that it never seemed effective.
He had a lot of former Communists in his government, and
many people didn't believe they had ever renounced communism. I used to receive lists of people in the government
who were Communists from Ernesto de la Fe, who had

started an anti-Communist movement at that time. He was no longer a friend of Batista. The story I had was that the Communists demanded, as the price for their not supporting Fidel Castro, that they be allowed to have their newspaper *Hoy* back, that no one in the party was to be molested, and that in the coming elections they were to get certain advantages by joining another party and using their influence in favor of the government. Batista reportedly turned thumbs down on the idea of *Hoy*, but agreed not to arrest any more Communists. As a matter of fact, the Bureau for Investigation of Communist Activities headed by Colonel Mariano Faget hadn't arrested a Communist for months. I cannot actually confirm the deal between Batista and the Communists, but later events made it seem quite probable that an agreement was reached.

The United States decided not to ship any more arms to the Batista government. That was certainly a real victory for Fidel Castro and his insurgents. Batista had been buying 1950 Garand rifles. A shipment was ready to be loaded, to leave the United States for Cuba, when the Batista government was informed that the shipment was suspended and advised not to make any more requests for permission to buy arms. It was not an actual embargo, but it had the same effect. Someone in the United States State Department had finally realized that there is a clause in the mutual defense pact of the American states which prohibits the shipment of arms to a country which uses them against its own people. The United States State Department said: "In authorizing shipments of arms to other countries under the mutual security program it has been our consistent practice to weigh carefully those consigned to areas where political tensions have developed. We wish to be assured, for example, that the arms are destined for uses consistent with the objectives of our mutual security legislation."

Well, that finished that. President Batista defiantly announced that Cuba "could buy arms in any country of the Americas or Europe." He was a little optimistic. During the months that followed, his agents had considerable difficulty in finding arms. Eventually they did, but it was too late by then.

Fidel Castro called the strike and the youthful rebels tried to stage it on April 9th. Labor did not respond. Forty young revolutionists were killed in street fighting. The Confederation of Cuban Workers, headed by Secretary General Eusebio Mujal, announced, "There is no general strike and all workers are at their jobs as usual." Near my office a bomb was thrown into a gas register destroying the main. Flames shot up and continued for hours. An American newspaperman trying to find out about it was beaten by police. Electric power was cut off in the old part of Havana and in Vedado's residential suburb. We had to use kerosene lamps again. My electric typewriters were useless. Big searchlights installed on the Presidential Palace swept the adjoining streets and cars of police and soldiers armed with machine guns patrolled the streets around my office.

The Communists helped sabotage the strike. One Communist, laughing, told Raul the next day, "Well, you didn't see any Communists get killed yesterday. We keep our heads." Several weeks later the Communists issued in their clandestine publication *Carta Semanal* an open letter to the rebels, pointing out that the April strike failed because the "26th of July" revolutionary movement had refused to form a united front with the Communists. They declared that only with Communist support could any general strike be successfully carried out in Cuba. They were perfectly correct.

The failure of the strike was a major blow to Fidel Castro. His right hand man, Faustino Perez, had been the head of the movement in Havana. Now, with the government searching for him, Faustino was useless to the rebels. Castro's own organization was angry, stating he was at fault over the failure of the strike. They could not realize, and probably Castro himself did not realize, that only a small portion of the people in Havana supported the rebels. Both Castro and his rebels had deluded themselves into believing that their popularity in the provinces was mirrored in Havana. Commerce and industry still clung to Batista.

Castro kept right on fighting. He had made an attempt to overthrow Batista suddenly, and had failed, but he remained as determined and defiant as ever. He ordered his rebels to get Faustino Perez out of Havana. With every policeman in the city looking for him, Faustino Perez left Havana and arrived safely in the Sierra Maestra. He even gave a press conference before he left. However, he did have a narrow escape. The police arrived at the house from which he had left, only five minutes too late. The police arrested many. Chief of National Police, General Pilar Garcia, one of the most hated men in Cuba, declared that "the police stations are full of prisoners."

The government put out the report that the "Castro movement is waning." It did look like it. The rebels were having setbacks on all fronts. Government forces were stepping up their attacks. There had been a large group of correspondents and photographers down from the States at the time of the strike failure. The Batista government, jubilant, told the foreign press they could send stories without censorship. I telephoned a story about the rebels taking control of the Moa Bay Mining Company. When the rebels attacked, the soldiers in the small army post fled aboard a navy vessel. The rebels bought food and supplies at the commissary. They even paid for the gasoline they had used in the jeeps and trucks of the company. Later they returned the "borrowed" trucks, welding equipment and road building machinery. They were building an airport.

The next day the censor in the telephone company called me and told me I could in the future send only official releases. He said I had sent a subversive story. I protested that it was the truth. He said, "Never mind the truth, the government doesn't like it." I then reminded him that the Prime Minister had said the foreign correspondents could send whatever stories they desired. The censor said he was not concerned with the Prime Minister, he was taking orders from the Minister of Interior. I called Dr. Guell. He was upset, not over the story the censor complained about, but a story I had sent about the police arresting and killing three young Catholic youth leaders. I asked him if he had read the story. He said he had not. He said he was dressing to go to the Presidential Palace for the presentation of credentials of some new ambassador and would call me again within a couple of hours. He did, telling me that there would be no more interference. I knew of course that President Batista gave that order. The President had always been very nice to me. He apparently liked me. I am sure that the censors would have stopped me from sending stories many times if it had not been for President Batista.

Camp Columbia army headquarters continued to issue communiqués telling how many rebels had been killed. No soldier casualties were ever mentioned. I mentioned in the *Times* that Batista's army was becoming known as the "bullet proof army." But the classic was an army communiqué stating that two hundred rebels had been killed and one soldier wounded in the hand. I hope that mention of such things will make it clear why correspondents find it difficult to give the American public the truth.

At the end of June, Raul Castro, Fidel's younger brother, had a brilliant idea, which apparently Fidel never did approve. Raul had left the Sierra Maestra with a rebel force and crossed the Central Highway. He established his headquarters in the Sierra Cristal Mountains, which do not offer as good protection as the Sierra Maestra. The mountains are more open, less jungle-like. However, Raul was an excellent commander. He had a natural talent for military action. He had been with the group General Bayo trained in the mountains of Mexico and he was one of the twelve who survived the first disaster of the expedition.

Raul is short and slight. He wears his hair long, caught in a sort of bun at the back, topped by a Spanish *boina*, or beret. He is not talkative, is a strict disciplinarian, and he and his men fought like tigers. The rebels had been complaining for weeks that Batista planes, which were bombing and strafing the rebels, were being refueled and given ammunition at the United States Guantanamo naval base. Raul decided to protest about this in a way which would upset the American government. He kidnapped forty-five Americans and three Canadians, whom the rebels probably thought were Americans. Within the space of a few days his insurgents had kidnapped twelve technicians from the Moa Bay Mining Company, two officials from the United States owned Nicaro Nickel plant, three officials of the United Fruit Company, two sugar mill managers and twenty-eight United States Marines and sailors. The personnel of the United States Guantanamo naval base were returning from the Cuban town of Guantanamo, which is fifteen miles from Caimanera, the small port where the sailors and marines take the launch to the base.

There never was an accurate description of the kidnapping—the United States Navy saw to that—but the best report I obtained was that the sailors and marines were in the regular Cuban bus which runs between Guantanamo and Caimanera. A couple of rebels armed with machine guns halted the bus on a lonely stretch of the road. The Americans, laughing and talking, some dozing, paid little attention. The rebels ordered the driver into a small side road and soon the sailors and marines found themselves going into the mountains. Apparently they accepted the matter as an adventure and soon the Americans and Cubans were good friends. The bus continued until the road was no longer passable. Then they had to get out and walk. The bus and its passengers disappeared without a trace. It was only when the rebels informed the United States Guantanamo base that anyone knew what had happened to them.

The story hit the front pages of newspapers all over the world. Raul Castro, with one act, had revived the flagging interest in their movement. The United States government was incensed over the kidnappings. The Cubans, long accustomed to worse things, didn't realize what the word kidnapping meant to the American people. President Eisenhower said in his press conference that the "United States is trying to get live Americans back." The rebels were shocked at the reaction of the American government and press. Some of the boys of the movement came into the office to tell me that the Americans were in no danger. I explained to them how the American people felt about kidnappings.

The Americans must have been well treated. One source informed me that Raul Castro gave the captives a swimming party and a barbecue one night in the hills and that two of the group, who were ill, were being given medical care by the rebel doctors. The rebels said the kidnapping was a protest against the policy of the United States naval base at Guantanamo in refueling and giving ammunition to the army planes. The United States authorities declared this had not been done. The American consul, Park Wollam, of Santiago de Cuba, went into the mountains to confer with Raul Castro. One of the political advisers was "Deborah," Miss Vilma Espin, who married Raul after the Batista regime fell. "Deborah" was a beautiful girl, about twenty-five, who had almost graduated from the Massachusetts Institute of Technology as an engineer. She speaks English and acted as one of the negotiators.

The Batista government, much chagrined, charged that the rebels were "taking strategic positions" during the time the Cuban government suspended all bombing in order not to injure the American prisoners. After much negotiation, during which the rebels demanded that American Ambassador Earl E. T. Smith or responsible officials of the United States State Department come to see them, the rebels finally began releasing the captives on July 2, 1958, a few at a time. They were flown in a United States navy helicopter from the mountains to the Guantanamo base. Oddly enough, almost all of the kidnapped men returned as confirmed *Fidelistas.* They had been shown every courtesy and consideration; the rebels had talked to them about the aims and ideals of the revolution. Even the marines and sailors talked favorably of Fidel Castro, although they were silenced by the navy. The rebels announced they had freed the servicemen because of the Lebanese situation. But the fact is that the rebels were afraid the Americans would send troops to Cuba or otherwise assist Batista. They did not understand that good treatment of the Americans still did not alter the fact that the Americans had been kidnapped. The rebels had been hoping that Americans would begin to understand that Batista was hated by the Cuban people. The rebels were puzzled by the American attitude toward them, by the American unwillingness to understand the reasons for the revolution. This accounts, in part, for Fidel Castro's distrust of the United States.

The anti-American campaign did not reach its peak until after the revolution, when Fidel Castro declared that "Cuba and Latin America should be neutral in any war between the United States and Soviet Russia." Many of the rebels who had been educated in the United States did not approve of this campaign. This was true also of the middle and upper classes, who realized that the United States was the island's greatest customer and supplier.

The United States has exerted tremendous influence during the past twenty-eight years on every phase of Cuban life. Thousands of Cubans fleeing from political persecution have taken refuge in the United States, particularly in Florida. The children of the middle and upper classes have attended American colleges and universities. Hundreds of doctors have served their internships in American hospitals; hundreds of youths fought with the United States armed forces during the Second World War and in Korea.

The United States is mirrored in every phase of Cuban life. The modern Cuban eats hot dogs, hamburgers, hot cakes, waffles, fried chicken and ice cream. It has become almost impossible today in Havana to find native foods such as *malanda, yuca, picadillo* or *ajiaco*. Spanish architecture remains only because of its indestructible bulk. The new apartment buildings could be mistaken for those in any American city, and the new private homes resemble those of Florida. Spanish furniture is becoming rapidly extinct. American made refrigerators, electric and gas stoves, and kitchen units have changed household customs.

Hundreds of English words have crept into the Spanish language. It would be impossible to describe a baseball game or a boxing match in Cuba without using English terms. A new composite language is emerging, evident in such words as *jonron* for "home run." The society pages are full of such words as "cocktail party," "bridesmaids," "birthday," "honeymoon," and others. Occasionally a publication in Havana rails against the increasing number of English signs, stores with English names, and the encroachment of the English language into Cuban life. But it is a hopeless battle. Words once given common usage cannot be eliminated. Most Cuban children think "sandwich" is a Spanish word. No waiter in a restaurant would know what to serve if asked for an *emparedado*.

Spanish influence is not nearly as strong in Cuba as in other Latin-American countries. The Spanish social customs have given way to modern ideas. A chaperon will soon be unknown in Havana, and Spanish courtship is laughed at by the young people. The Catholic Church remains powerful, but has far less control over the lives and morals of Cubans than in other Latin-American countries. Many lawyers, doctors and educated men do not agree with the rigid customs of the Catholic Church and rarely attend mass or directly participate in Church affairs.

There is little cultural influence of Spain in music, art or literature. Sculptors and painters look to the United States rather than Europe for recognition. "Cuba has developed its own music," according to Harold D. Schonberg, music critic of the *Times*. In literature Cuba has never accomplished much. Books must be published at the author's expense. The economic rewards of literature are so small that there is no reason to suppose that the new generation, so materialistic even in their ideals, will be attracted toward it. There is no theatre in the island. A number of small groups have launched experimental playhouses, but most of the plays are foreign productions translated into Spanish. A recent contest for the best play brought out many manuscripts, but none showed promise, according to the committee that read the plays. There are few trained actors and actresses and almost no audience. "Why make gloves for people who do not wear them?" one young man told me, when I asked him about the theatre.

Around the end of July the Caracas Pact was signed. Romulo Betancourt, now president of Venezuela, told the groups they must get together or Venezuela could not give them assistance. He said the Venezuelans were helping Cuba, not just one faction. Venezuela aided the revolution with money to buy arms and supplies in Florida. But the reports that Venezuela was sending arms and ammunition to the rebels by plane appears to have been inaccurate.

American marines landed in Cuba. The marines had landed to protect the water supply of the United States Guantanamo naval base. This action was taken in agreement with the Cuban government. The pipelines and pumping station are located on the Yateras River, six miles outside the base. The government had a detachment of soldiers guarding these installations, but with the rebels controlling the entire district, they were withdrawn for fear they would be killed. The American government then sent in the marines. Fidel Castro demanded over the radio withdrawal of the marines. His station was so weak at that time that we had to get the information through a rebroadcast from the *Continente* Station in Venezuela, which was re-transmitting the rebel broadcasts. Apparently this was a mobile radio unit, which the rebels moved from place to place to prevent location of their headquarters. The rebels then made an offer to guard the base water supply. On August 1, 1958 the marines withdrew. Later, the rebels cut off the supply two or three times for several hours explaining that the "necessities of war" required it. I never did find out what these necessities were.

The bodies of seven youths were found on the streets of Havana on the morning of August 2nd. Ten small bombs had exploded the night before in various sections of the town, causing alarm, but little damage. The police took seven boys who had been picked up days before the bombs exploded, killed them and threw their bodies at places where the bombs exploded. Photographers came to my office and showed me pictures of three bodies. Horrible pictures.

The rebels increased their attacks in Oriente Province. One army detachment was surrounded near La Plata on the south coast of Oriente Province. They were cut off from water and food. Reinforcements which the army sent out were annihilated. Planes tried to bomb the rebels but failed to do any damage. Finally, Major José Quevedo, in command of the army detachment, surrendered to the rebels. His detachment consisted of 246 men. The rebels immediately slaughtered a number of cattle to feed them, treated them with every courtesy, even letting their officers keep their side arms. When the rebels delivered the prisoners to the International Red Cross and Cuban Red Cross, the soldiers embraced the rebels when they left. People in Havana laughed and said that now Batista had 246 *Fidelistas* in his army. Major Quevedo joined the rebel ranks.

The delivery of these prisoners and wounded without exchange was the first of its kind in modern times. Fidel Castro had been urging the Red Cross to come to Cuba. Finally a representative, Pierre Jaquier, was sent out from Geneva. After receiving permission from President Batista, Jaquier took a group of ambulances from Havana, Santiago de Cuba, Bayamo, Manzanillo and other towns. I think they had about eighteen. After considerable difficulty, during which the army said Castro was lying since he had no wounded soldiers, the delivery was made. Later the Cuban Red Cross took over wounded soldiers and prisoners at intervals. We heard the arrangements being made at various times over amateur radios utilized by the rebels. On August 19, 1958, a broadcast from the Sierra Maestra rebel radio said that "hundreds of soldiers have been killed and wounded" and claimed to have delivered 442 wounded soldiers and prisoners to the Red Cross. Our contact in the Red Cross confirmed that.

15

About the middle of July, I decided we must have a really good radio to pick up all the broadcasts of the rebels. We listened regularly to Radio Continente of Caracas and Radio Rumbo of Caracas. Within a short time Fidel Castro increased the power of his rebel station so that we could hear it. The government interfered many times, but we taped the broadcasts and then played them over and over to get the information. In Havana, radio dealers were selling all the short-wave radios they had. Everyone wanted to hear the rebel broadcasts. The police ordered all radio dealers to report the name and address of everyone who purchased a radio. They arrested a number of people whom they found listening to the rebel radio. Sarita, who helped me check the broadcasts, used to turn on the air-conditioning, shut the doors of the office, and turn up the rebel broadcasts very loud.

The police in Havana were getting jittery. My daughter, Marta, was dancing at the Casino Parisiense of the Hotel Nacional. On her last night Ted Scott gave a party. That night, driving back alone along the Malecón Sea Drive, I saw a couple of police cars with a group of policemen armed with machine guns and rifles. They waved me to stop. I pulled up to the curb and got out of the car.

"Que pasa?" I demanded. One of the policemen said, belligerently: "Have you a driver's license?" I replied that I not only had a driver's license but I had credentials from the Presidential Palace. If they would come with me to the car I would be glad to show the credentials to them. There was a moment of silence and a policeman standing in the back, said, "Go ahead." I mention this because it was the kind of thing that happened day after day. It begins to have its effect on people. They begin to resent the very sight of the police.

Fighting broke out in Pinar del Rio, the province on the western end of the island. I had received the story several weeks before that a group was operating in the Organo Mountains. However, fighting was spasmodic. The rebels attacked transportation, burning buses, gasoline trucks, causing bus service to be suspended at intervals. One man told me the story of taking a bus at Bahia Honda on the north coast. It was late in the afternoon and the bus driver didn't want to travel at night. The army insisted that the bus must keep to its schedule and sent two jeeps full of soldiers as escort. As the bus went down a narrow road closed in by brush on both sides, the rebels fired a shot across in front of the vehicle. The soldiers in the two jeeps who were driving in front heard the shot and dashed back. The rebels killed or captured all of the soldiers. They burned the jeeps, loaded the soldiers into the bus, and told the driver to return to Bahia Honda. That ended travel at night.

President Batista sent word by Edmund Chester, his public relations man, that he was sorry to hear I was sending so many reports from the rebel radio. He said we had been friends for many years and he could not understand it. I sent word back that I was reporting *all* news from Cuba and since the army issued few communiqués and according to my reports from travelers in Oriente many of these reports were not accurate, it was necessary that I send in the news from rebel sources also. If I did not do so, I said, the *Times* would send down someone who would.

The rebels had been trying to get "belligerent status" in Latin America but they were never able to do so. If they had obtained this they could have purchased arms and ammunition from various countries. The rebels were really hitting hard at the army. On August 13, 1958 we had news that the Red Cross had received 170 wounded soldiers and buried 450 persons, including soldiers and civilians killed in the districts of Las Mercedes, Cerro Pelado, and other points near the Estrada Palma sugar mill.

The first part of August President Fulgencio Batista sent his propaganda chief, Señor Pizzi de Porra, to me. My husband, Phil, had saved his life during the 1933 revolution. Pizzi said the President had sent him to tell me that whenever I wanted any information which I found difficult to obtain I should call Pizzi, who in turn would see the President. In this manner I would be sure that the *Times* had the right information. He was getting worried about the *Times* stories. This contact proved useful. Later in the month the family of Dr. Orlando Cuervo Galano informed me that he had been arrested by the Military Intelligence Service (SIM). Orlando was the son of Dr. Pelayo Cuervo who had been killed the day the revolutionary group attacked the Presidential Palace. I called Pizzi and asked him if it were true that Dr. Cuervo had been arrested and, if so, what were the charges. Dr. Cuervo was immediately released.

Another case was the arrest of the wife of Dr. José Miro Cardona, first Premier of the present revolutionary government of President Manuel Urrutia. Mrs. Cardona had returned from Miami, where her husband was living in exile. Both she and her daughter-in-law were arrested. I called Pizzi. Within a couple of hours, an aide to President Batista called me to say that the arrest had been "in error." Her daughter called me twenty minutes later to tell me that her mother had just been released from Camp Columbia army headquarters.

Another instance of how useful this contact was: seventeen young revolutionists, freed by the Urgency Court, were again arrested by the police, just as they were being released at Principe Fortress Prison. I called Pizzi. Two days went by, then he called and said that all seventeen had been released. I was not always successful, however. At about this same time, I learned that two girls had been arrested after several boys had been killed in a gun battle with police in a Havana suburb. I called Pizzi. He said he would check into the matter. I learned later that the two girls, one of them from the Sierra Maestra Mountain headquarters of Fidel Castro, here on a mission, had been beaten to death by the police. Their bodies were almost unrecognizable when their relatives got them out of the morgue.

With the beginning of September the political parties, both government and opposition, were organizing for the November 3rd elections. None of them was too enthusiastic. There was little propaganda, no money was being spent on campaigns. In Santiago de Cuba a group of revolutionists tried to assassinate the candidate for mayor of Santiago. The candidate immediately withdrew. Then Dr. Ramon Grau San Martin started having trouble. His three representatives in Oriente Province, all of whom were members of the House of Representatives, and on whom he was depending to head his campaign there, suddenly resigned. One of them went to Miami. But Batista declared, in a speech to the armed forces, "Only God can prevent us from holding elections."

An incident occurred in Regla, the town across the bay from Havana. Regla was the headquarters of pirates of past centuries, and during the prohibition years in the United States it was headquarters for all the bootleggers who operated out of Havana. Today it is the center of the seafaring population of Havana and of stevedores and workers on the docks. In September a three day celebration is held, attended by thousands who pay homage to the Virgin of Regla, the only black virgin in the world. The Virgin of Regla is the patron saint of sailors. On September 8th the small ebony statue is taken from the old church and carried around Havana Bay in a colorful religious ceremony. Negro congas dance through the streets. The largest group are negroes of the Lucumi cult, although the Nañigo cult also participates.

On September 6th someone stole the virgin. We received the news at the office late in the afternoon. It was hard to check. Finally Sarita by sheer persistence got the priest of the church on the telephone. He told her that the virgin was still there, but he also told her that was all he could say. The police claimed that two boys had stolen the virgin, that a woman saw them and screamed. The boys dropped the virgin and fled. At any rate the virgin was there on the altar, but the story we had was that the virgin had really disappeared. It seems the police had rushed to a store and had purchased an imitation. The matter became a cause célèbre. The faithful claimed that the virgin in the church was not the real virgin, since it was taller. Finally the public became so aroused that it was necessary to suspend the traditional fiesta. This is what the rebels had wanted, since they contended that no fiestas should be held while the youth of the island were fighting and dying. The rebels were also well aware that the suspension of a religious holiday would reflect against the Batista government. The real virgin was put back on the altar the day after the Batista regime fell.

Elections were to be held under a suspension of constitutional guarantees for the first time in the history of the republic. The reason was that otherwise the courts of the island would function, habeas corpus would have to be recognized, and the courts would release hundreds of youths being held in jail without the slightest actual evidence.

President Batista shifted various high officers of his army. General Alberto Rio Chaviano was moved from Oriente Province to Las Villas province, where the *Directorio Revolutionario* rebels were highly active.

Reports from rebel sources convinced me that they were finally beginning to get together a considerable amount of arms and ammunition. According to the young rebels who fought in Oriente, numerous planeloads of arms and ammunition from the United States arrived during this period. However, the greater part of their arms was captured from Batista's soldiers. And the heavy amount of prisoners and casualties of government troops reported by the Red Cross, made me feel sure that Castro's forces were getting stronger. We heard radio broadcasts from the Sierra instructing those who captured arms to inventory them, to send them to headquarters where they would be given to recruits who still lacked weapons. I want to report here a little story that shows the spirit of the revolutionaries. Two boys were doing an inventory. One boy counted out ten rifles. "Ten San Cristobal rifles," he said. (Batista was buying San Cristobal rifles from Trujillo in the Dominican Republic.) The other boy, writing down the list, said: "More San Cristobal rifles? Junk!" "Yes," replied the one counting. "I think we made a mistake when we got the United States to stop shipping arms to Batista. Now we can never capture decent rifles."

The rebel radio announced that Fidel Castro was going to begin an offensive. They announced he was sending six columns out of the Sierra Maestra to defeat the Batista army. The radio gave the names of each of the six columns. I never could pin the revolutionists down to just how many men constituted a column but apparently it was about three hundred. General Francisco Tabernilla stated from Camp Columbia army headquarters that the "movement of rebels of Fidel Castro is of little importance." He even went further and said that "not a single rebel remains in Pinar del Rio Province."

Apparently the rebel columns had already marched, before it was announced. Three columns were marching westward. One was commanded by Major Ernesto Ché Guevara, the Argentine doctor, one by Major Camilo Cienfuegos, and one by Major Jaime Vega. These columns were marching across Camagüey province into Las Villas province to help the *Directorio Revolucionario* in the Escambray Mountains. They fought their way across Camagüey. Jaime Vega remained in Camagüey province near the border of Las Villas to protect the rear. Ché Guevara and Cienfuegos went into Las Villas where the decisive battle of the revolution was fought. Fidel Castro's idea was to reinforce the rebels in Las Villas and then to cut the island in two, stopping all transportation between Havana and the three eastern provinces. They fought hard to accomplish that, helped by the local "militia" in each of the towns.

On September 24th we heard that the buildings at José Marti International Airport were burning. It was reported by authorities to have been started by a short circuit. But it was quite clearly sabotage since it started in three places at the same time. The administration and passenger building was gutted and only the big hangars off to the right were undamaged.

I decided to interview the two opposition candidates. I called Dr. Carlos Marquez Sterling and went by to see him at his home. It was a comfortable house, but not at all luxurious. Dr. Marquez Sterling said his Free Peoples' Party would not withdraw from elections no matter what happened. Dr. Marquez Sterling comes of a very good family. He was well liked by everyone who knew him. He probably would have had a chance in any fair election. But I was sure that he was deluding himself if he thought he had any opportunity to win.

Next I went to see Dr. Grau San Martin, candidate of what was left of the old *Autentico* Party. Dr. Grau, 75 years old, is a thin professor type with prominent teeth and a flood of oratory which many Cubans find spellbinding. This practically indestructible old man sat in his Fifth Avenue mansion and talked about the election with a mixture of cynicism and enthusiasm. He had broken his hip several months previously, but could get around a little on crutches. He had just returned from Holguin in Oriente Province where he had held the only political rally which either the government or opposition had dared to hold in that rebellious province. He told Ted Scott, who went with me, that he believed twenty-five thousand people had died in the year and ten months of the Fidel Castro rebellion. He said that when he arrived in Holguin he was told that the rebels had several days before killed a government candidate running for the House of Representatives and that next day the bodies of five young men were thrown on the streets by the government.

I asked Dr. Grau if he thought the elections would be fair. He shrugged his shoulders. He said he had demanded that the government invite observers from the Organization of American States to oversee the elections. But he was sure nothing would be done.

Fidel Castro sent me an orchid. One night about midnight Sarita and I were in the office. She had just finished giving me information she had obtained from the last rebel radio broadcast that night and we were discussing it when Ernestina Otero arrived. Ernestina is a pretty, charming woman, one of the best reporters in Cuba. She was the only woman accredited to Camp Columbia army headquarters during the Batista government. Her information was always accurate. When she gave me information, for example, on the arrival of a boat with arms and ammunition for the government, she had the name of the boat, its date and hour of arrival, when it was unloaded, where the shipment was from, the cargo, and sometimes even the numbers of the bills of lading. She contributed much to the accurate information which Fidel Castro received out of Havana. Castro had an excellent espionage system here. Ernestina turned out to be a Captain in the "26th of July" movement and today is one of Fidel Castro's closest collaborators.

That night she arrived with a package wrapped in a newspaper. She opened it to reveal a lovely orchid. Sarita immediately knew it as a wild mountain orchid. It was still attached to the thick branch from which it had grown. Ernestina told me that Fidel Castro had sent it to me in a hand-woven basket made in the Sierra Maestra by the countrymen, but that she had discarded the basket, fearing to walk around Havana with it.

Later in October, Ted Scott recorded an interview with President Batista. One of the questions Ted asked the President was whether the twenty-five thousand figure of those killed was correct. The President said it was much exaggerated, but admitted that many had been killed.

Several weeks previously Fidel Castro had announced that the "26th of July" revolutionary army would levy a tax of fifteen cents per bag (two hundred fifty pounds) of sugar produced in "Free Cuban Territory" during the 1959 crop. Now the government announced a ten cents tax on each bag as a means of paying the expenses of combating the rebels. The American Embassy advised American sugar mills not to pay the rebel tax.

Fidel Castro's radio in the Sierra Maestra announced that all candidates in the November elections would be disqualified from running for office in the nation for the next thirty years. He gave the candidates ten days to withdraw from the race. Two government candidates running for seats in the House of Representatives withdrew and were ridiculed by all the others.

President Batista had been trying to buy arms all over the world ever since the United States had stopped shipments. He purchased some old tanks from Nicaragua, only to find that they needed special caliber ammunition which was made by Israel. A deal was almost made with Israel when the rebels found out about it and starting protesting. Israel hastily canceled the order for ammunition. Batista was luckier in the case of the British. He purchased seventeen Sea-Fury planes, a few tanks, and considerable ammunition. Fidel Castro issued Rebel Law No. 4 ordering the confiscation of all property of British citizens in "Free Cuban Territory" and ordered the arrest of all British citizens. Meanwhile, the Civic Resistance Movement called for a boycott of British goods, motion pictures and insurance companies.

The manager of the Shell Petroleum Company was accused of arranging for the purchase of the planes and tanks. A boycott on Shell gasoline was declared. I was told that it caused a drop of about 40% in sales in Havana, but was more effective in the interior.

The rebels were increasing their attacks on the army in Oriente Province. The rebels now controlled the country-side of Oriente, but the army still held the towns. The Texas Oil Refinery is located just outside of Santiago de Cuba. On October 20th we learned that the rebels had kidnapped two Americans and seven Cubans near the plant. The Americans were Charles E. Bennett, who had been raised in Mexico and Cuba, and a Texan, Kenneth D. Drewes. The United States State Department was greatly annoyed over the incident. Ambassador Earl E. T. Smith told the American consul, Park F. Wollam, who had negotiated the release of the forty-four Americans previously, to take a firm stand. The rebels released the kidnapped men in a couple of days.

Revolutionists in Havana explained to me how the kidnapping had occurred. It seems the rebel forces were in need of repair tools. A small detachment was ordered to capture the repair truck of the Texas Oil Refinery. They shut off the water in two wells being used by the refinery, then waited for the repair truck to arrive. When it did, they surrounded it and demanded that the seven Cubans and two Americans climb out of the truck. Bennett, who speaks good Spanish, argued so violently, stating that the truck was company property and that the rebels had no right to confiscate it, that the rebels decided to take the truck and its crew to their captain and let him settle the matter. The rebels claimed that they were merely giving Bennett an opportunity to argue his case with their leader, and the refinery reported the "kidnapping." The rebel captain kept the truck but released the men.

Raul Castro, in command of the rebels in the Sierra Cristal Mountains and eastward around Santiago de Cuba and Guantanamo, decided he needed a plane. His men had constructed two airports, one near Mayari and another further east. They had "borrowed" road building equipment and tractors and trucks from Moa Bay Mining Company and the Nicaro Nickel plant for this purpose. Early on the morning of October 22, 1958, in Santiago de Cuba, the Cuban Airlines plane took off as usual for the short circuit flight in the province. Its route was from Santiago de Cuba to Preston, Cayo Mambi, Moa Bay, Baracoa and back to Santiago de Cuba. It simply vanished after it took off from Cayo Mambi. Both the Cuban airlines and planes from the United States Guantanamo naval base searched for it. I got in touch with the father of the pilot who said that a friend of his had heard a broadcast from the Sierra Cristal telling what happened to the plane. The plane, with eleven passengers, had taken off from Cayo Mambi. Shortly after the plane was in the air, two of the passengers had taken revolvers from their coat pockets, forced the pilot to follow their instructions and land on the rebel airfield. The company also issued a statement saying the plane was in the hands of the rebels. It was several days before we found out that the rebels had loaded the passengers into a truck, driven them to the outskirts of Cayo Mambi and let them walk into town. The pilot, however, was held.

Mr. Josie Norman, the British musician whose hands had been tested for nitrate, came to see me. He was terribly upset. He and his wife had worked hard during the past four years, getting a long neglected coffee plantation back into production, building a better house, and improving the plantation in general. Now he told me that the rebels had burned his house, carried off all his books and music, all the things they had collected over a lifetime and of which they were very fond. The rebels distributed the clothes of his wife, himself, and his two sons among the Cuban villagers in the district. I was very sorry for him. His older son had come to Havana several months before. He was a tall, good-looking boy, about eighteen, studious and proficient in translating. He had been in my office for several days. Then the police had picked him up, beaten him and thrown him in jail. Fortunately, the British Ambassador, Stanley Fordham, intervened in the case, demanding his release. He was released, but only on condition that he left the country. This was the same policy the Batista regime used to get rid of Americans. So the father had suffered at the hands of the rebels, while the son was being kicked about by the government.

Norman wanted to see Fidel Castro and tell him about the burning of his house and other buildings on the plantation. Fidel Castro had issued public orders that any rebel caught burning property of the civilian population, unless it belonged to an official of the Batista regime, was to be shot.

I contacted Mario Hernández. He said that Julio Camacho, one of the top "26th of July" men, was in Havana, and to bring Norman to see him. Camacho is today Minister of Transportation. Julio Camacho was unknown to the Batista bloodhounds, and practically commuted between Havana and Castro's headquarters. His wife, a pretty girl and a very brave one, made all the trips back and forth with her husband. She used to tell me how beautiful the Sierra Maestra was and try to get me to go with them.

I took Norman to the house of Mario Hernández, where he told his grievances to Camacho. We arranged a meeting with Castro for Norman, his wife and their plantation overseer, who was in Bayamo. I asked Norman not to tell his wife or his young son—the older one had been sent to England—about the trip until an hour before they started. I was to contact them and tell them when to be in Bayamo.

When Mario came to tell me Camacho was leaving town it was late on a Saturday afternoon. I called Norman to the office and told him to leave that night and arrive in Bayamo the next morning. They told me that the next day Camacho and his wife picked them up in Bayamo. It was a dangerous business. Bayamo was the field headquarters of Batista's army. Mrs. Camacho had an uncle with a plantation near Bayamo, so apparently the army roadblocks and patrols didn't pay much attention to them. Norman was ostensibly going out to look over a piece of property they wanted to sell. At any rate, they got through the army lines and arrived at a house where horses were waiting. They started up the mountains on horseback. Norman's wife, Manuela, a very charming woman, has a heart condition. Frankly, I didn't think she should make the trip. Also, Norman had once had his back broken and wore a steel brace, but he never allowed this handicap to deter him. He was more concerned about his wife. He needed her along because his Spanish was not adequate. Also, it was her plantation, which she had inherited from her grandfather, General Calixto Garcia.

The trip was rough. They were forced to stay in a hut for two days, while it poured rain in the mountains. They slept on palm leaves. The old mountaineer who owned the hut also was the proud possessor of three books, an old arithmetic, an ancient book about diseases, and, of all things, a Protestant book on religion. Everyone read the books over several times while the rain poured outside and ran through places in the roof. Norman sat with his overseer, who was without any formal education, patiently trying to teach him how to solve problems in the fourth grade arithmetic.

Later, going up the mountains, they were strafed. Camacho told me that Norman and Manuela took the strafing with true British calm—they had been through the London blitz.

The last mountain was so steep and treacherous that the horses had to be abandoned. Manuela couldn't continue because of her heart. Norman refused to leave her there alone. The others went on. Fidel Castro was not at his mountain headquarters. One of his staff went down to talk with them about the plantation. They gave him all the facts, including the name of the rebel, Lieutenant Pena, responsible for the burning of the *batey*. The rebels promised to see that the plantation was restored and the lieutenant punished. But then came the big offensive, the end of the revolution, and to this day Norman still does not have his plantation back. However, after the revolution, he saw Lieutenant Pena appearing on television as a hero. Norman and his son rushed to the station, persuaded the "26th of July" to arrest him, and today he is in La Cabaña awaiting trial. I hope that some day they will get their plantation back since it is every thing they have in the world.

Mario Hernández was one of my best contacts throughout the revolution. His father was Colonel Blas Hernández, a tough old fighter who periodically used to take to the hills against Machado in 1933. His seven sons constituted a pretty good guerilla force. Mario was the youngest, good-looking, soft spoken and well educated, and was one of the old man's best fighters. Later, two of the boys were taken prisoner and murdered by Machado's men. Mario and his brothers promptly killed the group that did it. Then the old Colonel was shot down by a Batista officer after he was captured at Atarés Fortress. One can imagine how Mario has always hated Batista. One can imagine how he hates all forms of tyranny.

At the beginning of November I was informed that the rebels had occupied the United States government-owned Nicaro Nickel plant on the north coast of Oriente Province. This is a hundred million dollar plant built by the United States during the Second World War to furnish nickel for war industries. Later it was leased and is now operated by private industry. It was difficult to find out anything about Nicaro. The officials here in Havana hide under their desks any time anything happens. A little later statement came from the American Embassy that the American employees and their families were to be evacuated by a United States warship. The rebels had occupied the mines above the Nicaro plant, as well as the town. Everything was going along fine since the rebels did not interfere with operations.

The Cuban army launched an attack on the rebels at Nicaro. The government announced that their troops had cleared the Nicaro area of rebels. The rebels said they withdrew to prevent the army from bombing and killing Americans.

A United States warship finally evacuated fifty-nine Americans, leaving only five Americans at the plant, an official, his wife, and three other employees.

Later the army, which claimed to have cleared the district of rebels, bombed the Ocujal mines of the Nicaro in the hills behind the plant, which is located on the little peninsula, *Lengua de Pájaro* (Tongue of a Bird). The army destroyed a warehouse, the damage estimated at half a million dollars. The United States made an investigation to present a claim to the Batista government. But the claim was never filed. The Americans who had been evacuated from the Nicaro plant were sent to the United States. I never saw any of them. I heard they had been counseled by our government not to discuss the trouble at Nicaro.

The women of Oriente Province had been helping the Castro forces almost since the beginning of the revolution. But the first I heard of a detachment of all-women rebels was at the end of October. Fifty women, under command of Doctora Isabel Rojas, had a skirmish with soldiers near Holguin and killed several. The women had named their group *Mariana Grajales,* in memory of the mother of General Antionio Maceo. Reportedly every one of the women had lost some member of her family in the struggle against the Batista regime.

The rebels were now attacking transportation on the Central Highway which runs the length of the island. This was important news to me, since it indicated that the Batista forces could not adequately defend their main supply lines. I felt certain that victory for the rebels would come only after they managed to cut off the main supply lines of the army. Colonel James B. McCauley, a retired American air force officer, came to my office. He is a small wiry old man, over seventy, and he was very angry. He had just returned from Santiago de Cuba. Some thirty miles outside Santiago de Cuba, just as they rounded a bend in the road, his chauffeur stopped the car. In front of them was a milk truck and a bus surrounded by rebels dressed in their olive green uniforms. A young rebel came up to the car and told them to get out. The rebel ordered Colonel McCauley to set fire to the car. The Colonel said he was an American in Oriente Province on business, and was not going to destroy his automobile. "Besides," he said. "I have no matches." That seemed to confuse the rebel. He said something to the effect that he was only carrying out orders. Finally, the rebel told Colonel McCauley to go ahead. But just at that moment the bearded commander of the group approached and said that American or no American, the car was to be burned. He told the chauffeur to put the car against the bus, which had already started to burn. The young rebel helped McCauley and his chauffeur to remove their luggage.

The driver parked the car against the bus, and the bearded commander riddled it with a machine gun. He then ordered them to start walking down the road. They had walked only a short distance when they saw a group of people with their luggage. They were the passengers of the bus. Colonel McCauley looked back and saw the rebels trotting off down the road in the opposite direction. He ran back toward the burning bus. He jumped in the car. The keys were still in the ignition. Strangely enough, the tires had not been touched by the machine gun bullets. He started the car and backed it away from the bus. He got the car to a safe distance several minutes before the gas tank of the bus exploded.

After the bus had burned into a metal skeleton, Colonel McCauley ordered his chauffeur to maneuver around the bus, through a ditch, then back onto the road. They arrived in Havana with a car full of holes and shattered windows and the paint scorched on one fender. Oddly, the Colonel was not as angry about the car as about his briefcase, which the rebels had taken from him. He was sure he would never see it again and he said he had contracts and documents in the case. I told the Colonel I thought the rebels would return the briefcase, citing the incident of a jeweler whose car was burned by the rebels and whose sample jewelry had been taken away from him. The jewelry, quite valuable, was returned within a few days. The Colonel was skeptical.

About a week later Colonel McCauley came to tell me that he had received his briefcase through the American Consul in Santiago de Cuba. He was very much surprised.

On November 2nd a Cuban Airlines plane left Miami in the afternoon for Varadero, Cuba's famous blue beach on the north coast of Havana province. The plane had reported twenty minutes outside Varadero and then disappeared. There were sixteen passengers aboard and four crew members.

I sent the story and tried to get more information. At two A.M. New York called me to ask if there was anything new. Even under the best of circumstances, it is next to impossible to get information from the Cuban Airlines, and at that hour it was impossible even to get any of the officials on the telephone. I called Operations at the José Marti International Airport. Luck was with me. I learned that the plane had been found at Preston sugar mill on the north coast, where it had made a forced landing. I never knew to whom I had talked at the airport and the other correspondents who called there were told that the company knew nothing of the plane.

It was a terrible tragedy. The plane crashed killing thirteen of the passengers and all the crew. Only one American, who lost his wife and four children in the crash, a Cuban woman and a boy survived. The story was that four young rebels had taken over the plane. They had tried to force the pilot to land at the rebel airport in the Sierra Cristal, but the landing strip was too short. Then the pilot flew to Preston. Owing to lack of runway lights the plane had overshot the field and crashed into the bay. Another version was that, as the pilot attempted to land, soldiers stationed at

Preston had thought it was a rebel plane and had shot a fusillade of bullets at it, causing it to crash into the bay. There were many stories, none of which have ever been confirmed. The plane struck in shallow water and the bodies were removed by divers from the United States naval base in Guantanamo. The three survivors were put in the hospital at Preston. The American was brought to Havana and then spirited away to the States. He never talked with anyone here. The two other passengers who survived also were unavailable.

I have heard that three of the rebels who seized the plane survived. One reporter claims he saw one of them in jail in the Sierra Maestra mountain headquarters of Fidel Castro where he was going to be tried for the insane attempt to seize a Viscount, with no place to land it. It was bad publicity for the rebel cause. Everyone was indignant. The rebel government has not yet hauled the plane out of the bay nor clarified whether the plane was shot down.

Election day, November 3, 1958, resulted in the quietest election I have ever seen. There was little traffic. It was so quiet that even in the office I realized it and went out on the balcony. Only a few people were on the streets. I saw President and Mrs. Batista walking down Refugio Street from the Presidential Palace surrounded by officials and bodyguards. They went around the corner on Morro Street to cast their vote in the small precinct there. Gene Carrier of NBC dashed down to take a picture. Various other photographers were there and a picture of Batista voting appeared on the front page of the *New York Times* the next morning. There were only a few people standing around and they applauded the President weakly.

Raul Casanas and I made a tour of the city. He drove so I could better see what was taking place. We drove through Old Havana, out into Vedado residential section and circled back. I saw only five or six persons at each of the polls, in addition to the two armed police who always guard each precinct. There were no long lines of voters. It was apparent that the people were not going to vote. That was about one o'clock in the afternoon. The same situation contined until the polls closed at six.

By seven o'clock we were getting reports from Camp Columbia army headquarters—of all places—concerning the lead being run up by Dr. Andres Rivero Aguero, the candidate of the four-party government coalition. Ernestina Otero, the only woman reporter authorized in Camp Columbia, called me at intervals giving information. She said they had a big bulletin board with batteries of telephones and they were really doing a fine job of tabulating votes, as they were telephoned in from each military post.

I had been told that in the Oriente and in Camagüey and Las Villas, the three eastern provinces where the rebels were determined not to permit elections, the votes had been filled in long in advance and even packaged and made ready for shipment to the superior electoral board in Havana. The candidates worked at night in the electoral boards under heavy guard of soldiers, making out the votes, and I heard that some of the soldiers were even pressed into service to help fill them out. One funny story was told by a government candidate who said he had been working for many hours at this task in Oriente Province with various other candidates. He was a member of the four-party coalition. He became so exhausted he went to sleep. When he woke up, he said, his fellow candidates had double-crossed him and counted him out. That is a typical Cuban story and probably not true but it is indicative of the Cuban attitude toward elections under the Batista regime.

Before midnight the government announced the sweeping victory of Dr. Andres Rivero Aguero. Dr. Grau San Martin called me personally to say that the elections were fraudulent and he went on to tell me what had happened. I can never imagine why he thought the government wouldn't rig the elections. He sounded highly indignant. Then Dr. Carlos Marquez Sterling sent me a message along the same lines. Dr. Rodolfo Mendez Penate, his running mate, made the strongest statement of the group. "Fidel Castro has won the elections. He was right and we were wrong."

It was all over. The coalition candidates were elected. Of course, the parties of Dr. Grau and Dr. Marquez Sterling automatically won five senatorships in each province according to the electoral law. Dr. Marquez Sterling received more votes than did Grau—according to the government count—so his party had three senatorships.

It seems strange that Grau and Sterling could have deluded themselves into thinking the people would go to elections and, if they did, that the Batista government would permit the oppositionists to win. A few days before elections a cousin of Dr. Marquez Sterling dropped into my office late at night. He asked me if I thought Marquez Sterling had a good chance. I just looked at him and said, "He hasn't a chance in the world and neither does Grau." He was a little shocked and said, "How can you be so pessimistic?"

Weeks went by. If the superior electoral board ever announced which candidates had won I never heard about it. We did know of course that Dr. Rafael Guas Inclan, Vice President, had won the mayorship of Havana. Dr. Gaston Godoy, President of the House of Representatives, was elected Vice President. The government claimed that 80% of the people voted. More reliable reports indicated only 30% voted, and as low as 10% in some districts. These elections were the most colossal fraud in the history of Cuba.

The day following the elections another plane disappeared. It was a Cuban Airlines plane, a DC-3, which left Manzanillo with two crew members and twenty-five passengers. It vanished into thin air. Within a few hours the rebels radioed that they had the plane, that it had landed at their airport in the Sierra Cristal Mountains and that all were safe. About a week later the rebels delivered the passengers and crew, except for one child who had been very ill when the plane was seized and whom the rebel doctors could not save. Also, they released the pilot of the plane which had been hijacked outside of Cayo Mambi.

On November 12th Fidel Castro said his columns were in position to launch their greatest offensive against the armed forces of Batista. He ordered transportation halted throughout the three provinces, towns captured, military posts attacked in an all out war. He also told the rebels when they captured a town to do so at night and to leave the town before daylight to prevent army planes from bombing the civilian population. However, the army continued to bomb and strafe towns.

Here is a curious thing. I tried to check how many people had been killed by bombing and strafing. I was told hundreds but I never could pin down the amounts or the specific places. A person who had been in one of the towns bombed told me the bombs were ineffective and that strafing killed very few. I was told by another source that the reason for the few people killed was because the minute the rebels took a town the population fled to the hills. I saw pictures of Sagua de Tanamo which was practically destroyed.

When forty-three airmen were tried in Santiago de Cuba in February and March, 1959, the only deaths the prosecutor could prove in that section numbered eight, with seventeen wounded. There were countrymen and their families killed in isolated places, but the claims of "hundreds" of civilians killed were not true. The British airplanes, which the rebels protested so vigorously, did little damage. Planes bombed Santa Clara in the last decisive battle of the revolution, destroying many houses. However, even today I cannot obtain an official casualty list. It would appear that the air force of the Batista regime was practically useless in the type of warfare fought in Oriente Province.

The fighting became fierce. Raul Castro's men, together with the three columns moving down the Central Highway, were attacking town after town. Over in Las Villas Province Major Ché Guevara and Major Camilo Cienfuegos had joined the *Directorio Revolucionario* forces. They began to capture territory and to hold it instead of the hit-and-run tactics of previous months.

As this was being written, three girls came into my office. Two were from Santiago de Cuba and had been in the mountains with the rebels. The third was a school teacher from Sancti Spiritus in Las Villas Province who had been with Fidel Castro. One was a student nurse and she told me about the emergency hospitals. The last one she was assigned to was *Mata Jague,* located in the Sierra Cristal Mountains. She said that after one battle fifty wounded soldiers from Batista's army had been brought in. Although some of them had their arms or legs shot off, all of them recovered. I asked her how many rebels were wounded in that battle. She said, "Six."

16

For weeks I had been receiving reports that the Batista soldiers were not fighting. When a group of rebels moved into a small town, the soldiers did not stir outside of their garrison post until they had gone. When sent out on patrols, the soldiers tried to avoid contact with the rebels. I talked with a correspondent who had been with the rebels. He said that when the soldiers were cornered they fought, but otherwise they retreated or surrendered.

In Havana a group of youths killed four policemen and wounded fifteen. The policemen were standing just outside the Fifteenth District police station, waiting for a bus. The police that night took eleven prisoners, machine gunned them and threw them into the street in front of the police station for the public to see. The police claimed they had been killed in gun battle when the youths attacked, identifying them only as of various ages and races. Some were negro youths. A woman who lives close to the station told me they must have killed the prisoners in three groups, as she heard three bursts of a machine gun fire inside the patio of the police station during the night.

I heard the next day that the rebels who had killed the police in the attack had returned to Las Villas. I never did find out the reason for this killing. I had been told weeks before that Fidel Castro had sent orders to his "26th of July" movement in Havana to stop terrorism since it was ineffective.

For the third time in 1958 Congress declared a state of national emergency which gave the President unlimited powers over every phase of national life. The rebellion had begun to take its economic toll. Transportation was practically cut off between Havana and the three eastern provinces. Trains from Havana ran only as far as Camagüey and the December dynamiting of a big bridge on the main railway line in Calabaza in Las Villas province halted the trains at Santa Clara. Manufactured goods piled up on the shelves of industrial plants in Havana. Wholesalers of groceries, drug companies, machinery firms and others were unable to ship anything to their former customers. Business was beginning to come to a stop.

Telephone service in the three eastern provinces was paralyzed. Telephone and telegraph communications between Havana and Santiago de Cuba had been cut off for two months, and now the rebels began to systematically cut the service to all towns in these provinces. At Iguara, Camagüey province, rebels carried off the entire telephone exchange and all the repair equipment. For months the rebels had been constructing a telephone system of their own in places where no telephones had existed. In the Sierra Maestra and the Sierra Cristal they had a system which provided communication between headquarters in the mountains and the foothills. One man in Havana bragged to me that he could relay a telephone message to Fidel Castro within an hour by using the telephone to Bayamo, and thence from near Bayamo to Fidel Castro's headquarters. I noticed they were careful not to cut Bayamo off from Havana until just at the last of the rebellion, when they had sufficient radio stations in operation. I had a list of twenty-two radio stations in Oriente Province. We heard from such stations as *Indio Azul* and *Indio Apache*.

The British Sea-Fury planes, purchased by Batista, arrived in Havana aboard a British ship and were unloaded. The greatest possible precautions were taken to prevent sabotage. The stevedores who unloaded the planes and ammunition were forced to strip to the waist and wear shorts and shoes only. It was the first time shorts had been seen on the docks in Havana, and the shouts of laughter and jeers of the stevedores looking on at the operations hampered the unloading operations. Then the big army trucks, loaded with the planes, which were to be assembled in Camp Columbia army headquarters, roared through town with an enormous military escort.

The sugar industry was extremely worried. Mill owners said they could not grind in the three eastern provinces, where 75% of Cuba's annual crop is produced. They pointed out that none of the mills had sufficient gasoline to run their trucks, nor oil to operate their narrow-gauge railways, which brought the cane in from the outlying districts to the mill. There would be no hope of shipping the sugar, since railway service was nonexistent and the highways were badly damaged by rebel sabotage. I had many stories about the rebels. They were taking bulldozers and scooping out whole sections of roads, even at some places along the Central Highway.

About midnight one night a couple came to see me. The man was an American, the woman, Cuban. They had been married many years before and had divorced, but the man had flown in from Puerto Rico when his ex-wife informed him that their son, a young engineer educated in the United States, was in danger of his life. The woman and her son were living on a cattle ranch near Guaimaro, Camagüey province. The district was under control of Colonel José Maria Salas Canizares, the "Butcher." His troops were trying to get convoys of food and supplies through the National Highway to towns in Oriente.

The woman told me that the government troops and rebels had fought a number of skirmishes on her ranch several days before. She, her son and her twelve-year-old daughter had been forced to hide in a bathroom during the battles which went on all afternoon. Even around midnight firing broke out and bullets smashed through the windows and walls. At daybreak she decided to go to Guaimaro, despite the threat of the rebels to shoot at anything that moved. She and her children and the servants took two cars and were able to escape.

When they arrived in Guaimaro, Colonel Salas Canizares arrested her son. One of the government soldiers accused the boy of shooting at him out of the window. Colonel Canizares told the woman he was going to execute her son when he returned from a trip to Holguin.

The mother rushed to Havana and appealed to everyone she knew in the Batista government to save her son. Her husband was a distant cousin of Dr. Andres Domingo Morales del Castillo, Secretary of the Presidency. She appealed to him. The Argentine Ambassador in Havana was a friend of her family. She asked him to help. Her ex-husband, having flown in from Puerto Rico, had gone to the American Embassy. The embassy said they could do nothing since the boy was now a Cuban citizen. The father of the boy insisted on coming to see me that night, as a last resort. I called Pizzi de Porra and told him that I thought such an incident was incredible. He agreed with me. He said he would guarantee that the boy would not be executed. And then we were notified, within a few hours, that the boy would be released. His father flew to Guaimaro the next day when they released him, and immediately took him to Puerto Rico, "A sane country," he said bitterly.

The rebel radio announced the arrival of Dr. Manuel Urrutia, Fidel Castro's choice for provisional president, who had been living in exile in the United States. Dr. Urrutia made a statement to the effect that the rebels had no intention of interfering with the harvesting of the sugar crop. With railway and highway transportation halted, the sugar mill owners were inclined to disbelieve that statement.

United States Senator Allen J. Ellender of Louisiana came to Havana. He gave a press conference at the American Embassy and declared that he was in favor of selling arms to the Batista government for the purpose of "internal security." The interview was held in a small conference room off the Information Department of the embassy. The foreign press and one reporter from each newspaper had been invited. The embassy had taken care that the local reporters invited spoke English so there would be no need for an interpreter. The press looked at Ellender in surprise after that statement. One Cuban reporter ventured to ask him if he thought that was a correct policy in the present civil war in Cuba. Ellender replied promptly: "I haven't heard of any fighting," and added that he hoped "civil war does not break out." The Cuban reporters were stunned.

A couple of the American correspondents baited the Senator, who was perfectly willing to express an opinion about anything and everything, although he prefaced each statement by saying: "I know nothing about this but . . ." It seems incredible that a United States Senator should express such ignorance of the domestic and political problems of an island lying only ninety miles from the shores of the United States.

When I returned to my office, the information department at the embassy called me to ask what I thought of the interview. They knew of course that Senator Ellender had not endeared himself to the Cubans. I told them that I had not been so entertained for a long time.

The New York Times did not publish from about December 10th to 27th due to a strike of the delivery unions. People in Cuba were disturbed. My telephone rang day after day as the public asked when the *Times* would again be published. The Cubans seem almost more concerned whenever American newspapers are not being circulated than when their own are closed down.

I received a call from Dickie Chapelle. She had just returned from spending three weeks with Fidel and Raul Castro, having come down from the Sierra Maestra headquarters when the rebels launched their big offensive. She was writing a story for *Readers Digest*, while nursing a sprained ankle caused by a jeep accident. She said if the revolution failed it would be because the Castro rebels never repaired their equipment. In all the time she had been with the rebels she never saw a jeep with brakes. I was delighted to find out through her that my information about the progress of the rebel forces was essentially correct. She said the rebels, at least the ones she was with, were living on rice and milk and sometimes just rice. They were advancing too rapidly for their supplies to catch up with them. One thing that impressed her was the rebel awareness of all the movements of the government soldiers, of reinforcement and supply columns. The entire civilian population of Oriente was acting as spies for the rebels.

Dickie said the Batista soldiers were not fighting with any spirit and were mostly retreating. When Ted Scott interviewed her on NBC, she stated that she didn't see any possibility of the Batista army stopping the rebels.

Raul Castro's forces, which now controlled the eastern half of the province, except the larger towns, moved in to help the columns moving eastward from the Sierra Maestra. Santiago de Cuba was already surrounded by the insurgents of Raul Castro, who had trapped and isolated nearly six thousand soldiers of the Batista army. The army had sent reinforcements by sea, landing them, along with British tanks, at Santiago de Cuba. But every time the army tried to move these reinforcements out of Santiago, the rebels turned them back.

Raul Castro is a small thin man with a Spanish face, his long hair pulled into a sort of a bun. With his Spanish *boina,* he has the appearance, some Cubans say, of having stepped out of a painting of the Spanish pirates. His men live under a strict code of both military and moral discipline. They are under oath not to drink any alcoholic beverage while in uniform. Their code penalizes by court-martial any rebel who even talks back about an order. The people of Santiago de Cuba, although they admire Raul Castro and his disciplined, hard-fighting rebels, have some reservations about him. They feel that he is more dangerous in his thinking than his brother, and perhaps more influenced by his trips into countries behind the Iron Curtain. Cubans do not trust a man of silence or a man who gives his views with directness and without qualifications, and Raul Castro has both of these traits. The people of Santiago also remember that it was Raul Castro who ordered the trial of the seventy-one Batista soldiers, all of whom were executed in a single day.

While Raul Castro was keeping the government troops from sending reinforcements out of Santiago, a portion of his forces and the columns from the Sierra Maestra moved eastward from Bayamo onto the Central Highway. Directed by Fidel Castro, they stormed through Jiaguani, Baire, Contramaestra and Palma Soriano. Fighting was fierce around San Luis, Alto Songo and El Cristo during the last part of December. Fidel Castro was out of the hills and fighting to get control of the towns. The inability of the Batista army to match strategy with the rebels is plainly shown by the fact that no troops moved out of Bayamo to attack the rebel columns from the rear. In the seventy mile stretch between Bayamo and Santiago de Cuba, the rebel radio said that 600 soldiers were killed, wounded and captured. At Maffo 150 soldiers surrendered after the rebels had surrounded them. This battle went on for several days, with the rebels finally using mortars. Large quantities of arms and ammunition were captured by the rebels and for the first time Castro's men had all the weapons they needed.

The rebels used their radio stations very effectively. Daily broadcasts informed the Batista armed forces that the rebels felt no animosity toward them and urged them to join the rebels to "save" the country. The rebel speakers expressed sympathy for the government troops, who were eating limited rations because their officers were stealing the money

allotted for food. "Those who are asking you to do their
fighting and their dying are living in the greatest of luxury
in Havana." In addition to such obvious propaganda (and
its effectiveness must not be overlooked), the rebel radio
gave accurate figures on government expenditures, which
were furnished to them by informants in the government
departments. They also gave accurate accounts of battles,
sometimes reporting the entire list of casualties. The underground civic resistance issued clandestine publications, trans-
lations of stories published abroad, and lists of those killed
and tortured. Castro's representatives abroad both in the
United States and Venezuela kept the name of Castro in the
press as much as possible. A kind of myth was built up
around him which has since had tremendous effects in Latin
America.

There can be little doubt that this barrage of propaganda
lowered the morale of Batista's soldiers, especially when they
knew that the rebel reports on casualties and the outcomes
of battles were more accurate than the army communiqués.
The soldiers began to realize that they were fighting a civil
war and that their own people were against them. Batista's
power in the armed forces had always stemmed from the enlisted men, who so admired him. But this admiration faded
as the casualties began to mount, as the supplies diminished,
and as the war promised to last indefinitely.

Several days before Christmas the rebels in Las Villas
province, which included the *Directorio Revolucionario,* the
Second National Front, and the insurgents of Major Ché
Guevara and of Major Camilo Cienfuegos, started a strong
offensive against government troops there. Within a few
days they had captured eighteen towns, including Sancti
Spiritus, second largest town of the province, and Caribairen,
one of the largest sugar shipping ports.

Batista announced that two thousand reinforcements were
being sent from Havana to Las Villas. I had heard about the
trains being armored in the shops of the government-owned
railway. Now the army was going to use them. One train

left Havana. It was preceded by an engine for fear of track sabotage. The engine in front was running along at high speed, and the engineer claimed he did not see the bridge at Santo Domingo burning until he was almost on it. He braked. The troop train rammed into the engine, throwing various cars of the troop train off the track. It took many hours to get the train back on the track and tied up the line during that period.

There was no celebration of *Noche Bueno,* the traditional Christmas Eve feast. Few families ate the special dinner of roast pig, rice, black beans, wine and other delicacies. There was not a Christmas tree to be seen. Some American families had trees, but the lavishly decorated trees behind big picture windows and the lighted trees in gardens were nonexistent. The streets had not been decorated as in former years and the merchants said no one was buying Christmas presents. The big clubs held none of the usual fiestas. Only a few private parties took place.

In Las Villas the rebels announced only two towns were left in hands of the army, Cienfuegos and Santa Clara. The rebels attacked Santa Clara, which had some five thousand soldiers, the strongest garrison in the province. Rebels in Camagüey moved toward the border to prevent reinforcements from coming in from the east. Other contingents moved westward to prevent reinforcements from Havana. Santa Clara is located on the Central Highway, almost in the center of the province. There was no way for the government to get reinforcements into Santa Clara.

It was the decisive battle of the revolution. Sarita stayed by the radio hour after hour listening to the radio stations of the rebels talking among themselves, giving orders, calling for reinforcements, sending troops to various points, sometimes openly and sometimes in code. We followed the battle as best we could from this information as there was nothing from the government and only a bulletin now and then from the Sancti Spiritus radio station, which had been taken over by the rebels.

The army was savagely bombing the outskirts of Santa Clara. One soft drink plant was almost completely destroyed. We heard from the rebel radio reports of hospitals and first aid stations in towns surrounding Santa Clara being prepared for the wounded. There were no army communiqués. But the Presidential Palace kept saying that the army was pushing the rebels out of Santa Clara and government reinforcements were arriving. It didn't look that way to me. The rebels captured an armored train with three hundred soldiers aboard just outside Santa Clara.

The Minister of State, Dr. Gonzalo Guell and the Minister of Labor, Dr. Suarez Rivas, suddenly flew to the Dominican Republic the day after Christmas. The rebel radio immediately charged that Batista and Generalissimo Rafael Trujillo were planning to bring in thirty planes with Dominican pilots and a considerable number of troops to fight against the rebels. The Presidential Palace assured the people that the two Ministers had gone to the Dominican Republic to be present at the opening of the new Cuban Embassy there. As it turned out, neither the rebels nor the palace were right.

Meanwhile, in Oriente Province, General Eulogio Cantillo, in command of government forces in Oriente Province, sent a message to Fidel Castro, asking for a meeting with him "to discuss the situation." Cantillo arrived by helicopter. Fidel Castro demanded that Cantillo surrender Santiago de Cuba. Cantillo then flew to Havana and told the general staff that Castro was demanding the surrender of Santiago de Cuba. General José Pedraza, whom President Batista had brought back into the army to take charge of operations against the rebels, flew to Santiago de Cuba and to Santa Clara. Reportedly he came back to Havana and told Batista bluntly that his army was not fighting and it would only be a matter of time until the rebels marched into Havana. General Francisco Tabernilla and the general staff confirmed the rapid deterioration of the army.

President Batista prepared to leave the island which he

had ruled by military force since 1933, with exception of the eight years of government of Dr. Grau San Martin and Dr. Prio Socarras. He sent Dr. Gonzalo Guell to the Dominican Republic to arrange for his asylum. It was a bitter ending for a man who had wielded power in Cuba for many years.

A big party was always held in Camp Columbia army headquarters on New Year's Eve. However, this year there was no enthusiasm for the fiesta and no advance preparations had been made. Batista invited a small, select group to a party at the camp. When one of the invited appeared reluctant to attend, he was told that it was highly important that he be there. The whole thing was kept a close secret. The cousin of the Minister of Treasury told me that he had been talking with the Minister at one o'clock on New Year's morning and that the Minister knew nothing of the plans of Batista. The younger officers in Camp Columbia were called to a staff meeting to keep them from suspecting what was going on. Batista and his military chiefs met and handed the army over to General Eulogio Cantillo. They tried to give it some form of legality by saying that the President resigned. But there was no time for formalities that night.

Plane after plane was lined up on the runway, and the chosen few, frightened military and civilian collaborators of the Batista government, embarked. Four planes took off for the Dominican Republic. Other planes went to the United States. Ironically, Batista fled, leaving behind the largest army he had ever controlled, 46,000 soldiers, including 15,-000 new recruits, and big shipments of arms and equipment only recently arrived.

There was little celebration of New Year's. The private clubs suspended their traditional fiestas. However, tourist hotels like the Hotel National, the Riviera, the Capri and the Habana Hilton, were holding dinner dances with their usual floor shows. Herbert and Nancie, Ted Scott and I had been invited by Colonel Charles Barron of the Habana Riviera to have dinner with him. That afternoon I called the hotels to find out about their reservations. Two days before they had all told me that reservations were pouring in. But that afternoon the Habana Riviera informed me in a puzzled tone that they had received some two hundred cancellations that day.

Ted Scott, who had been trying to see Dr. Gonzalo Guell, Premier and Minister of State, since he had returned from the Dominican Republic, went over to the palace. That evening as we were driving out to the Hotel Habana Riviera Ted asked me if I knew what "Cheyne Stokes breathing" was. I admitted that I had only a vague idea. He said that was what existed at the palace.

It was a strange New Year's Eve. There was little traffic, few people on the streets. The tension which had been mounting for days was almost a tangible thing to one who has lived in Cuba a long time. The Copa Room of the Habana Riviera was about one-fourth filled by the time we started dinner. The orchestra played energetically. We began to relax and forget about the desperate battle going on in Santa Clara. I had left Sarita in the office to listen to the rebel radios. Raul was checking the palace. Just before midnight, one of the guests at our table remarked that he had seen a curious thing. He lived near Camp Columbia and he said that he had noticed just before he left home a number of cars filled with women and baggage, escorted by SIM cars. Ted Scott looked at me and said: "Here we sit having dinner and the government is falling. Let's get out of here!" Ted had barely finished speaking, when the New Year came in with a blast from the orchestra, and the customary hurrahs and shouting. But there was no real air of merriment. The hats, noisemakers and serpentines provided by the hotel were used half-heartedly. We quickly told our host goodnight and left.

Dropping Herbert and Nancie at their hotel, we went to the office. Sarita was gone. I tried to check with other sources. All the newspapers were closed, everyone had vanished, as is usual on New Year's Eve. I decided to call it a night, to celebrate by getting to bed early for once in my life. I drove home through completely deserted streets, seeing only one or two cars. Even at the tunnel I didn't see the usual police. When I arrived home my sister was still reading. As we were talking, Sarita called and said she and Raul had received a tip that something unusual was going on in Camp Columbia. I live just beyond the airfield of the camp and as I finished talking with Sarita I heard three planes take off, one after the other. I remarked to Irma that it was strange for planes to be taking off at that hour. We were accustomed to hearing them just before daybreak, but night flights were rare. Then my phone rang. It was Ernestina Otero, and she was wildly excited. "They've gone! I know it!" she said. She went on to say she had just called General Tabernilla's house and someone had answered, jabbering almost incoherently. Tabernilla had fled or something. "But check it," she said, and hung up. I didn't even have time to tell her about the planes I had heard.

It was almost impossible to get information. I called Ted and asked him for the private number of a general he knew. Practically all telephone numbers in Havana are private numbers not listed in the directory. One has to keep a private list and frequently revise it. This in particular applies to government officials and military men, who not only have private numbers, but change them quite often.

Then the telephone rang again. It was Paul Bethel, the information officer of the American Embassy. He said that President Batista and his family had fled and had taken most of his top officials, both military and civil, with him. The news spread like wildfire. My telephone rang constantly as people demanded confirmation. One man laughed and laughed and said that the next day he would be in my office with a bottle of champagne.

In the morning Havana was strangely quiet. The police and soldiers had disappeared. I didn't see a single police or SIM car. There was no one on the streets. After seven years of military rule, people were apparently afraid to trust their liberation. They were afraid of the empty streets and the silence.

But about ten o'clock in the district around my office I heard the roar of a crowd. Then began the destruction of the parking meters, which had long been unpopular, but which also contained a considerable amount of nickels. It seems to me significant of what ordinary people in Havana consider to be liberty that the parking meters should have been their first act of vengeance. Then the mobs of the lower classes which always start destroying, looting and burning in every revolution in Cuba, began on the tourist stores, the airplane ticket offices and other establishments on the Prado Promenade, just a block from me. They rushed into the Sevilla Biltmore and destroyed the casino, broke the big plate glass windows of the hotel and all the adjoining establishments. Over on San Rafael, in the shopping district, the crowd broke plate glass windows and stole everything in the displays. Out in the suburbs, mobs were storming the houses of former officials of the Batista regime, looting and carrying off everything they could get hold of. I had seen this before in 1933. It was, for me, like sitting through a bad movie a second time. Mobs speak with the same voice in every generation.

However, now the "26th of July" militia moved in, and started shooting the looters. A truck with loud speaker moved down the Prado and into the business district with the message: "Get off the street or be killed." This was something new in the history of Havana, a volunteer group determined to keep order and protect property. The militia were youths of the underground "26th of July." They had walked into each police station, the majority without arms, early in the morning, telling the police on duty they were taking over—and they did. They installed a group in each police station to take command and then armed the youths who were to patrol the city in the police cars. It was an excellent job of organization. Some of the looting mob were killed, but within a few hours most of them had been dispersed. The headquarters of the patroling militia was established at the CMQ Radio Station and we listened on the radio to the orders given to the militia.

Out in the suburbs mobs still gathered and attempted to loot homes of the Batista officials, but the CMQ headquarters were notifying patrol cars wherever a mob was reported. My sister called me late that night to say that on Ninety-Sixth Street in Miramar suburb an American woman had called her to say that a mob was systematically looting every house on the street and would soon be at her house. Sarita called militia headquarters and we heard immediately the call for police cars to go to Ninety-Sixth Street to disperse the mob. This method was so effective that not over fifteen houses in the whole of Havana were looted, in comparison to hundreds in the revolution of 1933.

About noon rifle and machine gun fire broke out in Central Park. It sounded like a major battle. Soon a tank moved in. The militia had surrounded the Manzana de Gomez building, where a group of the private army of former Senator Rolando Masferrer had holed up. The battle continued for an hour before the Masferrer men surrendered and were dragged out of the building.

Throughout the day the militia dispersed mobs and tightened control. That night, roadblocks made it impossible to travel throughout the city. I was busy. I stayed at my office for eleven days after the fall of Batista. Fortunately, I had clothes here and a room where I could sleep, what little sleep I got.

General Eulogio Cantillo, early that morning, began forming a "government junta," composed of military and civic figures. The oldest member of the Supreme Court, Dr. Carlos Piedra, who was now in theory at least, President, went to the palace. The Supreme Court refused to administer the oath of office. Late in the afternoon, after consulting with American Ambassador Earl E. T. Smith and Manuel Cardinal Arteaga, he left.

Fidel Castro declared that his insurgents would remain on a "war footing" and would not accept the designation of Dr. Carlos Piedra as President. Fidel Castro said that only Dr. Manuel Urrutia could be provisional president of Cuba. He called a general strike until Urrutia was installed in office. The situation was one of the greatest confusion.

Colonel Ramon Baraquin, who was in prison in the Isle of Pines Penitentiary, was brought to Havana by plane that afternoon, under orders of General Eulogio Cantillo, and given the position of Chief of Staff of the Cuban armed forces. He had conspired against President Batista two years before and had been sentenced to six years in prison. He had been the military attaché of Cuba in Washington, at the time he carried out this conspiracy. Barquin had never had any close association with Fidel Castro. He issued a public statement that he considered his position, as well as that of the officers he had appointed, as temporary.

The people responded to the call from Fidel Castro for a general strike. Commerce and industry had not opened on New Year's Day of course and restaurants, hotels, cafés and other establishments which usually operate on holidays closed their doors. International and domestic plane service was suspended at the José Marti International Airport. Vessels arriving in Havana were unable to dock due to the fact no port workers were working. Some 2,000 American tourists were caught. They soon found that living in hotels without any employees was highly uncomfortable. The closing of the restaurants and hotel dining rooms made it almost impossible for them to obtain food. Most of the hotels continued to serve sandwiches and coffee. The sale of alcoholic beverages had been prohibited by the authorities. The American Embassy announced that Ambassador Earl E. T. Smith was attempting to arrange transportation to evacuate the tourists.

Since there were no automobiles for hire on account of the strike, the embassy personnel loaned their automobiles to take the tourists to the docks where they were put aboard the ferry "City of Havana" and later sent out by plane. The American marines guarding the embassy escorted the tourists to the docks and the airport.

Political prisoners were being freed all over the island. At Principe Fortress jail not only the political prisoners were released but all the common criminals who were serving sentences of from one to three years. Four Americans appeared at my office stating they were among the political prisoners and telling about how the guards had been killed after they had killed several prisoners. The stories did not sound true to me. However, some of the foreign correspondents accepted the Americans at face value and cabled the tale of their "political persecutions" to the States. I had a talk with Peter, a German boy who had been in prison with the Americans. Peter had been serving a three-year sentence for forging doctor's certificates to buy cocaine. Peter told me that the four Americans were common prisoners, not political prisoners. The actual crime which two of these Americans had committed was to kidnap the Manager of the American Club, take his money and throw him, tied hand and foot, into a ditch along the road to Matanzas. They had been captured and sentenced to three years.

At one o'clock in the morning of January 2nd, Fidel Castro proclaimed Dr. Manuel Urrutia as president of Cuba in a ceremony in Santiago de Cuba, before a cheering crowd of thousands. Fidel Castro declared that Santiago de Cuba was the capital of the nation. He was later forced to revoke this proclamation when he realized that the huge ministries with their thousands of workers could not be moved to Santiago de Cuba. Santiago simply did not have sufficient buildings to accommodate the public employees.

About noon on January 2, 1959, the first rebels arrived in Havana from Santa Clara, Las Villas Province. The public went wild with joy. The trucks, filled with long-haired, bearded youths called *barbudos* could hardly move through the streets because of the cheering populace that swarmed around them. Major Ernesto Ché Guevara rolled into Havana with his troops and took over Cabañas Fortress across the bay from Havana. Major Camilo Cienfuegos marched into Camp Columbia army headquarters and took command.

General Eulogio Cantillo had taken over the army when Batista fled. Fidel Castro, angered because Cantillo had come to Havana instead of surrendering Santiago de Cuba, had the general placed under arrest. He also blamed Cantillo for having allowed Batista and his cohorts to leave the island.

The presence of the *barbudos* in Havana had a strong disciplinary effect upon the populace. People regarded the young veterans with awe and respect. The Boy Scouts volunteered to handle traffic. It was, I thought, in contrast to the rugged veterans of the rebel forces, highly amusing to see youngsters in short pants directing traffic. Drivers who a week previous would not have respected a major general in full uniform obeyed these children without question.

The rebel discipline and the admirable conduct of the young veterans who marched into Havana greatly surprised the public. There was no drinking: The *barbudos* took coffee and soft drinks, and spoke with courtesy and friendliness. They did not hesitate to enforce the laws, but they were gentle and kind to offenders. One had the feeling that they would not hesitate to shoot a Batista supporter, but he would be shot with the greatest courtesy. They so impressed the people of Havana that even the pickpockets and petty thieves took a holiday from their accustomed activities. Ted Scott and I went over to Cabañas, and while we waited to see if Major Guevara was at the Comandancia, one of the guards brought us a bench and offered it to us to sit on. It was certainly a contrast to the snarling, arrogant soldiers of Batista.

The militia and *barbudos* were taking over the various departments of the police, who were being held in quarters in Cabañas and Camp Columbia army headquarters. The hunt for members of the armed forces who had tortured and killed began.

At the José Marti International Airport, planes of the Cuban Airlines were busy bringing political prisoners and exiles from the Isle of Pines Penitentiary and from Miami. Hundreds poured into Havana. They were getting their first taste of freedom in many years.

All officials of the government were arrested. Dr. Joaquin Martinez Saenz, president of the National Bank of Cuba, and Dr. Emeterio Santovenia, president of the Agricultural and Industrial Development Bank, were also placed under arrest.

The rebels occupied all radio stations. Only news of rebel activities was broadcast. All regular programs were suspended. Food became scarce. The rebels authorized grocery stores throughout the city to open for two hours each day. The militia stood guard and permitted only two persons to enter a store at one time. Only canned goods were on the shelves. There was no bread, milk, vegetables, or fruits.

Fidel Castro announced from his Santiago de Cuba headquarters that he would "protect the economy of the Republic." The sugar crop would start immediately. The first thing to be done was to repair the highways and railways.

Some of the young veterans went to the big tourist hotels to find lodging. The *Directorio Revolucionario* took over Havana University, 600 rebels slept in the Habana Hilton ballroom. The Hotel National accommodated another large group, as did the Habana Riviera and the Capri.

President Urrutia, in Santiago de Cuba, appointed cabinet ministers. Dr. Roberto Agramonte, presidential candidate in the June, 1952, elections which were never held due to the military coup of Batista, was appointed Minister of State. Minister of Treasury was offered to Raul Chibás. However, he refused to accept the portfolio and Lopez Fresquet, well known economist, was appointed. The Minister in charge of the Recovery of Stolen Government Property, a newly created Ministry, was Faustino Perez.

Provisional President Manuel Urrutia arrived in Havana by plane on January 5th. He was greeted enthusiastically at the Airport. Instead of going directly to the palace, he stopped at Camp Columbia army headquarters. United States Ambassador Earl E. T. Smith and other members of the diplomatic corps called on President Urrutia that night.

Fidel Castro announced the strike was ended. Havana returned to normalcy quickly. The strike had served the purpose of keeping people in their homes, thus permitting the militia to disperse any crowds which gathered. It had permitted the arrest of many fleeing members of the Batista regime, and had given the young revolutionists time to establish their control of the city.

Top officials of the Batista regime had sought refuge in the embassies of Latin-American countries, using the protection of the political asylum pact. Every Latin-American embassy was overflowing. The Chilean Embassy had eighty-five and was forced to rent a house next door to lodge them. The new Cuban government was reluctant to give these officials and collaborators of the Batista regime the usual safe conducts to leave the country. However, when the diplomatic corps in Havana demanded that Cuba comply with the terms of the pact, the permits were issued. The Panamanian Embassy was the first to get their "guests" off to Panama.

Havana waited impatiently for Fidel Castro to arrive. Reports that he was coming by plane circulated every day. Havana was swarming with correspondents from the United States, Great Britain, Mexico, Venezuela and France. Then Fidel Castro started his triumphant march from Santiago de Cuba up the Central Highway to Havana. Accompanied by five thousand of his rebels, Castro moved along the highway with trucks, tanks, jeeps and automobiles. In towns and villages the people hysterically welcomed the victorious young leader.

In Havana, Major Camilio Cienfuegos, was tightening control on Camp Columbia and on the police installations. He was replacing the militia with his own soldiers. With the *Directorio Revolucionario,* the Second National Front of

Escambray, and the "26th of July" rebels, there were now several thousand troops in the city. Herbert Matthews and Gene Carrier flew in an army plane to Camagüey. On their arrival they learned that Castro and his forces were approaching. An hour or so before Castro arrived a gun battle broke out between a group of the Masferrer private army and the rebels. The Masferrer men had barricaded themselves in a school building and it was necessary to bring up artillery to dislodge them.

Matthews had hoped to talk with Fidel Castro; however, it was physically impossible with the masses around the young rebel leader and the utter state of confusion caused by the thousands who insisted on seeing and greeting the most popular hero in the history of the island. Fidel Castro started his speech-making on that trip. This was the beginning of an unending series of Castro talks on television, at labor meetings, luncheons, dinners, and press conferences. The way Castro drives himself, his whirlwind activity would exhaust a giant. This was a televised revolution. All the rebel leaders appeared on television, all day long in Havana. Newscasts were now more complete on television than on the radio.

With the triumph of the revolution, the revolutionary radio began playing the "Cancion de Libertad," composed by José Obelleiro Carvajal. Played in march time, it is one of the most inspiring pieces of music ever composed in Cuba. In the mountains the rebels had marched to the "Hymn of the 26th of July," composed by Agustin Diaz Cartaya. It was sung around the fires of many a camp.

Fidel Castro and his rebels arrived in Havana on January 8, 1959. Never in the history of Cuba has anyone received such a welcome. The ovation was of such magnitude that it was a little frightening. The majority of Havana's one million inhabitants must have turned out. Crowds gathered along the entire route to the Presidential Palace, where he paused to greet President Manuel Urrutia, and then went on to Camp Columbia army headquarters. The television stations of Havana did a magnificent job. They had cameras and mobile units along the route.

The insurgents rode into town on trucks, tanks, jeeps and automobiles, greeted by shouting crowds which became hysterical at the sight of Fidel Castro. The column entered the city at the Shrine of the Virgin of the Road, where the Via Blanca Highway ends, and moved past ancient Atáres fortress where Major Crittinden, who brought an American expedition to Cuba to free the island, died before a firing squad 108 years ago. But, now Cuba had her own hero, a young man of unusual stature and oratorical powers, who did not hesitate to announce himself as a liberator, and who proclaimed that Cuba was a free nation for the first time in history.

Along the Avenida del Puerto the crowd showered the triumphant rebels with confetti and serpentines, waved the Cuban flag and the black and red flag of the "26th of July" revolution, and shouted "Viva Fidel!" Some of the youthful fighters had already shaved their beards, but the majority still wore their hair long, and their beards gave them the appearance of North Carolina mountaineers. Army planes flew overhead. Castro, riding in a jeep, responded to the shouts of the crowd with a rare smile. The young leader's face was drawn with fatigue. For the past few days he had hardly eaten or slept. The rebels obviously were enjoying the sensation of being heroes. After spending two years in the mountains, the gaily decorated city and the crowds shouting looked like a veritable paradise to them.

Two Cuban warships steamed into the harbor, firing salutes. The column halted opposite the Presidential Palace and Fidel Castro, accompanied by Major Camilo Cienfuegos, who had taken over control of Camp Columbia army headquarters, walked through Misiones Park to the palace. In the Presidential Palace, crowded with revolutionists, the bearded rebel leader sat beside President Manuel Urrutia. He wore the square French cap, utilized by most of the rebel officers, his campaign shirt open at the throat. He held his famous telescopic rifle in his hand as he talked. Fidel Castro's face wears a serious intent expression at all times. He rarely smiles. He did not smile that day. He sat wearily, exhaustion showing in every line of his face. Nearby was Celia Sanchez, who had shared the struggles of the long months of rebellion.

A few minutes later, Fidel Castro, with his rifle slung over his shoulder, spoke from the palace terrace to the massed thousands in the street and in Misiones Park.

As I watched Castro I realized the magic of his personality, the fanatic loyalty of his insurgents. He seemed to weave a hypnotic net over his listeners, making them believe in his own concept of the functions of government and the destiny of Cuba. When he finished his informal talk, he asked that a passage be opened by the crowd to permit him and his escort to walk to the jeep at the foot of Misiones Park. The obedience of the crowd was amazing. Without the need of soldiers to push them back as was usually the case, they opened a wide avenue for Fidel Castro to walk through. Trivial as this act was, it made a deep impression on me. Many politicians in Cuba had been able to arouse the people, to awaken their passions, but never before had I seen such respect and awe.

Five hours after he entered Havana, Fidel Castro reached Camp Columbia. There he spoke over a national television and radio hookup to the people all over the island and to the public which had been permitted to enter Camp Columbia without restrictions for the first time in history. President Manuel Urrutia and his cabinet, government officials and the rebel leaders all sat in attendance. As Castro spoke, someone in the crowd released two white doves. One of them lighted on the collar of the tall bearded speaker and remained there, much to the delight of the crowd. The Cuban people are deeply moved by such omens. It is hard for an American to realize the deep significance which Castro had at that hour to his countrymen. He stood there before them, proof that the power of the Cuban army had been broken by the people themselves. He stood there before them, unentangled and uncompromised, free of all the factious political parties. The revolution was won. Now Fidel Castro was ready to begin the program of reforms which was designed to change the political, economic and social structure of the Republic.

17

Dr. Fidel Castro and his "26th of July" revolutionary armed forces have been in control of Cuba since January 1, 1959. With his rifle in one hand and a list of reforms in the other, he is determined to cure the ills of centuries within a few short months, frequently by resorting to the firing squad. The new revolutionary regime is a one man government. President Manuel Urrutia and his cabinet sit in the Presidential Palace dutifully approving legislation which Premier Fidel Castro has already announced to the public in nationwide televised speeches.

A feeling of apprehension and uncertainty is growing in the island as Castro's reforms are enacted, one by one. The announcement by Fidel Castro that Cuba is to be a country with a middle-class only, with neither rich nor poor, has shaken the highly individualistic, pleasure loving Cubans.

Since the victory of the revolution, Fidel Castro has directed his speeches and appeals for support to the masses, the same masses that never supported him during his lonely, sometimes heartbreaking two-year armed rebellion. Labor had twice refused to walk out in a general strike which might have spelled the end of the Batista regime. These masses—except for a small group—steadfastly supported Batista. It was the members of the much maligned middle-class that supported Castro. They fought side by side with the young rebels, poured out their meager financial resources to buy arms and ammunition, medicine and equipment for the rebels, abandoned their professions and lost their practices to help the revolution, and now see themselves ignored or acidly criticized by Castro. If the reforms continue they will be caught in the economic juggernaut and crushed, together with the wealthy class, which Castro appears to have as his principal target. Students of political philosophy can see clearly the significance of Castro's attitude toward the middle-class, the bourgeoisie, which is the heart of any democratic land.

The reforms of Fidel Castro are almost exactly those he proposed in 1953 when he stood before the court in Santiago de Cuba and audaciously denounced Batista as a dictator. At least six hundred members of the armed forces and collaborators of the Batista regime have died before the firing squads of the revolutionary government in the manner promised by Castro in his speech in 1953. And there is no indication when these executions will stop.

When Batista fled the country, the "26th of July" militia did an admirable job of maintaining order and holding the mobs in check until the arrival of the bearded veterans from the battle fronts. It was apparent, however, that these masses wanted blood, demanded retribution. There is no doubt that hundreds of Batista's supporters would have been torn to pieces in the public plazas had it not been for Castro. Castro himself would have been powerless had he not promised summary trials and executions of the guilty.

At first the executions following the trials, characterized by the admission of hearsay evidence which would never have been accepted in Anglo-Saxon courts, were given wide public support because the executed were known to be killers of the Batista regime. Americans must keep in mind that concrete evidence of guilt is not important to Latin Americans, who do not believe guilty men should escape punishment simply because of insufficient evidence. The Napoleonic code on which Latin law is founded makes this kind of justice possible.

However, the statement by Fidel Castro that those convicted of traffic in narcotics, illegal gambling, misappropriation of government funds and counterrevolutionary activities would also be executed disturbed the people. Without there being any legislation to cover these crimes, a military court sentenced a marijuana seller to death before a firing squad, citing Article 16 of the rebel criminal code as its authority. This code was drawn up by Castro and his officers in his Sierra Maestra headquarters during the rebellion. The public was shocked. It became clear that only the will of the revolutionary government stood between any offender and the firing squad—and the will of the revolutionary government was in reality the will of one man—Fidel Castro.

Several thousands accused of torture and killing are still in the island's prisons awaiting trial. Many of them will be executed. Also, hundreds accused of graft and collaboration with the Batista regime are being held. Four months after the victory the civil courts are still not functioning. The civil court is undergoing a process of reorganization, and a great number of judges and court personnel have been dismissed. In one notable case, a Judge of the Urgency Court which tried terrorists and anti-government offenders during the Batista regime, was executed in Pinar del Rio Province for the crime of collaboration and being an informer. People are asking whether "collaboration," a term still undefined by the revolutionary government, will be considered a crime punishable by death. There is no tradition for such executions in Cuba. Once free of the Spanish rule, the Cuban people abolished capital punishment. The constitution of 1940, which Fidel Castro has declared in effect, except as modified by the revolutionary government, prohibits capital punishment. Since the birth of the Republic in 1902, only six men have been executed by order of a legal court and in each case the crime was murder. Revolution or counterrevolution in Cuba has never before been considered a crime punishable by death. Castro himself was sentenced to fifteen years imprisonment in 1953 when his revolt in Santiago de Cuba failed.

Many of the reforms of Castro, such as the promise of honesty in administration, the suppression of illegal gambling, the campaign against prostitution, narcotics traffic and other vices, have been applauded by the public. His agrarian reform law to give land to the tenants and squatters has long been considered necessary by economists. Cuba has thousands of acres of government land lying idle. At the same time, there are many huge estates held by families for generations, without development, vast lands which the wealthy owners have never bothered to develop, and which they can afford to keep undeveloped because of the almost nonexistent taxes. The expropriation of sections of these estates is regarded by many as being desirable. However, when Castro then stated that all land which the government considers as not being efficiently cultivated would also be seized, and that a limit would be placed on the amount of land any individual or company could own, cane planters, tobacco plantation owners, and cattle ranchers expressed their concern.

The reduction of rents by 30% to 50% is considered just by the tenants but unreasonable by the owners of property. Rents have long been excessively high in Havana, where few people own their homes. Many of the great fortunes in Cuba are based on real estate. But in recent years, following the Spanish tradition of investing in land and houses, many of the middle-class have poured their savings into small apartment houses, most of which are mortgaged. Rent reductions placed these properties in jeopardy, since the mortgages were based on higher rent income. The government, to counteract this, reduced mortgage interests and taxes on rental properties.

The owners of vacant lots in all towns have been ordered to sell them to anyone who wants to build a home. The only other choice the owners have is to sell the vacant lots to the government. The price of land in the island has always been extremely high, since it is in the hands of a relatively small group compared with the total Cuban population. But the statement by Fidel Castro that no land in the island is worth more than four dollars per *vara* (33″ x 33″—the old Spanish measurement) caused not only the wealthy but the middle-class to regard their investments with concern. In Havana, where land is more expensive than in any other part of the nation, lots sell from ten dollars in the outskirts to as high as five hundred dollars per *vara* in the center of the city.

The reason for this drastic reform, according to Fidel Castro, is to force capital to stop investing in real estate and to establish industries to give the unemployed—estimated by Castro at 700,000 in a nation of six million—a chance to secure employment. The measure was immediately effective. All real estate transactions stopped and the building industry, for many years a bright spot in Cuba's economy, was paralyzed, throwing thousands out of work. The large American-owned Cuban Portland Cement plant at Mariel, some twenty-five miles from Havana, closed down, its silos filled with cement for which there were no purchasers.

Dr. Fidel Castro has promised the workers they will receive higher wages and that living costs will be reduced. This has resulted in a wave of labor demands in every industry. Employers find it impossible to grant wage increases in the present critical economic situation. Cuba already has one of the most modern labor codes in the world and wages must depend on sales and general prosperity. As soon as the harvest of sugar, the principal industry of the island and the barometer of its economy, ends in April, the sugar workers will present new demands. They were persuaded by Dr. Castro in January to harvest the crop and present their demands later. Now, the sugar industry, faced with the lowest price in years for its product, is in no condition to meet further labor demands.

The imposition by the revolutionary government of currency controls and restrictions of imports—for the first time in the history of Cuba—has further disturbed and handicapped commerce and industry. Without doubt, the enormous amount of capital that was taken out of Cuba during the last months of Batista's government, the tremendous expenses of the civil war, and the looting of the treasury by the fallen regime, made it necessary for Castro to impose controls and restrictions. Castro must not be blamed for this. He is trying to save the nation's reserves. His government suffers from all the evils for which Batista was responsible. Thousands of bank accounts have been frozen and hundreds of safety deposit boxes sealed in an effort to prevent more money from being taken out of Cuba by friends or agents of the former regime.

The confiscation of funds and property of the members of the past regime is considered just by many Cubans. However, when this measure was amplified to include every person who had been in the Batista government since 1952 or who had been a candidate for a public office, including those who had opposed Batista at the polls in the elections of 1954 and 1958, "justice" begins to take on an ominous overtone. Many of these people inherited their properties or obtained them by their own hard work and frugality. For instance, the members of the State Advisory Council, named by former President Batista when he seized control of the government in 1952, have been included in the confiscation legislation.

Such drastic measures as these have caused the termination of credit by foreign exporters to merchants and industrialists. The exporters of the United States and Europe want to see where Cuba stands before they extend further credit.

Few voices have been raised in criticism of the revolutionary government. The press has been silenced by economic pressure of the Castro regime. Since the beginning of the Republic, all publications in Cuba have received subsidies and sinecures from every administration. Now these subsidies and sinecures have been canceled by the revolutionary government, leaving both the publications and the newspapermen in a vulnerable position, which makes them afraid to criticize the regime. Thus a kind of censorship of the press exists. This censorship is the result of fear. While Castro is right in saying that his regime does not impose censorship, nevertheless he has, in addition to destroying their financial backing, declared a policy of "don't read them and don't support them." The result is that if Fidel Castro expresses serious disapproval of any given newspaper or magazine, advertisers, the only other real source of income, are afraid to deal with the paper.

Like so many reformers, Fidel Castro is enraged by criticism. He has little sense of humor and reacts violently to cartoons lampooning the new government, no matter how gentle the humor. He is carrying out a campaign against the foreign news services and publications in the United States which he accuses of deliberately distorting the facts of the Cuban revolution.

Fidel Castro is a phenomenon, a silver-tongued orator with a persuasiveness and personality, even on television, which has never been equaled in Cuba. His marathon speeches sometimes hours in length, are listened to eagerly by the public, which is swept by his words to the Utopia he so vividly describes. However, as soon as the magic of his personality subsides, the old doubts again rear up against the violent reforms.

The constant whipping up by Fidel Castro of an extreme nationalistic spirit is regarded by many Cubans as ill advised in an island which depends on exports for its economic life and must import the greater part of its food. "Economic independence" has been a catchword of politicians in Cuba since the dawn of the Republic, but the majority of Cubans realize that it is an impossible dream, since Cuba is inevitably tied economically to the United States—its best customer and largest supplier. Except in time of war, there is usually a world surplus of sugar. The United States purchases nearly three million tons of sugar from Cuba yearly and pays two cents per pound premium over the world market price. It is this which makes the sugar industry so profitable in Cuba and brings in the American dollars necessary for imports. The cost of sugar production has risen so sharply that at present there is little profit in selling sugar on the world market. Thus the dream of sugar producers is an increase in the quota of the American market. Cuba also wants the assignment of her percentage of the American market put into a permanent commercial treaty. This would remove it from a precarious dependency on the United States Congress and the tremendous pressures exerted by other foreign suppliers trying to obtain greater quotas.

This year, with the low price of sugar on the world market and the slow sales, the island—according to predictions in sugar circles—will have a reduction in income of about $1,250,000, unless some emergency causes the world market to rise. The economic problems of the Castro government therefore threaten to multiply.

The responsible classes of Cuba are worried about the anti-American sentiments expressed by Fidel Castro, his brother Raul, who is Commander of the land, sea and air forces, and many of their principal followers. Even Cubans in the lower classes take a critical view of these attacks on the United States. The reaction of the people to the statement by Fidel Castro that Cuba will remain neutral in case of a war between the United States and Russia was not what the Castro-Urrutia government expected. The night Castro made this pronouncement the crowd applauded, but in the sober light of morning they shook their heads in disapproval. This historic incident was provoked by José Figueres, former president of Costa Rica, who was in Havana as an official guest of the government. Figueres spoke at a demonstration of five hundred thousand workers. He declared that in case of a war between the United States and Russia, Latin-American nations should be on the side of the United States. The Cuban people showed their support of Figueres' sentiments by applauding him in newsreels shown in the theatres of the Republic. The Figueres-Castro declarations have had hemispheric repercussions.

Approximately one billion American dollars is invested in Cuba in sugar mills, railways, industries, commercial establishments and other enterprises. Included in this is the one hundred million dollar United States government-owned Nicaro Nickel plant. Millions more are needed for further development of the island's resources. However, the present attitude of Dr. Fidel Castro and his followers has not been conducive to inspiring confidence. His violent attacks on the United States and its "vested interests," on American companies operating in Cuba and on the American press, have brought about a feeling of suspicion in relations between the two countries.

The most debated question in Cuba today is just how much Fidel Castro is being influenced by the Communists. Although the "26th of July" steadfastly refused throughout the two year rebellion to join the Communists, the resurgence of communism in Cuba today is notable. During the last months of the revolution the *Carta Semanal*—a clandestine Communist publication—printed a letter signed by Juan Marinello, former president of the Communist Party, pointing out to the "26th of July" that it had twice failed to bring about a general strike because it had refused to make a united front with the Communists.

Within a few hours after the fall of the Batista regime, the Communists in Havana, through their organized underground, seized the small gambling places and the political headquarters of various government parties, and hung out signs, *Partida Socialista Popular*, the euphemism under which the Communists operate in Cuba. At the same time, Communists seized union headquarters and declared themselves in control not only in Havana but in the provinces. Some of these groups were dislodged by the rebels, but many remained in control. Within a few days, the Communist newspaper *Hoy*, which had been banned by Prio Socorras and Batista, appeared on the streets. A campaign to collect $150,000 to buy new shops for the newspaper was highly successful. Today the Communists are in the market to purchase a new print shop.

The old familiar faces of the Communist Party have returned to Havana. Blas Roca, top leader, and Lazaro Peña, hoarse-voiced labor leader who controlled island labor for years, are conspicuous examples. Juan Marinello, dashed off to Moscow right after the fall of Batista to report on conditions and make recommendations on policy. There is no doubt that the Communists wield tremendous influence in the Castro government and in the labor unions. Their methods of placing men in key posts are extremely effective.

Ironically, Fidel Castro stands as a possible bulwark against Communism, not because of his "reforms," but because of his highly individualistic personality. He is a strong willed young man who will take advice from no one. He has his own ideas of what Cuba needs and he is not afraid that anyone will wrest control of the island from him. He points out that the great democracies—the United States and Great Britain—have legal Communist Parties and he cannot understand why anyone is worried about Communist influence in Cuba. What Castro does not realize is that in a small country, determined and dedicated Communists can get control of a surprising number of posts in key positions, thus exerting a disproportionate influence in national affairs. Furthermore, propaganda directed to the uneducated masses is more effective than in the United States and Great Britain, where the educational level makes it difficult for the Communists to win followers by stereotyped arguments.

At present the Communists are merely applauding the reforms of Castro. Ironically, he has outflanked their appeals to the Cuban people by instituting his own reforms. In fact, Castro considers the old time Communists as sheer reactionaries and is not interested in their advice. Many people in Cuba believe that the Castro reform program is in the tradition of the communist pattern, but others believe that the parallel with communist procedure is coincidental. Whatever Fidel Castro's basic motives, the primary question is whether he will destroy the economy of the island, bringing economic ruin; or whether he will build a solid and sound economy. The number of Cuban people who believe the latter is daily growing fewer. Most Cubans look to the future with fear and uncertainty, though clinging to the hope that Fidel Castro will realize what is happening, moderate his drastic reforms, and reestablish confidence in the island's future. Cuba, rich in resources, can have a wonderful future, if given a chance.

The United States views the situation in Cuba with alarm. Cuba is the key to the Gulf of Mexico. The largest naval base of the United States in the Caribbean is located at Guantanamo. The demand that this base be abandoned has already been voiced in Cuba. The scattered protests of today have a habit of becoming the thundering voices of tomorrow. The military strategists of the United States are definitely worried. They know that the trackless, almost impenetrable Sierra Maestra would make an ideal spot for the launching of rockets against the United States. An enemy in Cuba, with the many excellent harbors, could be supplied effectively by submarines. The highest interests of the United States and of hemispheric defence require that no enemy power obtain control of any portion of Cuba.

Rising anti-American sentiment in Latin America is the harvest being reaped from years of vacillating, hesitant and cowardly policy by the United States government. The objective of the American government should be to weld the Western Hemisphere into a solid bloc through common interests—commercial and political—and the creation of an awareness in Latin America of the need for mutual defence. This should be the basis of our Latin American policy.

The United States is confronted with a problem of survival in the face of the Russian military conspiracy to gain control of the world by force. There is no doubt that our foreign policy at the present time will be the determining factor in our continued existence as a sovereign, independent nation. Anti-American sentiment in Latin America is directly related to the United States' failure to support and encourage the establishment and maintenance of democracy. Latin Americans are bewildered by the American foreign policy. They see the United States striving to establish democracy in distant lands, such as Japan, Germany and Korea, while failing to support democracy in Latin America, where people are striving for participation in their national affairs.

For many years the United States has recognized any dictator who managed to seize a country in Latin America. I point out two examples—Trujillo and Somoza—who were supported by the administrations of Franklin D. Roosevelt, Harry Truman, and now by President Eisenhower. Recognition of any government in Latin America implies *approval*, despite anything the United States Department of State might say, and no Latin American will ever be convinced to the contrary. The United States should never recognize any government in Latin America which obtains power by force of arms, without regard to whether the leader is a "dictator" or a "liberator." An announcement should be made to the world that the policy of the United States has changed, that new governments will be recognized only after a period of one year, during which it will be observed whether the liberator calls for elections and gives the people a chance to choose their government.

The shameful support to existing dictators in Latin America should be withdrawn. No loans should be made to these dictators. All shipments of arms and ammunition from the United States should be halted. The dictators should be advised in an open note, made public to the world, that the United States looks with disfavor on the disregard for human rights in their territories. This policy must be maintained regardless of world political situations. It would increase United States' prestige with the people of Latin America and give them confidence that their big neighbor to the north has decided at last to see to it that democracy came into being below the Rio Grande.

The highly touted "economic assistance" which the American liberals state is the answer to Latin-American problems is a dangerous policy. Loans and gifts have created hatred of the United States in most of the countries of the world. The money is, almost invariably, drained off in graft by the administration in power. Latin-American countries need financial assistance in developing their resources. Make no mistake about that. However, this assistance should be handled by an Inter-American Development Bank in which all the countries are stockholders. Loans should be given only on projects which have been checked and verified by experts as to their cost, usefulness and suitability to the country in question. Control of the money spent on these projects should be retained by the bank. There should be no gifts.

The decision of the United States to send arms and military missions to Latin-American countries was an unfortunate one. The basic idea behind it was that these countries should learn to defend themselves and to help the United States in time of war. Although excellent in theory, in practice it became one of the greatest hindrances to friendly relations with the people of Latin America. These arms have been used again and again to oppress and enslave the people of the countries that received them. The United States military missions have inadvertently trained the armies, navies and air forces of these countries only to fight against their own peoples, not a foreign enemy. Cuba and Venezuela are sad examples of the evil such a policy can produce. Army, navy and air missions of the United States should be immediately withdrawn from Latin America. Officers of these countries could be trained in the United States if so requested by the countries. The United States should realize that the Latin American countries will not at the present time contribute troops to any war in which the United

States may be involved. Perhaps if the proper policy were followed Latin Americans might one day consider any war in which the United States was involved as *their* war.

The prestige of the United States is today at its lowest ebb in Latin America. This is due in no small measure to the failure of the United States government to protect United States citizens and their property. The hesitancy and reluctance on the part of our diplomatic officials to extend to American citizens the rights due their nationality is almost unbelievable. It would appear that today all the large and powerful nations fear to assert their legitimate rights in any dispute with a small nation. This hesitancy, this timidity, this apology for their existence, is regarded in Latin-American countries as a weakness which can be exploited to considerable advantage. It makes Latin-American countries contemptuous of us. Throughout the hemisphere, United States citizens are thrown into jail, held for long periods without trial or formal charges. These abuses have been notable under the Castro government, but they also occurred under Batista. United States diplomatic officials take the attitude that any American who has been arrested is already a criminal. Their position seems to be "do not rock the diplomatic boat." A firm, calm, just attitude should be taken in cases of American citizens arrested in any foreign country. The crime with which they are charged should have no bearing on the action of the American diplomatic representatives, whose explicit duty is to see that the persons arrested have been placed under arrest through proper legal procedure and are given proper treatment and prompt hearings.

The protection of property of United States' citizens is a vital point in Latin-American relations. The United States should overcome its sensitiveness to the cry of imperialism. It should be realized that the era of the "exploitation" of poor natives by American capital has passed. The average American who goes to a Latin-American country is willing to invest his money to obtain a reasonable profit. However, he wants to feel that he has some protection from changing administrations, and certainly his American passport should have some value when he is in trouble.

Bilateral treaties should become the basis for the investments of American citizens abroad. Any Latin-American country which desires American investments should be willing to agree not to expropriate or confiscate these investments. Through such a treaty the United States government, which strictly regulates its own industries and commercial firms, could subject its foreign investments to such regulations as would insure that no abuses would be committed by American capital abroad. If any Latin-American country is not in accord with such a treaty, it should be considered as not desiring the investment of American capital, and this fact should be publicized throughout the United States. Then, any American who wished to invest would do so at his own risk.

The policy of the United States in sending political appointees to Latin America as diplomatic representatives is one of the great hindrances to friendly relations with these countries. The businessman is almost always a failure as a diplomat. He knows little of the country to which he is assigned, its background or its language, and, furthermore, usually is so close to the President that his usefulness is considerably diminished. How can this kind of ambassador or minister be able to form a sound judgment of the situation in any country? On the other hand, the professional diplomat is too often concerned only with furthering his own career. He is afraid to express an opinion or take a definite stand on any question in which the United States State Department needs guidance. Unfortunately, his career does not depend upon positive results. Instead, it requires that he make no mistakes; this, in turn, requires that he make no important decisions. "If I do nothing, I can do nothing wrong!"

One of the major reasons for the blunders of the United

States Department of State in Latin America—as in the rest of the world—is the lack of accurate information upon which to base its policy. It is imperative that the Ambassador of the United States in any country be able to furnish the State Department with accurate information on the situation in that country. He should even be able to predict with a high degree of accuracy the probable future. If trouble is brewing he should know it and know the reasons behind it. The surprise so often expressed by our State Department reflects the incompetence of our representatives in foreign countries.

The visits of Congressmen and high officials of the United States government to Latin America in publicized investigations are useless, and have resulted in incidents detrimental to relations between the United States and Latin American countries. Any official mission will be received and entertained by the government in power. Since the members of these United States missions are never trained investigators, the information they obtain is exactly that which the government of the country in question desires them to receive.

The tremendous propaganda campaign carried on by the Soviet Union against the United States in Latin America has never been effectively combatted. The United States is steadily losing the "cold war" in these countries. The present American propaganda in Latin America is useless to combat Communism. You cannot fight Communism by being apologetic about your own way of life. We fail to draw sufficient attention to such excellent enterprises of the United States as the Point Four Program, the exchange of students, and the enormous financial aid. Our so-called information does not reach the lower classes, where the greatest anti-American sentiments lie. The propaganda of the United States should be aggressive, not defensive, as it is at present. It is necessary to attack communism, not defend the American way of life. The United States is shown to the Latin Americans by the Communists as an imperialistic nation attempting to gain control of their governments in order to exploit them. Little effective effort is made by the United States to combat this propaganda.

Today, revolutionary forces are on the march in Latin America. The determination to overthrow the remaining dictators is mounting. These forces are not Communist, although they have within their ranks many Communists who hope to control the movement once it succeeds in the field of battle. But if the majority of these revolutionaries are not Communist, they are anti-American, because the United States has consistently allied itself with the dictators.

The antagonism of these revolutionary forces can be overcome only by a major change in American foreign policy. The United States is at present manifestly helpless against this kind of internal revolt. Small guerrilla bands entering any country to fight as Castro did in Cuba is something which the United States cannot prevent. This is what makes our support of men like Trujillo ridiculous, for we glean not merely the hatred of the oppressed people in the Dominican Republic, but once the revolutionaries succeed, our influence is destroyed. The United States can combat this only by disowning all dictatorships, withdrawing material and moral support from them, and bringing pressure to bear to see that free elections are held. If we would reward those countries which *do have* representative governments, the need for revolutionary movements would soon come to an end, and we would win the gratitude and friendship of the *people* of Latin America.

Two countries—the so-called Dominican Republic and Nicaragua—which have been supported by the United States government for many years, will soon be torn by disorders and civil war. Is it possible that the United States Department of State can believe that any armed victory in these countries will bring to power a group seeking or admitting of the desirability of friendly relations with the United States?

Hurricane warnings are already displayed all over Latin

America. Panama will soon explode. The United States must change its policy or find active enemies at its back door. One of the present problems is the possible loss of the Panama Canal. To take control of the Canal is the avowed intention of revolutionary forces moving in Panama. There is already a precedent for the taking over of the Panama Canal. Mr. Foster Dulles provided that when he declared that Egypt had the right to seize the Suez Canal. At the same time, several years ago, the Panama Canal was removed from the jurisdiction of the American army and placed under the control of the Panama Canal Company, patterned after the company which operated the Suez Canal. Could anything be more advantageous to those who hoped to wrest control of the Panama Canal from the United States government?

Unless the United States adopts a firm attitude that treaties are treaties and not scraps of paper, and becomes impervious to the shouts of "imperialism" in the interest of its self-defence and its own unchallengeable rights, our great American nation will find itself crippled in its efforts to hold the line against the rising influence of Soviet Russia.

Whether the future of Cuba and of all Latin America shall be decided from Moscow and not by the countries of this hemisphere themselves is a question in which the United States can and should be the decisive factor.

Index

ABOUT THE AUTHOR

Ruby Hart Phillips was born in Okeene, Oklahoma. She went to school in a dozen different towns, being raised in Oklahoma, Texas and New Mexico. She became interested in foreign and national political affairs at an early age. She learned Spanish and decided to see Latin America. She arrived in Havana on the same day as James Doyle Phillips, whom she later married. Mr. Phillips became correspondent of the *New York Times* in 1931, and a short time later Mrs. Phillips became correspondent for Times Wide World Photographic Service.

During the next six turbulent years in Cuba, the two worked very closely together. In August, 1937, James Doyle Phillips was killed in an automobile accident in California. In the same accident their daughter, Marta, was badly injured. However she recovered and is now a successful professional dancer. As soon as she knew her daughter would live, Mrs. Phillips took over her husband's work in Havana. Since then she has covered not only the dramatic political events, but economics, sports, entertainment, etc., for *The Times*.

Her office is an old Spanish building, a block from the Presidential Palace in Havana. Since she is the dean of the foreign press in Cuba and the only full-time foreign correspondent there, her office is the meeting place for correspondents all over the world when the news is hot. She says, "At the same time, American business men, and current revolutionists, government officials, oppositionists of the regime in question, politicians, observers, Latin American journalists, sometimes revolutionists, exiles and Europeans come to see me. All this, of course, is very fortunate since news comes to me from every source." She does have a hideaway, however —a house in the outlying district of Miramar, which she had built herself and stocked with animals, birds and fruit trees.